The Government and Politics of Spain

The Government and Politics of Spain

Paul Heywood

St. Martin's Press   New York

St. Martin's Press, Scholarly and Reference Division, 175 Fifth Avenue, New York, N.Y. 10010

First published in the United States of America in 1995

Printed in Great Britain

ISBN 0–312–15796–7 (cloth)
ISBN 0–312–15804–1 (paper)

Library of Congress Cataloging-in-Publication Data applied for

For Mary –
who deserves much better, but
without whom this would have
been much worse

Contents

List of Tables, Figures, Exhibits and Maps

Tables

Figures

Exhibits

Map

Acknowledgements

This book has taken far longer to complete than I anticipated when I set to work on it in 1989. The reasons can be attributed not just to the ever-increasing incursions made into research time by the demands of resource-starved academe, but also to the nature of the task itself. In contrast to other major European countries, there are no standard interpretations of Spain's contemporary political system upon which to build or against which to argue. As a result, this study has involved considerably more original research – and hence time – than might be expected of an analytical introduction to the government and politics of Spain.

In the course of researching and writing, I naturally incurred a number of debts which it is a pleasure finally to acknowledge. I owe most to Paul Preston and Elías Díaz, two scholars from whom I have learned much that I know about contemporary Spain and from whom I have enjoyed unfailing support. Vincent Wright commissioned the volume, and offered constant encouragement and critical insight – as well as demonstrating considerable patience – throughout the project. Steven Kennedy proved to be equally phlegmatic over the numerous requests for deadline extensions.

I benefited enormously during the course of working on this book from a period spent between 1989 and 1992 writing quarterly country reports on Spain for the Economist Intelligence Unit. Charles Jenkins was a rigorous editor who asked unfailingly probing questions: I hope he finds some of the answers here. Rory Clarke brought to bear both help and humour. I am grateful to the Economist Intelligence Unit for permission to reproduce the table on Spanish privatisations from the EIU Country Report No.4 (1992).

In visits to Spain over the years, I have derived much benefit from conversations with Gayle Allard, Pepe Bolorinos, Isabel Espuelas, Ana Guerrero, Jesús Leal, Enrique Moradiellos, Antonio Oporto, Florentino Portero and Maite Villar. Mariano Aguirre and Isabel Sánchez provided valuable information and assistance via the Centro de Investigaciones para la Paz. Amongst fellow Hispanists, Sheelagh Ellwood, Sebastian Balfour and Jordi Molas have more than once come to my rescue with their expertise. Bill Miller and Stephen White were instrumental in creating a stimulating academic environment in the Department of Politics at the University of Glasgow. James Kellas's teasing queries forced me to think more deeply about Spain's system of regional government. Matthew Wyman helped keep me sane. Amongst other colleagues who provided essential encouragement, Dave Edgerton and Nick Ellison showed a keen interest in the book's development. Laura Cram was kind enough to offer expert comment on the chapter on the policy process.

Finally, I wish to thank my wife Mary Vincent, to whom this book is dedicated. She most certainly did not type the manuscript, but she did provide constant intellectual stimulation, a razor-sharp critical eye, and – most important – the emotional support which made writing this book less painful that it otherwise would have been.

PAUL HEYWOOD

Glossary of Spanish Words

abertzale	left-leaning Basque nationalist
administración periférica	provincial administration, prior to establishment of Autonomous Communities
aperturista	Francoist in favour of 'opening up' the regime to reform (hence *aperturismo*)
ayuntamiento	town council/town hall
beautiful, los	'beautiful people', an interconnected group of wealthy individuals, mostly associated with the Socialist Party in office, who became the focus of media attention in the late 1980s
búnker	Francoist members of the extreme right, mainly within the military, wholly opposed to reform
cacique	local political boss
caciquismo	the practice of political clientelism, especially electoral fixing
caja de ahorros	savings bank
cesantes, los	suspended civil servants in the era of political appointments to the public administration
Comunidades Autónomas	Autonomous Communities, Spain's seventeen regional governments
Congreso de los Diputados	Congress of Deputies (parliamentary lower house)
consignas	instructions or orders
Cortes [Generales]	Spanish parliament
Cortes Constituyentes	constituent assembly
cuerpos	specialised corps within the public administration
cultura del pelotazo	'sleaze culture', a term used to describe the political atmosphere of the scandal-ridden 1990s [from the term *'cogerse un pelotazo'*, meaning to get drunk or high, and intended to convey a get-rich-quick attitude, high-living and corruption]

Defensor del Pueblo	Ombudsman
desencanto	disenchantment, disillusion – a term used in the press to describe attitudes to the political system in the late 1970s and early 1980s
desgobierno	lack of government
Diputación	Council
estado de derecho	state of law, in the sense of the state being legally established and accountable
etarra/s	members of the Basque separatist organisation, E.T.A.
Euskera	the Basque language
felipistas	supporters of Felipe González, first elected prime minister of Spain in October 1982
fontaneros	plumbers, a term used to decribe Adolfo Suárez's inner circle of advisers
fueros	ancient code of laws in Basque Country and Navarra
Galega	the Galician language
Generalitat	the Catalan regional parliamentary assembly
golpe	military coup
golpismo	the practice of plotting coups against the government
guerristas	supporters of Alfonso Guerra, deputy prime minister in the Socialist administrations, 1982-91
Hispanidad	the essence of Spanish identity (literally, 'Spanishness')
la lucha	'the struggle', in the sense of Communist opposition to Franco regime
maketos	a Basque term of abuse to denote Spaniards
movida, la	Madrid nightlife in the 1980s, associated with the city's post-Franco renaissance
Movimiento	the Franco regime's institutional framework
oposiciones	competitive examinations for public sector posts
patria	fatherland
patria chica	home town or local area
pistolerismo	gun-law
pluriempleo	the practice of holding down several jobs at one time
poderes fácticos	centres of power with major political influence, such as the army, banks, Catholic Church, etc.
ponencia	a report, or the committee which draws it up

procurador/es	a member of the Francoist *Cortes*
pronunciamiento	military insurrection
Renaixença	Catalan cultural renaissance in the late nineteenth century
renovadores	members of the Socialist Party in the late 1980s and early 1990s in favour of market-led policies
revistas de corazón	glossy society magazines, such as *¡Hola!*
Rexurdimento	Galician cultural renaissance, similar to *Renaixença*
sector crítico	leftist opponents of the Socialist Party's abandonment of Marxism
Senado	Senate, the upper house in the *Cortes Generales*
Tejerazo	the attempted coup of 23 February 1981 led by Lieutenant-Colonel Antonio Tejero
tertulia	a gathering of friends to discuss issues of mutual interest
una, grande y libre	'one, great and free', a shibboleth of the Franco regime to describe the Spanish state
Xunta	the Galician regional parliamentary assembly

List of Abbreviations

AEB	*Asociación Española de Banca Privada* (Spanish Banking Association)
AES	*Acuerdo Económico y Social* (Economic and Social Agreement) – tripartite pact between government, employers and unions
AGM	*Academia General Militar* (General Military Academy)
AMI	*Acuerdo Marco Interconfederal* – agreement between employers and unions on framework for collective bargaining
AP	*Alianza Popular* (Popular Alliance)
ARE	*Assemblé des Régions Européennes* (Assembly of European Regions)
BNG	*Bloque Nacionalista Galego* (Galician Nationalist Bloc) – established in 1986 following split in CG
CAP	Common Agricultural Policy
CC.AA.	*Comunidades Autónomas* (Autonomous Communities) – Spain's 17 regional governments
CC.OO.	*Comisiones Obreras* (Workers' Commissions) – trade union federation with historic links to Communist Party
CDC	*Convergència Democràtica de Catalunya* – component part of the CiU
CDS	*Centro Democrático y Social* (Social and Democratic Centre Party) – founded by Adolfo Suárez in 1982
CEIM	*Confederación Empresarial Independiente de Madrid* (Madrid-based employers' group, affiliated to CEOE)
CEM	Council of European Municipalities
CEOE	*Confederación Española de Organizaciones Empresariales* (Spanish employers' organisation)
CEPYME	*Confederación Española de la Pequeña y Mediana Empresa* (Spanish employers' organisation of small and medium-sized firms)

CES	*Consejo Económico y Social* (Social and Economic Council) – a non-governmental agency established in the early 1990s
CFSP	Common Foreign and Security Policy
CG	*Coalición Galega* – Galician nationalist party
CGPJ	*Consejo General del Poder Judicial* (General Council of the Judiciary)
CiU	*Convergència i Unió* (Convergence and Union) – right-leaning Catalan nationalist party
CNC	*Confederación Nacional de la Construcción* – construction industry employers' organisation, affiliated to CEOE
CNT	*Confederación Nacional del Trabajo* (National Workers' Alliance) – historic anarchist organisation
CONFEMETAL	*Confederación de Organizaciones Empresariales de Metal* – metal industry employers' organisation, affiliated to CEOE
COPE	*Cadena de Ondas Populares Españolas* – radio station owned by the Catholic Church
CSCE	Conference on Security and Co-operation in Europe
CSIF	*Confederación de Sindicatos Independientes de Funcionarios* (independent union for government employees)
DGPE	*Dirección General del Patrimonio de Estado* – state holding company
EA	*Eusko Ta Alkartasuna* – Basque nationalist party formed in 1986 as breakaway from PNV
EAGGF	European Agricultural Guidance and Guarantee Fund
EC	European Community
ECB	European Central Bank
EDF	European Development Fund
EE	*Euzkadiko Ezkerra* (Basque Left) – Basque nationalist party, absorbed by PSE-PSOE in 1993
EEC	European Economic Community
EFA	European Fighter Aircraft
ELA–STV	*Eusko Langileen Alkartasuna–Solidaridad de Trabajadores Vascos* – left-leaning Basque union federation
EMS	European Monetary System
EMU	Economic and Monetary Union
ERC	*Esquerra Republicana de Catalunya* (Catalan Republican Left) – radical nationalist party, founded in 1931
ERDF	European Regional Development Fund
ERM	Exchange Rate Mechanism

ESCB	European System of Central Banks
ESF	European Social Fund
ETA	*Euskadi Ta Askatasuna* (Basque Homeland and Liberty) – radical nationalist separatist organisation
EU	European Union
FII	*Fuerzas de Intervención Inmediata* – armoured mobile units
FLN	*Front de Libération Nationale* (National Liberation Front) [Algeria]
FLP	*Frente de Liberación Popular* (Peoples' Liberation Front) – anti-Franco opposition group
FTN	*Fomento del Trabajo Nacional* – Catalan-based employers' group, affiliated to CEOE
GAL	*Grupos Antiterroristas de Liberación* (Anti-terrorist liberation groups) – engaged in 'dirty war' with ETA between 1983 and 1987
GDP	Gross Domestic Product
GDR	German Democratic Republic
GIL	*Grupo Independiente Liberal* – political party established by Jesús Gil
GNP	Gross National Product
HB	*Herri Batasuna* – radical Basque nationalist party, seen as political wing of ETA
HOAC	*Hermandad Obrera de Acción Católica* (Workers' Brotherhood of Catholic Action)
IFA	*Instituto de Fomento de Andalucía* – body established to promote the economic development of Andalucía
IGSAP	*Inspección General de Servicios de la Administración Pública* – non-governmental agency which evaluates public administration
INE	*Instituto Nacional de Estadísticas* (National Institute of Statistics)
INEM	*Instituto Nacional de Empleo* (National Employment Institute)
INH	*Instituto Nacional de Hidrocárburos* – state holding company
INI	*Instituto Nacional de Industria* – state holding company
INTG	*Intersindical Galega* – moderate Galician union federation
IU	*Izquierda Unida* (United Left)
JOC	*Juventud Obrera Católica* (Catholic Workers' Youth Movement)

JUJEM	*Junta de Jefes de Estado Mayor* (Joint Chiefs of Staff)
LOAPA	*Ley Orgánica de Armonización del Proceso Autonómico* (Organic Law on the Harmonisation of the Autonomy Process)
LODE	*Ley Orgánica del Derecho a la Educación* (Organic Law on the Right to Education)
LOGSE	*Ley de Ordenación General del Sistema Educativo* (Law on the General Organisation of the Education System)
LOPJ	*Ley Orgánica del Poder Judicial* (Organic Law on the Judiciary)
MERCOSUR	Free Trade organisation involving Brazil, Argentina, Paraguay and Uruguay
META	*Plan de Modernización del Ejército de Tierra* (Plan to Modernise the Army)
NATO	North Atlantic Treaty Organisation
OECD	Organisation for Economic Co-operation and Development
ONUCA	United Nations Observation Group in Central America
ONUSAL	United Nations Observation Group in El Salvador
OPEC	Organisation of Petroleum-Exporting Countries
ORGA	*Organización Republicana Gallega Autónoma* – Galician political organisation in the 2nd Republic
OSI	Operational Services Inspection [*Inspección Operativa de Servicios*, IOS]
PAD	*Partido de Acción Democrática* – short-lived christian democratic party
PCE	*Partido Comunista de España* (Communist Party)
PDL	*Partido Democrático Liberal* – short-lived liberal party
PDP	*Partido Democrático Popular* – conservative christian democratic party set up in 1982
PNV	*Partido Nacionalista Vasco* (Basque Nationalist Party)
PP	*Partido Popular* (Popular Party)
PRD	*Partido Reformista Democrático* – short-lived centrist party set up by Miquel Roca in 1983
PSC-PSOE	*Partit del Socialistes de Catalunya* (Catalan branch of the PSOE)
PSE-PSOE	*Partido Socialista de Euskadi* (Basque branch of the PSOE)
PSOE	*Partido Socialista Obrero Español* (Socialist Party)

PSP   *Partido Socialista Popular* – small socialist group led by Enrique Tierno Galván

PSUC   *Partit Socialista Unificat de Catalunya* (Catalan Communist Party)

Pta   Peseta

RTVE   *Radio-Televisión Española* – state-owned television and radio network

SEA   Single European Act

SPP   *Sindicato* [formerly *Asociación*] *Profesional de Policía* – police trade union

TSJ   *Tribunal Superior de Justicia* (Higher Court of Justice) – regional court

UCD   *Unión de Centro Democrático* (Democratic Centre Union) – a right-wing coalition which governed Spain between 1977 and 1982

UDC   *Unió Democrático de Catalunya* – component part of the CiU

UGT   *Unión General de Trabajadores* (General Workers' Union) – historically associated with the Socialist Party

UK   United Kingdom

USA   United States of America

USO   *Unión Sindical Obrera* – small scale trade union

USP   *Unión Sindical de Policías* – police trade union

VAT   Value-added tax [*Impuesto Sobre el Valor Añadido*, IVA]

WEU   Western European Union

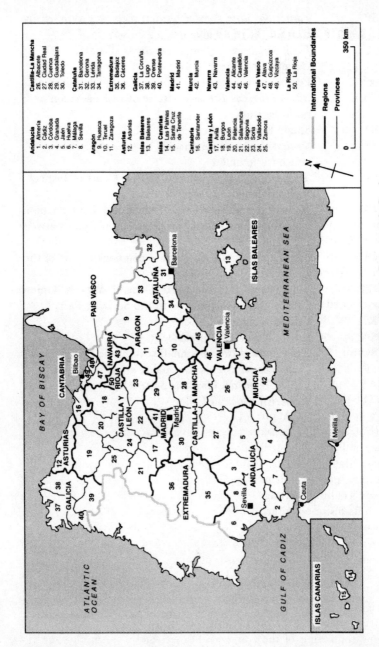

Autonomous Regions and Provinces in Democratic Spain

Andalucía	**Castilla–La Mancha**
1. Almería	26. Albacete
2. Cádiz	27. Ciudad Real
3. Córdoba	28. Cuenca
4. Granada	29. Guadalajara
5. Jaén	30. Toledo
6. Huelva	
7. Málaga	**Cataluña**
8. Sevilla	31. Barcelona
	32. Gerona
Aragón	33. Lérida
9. Huesca	34. Tarragona
10. Teruel	
11. Zaragoza	**Extremadura**
	35. Badajoz
Asturias	36. Cáceres
12. Asturias	
	Galicia
Islas Baleares	37. La Coruña
13. Baleares	38. Lugo
	39. Orense
Islas Canarias	40. Pontevedra
14. Las Palmas	
15. Santa Cruz	**Madrid**
de Tenerife	41. Madrid
Cantabria	**Murcia**
16. Santander	42. Murcia
Castilla y León	**Navarra**
17. Avila	43. Navarra
18. Burgos	
19. León	**Valencia**
20. Palencia	44. Alicante
21. Salamanca	45. Castellón
22. Segovia	46. Valencia
23. Soria	
24. Valladolid	**País Vasco**
25. Zamora	47. Alava
	48. Guipúzcoa
	49. Vizcaya
	La Rioja
	50. La Rioja

International Boundaries
Regions
Provinces

0   350 km

Introduction: Analysing Spanish Politics

On 26 July 1992, with a massive police escort and amid considerable controversy, Pablo Picasso's *Guernica* was moved from the Casón del Buen Retiro at Madrid's Prado Museum to the city's newly-opened modern art gallery, the Centro de Arte Reina Sofia. At Picasso's behest, *Guernica* – a searing condemnation of the Civil War atrocity in which Nazi aeroplanes, on behalf of General Franco, bombed the undefended Basque market town to destruction – had come to Spain only after the restoration of democracy. Picasso, who died in 1973, never saw his wish fulfilled; Franco outlived him by two years, and not until 1981 was *Guernica* finally shipped from New York's Museum of Modern Art (where it had remained on extended loan since 1939) to be displayed in its own special gallery at the Prado.

The painting's subsequent relocation within Madrid was symbolic in a double sense. At one level, it signified a coming to terms with the terrible tragedy represented by the Civil War: rather than emphasise the conflict's continued capacity to divide Spaniards more than fifty years after its end by exhibiting *Guernica* in a unique setting, the painting now took its place amidst other works which formed part of Spain's cultural heritage. *Guernica* could henceforth be appreciated in both its historic and artistic context, much as Goya's powerful works document an earlier period of Spanish history. At another level, however, the fact that the relocation of *Guernica* not only aroused impassioned feelings, but also that the painting remains behind bullet-proof glass to protect it from right-wing extremists – as it has done ever since it arrived in Spain – is indicative of the continued weight of the country's past in contemporary Spain.

To understand the politics of democratic Spain, it is necessary to know something of the country's history. Spain's current constitutional arrangements have been profoundly conditioned by its

1

historical legacy – most notably the experience of civil war and dictatorship during the twentieth century, in turn the product of deep social divisions. Yet, the country's longer-term historical experience has also helped shape contemporary aspirations: Spain's determination to play a central role in the construction of an integrated Europe reflects a desire to avoid experiencing ever again the political marginalisation which had followed the loss of empire. Between Spain's imperial heyday in the sixteenth century and the 1930s' conflicts which led to civil war, the country was relegated in political terms to the status of a European backwater. Thereafter, the Franco dictatorship (1939-75) ensured that Spain would remain a marginal force in democratic Europe. Only with the post-Franco transition to democracy did Spain begin to re-establish a significant international presence.

From Empire to Isolation

That Spain should have experienced such an extended period of political isolation was remarkable for a country which had been at the very heart of Europe's expansionist hegemony in the fifteenth and sixteenth centuries. 1492 – a date familiar to all Spanish school-children – marked the beginning of imperial dominance. Granada, the last Muslim kingdom on the Iberian peninsula, fell that year to the 'Catholic kings', Ferdinand and Isabella, whilst the great voyage of Columbus laid the foundations for Spain's maritime empire. Under the Habsburg monarchy, particularly Philip II (1556–98), Spain not only became the staunchest defender of the Catholic Church against Protestant reformers, but also extended her European possessions. Yet paradoxically, in spite of its imperial reach, the Spanish state remained poorly integrated and weakly developed. By the time Philip II's great-grandson bequeathed his throne to the house of Bourbon in 1700, Habsburg grandeur was fading fast. Territorial losses in Europe and the revolt of both the Portuguese and the Catalans in 1640 had severely weakened the Spanish throne, further evidenced by the Treaty of Utrecht (1713), which ceded Gibraltar to the British. Under the Bourbons, Spain underwent a process of long-term decline, and the old regime finally crumbled before Napoleon's invading armies (1807-8). Although the French Revolution had some impact in the peninsula – notably in the 1812 'liberal' *Cortes* of Cádiz – when the monarchy was restored in 1814, Ferdinand VII's absolutist rule ushered in a period of revolts and the loss of the American colonies.

In the early nineteenth century, two antagonistic blocs – which were to dominate Spanish history for well over a century – began to crystallise. Forces of reform, which sought to bring Spain's political structure into line with its evolving social structure, were repeatedly confronted by reactionary elements reliant upon military force to maintain the power balance in their favour. A tradition of *pronunciamientos* (military risings) emerged, which effectively left the choice of government in the hands of the army. Unlike in Britain and France, there was no establishment during the nineteenth century of a relatively democratic polity able to adjust to and absorb new social forces. Instead, the Spanish state maintained the power of the monarchy, the landed nobility and the Catholic Church basically intact until well into the twentieth century. Following the overthrow of the First Republic (1873-4), a 'reactionary coalition' became established between this ruling oligarchy and a politically weak commercial and manufacturing bourgeoisie.

The political system of the 'Restoration Monarchy' (1875-1923), known as the '*turno pacífico*', was designed to maintain the configuration of political power in Spain basically unaltered whilst presenting a façade of parliamentary democracy. Two political parties, the Conservative and the Liberal, alternated in power, keeping their position through the actions of *caciques* – local political bosses who, through a variety of more or less corrupt means, ensured that electoral results approximated to the predetermined outcomes decided upon in Madrid. Challenges to the system did emerge, however, from the burgeoning working-class movement, both socialist and anarchist, and the regional nationalism which was becoming a potent political force in Catalonia and the Basque Country. By 1917 the country was starkly divided between mutually hostile groups.

The counterpoint between the forces of reform and reaction spilled into an escalating spiral of violence between 1917 and 1923, brought to an end only by the dictatorial intervention of General Miguel Primo de Rivera. Primo, though, proved unable to construct a viable replacement for the *turno* system, and he was forced to resign in 1930. The Second Republic, which was proclaimed on 14 April 1931, represented a bold reformist experiment aimed at modernising Spain's political structure by establishing the country's first genuine democracy. During the course of the Republic, however, the divisions in Spanish society which had developed over the course of the previous hundred years hardened into a series of bitter confrontations which pitched republicans against monarchists, anti-clericals against the Catholic Church, regionalists against centralists, workers against employers. By 1936, war appeared inevitable. General Franco's uprising on 18 July, and the savage civil war which ensued, represented the ultimate expression of reactionary forces in Spanish politics seeking to crush any threat to their privileged status.

The Franco dictatorship made no attempt at national reconciliation. Instead, the rhetoric of the regime, which emphasised the distinction between victors and vanquished, confirmed the long-term divisions which had marked Spain's troubled history. Through a centralised and heavily bureaucratic political structure, Franco sought to impose his vision of a unified Spain – '*una, grande y libre*' – fashioned in the image of imperial greatness. Although the face of the regime became less repressive over time, with ideological justification drawn from Catholicism rather than the fascism of Franco's sponsors during the civil war, Hitler and Mussolini, all forms of political pluralism remained proscribed. Significant economic growth during the 1960s helped further ameliorate the regime's image, and Franco was able to pose as the avuncular patron of Spain's socio-economic modernisation. Yet, when the regime's opponents (now including sections of the Catholic Church) began to mount increasingly serious challenges to its survival in the late 1960s, Franco reverted to the harsh repression which had marked his early years in power: political executions took place as late as 27 September 1975. The dictator's death two months later, on 20 November 1975, closed one the darkest chapters in Spain's history, but left the country once more seemingly facing the abyss of irreconcilable political division.

The Transition to Democracy and the Analysis of Spanish Politics

In the event, Franco's death was followed not by bloody conflict, as had been feared by many, but by a remarkably rapid and skilfully engineered transition to democracy. The success of the transition generated a massive outpouring of literature, much of it seeking to explain how the divisions which had characterised Spain's political development for centuries had been kept in check in the aftermath of the Franco regime.[1] Interest in Spain's transition to democracy was further stimulated by the collapse of communist regimes in Eastern Europe and the Soviet Union between 1989 and 1991: the Spanish 'model' was seized upon by many academics and politicians as holding the key to the successful construction of democratic states in the post-communist world (Di Palma, 1990: 185; Maxwell, 1991; Huntington, 1991/92: 592; Mainwaring *et al.*, 1992: 5; Cuenca Toribio, 1994). Such analyses tended to overlook crucial differences between the Spanish experience and that of the former communist regimes – not least, the significance of a general desire to avoid re-opening the wounds created by the civil war and its aftermath, as well as the fact that Spain's economy had been integrated into the market-based western capitalist framework long before Franco's death, thereby allowing the embryonic emergence of a pluralist civil society.[2] Nevertheless, academic interest in contemporary Spain has remained very firmly focused on the success of its political transition from dictatorship to democracy.

Far less attention has been paid to the subsequent development of Spain's democracy. With a few notable exceptions, political scientists have by and large ignored the government and politics of contemporary Spain. Moreover, those political scientists who have devoted extensive attention to Spain – such as Ramón Cotarelo, José Ramón Montero, Lourdes López Nieto, Joan Botella, Richard Gunther and Samuel Barnes – have tended overwhelmingly to concentrate on specific aspects of the Spanish political process, notably parties, electoral behaviour and opinion surveys. The territorial organisation of the post-Franco Spanish state has also been the focus of a number of studies. However, as yet – and in marked contrast to the myriad texts on the politics of other European states like Britain, France, Germany and Italy – there has been no synoptic analytical overview of the government and politics of Spain. Such volumes as do exist on the politics of contemporary Spain have generally been edited collections, often compiled by historians or sociologists (Carcassonne *et al.*, 1979; Abel and Torrents, 1984; Payne, 1986; Giner, 1990; Vidal-Beneyto, 1991a, 1991b; Cotarelo, 1992). Despite their many virtues, these collections face inevitable problems of imbalance in the treatment of different issues, inconsistent approaches, and repetition of basic material.

There are two main reasons for the lack of attention paid to Spain by academics working in departments of political science. First, and most obviously, very few political scientists are Hispanists; secondly, very few Spanish academics are political scientists. Area specialists working on Europe, notably in the English-speaking world, have understandably tended to focus on the 'major' countries, a community of which Spain did not form part until very recently. In turn, comparativists have often lacked appropriate points of reference for including Spain within wider studies. Meanwhile, the study of politics within Spain has developed within a distinctive European tradition, shaped by its location mainly within faculties of law (*derecho*), which has led it to focus primarily on political theory and constitutional issues. Indeed, the discipline of political science was not specifically recognised in Spanish academe until the University Reform Law of 1984 (Colino Cámara *et al.*, 1994: 527). As a result, Spanish studies of the political system have often been characterised by minute analysis of the 1978 Constitution, rather than its translation into practice[3] (Alvarez Conde, 1990; Aparicio, 1988; Baena del Alcázar, 1988; López Pina, 1987; Blas Guerrero, 1983). Other areas, such as core executive decision-making, the impact of institutional arrangements on the political process, policy styles and environments, and the political influence of the judiciary, have barely been identified as key issues.

The present volume seeks to provide a broad overview of government and politics in contemporary Spain. The central theme of the volume is that, for the first time in modern history, the organisation of the Spanish state combines functional efficiency with recognition of the country's social composition. State and civil society are no longer in serious conflict, as they have been so often in Spain's past. The key to the central state's effectiveness has been the provision in the 1978 Constitution of a very high degree of executive power, based on formal mechanisms of accountability (even though, in practice, these have often failed to operate as envisaged by Spain's constitutional architects). However, the existence of a strong executive, which has provided for governmental stability, has been counter-balanced by two developments which are of growing significance in contemporary Spain and which form the sub-themes of this study: the territorial organisation of the state and integration into the European Union (EU).

Spain's system of seventeen regional governments, which enjoy extensive (and increasing) powers in their own right, has acted as a check on the central state. Whilst the relationship between central and regional governments has often been troubled and continues to be the source of political conflict, Spain's current territorial organisation represents the most effective solution to the regional issue ever attempted. A further constraint on the power of the central state derives from the trend towards European economic integration, as evidenced most obviously in the 1987 Single European Act and the 1992 Maastricht Treaty. Spain's entry into the European Community (EC) in 1986 represented a formal return to Europe's political mainstream, thereby bringing to an end nearly two centuries of international isolation. However, the political process in Spain, particularly in regard to macroeconomic policy, has been profoundly conditioned by the broader demands of European integration. Spain's membership of Europe has resulted in increased influence on the international stage only at the expense of a decreased capacity to shape the broad parameters of domestic policy. In this regard, Spain finds itself in a similar position to that of most of the EU's member states.

It is a central argument of this study that contemporary Spain should be seen as an established European democracy: naturally, Spain's democracy has distinctive elements, but its political structure shares many features in common with various European partners, its political challenges are those which face all European democracies. However, in spite of the remarkable success of its transition to democracy – a success which few observers would have believed possible in 1975 – Spain's political health has increasingly been called into question during the 1990s. Particular concern has been expressed in Spain over such issues as a perceived lack of executive accountability, the ineffectiveness of parliament, the loss of policy autonomy as a result of European integration and the resultant 'democratic deficit', and – most tellingly – the widespread existence of political corruption. These are all real and serious problems which, if not confronted and tackled by the political class as a whole, could undermine the legitimacy of the democratic process. Yet, significantly, these problems mirror similar concerns which exist throughout Europe. This is not to seek to underplay their importance, but rather to suggest that they neither derive exclusively from the organisation of the Spanish state, nor are they open to simple solutions. It is to be hoped that the sense of political responsibility which facilitated the success of the transition to democracy will safeguard its achievements as Spain approaches the next millenium.

The book is divided into three parts. Part 1 looks at how the organisation of the contemporary Spanish state has been conditioned by the country's historical legacy, with particular regard to the regional issue. The changing role and influence of major social institutions – such as the military and the Catholic Church – are also discussed, as is the elaboration of the 1978 Constitution. Part 2 of the book analyses the political organisation of the democratic state. Attention is paid to executive, legislative and judicial institutions, as well as to the modernisation of the public sector. Thereafter, a detailed analysis of the structure of Autonomous Communities is followed by a discussion of political parties and the electoral and party systems. Part 3 assesses Spain's emergence as an international power, laying emphasis on its economic transformation since the return of democracy, the evolution of the policy process, and the development of a significant profile on the international stage. Given that several of these issues are dealt with in a systematic manner for the first time in this volume, it is inevitable that there will be errors of fact and interpretation in what follows. Naturally, the responsibility for any such errors is mine alone.

Part I
The Legacy of History

1

Reconciling State and Nation: The Politics of Regional Diversity

Spain is one of the oldest states in Europe, having occupied the same boundaries for some 500 years. Yet, in spite of the political dominance of Castile and the Castilian language, regional differences hold the key to understanding the modern Spanish state (see Exhibit 1.1). Since the nineteenth century, regional demands have constituted one of the central issues in Spanish politics. The few occasions on which they have been answered – such as during the First and Second Republics[1] – have generally been followed by periods of more or less rigid centralism. General Franco, who ruled over Spain from 1939 until his death in 1975, imposed an unbending and repressive policy of state centralism throughout his period in power. Thus, at one level, the emergence of regionalism as a paramount political issue in contemporary Spain is an obvious and direct legacy of the Franco regime insofar as it represents a reaction to his stultifying rule. However, regionalism has much deeper roots, and any attempt to understand its continued significance must consider the context within which Spain became a unified state.

'Regional Nationalism' and the Emergence of a Modern State

The dual process of state-building and nation-building has been of fundamental importance to the territorial structure and identity of modern Spain. It has been argued that Spain's unity was largely

EXHIBIT 1.1

The Spanish Regions

Region[a]	Provinces	Capital city	Size (km^2)	Population (million)
Andalucía	Almería, Cádiz, Córdoba, Granada, Jaén, Huelva, Málaga, Sevilla	Sevilla	87,268^2	6.44
Aragón	Huesca, Teruel, Zaragoza	Zaragoza	47,669^2	1.2
Principado de Asturias	Asturias	Oviedo	10,565^2	1.13
Islas Baleares	Baleares	Palma	5,014^2	0.66
Canarias	Las Palmas, Santa Cruz de Tenerife	Las Palmas de Gran Canaria	7,273^2	1.37
Cantabria	Santander	Santander	5,289^2	0.51
Castilla y León	Avila, Burgos, León, Palencia, Salamanca, Segovia, Soria, Valladolid, Zamora	Valladolid	94,147^2	2.54
Castilla-La Mancha	Albacete, Ciudad Real, Cuenca, Guadalajara, Toledo	Toledo	79,226^2	1.65
Catalunya (Cataluña)	Barcelona, Gerona, Lérida, Tarragona	Barcelona	31,930^2	5.66
Extremadura	Badajoz, Cáceres	Mérida	41,602^2	1.06
Galiza (Galicia)	La Coruña, Lugo, Orense, Pontevedra	Santiago	29,434^2	2.81
Comunidad de Madrid	Madrid	Madrid	7,995^2	4.69
Región de Murcia	Murcia	Murcia	11,317^2	0.96
Comunidad Foral de Navarra	Navarra	Pamplona	10,421^2	0.51
Comunidad Valenciana	Alicante, Castellón, Valencia	Valencia	23,305^2	3.65
Euskadi (País Vasco)	Alava, Guipúzcoa, Vizcaya	Vitoria (Gasteiz)	7,261^2	2.14
La Rioja	La Rioja	Logroño	5,034^2	0.25

[a] Regions listed by official title, with Spanish equivalent indicated where relevant.

artificial until well into the nineteenth century (Fusi, 1989: 14). According to Juan Linz (1973), Spain became a nation-state – in the Weberian sense of commanding loyal solidarity over and above its claim to a monopoly of the legitimate use of force – only slowly and sporadically.

It was not until the eighteenth century that there emerged the first manifestations of genuine 'Spanish' identity, seen through developments such as a concern with the historical sense of the notion of Spain, the creation of national cultural institutions, and the development of governmental projects at national level. Prior to that date, the Spanish state had been composed of a series of distinct kingdoms, united formally through dynastic marriages and military conquest, but with no overall national identity. At the same time as this national identity began to emerge, however, equivalent processes were taking place at regional level. In the Basque Country, for instance, studies were published in the early eighteenth century which sought to codify the national language, and a royal society was established in 1765 to promote indigenous culture. Similar developments took place in Galicia and Asturias, adding emphasis to the fact remarked upon by one observer in 1846 that Spain was the country of the '*patria chica*', made up of various different regions with their own languages, customs, and social traditions (Ford, 1974: 13).

A real sense of popular patriotism became evident only with the Napoleonic invasion of 1808, but even then it was often fragmented and localist in character. The construction of a centralised state was a lengthy process, less the result of political nationalism than of gradual adaptation to the evolving machinery of the state. Until well into the twentieth century, the province remained the primary focus of identity; in the view of José Ortega y Gasset (1931), the Spanish philosopher, the province represented the most authentic social reality in Spain upon which any sense of national identity would have to be constructed. Spanish nationalism was thus very weak as a force for social cohesion. Indeed, social and economic fragmentation remained marked until a cohesive national political and administrative system was finally achieved.

The emergence of such a system was dependent upon developments such as the growth of trade, markets, and population centres, the construction of a communications infrastructure, and the creation of a common educational plan. The major growth in population centres and railways occurred at around the same time, between 1840 and 1860 (Shubert, 1990: 16–19, 43–56). Other important stages along the road towards national cohesion were the modernisation of the central administration through the adoption in 1823 of a ministerial system of government, the establishment of a uniform system of local government through the reform of provincial administration in 1833, the creation of the Civil Guard in 1844, the development of penal codes in 1848 and 1879, and the adoption of national systems of secondary education in 1845 and 1857. Only through the combined effect of all these developments did a 'national' sense of Spanish identity emerge towards the end of the nineteenth century, capable of acting as a force for social cohesion. A key moment in this process occurred – perhaps paradoxically – with the so-called 'disaster of 1898', when Spain lost Cuba, Puerto Rico and the Philippines, her only significant remaining colonial possessions. The disaster provided a major stimulus to a nascent, but growing, concern amongst Spanish intellectuals to identify the nature of *Hispanidad*, or 'Spanishness'. Leading figures amongst 'the generation of '98', such as Miguel Unamuno and Rafael Altamira, attempted to confront the question of just what it was that constituted the essential nature of Spain.

Their concern derived in part from the lack of cultural homogenisation in Bourbon Spain. In a sense, Spain was out of synchrony with other European states in terms of the development of a distinctive national consciousness. In Britain and France national bonding was fostered in part by colonial aggrandisement, and in Germany and Italy unification in the mid-nineteenth century gave rise to a wave of romantic nationalism. In Spain, however, nationalism was primarily a *local* phenomenon. Thus, the nineteenth century saw not only the extension of an idea of the nation and national sentiments, but also the confirmation of the province as the focus of political identity. Provincial capitals became centres of regional affairs, while *diputaciones* (local councils) – although limited in number – began to consolidate their power bases. During the mid-nineteenth century there began to emerge a clear sense of regional identity in areas such as Andalucía, Catalonia, the Basque Country and the capital, Madrid. One indication of this development was the importance of local, as opposed to national, newspapers – most notably in the emerging industrial centres, Barcelona and Bilbao, where titles such as *La Vanguardia* and *El Liberal* started to exercise political influence.

Moreover, it can hardly be overstressed that the central Spanish state remained weak, being both financially poor and administratively inefficient. This fact helps to explain a development of crucial significance to the strength of regional nationalism in the nineteenth and twentieth centuries: the appropriation of state functions by *caciques* and local oligarchs. In common with most of Mediterranean Europe where the central state was omnipresent but weak, regional brokers arose – *caciques* in Spain, *mafioso* in Italy, *comatarhis* in Greece – to mediate between centre and periphery. The patron-client relationships upon which the brokerage system rested served as a mechanism of social order. However, once economic modernisation was under way in regions such as Catalonia and the Basque Country, so the network of regional brokerage began to be undermined: the political centre found it ever harder to impose its will on economically more powerful regions, and specific nationalist demands increasingly sought satisfaction from Madrid (Heiberg, 1989: 234ff. ; Gellner and Waterbury, 1975). Yet, the central administrative apparatus remained small, with just eight central ministries by 1900. Furthermore, central state expenditure was overwhelmingly directed towards either military purposes or servicing the national debt, with little devoted to the building of a modern state infrastructure.

Thus, what little industrial development did take place was concentrated in particular regions, most notably Catalonia and the Basque Country. In the former, textile manufacturing served as the motor of economic growth during the nineteenth century, whilst iron ore, metallurgy and ship-building underpinned the latter's slightly later emergence as Spain's leading industrial centre. Although Madrid remained the political centre, economic hegemony shifted decisively to Barcelona and Bilbao, where it would remain until the late twentieth century. Catalonia established close trading links with Cuba, where textiles enjoyed preferential treatment. When Cuba was lost to the United States of America in 1898, the deep structural crisis which resulted within the Catalan economy provoked major social tensions and served as a stimulus to the emergence of militant nationalism. In the Basque Country, economic expansion occurred more rapidly and was linked to northern Europe rather than colonial markets. Here, appalling working conditions, combined with the social stresses related to a vertiginous growth in the population, engendered a distinctive brand of nationalism which married elements of racism with anti-industrialism and fervent Catholicism.

The emergence of Catalan and Basque nationalism as potent political forces represented a crisis for the restored Bourbon state's territorial structure. From the last quarter of the nineteenth century, the national question attained a decisive importance in Spanish politics and became one of the major dynamics in the country's troubled development. Even before the 1898 'disaster' provoked a wave of anti-Madrid nationalism, pressure had been exerted on the central state to recognise regions in addition to provinces. Reform projects by Segismundo Moret (1884) and Francisco Silvela (1891) created thirteen regions with their own governments and councils which – with the exception of León and Murcia – coincided with the historic kingdoms. Further measures by Antonio Maura in the first decade of the new century paved the way for the creation of the *Mancomunitat Catalana* in 1914, a form of regional government which encompassed the provinces of Barcelona, Gerona, Lérida and Tarragona. Its first president was Enric Prat de la Riba, a leading theorist of conservative Catalan nationalism in the *Lliga Regionalista*, which had been founded in 1901 'to work by all legitimate means for the autonomy of the Catalan people within the Spanish state'. In the Basque Country, meanwhile, nationalists won the 1907 mayorial contest in Bilbao, and took control of the Vizcaya local council in 1917.

Regional nationalism severely challenged the political order established under the Restoration Monarchy. However, the generic term 'regional nationalism' obscures the fact that its various specific manifestations were far from uniform in nature. Catalan and Basque nationalism may have emerged as significant political movements in the same period, but their origins, characteristics and demands were divergent. By the same token, the emergence of nationalist consciousness in regions such as Galicia and Andalucía followed distinctive patterns which reflected their own particular historical logic. None the less, one factor which unites the so-called 'historic regions' of Catalonia, the Basque Country and Galicia is that each has a separate language, a potent element in the construction of the primordial identities often associated with regional nationalism.[2] In short, the development of Spain's nationalist movements reflects the interlocking influence of both economic and cultural imperatives, the relative balance of each varying according to the region in question.

Until well into the twentieth century, the Spanish state could be seen as 'weak, yet heavy'. Political power was concentrated in the hands of an oligarchic and labour-repressive 'reactionary coalition' (Moore, 1967: 433–52) comprising the monarchy and landed classes together with religious and military elites; however, the diffuse regional composition of the country generated a network of patron-client relationships – backed up by the threat (and occasional use) of force – through which the central state sought to impose its rule. The intrusive, yet ineffective, central state in turn inhibited the emergence of a strong civil society which could provide a counter-balance to its centralising tendencies. A combination of weak state and weak civil society provided a fertile soil in which germinated the seeds of division that culminated in the Spanish Civil War (1936-9). Only under the Franco dictatorship did the central state begin to function as an *effective* instrument of political control, albeit at the cost of repressing all manifestations of societal incorporation.

Over time, however, the Franco regime underwent a significant transformation from what might be termed 'Hobbesian domination' during its period of economic autarky (1939–59) towards gradual integration into the western liberal capitalist framework. The consequent internationalisation of Spain's economy undermined the bases upon which the Franco state rested, highlighting the growing contradiction between political repression and the demands of economic liberalisation. The regime's loss of legitimacy was reflected in the growth of popular discontent and organised opposition within Spain, and the hesitant emergence of societal initiatives which would lay the basis for the post-Franco transition to democracy (Pérez-Díaz, 1993). The regional dimension of these initiatives, which derived major impetus from the activity of Basque nationalists in particular, was of inestimable importance.

Nationalism and Cultural Identity

The cultural component of nationalist claims has given rise to powerful myths. In the search for an identity which surpassed mere territoriality, many nationalists were prone to emphasise the supposed individuality of their regions – a tendency which was lent added weight by the widespread practice of cultural stereotyping. The two most obvious examples of this phenomenon concern Catalonia and the Basque Country: both regions have seen various nationalist attempts to construct theories of racial or genetic uniqueness. Yet, Galicia too has increasingly emphasised its cultural distinctiveness, a pattern which has been mirrored in many of Spain's regions since the post-Franco restoration of democracy.

Catalonia: A Distinctive National Identity

In Catalonia during the nineteenth century, Dr Bartolomeu Robert i Yarzábal, mayor of Barcelona from 1899 until his death in 1902, carried out anthropometric studies which purported to prove, via cranial measurements, that Catalans were a superior race. His findings prompted the Catalan nationalist politician, Antoni Rovira, to write in 1916, 'If a different cranium predominates in the north-east of the country, we Catalans are not going to deform our skulls just to support Spanish unity' (Rovira i Virgili, 1916: 24; see also, Hughes, 1992: 494–7; Temprano, 1988: Ch. 6). In the early twentieth century considerable emphasis was placed on the purity of the Catalan race by nationalists, including the bishop of Vic, Josep Torras i Bages, who attributed Catalan superiority to divine design (Hughes, 1992: 317–22). As in the case of early Basque nationalists, such claims to racial distinction smacked of xenophobia.

However, the main focus of cultural identity in Catalonia has been language. Indeed, it was mainly through a nineteenth-century literary renaissance (*renaixença*) that Catalan nationalism first took root among the region's intellectuals and middle classes. The most renowned expression of a distinctively Catalan culture came through the architectural style known as '*Modernisme*', which emerged in Barcelona at the turn of the twentieth century in response to dramatic demographic expansion: the city's population rose from 272 000 in 1887 to nearly 547 000 by the turn of the century, giving rise to feverish town-planning activity. '*Modernisme*', which encompassed the genius of such architects as Antoni Gaudí, Josep Puig i Cadafalch and Lluís Domènech i Montaner, sought to synthesise traditional Catalan architecture with modern European currents, utilising the latest technological and engineering advances to create 'total works'. The movement was instrumental in the reconstruction of Barcelona as a distinctively Catalan capital city.

Because Catalan nationalism arose from a cultural movement, its political formulation evolved in a gradual and fluid manner, conditioned both by external references and local circumstances. Significantly, under the Restoration Monarchy (1875–1923) Catalonia underwent a process of modernisation which highlighted differences between the region and the rest of Spain in terms of economic, social, political and cultural development. By 1900, 40 per cent of Spain's industrial production was concentrated in Catalonia (De Riquer Permanyer, 1989: 380). As the economy developed, so a distinctively Catalan civil society emerged – reflected in a major growth of associational activity – which first began to organise politically in an era of intensive class struggle. If Catalonia saw the early development of regional nationalism, it was equally a major centre for the growth of republican, radical and syndical movements.

The bourgeois intellectuals who led Catalan nationalist demands initially favoured a strong central state, able to defend their interests from the twin threats of revolutionary insurrection and the ultra-reactionary recidivism represented by Carlism.[3] However, the ever more apparent failings of the central state – which reached their nadir with the 'disaster of 1898' – prompted a more pragmatic approach. Although still conservative in economic and political terms, Catalan nationalists began in the early twentieth century to organise actively in defence of their own interests and against Madrid-based governments. Many of the nationalist movement's key leaders – figures such as Prat de la Riba, Francesc Cambó and, in recent years, Jordi Pujol – have sought to represent and defend Catalan business interests. Equally, the most successful nationalist organisations, such as the *Lliga Regionalista* (founded in 1901 and active until the Civil War) and Pujol's post-Franco coalition, *Convergència i Unió* (CiU), have been politically conservative, despite their demands for Catalan autonomy.

The conservatism of early Catalan nationalists is accounted for, in part, by the radicalism of the region's labour movement. The anarcho-syndicalist *Confederación Nacional del Trabajo* (CNT), founded in 1910, achieved its greatest impact in Catalonia. Between 1916 and 1920, Barcelona's industrial zone experienced the highest incidence of strikes in western Europe, provoking an extreme employers' backlash which in turn led to an intense spiral of violence. The collapse of social order was ended only with the dictatorial intervention in 1923 of Catalonia's captain-general, General Miguel Primo de Rivera, whose rule was marked by the repression of nationalist demands (Ben-Ami, 1983). However, during the Second Republic, the region gained its first experience of democratic autonomy. The *Esquerra Republicana de Catalunya* (Catalan Republican Left), a moderate, left-leaning nationalist party with a cross-class appeal, became the dominant force in the *Generalitat*, the Catalan parliament created in 1932. Francesc Macià, founder of the *Esquerra*, and Luis Companys, who succeeded him as leader, were key figures not just in Catalan politics, but also at a national level – most notably in October 1934 when Companys launched an abortive move for Catalan independence. The *Esquerra* subsequently re-emerged in the post-Franco period, adopting an ever more radical stance which led in 1992 to its calling for Catalan independence.

Following the post-Franco transition to democracy, the reconstituted *Generalitat* has been dominated by the CiU, whose leader Jordi Pujol has governed the region since 1980. Under Pujol's leadership, Catalan claims to the status of 'nation' have been relentlessly pursued. Partially as a reaction to the enforced use of Castilian during the Franco dictatorship, it has become virtually *de rigueur* to speak in Catalan: the *Generalitat* not only promotes the use of Catalan as part of its policy of *fer país* (literally 'nation-making'), but has made promotion to some posts in the public sector dependent upon passing a language proficiency exam. In 1986, the Information and Documentation Consortium of Catalonia conducted a Language Census, which sought to analyse the population's knowledge of the regional language. It showed that 31.5 per cent had a full working knowledge of the language, including being able to write in it, 60.5 per cent could read it, 64 per cent spoke it, and 90.4 per cent understood it (Puigjaner, 1989: 52–6). The 1983 Law of Linguistic Normalisation sought to defend a language which was defined as being in a precarious situation, and confers on all citizens the right to choose to communicate in Catalan or Spanish with any public institutions. The *Generalitat* announced in November 1993 that, under the terms of the 1983 law, up to 50 per cent of all films shown in Catalan cinemas must be either in the regional language or else subtitled.[4] However, the region's leading newspaper, *La Vanguardia*, is still published in Spanish, reflecting the fact that a significant minority of Catalonia's population does not use the vernacular.

The Basque Country: In Search of Cultural Definition

Prior to the Franco regime, Catalonia rather than the Basque Country had been the main source of regionalist challenges to Madrid government. Only with the emergence of violent protest against the dictatorship did the Basque Country come to represent the principal threat to the vision of a unitary Spain. However, in contrast to Catalonia, the issue of identity in the Basque Country has been complicated by a lack of consensus over what the definition of 'Basque' entails, and no agreement on the criteria by which it may be defined, nor even who may rightfully lay claim to the distinction (Clark, 1990a: 78).

Basque nationalism as an organised political movement emerged relatively late: nationalists themselves date the origins of their political struggle to the 1890s when a series of violent incidents in Bilbao provided the impetus for the formation of the *Partido Nacionalista Vasco* (PNV, Basque Nationalist Party). Outside the province of Vizcaya, Basque nationalism failed to establish a significant presence until nearly a decade into the twentieth century. Moreover, the three Basque provinces of Guipúzcoa, Alava and Vizcaya have never been united as an independent political entity, nor even an administrative unit. From the thirteenth century onwards, they have been under some form of Castillian tutelage (Fusi, 1984: Ch. 10).

None the less, the Basque Country does have a legitimate claim to a distinctive identity within the Spanish nation. Both language and its own peculiar administrative structure, the so-called foral system, have underlain the continuity of a Basque sense of differentiation from the rest of Spain. The foral system has been subject to considerable misinterpretation. Rather than a uniform, rigid and closed administrative system which granted specific rights to the Basque regions and Navarra, this medieval privilege entailed a collection of disparate juridical dispositions which varied considerably according to the area in question. Moreover, foral rights never took precedence over Spanish national legislation. Thus, although foral rights encompassed a wide-ranging and distinctive series of provisions, they never amounted to codes of sovereignty as was later claimed by Basque nationalists. None the less, their abolition by stages during the nineteenth century (finally consummated in 1876) elevated them into a powerful symbol of a distinctive Basque identity (Fusi, 1984: 188–93).

Language provided equally potent symbolism. Federico Krutwig, author of *Vasconia* (1963), a key text in the ideological definition of the Basque separatist organisation, ETA (*Euzkadi Ta Askatasuna*: Basque Homeland and Liberty), claimed that language was the most important factor of Basque identity. However, such an emphasis came late in the development of Basque nationalism. The origins of *Euskera*, the only anciently-established non-Indo-European language extant in western Europe, remain obscure. Its peculiarity is such that it has so far defied scholarly agreement even as to its classification (Collins, 1986: 8–12). The very obscurity and consequent poor diffusion of the language led to its being largely overlooked by nationalist intellectuals in the earliest phase of the movement: few of them actually spoke *Euskera*. In contrast to Catalan, the inherent difficulty and lack of direct connection to Spanish or Portuguese continues to militate against the adoption of *Euskera* as the *lingua franca* of the Basque Country, although the autonomous government has promoted its teaching in the region's schools. Indeed, figures produced by the Ministry of Culture in 1990 show high levels of comprehension of the vernacular tongue in all regions except the Basque Country (see Table 1.1).

TABLE 1.1

Percentage of population resident in 'historic regions' with knowledge of vernacular language, 1990

	Catalan	Basque	Galician
Understand well	86	28	84
Speak well	68	26	63
Read well	64	25	52
Write well	31	20	30

Source: based on Ministerio de Cultura, *Encuesta de equipamiento, prácticas y consumos culturales* (Madrid, 1990).

Lacking a clear linguistic focus, the development of Basque nationalism was characterised by a lack of definition and continuity in its choice of primordial identity and values (Conversi, 1990). The founder of Basque nationalism, Sabino Arana (1865–1903), developed a theory of Basque identity which was essentially racist in nature, melding a theocratic vision of Basque ethnic superiority with a rejection of the moral perversions which characterised the rest of Spain (Jáuregui Bereciartu, 1985: 13–22; Sullivan, 1988: 5–9). Arana regarded Spaniards as *maketos*, a term of racist abuse intended to emphasise Basque purity as opposed to the irreligiosity and immorality of the Spanish. Insofar as the Basque language served a purpose in Arana's independence demands, it was to act as an ethnic border, a protection against the contagion of the Basque identity by 'foreigners'. The importance of *Euskera* lay not so much in its intrinsic merits as in its symbolic differentiation from Spanish. Such a strategy was in part dictated by the fact that in Bilbao, where Arana established the *Partido Nacionalista Vasco* in 1895, *Euskera* was hardly spoken. Indeed, Basque nationalism initially found greater support amongst those sectors of the population which did not speak *Euskera*; the vast majority of nationalist publications at the turn of the century were in Spanish.[5]

The Basque claim to racial superiority and ethnic uniqueness found its origins in the ancient concept of 'collective nobility' (*hidalguía colectiva*): 'any Basque able to prove birth of Basque parents . . . was automatically recognised as noble by virtue of purity of blood' (Greenwood, 1977: 86). In more recent times, claims to Basque racial uniqueness have been based on studies which purport to show an unusually high percentage of blood group O amongst the indigenous population, as well as tests conducted via the rhesus system and other supposedly distinctive physiognomic features such as cranial formation, and hair and eye colouring.[6] Nationalist claims which built upon such exclusivist criteria inevitably restricted the movement's potential appeal and ultimately proved to be untenable in political terms as large-scale internal migration – especially in the 1960s – brought an ever greater number of non-Basques into the region. The racist theories of Arana have now been abandoned by all Basque nationalist parties.

However, nationalist parties have become the dominant political force in the Basque Country. As in Catalonia, the post-Franco return of democracy has seen a politically conservative nationalist party – the PNV – come to prominence in the regional parliament. Unlike the CiU, however, the PNV has usually had to rely on coalitions with the Socialist Party. Moreover, the political situation in the Basque Country has been immeasurably complicated by the existence of hard-line separatist groups, notably ETA and its political wing, *Herri Batasuna* (HB, United People). The Basque equivalent to Sinn Féin in Northern Ireland, HB has regularly won notable support in regional elections: in both 1986 and 1990 it secured 13 out of the 75 seats with nearly 20 per cent of the vote, although the elections of October 1994 saw it lose two seats as its vote slipped to 16 per cent. *Eusko Alkartasuna* (Basque Solidarity, founded in 1986 as a breakaway from the PNV) and *Euskadiko Ezkerra* (Basque Left, founded by ETA dissidents in 1976)[7] have also attracted significant backing in elections to the Basque parliament. Taken together, nationalist parties won over 67 per cent of the votes at the 1990 Basque regional elections, reflecting the fact that greater autonomy – and even independence – remains the aspiration of a clear majority of citizens (see Table 1.2).

TABLE 1.2

**Preferences concerning the form of state,
Basque respondents, 1976, 1979 and 1987**

	1976	1979	1987
Centralism	26	10	3
Autonomy	48	38	34
Federalism	12	15	20
Independence	11	30	31

Source: based on López-Aranguren and García Ferrando (1991: 120); Gunther
(1992)

Spain's Celtic Periphery: Continuity and Change in Galicia

Although the Basque Country and Catalonia tend to be the principal
focus of regional studies on Spain, they are far from unique in having
a strong sense of national identity. Galicia, in the north-west of the
country, is the third of Spain's so-called 'historic' nationalities, with
its own distinctive language and culture. Yet, Galicia has always
remained in northern Spain's economic shadow (Villares, 1989: 482–
3). In 1992, 36 per cent of the resident population was employed in
fishing or agriculture, even though this sector's contribution to the
region's GDP was no more than 9.5 per cent. In the words of the
regional president, Manuel Fraga Iribarne, 'its still abundant
farming population and the small-farm structure of its land confers
on Galicia the features of a unique individualism' (Fraga, 1992: 12).

A backwater during the height of Spain's imperial dominance,
Galicia was the source of many emigrants to the colonies; the term
'*gallego/a*' is still used colloquially in several South American countries
to describe poor immigrants. In the nineteenth century, famine drove
tens of thousands more to migrate, most taking lowly jobs in the
major Spanish cities. Like the Irish in mainland Britain, Galicians
were often branded as dullards and became a standard butt of
Spanish humorists. They share with all Celtic races a reputation for
romanticism, poetic genius, love of music and a melancholy character
reflected in a fascination with death. Such crude characterisations
were reinforced by the emergence in the late nineteenth century of a
distinctive cultural nationalism, built around the Galician language.
As in Catalonia, the rise of Galician nationalism ran parallel to a
literary revival. The literary critic and scholar Ramón Menéndez

Pidal was a leading figure in the so-called *rexurdimento*, the rediscovery of Galician literature which matched, and to some extent imitated, the Catalan *renaixença* (Brenan, 1963: 316–24).

The region's isolation, exacerbated by an underdeveloped communications infrastructure, has helped Galicia to maintain its culture, customs and traditions. Language continues to form the principal focus of Galician culture, reflected in a literature which has flourished since the end of the Franco dictatorship.[8] In response to the growing use of the language, Galicia's Royal Academy (founded in 1906) and the *Instituto de Lingua Galega* (founded in 1971) have recently produced for the first time a guide to the orthographic and morphological norms of *Galego*. However, a 1987 study found that although nearly all children understood *Galego*, only half could speak it. Three-quarters of teachers use Castilian – possibly on account of its continued association with social advancement in Galicia, where it remains the language of the region's elites (Villares, 1989: 508; Hooper, 1986: 246).

In common with the Catalan and Basque pattern, Galician nationalism has been divided historically between the 'moderate' approach of bourgeois liberals, stressing regional identity within the Spanish state, and a more radical, culturally-chauvinist conception which emerged with the launch in 1916 of the *Irmandades de Fala* (Fala Brotherhoods).[9] Although the dictatorship of Primo de Rivera put a temporary halt to nationalist activity, in 1929 Santiago Casares Quiroga, future prime minister under the Second Republic, set up the *Organización Republicana Gallega Autónoma* (ORGA), an expressly political body which played down the cultural component of nationalism favoured by the *Irmandades*. Once the Republic was established in 1931, the *Partido Galeguista* was created with the aim of bringing together all nationalist currents in one, inter-class, party. After some initial success, the party followed the pattern of most Galician nationalist movements and split (Máiz, 1986; Máiz and Portero, 1988). The Civil War, in which Galicia was overwhelmingly pro-Franco, put an end to all regional initiatives until after the dictator's death, although the *Partido Galeguista* maintained a clandestine existence until 1950.[10]

Galician nationalism has never represented a challenge to the Spanish state similar to that posed by its counterparts in the Basque Country and Catalonia. Indeed, nationalism in Galicia has consistently been less radical than that in the other two 'historic' nationalities, with more emphasis placed on defending the region's cultural heritage than seeking political independence. In the post-Franco period, although Galicia was one of the first regions to be granted autonomous status, there was a conspicuous lack of enthusiasm amongst the population: in the December 1980 referendum on the autonomy statute, 71 per cent abstained and, of those who voted, only 73 per cent supported the statute creating the *Xunta de Galicia* (Galician parliament). Equally, in both national and regional elections since the return of democracy, there has been little evidence of significant support for Galician nationalist parties. In the regional elections of October 1981 the abstention rate was 53.7 per cent and regional parties won less than 10 per cent of the votes cast (Alvarez Conde, 1990: 751).

There is thus a dissonance between the relatively low level of support for political nationalism in Galicia and the strong sense of cultural identity within the region. Amongst the reasons put forward for the conservatism of the Galician population has been the influence of the Catholic Church (Villares, 1989: 481–5). With its low level of urbanisation – in 1990, 76 per cent of the population lived in sub-municipal units of under 2 000 inhabitants and only seven towns had more than 50 000 – Galicia is classic Catholic territory. However, religion alone offers an inadequate explanation of Galicia's lack of radical nationalism. Levels of religious practice have also always been very high in the Basque Country, where the Catholic Church has often lent its support to nationalist demands. Of more significance is the specific combination of high levels of religious practice and a low level of economic development, with a concomitant lack of urbanisation. In contrast to the Basque Country and Catalonia, Galicia was neither fiscally discriminated against by the central government, nor proselytised by radical workers' movements. Instead, it was left to continue in its traditional forms of social organisation, isolated from developments in the rest of Spain. None the less, Galicia's distinctive culture – together with the 1936 promise of home-rule – ensured that it would be accorded similar treatment to that demanded by both Catalonia and the Basque Country in the post-Franco era. Radical nationalist movements were thus no prerequisite for achieving autonomous status in democratic Spain.

There are no nationalist parties in contemporary Galicia equivalent in size or importance to the CiU or the PNV, although the *Coalición Galega* (CG) did win one seat in the *Cortes* in 1986 and two seats in the regional parliament in 1989. Splits within the CG led to the emergence in October 1986 of the *Bloque Nacionalista Galego*

(BNG). By the end of the 1980s the BNG had begun to establish a significant presence in Galicia, winning five deputies in the 1989 regional elections, a figure which rose to 13 four years later – the most successful showing by a nationalist party in any Galician election. In addition to mainstream nationalist parties, there is a tiny terrorist organisation, *Ejército Guerrilleiro de Pobo Galego Ceibe*, based on its namesake in Guatemala, but more similar in aims and impact to the Welsh Sons of Glendower group.[11] Whilst evidence from both national and regional elections in 1993 suggests that nationalist concerns are beginning to make a political impact, Galicia remains one of the heartlands of the conservative *Partido Popular* (PP). Manuel Fraga, the PP's founder, retired from national politics to assume the presidency of Galicia in December 1989 with 44 per cent of the vote in the regional elections, a figure which rose to over 52 per cent in the elections of October 1993.

The Politics of Ethnic Conflict: Nationalism, Separatism and Violence

Since the early 1960s, the Basque separatist group, ETA, has represented the most visible manifestation of intransigent nationalist sentiment within Spain. Its campaign of violence against the Spanish state has given the organisation a continued protagonism, serving to highlight the intractability of its demands. During the Franco regime, ETA claimed responsibility for 57 deaths, mostly policemen. In the period of democratic transition, 1975–7, it claimed a further 134 victims. Between 1978 and 1994, more than 700 people – a great many of them civilians – have fallen victim to ETA's terrorist tactics. ETA remains a major threat to state organisation and stability in contemporary Spain.

The internal migration to the Basque Country which accompanied the economic growth of the 1960s served as the catalyst to the emergence of ETA's hard-line form of nationalism. It is no coincidence that ETA was born in this period as a breakaway from the PNV. Although ETA subsequently developed a political identity which borrowed from 'progressive' ideologies such as Marxism, its initial appeal was based on the need to protect the Basque people from being submerged by immigrants (Jáuregui, 1985: 87–147; Sullivan, 1988: Ch. 2). Whereas the PNV continued to build upon a post-Arana tradition of populist Christian democracy, whose possibilism in the political sphere led it to adopt a call for autonomy within Spain rather than outright independence, ETA stood unequivocally for separatism.

The issue of why radical separatism, championed by an organisation using the tactics of terror, should have emerged in the Basque Country and not in Catalonia has provoked considerable scholarly attention. Three broad approaches can be outlined, stressing in turn a reaction against repression by the central state, the particular cultural background of the Basque region, and specific economic factors.[12] There can be no doubt that the stultifying centralism of the Franco dictatorship not only acted as a spur to regional demands, but also intensified them. However, the fact that Catalan was deeply rooted and, in private, widely spoken meant that Francoist repression posed less of a direct threat to Catalonia's identity, whereas the cultural imprecision which – as has been shown – characterised Basque nationalism made it seem more vulnerable to official proscription (Castells, 1989: 763). Equally, though, important social transformations took place in the Basque Country as a result of the region's industrial development during the 1950s and 1960s. Up to 900,000 migrants entered the Basque Country between 1950 and 1975, a period in which one of the key elements of Basque tradition, a profound commitment to Catholicism, was undermined by the widespread process of secularisation evident throughout Europe at the time.

The emergence of ETA in 1959 reflected all these factors, but was also prompted by the seeming inactivity of the PNV in opposing the Franco dictatorship. The separatist movement's initial model of nationalism, which derived from the conviction that the Basque Country was an occupied territory, lacked precision. This contributed to the ideological and tactical inconstancy which has characterised the movement since its inception. Until the late 1960s, ETA remained a marginal organisation which appealed to a few young activists whose cultural nationalism was mainly expressed through wall daubings and propaganda efforts. However, there then occurred a radical shift in the movement's tactics, triggered in part by the sharp rise in immigration to the Basque Country (Letamendía Belzunce, 1994, vol. 1: 267–79). In response to the PNV's grudging acceptance that immigrants should play a part in Basque politics, ETA sought their full-scale integration via the adoption of a Marxist framework which rejected exclusivist nationalism. By doing so, ETA created a tension between the need to maintain its activist support amongst the lower middle-class population of small towns in the provinces of Guipúzcoa and Vizcaya, and the need to build up a mass movement by winning the support of a mainly immigrant, non-Basque-speaking working class. Parallel to this conflict was a further division between proponents of guerrilla warfare, who idealised the countryside as the cradle of authentic Basque values, and proponents of urban, working-class agitation, who emphasised proletarian internationalism.

ETA was born when the Algerian struggle for independence, led by the *Front de Libération Nationale* (FLN), was at its height. However, Basque nationalists have looked to a variety of different models since the start of the Franco regime, including those of *Irgun*, the Jewish national liberation movement led by Menachem Begin, the Irish Republicans under Eamonn De Valera, and Habib Bourguiba's Tunisian independence movement. ETA's *Libro Blanco* (White Book), which synthesised the organisation's ideas, contained just one Basque source. ETA's action–repression–action theory, adopted in 1965 and according to which the separatist organisation aimed to unleash an escalating cycle of violence which would ultimately culminate in a popular uprising, drew heavily on the insurrectionist model of Franz Fanon. Indeed, ETA theorists have often drawn a parallel between the Algerian revolution and the Basque struggle for self-determination.[13] The experience of Algeria appeared to prove that the strategy of violence could lead to success, a view which was reinforced by the impact of several Third World liberation struggles on European youth movements during the 1960s. Repression under the Franco regime served to emphasise further the liberation aspect of ETA's strategy.

However, the international models upon which ETA built never remained constant. By the time of Franco's death and the subsequent transition to democracy, the Basque organisation was increasingly deprived of its sources of external inspiration and legitimation. In particular, the post-revolutionary Cuban and Algerian experiences gradually undermined the image of these regimes as champions of the oppressed, whilst Middle Eastern developments in the 1980s offered little of practical relevance to the Basque situation. Since the return of pluralist politics to Spain, ETA ideologues have been forced to develop self-referential justifications for their tactics – a process which has intensified the organisation's propensity for bitter splits (the most notable of which occurred in 1974 between ETA-m, the exclusively military wing, and ETA-pm, the political–military wing).

In very broad terms, divisions have tended to be generational, focusing on the relationship between the armed struggle and mass activity. Most ETA activists are young, single males; as militants grow older they come to question the efficacy of violence and call for greater emphasis to be placed on political negotiation. As one *etarra*, jailed in France, put it: 'It's more difficult to be a terrorist at 40 than it was at 21' (quoted in The *Guardian*, 1 May 1992). The readiness of older ETA members to contemplate the renunciation of violence in turn provokes the adoption of more radical stances by hardline activists. Violence can thus become a self-generating phenomenon, a vicious circle which is virtually impossible to stop. An indicative example of this dynamic occurred in the case of 'Pertur' (Eduardo Moreno Bergareche), inspiration behind the *Ponencia Otsagabía* in 1976, which called for the establishment of an autonomous political party and the downplaying of military activities by ETA-pm (Letamendía Belzunce, 1994, vol. 1: 447–51). Pertur was murdered as a result, almost certainly by ETA-m, but his initiative boosted the emergence of the so-called patriotic or *abertzale* left, key protagonists in the Basque struggle (Sullivan, 1988: ch.6).

During the 1980s, as a new generation of separatist activists with no direct memory of Francoist repression began to emerge, so the generational division became more acute. Members of *Jarrai*, the separatist youth corps, learn the tactics of terror from propaganda and explosives manuals. Many of them are the children of immigrants, desperate not just for something to do in a period of scarce job opportunities, but also anxious to prove their belonging in their adopted home. In late 1991, after a spate of atrocities in which innocent by-standers had been killed or maimed, jailed ETA leaders Juan Antonio Urrutia Aurteneche and Isidro Etxabe Urrestrilla bitterly criticised the tactics of 'four imbeciles at the top', whom they accused of killing children for sport. Concerned that 'active duty' members were creating such hatred that ETA would lose support even in its Basque heartlands, up to 70 of the movement's more than 300 prisoners in Spanish gaols initiated a debate in a document which called for an end to the military struggle.

A major step on the road to isolating ETA was the Pact of Ajuria-Enea, signed on 12 January 1988 by all mainstream Basque parties in opposition to the use of violence. Spanish authorities were also able to draw encouragement in late 1990 from the withdrawal from active politics of the European deputy, 'Txema' Montero Zabala. Montero, who had served as a defence lawyer in many ETA trials, had once argued that selective 'ethnical' violence was socially legitimate and imaginative, but subsequently came to oppose the use of terrorist tactics.[14] An indication that the tide of public opinion seemed to be ebbing away from ETA even in the Basque Country emerged in the early 1990s as growing numbers of young people gathered at rallies organised by a new, non-aligned movement, *'Gesto por la paz'* (Peace gesture), to express their revulsion at violence. The eloquence of their silent demonstrations, which in Bilbao attracted up to 200,000 sympathisers, provoked disquiet within *Herri Batasuna*, some of whose leaders came to argue that violence was becoming counter-productive. Indeed, opinion surveys in the early 1990s suggested that up to a quarter of HB's own members opposed the use of violence. None the less, given the nature of terrorist struggles, it is probable that an end to the violence will depend as much on the success of the security forces in disarticulating ETA cells as on the moral repugnance of Basque citizens.

It is important to stress that violence is not an innate, atavistic characteristic of the Basques. Robert Clark (1984: 278) has argued that violence plays virtually no role in Basque political culture and that traditional Basque culture does not support ETA's actions. Violence, though, has proved to be an effective substitute in the Basque Country for cultural aspirations – especially language – since it has allowed for ever-wider sections of the population to be subsumed within nationalist goals. Evidence suggests that second generation immigrants are easily integrated into Basque nationalist politics, with instances of strong support for *Herri Batasuna*, ETA's political wing, in areas with an overwhelming immigrant population (Clark, 1984: 147–9). However, recent studies have cautioned against the search for a specific, identifiable 'cause' of violence, particularly since research on terrorism often blurs the distinction between normative and factual propositions. Thus, it has been argued that, since ETA defines itself as a movement of political liberation rather than a political party and therefore engages in activity which is not exclusively political, it is inappropriate to analyse it in conventional political terms by assessing its strength through electoral results and public opinion surveys. Rather, according to this view, ETA should be seen as a 'concept' just as much as a structure, whose existence conditions all actors' political calculations (Douglass and Zulaika, 1990).

Methodological issues notwithstanding, nationalist violence in Spain has not been confined to the Basque Country. The most extreme example of violence being justified under the banner of nationalism occurred during the Spanish Civil War and its aftermath, as General Franco engaged in a deliberate policy of ruthless vengeance on his opponents (Preston, 1993: 164–5, 222, 227). Indeed, state-sanctioned violence has been a recurring theme of Spanish politics since the late nineteenth century and cannot be divorced from the reactions it has often provoked. Thus, violence has also been marked in Catalonia, particularly in the early part of the twentieth century – for instance, during the so-called 'Tragic Week' of 1909, when a general strike escalated into a widespread attack on Church properties, and in the period 1917–23 when *pistolerismo* (gun-law) was rife. Although no equivalent to the Basque separatist struggle emerged in Catalonia during the Franco regime, *Terra Lliure* (Free Land), a terrorist group with links to ETA, briefly came to prominence in the mid-1980s. However, its sporadic activities came to an end in 1991 when the organisation disbanded and its members joined *Esquerra Republicana*.

The precise reasons for nationalist violence remain unclear. Although violence can be self-sustaining, quickly entering a deadly spiral of action and reaction, its intensity may also be linked to disputed territorial boundaries. Thus, whereas Catalan separatists seek to transform their currently-defined administrative region into an independent state, Basque separatists have a further territorial claim on both Navarra and the French Basque provinces. Such a stance implies a need to conquer and may help crystallise the sense of being at war with the central Spanish state. Equally, for all hard-line separatists, the stakes are zero-sum: there can be no accommodation with their opponents, since independence is a non-negotiable aspiration. Moreover, so long as there remains a bedrock of support, organisations such as ETA can continue to operate on the basis of very small memberships.

Spain in the 1990s: A State of Many Nations in a Europe of the Regions

The greatest challenge faced by the post-Franco architects of democracy was to construct a polity which reconciled the central state with regional demands. It is a measure of the contemporary Spanish state's *strength*, in contrast to its historic weakness, that the challenge was successfully confronted. Spain's system of Autonomous

Communities has ensured that regions have assumed ever-increasing importance in Spain's political structure (see Chapter 7). All seventeen Communities have developed a strong sense of regional identity since the early 1980s, with *diputaciones* and *ayuntamientos* often acting in concert with local businesses (especially *cajas de ahorro*) to promote and support a wide variety of cultural events. Regional languages have been recognised as co-official languages with Castilian Spanish. The prodigious expansion in the number of regional studies available in bookshops represents one of the few major growth areas for the publishing industry in the 1980s and 1990s. Self-government has thus provided a stimulus to the emergence of distinctive regional feelings throughout Spain. Naturally, such feelings are most intense in the three 'historic' regions (see Table 1.3). Survey research in 1988 generally showed an increase in nationalist self-identity compared with earlier in the decade (López-Aranguren and García Ferrando, 1991: 122–4; Giner and Moreno, 1989: 188–91).

There are, of course, great disparities between the regions in terms of size, socio-economic structure, level of development and wealth. Spain's largest region, Castilla y León, covers an area of 94,147 km – more than Denmark, the Netherlands, Belgium or Portugal – and agriculture remains an important component of its economy.[15] At the opposite extreme in regard to size, La Rioja – renowned for its viniculture – is smaller than the county of Norfolk in Britain. Table 1.4 shows how the regions' productive structure and levels of income per capita vary, ranging from Extremadura with a GDP per capita at 65.9 per cent of the national average and 52.5 per cent of the EU average, to the Balearic Islands, with equivalent figures of 142.1 per cent and 113.1 per cent respectively. Six regions (Catalonia, Madrid, Andalucía, Valencia, the Basque Country and Castilla y León) account for 70.3 per cent of Spain's entire GDP, whilst the nine poorest regions have EU '1st Objective' status, requiring urgent investment measures in infrastructure and productive capacity (see Chapter 7). Fully 80 per cent of foreign direct investment is channelled to just two regions: Madrid and Catalonia (Chislett, 1994: 134).

Between 1985 and 1989, many of Spain's regions experienced economic take-off: the Balearic Islands, the Canary Islands, Valencia, Murcia, Aragón, Catalonia, Navarra, La Rioja and Andalucía all posted annual GDP growth during that period of at least 4.9 per cent (Alonso Zaldívar and Castells, 1992: 156-7). The case of Andalucía is

TABLE 1.3

National/regional identity in selected Autonomous Communities
Percentage replies to the question, 'I see myself as. . .'

Catalonia	1984	1988
– Spanish only	11	13
– More Spanish than Catalan	11	8
– As much Spanish as Catalan	45	35
– More Catalan than Spanish	22	25
– Catalan only	8	16
– Don't know/no answer	3	3
	(1,484)	(2,900)

Basque Country	1984	1986
– Spanish only	9	8
– More Spanish than Basque	4	5
– As much Spanish as Basque	36	27
– More Basque than Spanish	25	23
– Basque only	24	31
– Don't know/no answer	2	6
	(1,515)	(1,191)

Galicia	1984	1985
– Spanish only	7	5
– More Spanish than Galician	6	7
– As much Spanish as Galician	51	52
– More Galician than Spanish	21	27
– Galician only	9	6
– Don't know/no answer	6	3
	(2,999)	(3,987)

Andalucía	1982	1986
– Spanish only	11	8
– More Spanish than Andalucían	10	6
– As much Spanish as Andalucían	57	66
– More Andalucían than Spanish	3	3
– Andalucían only	3	3
– Don't know/no answer	6	3
	(2,000)	(1,801)

Source: based on López-Aranguren and García Ferrando (1991: 123–4).

TABLE 1.4

Per capita **GDP of Spain's Autonomous Communities**

	GDP *per capita* (national average = 100)		GDP *per capita* (EU average = 100)	
	1989	1993	1989	1993
Andalucía	70.7	69.1	54.4	55.0
Aragón	109.1	107.5	83.9	85.6
Asturias	87.9	87.9	67.6	70.0
Balearic Islands	136.7	142.1	105.2	113.1
Basque Country	109.3	107.9	84.1	85.9
Canary Islands	101.7	99.1	78.2	78.8
Cantabria	90.5	92.1	69.6	73.3
Castilla-La Mancha	79.8	79.5	61.3	63.3
Castilla y León	87.0	91.5	66.9	72.8
Catalonia	128.6	126.8	98.9	100.9
Extremadura	64.0	65.9	49.2	52.5
Galicia	7 9.8	84.0	61.4	66.8
Madrid	127.6	129.7	98.1	103.3
Murcia	82.9	81.3	63.7	64.7
Navarra	111.2	116.4	85.5	92.6
La Rioja	107.2	110.6	82.5	88.0
Valencia	105.6	103.6	81.2	82.4

Source: Alonso Zaldívar and Castells (1992: 153); Chislett (1994: 134).

particularly noteworthy. This massive southern region – larger than Austria – with a population of over 7 million (more than that of several European member-states) is the part of Spain from which most of the country's stereotypical clichés derive. Yet, Andalucía's tourist image of sun-soaked beaches, hot-blooded flamenco dancers and Moorish citadels belies the reality of its diverse regional economy. Between 1985 and 1989, Andalucía's levels of industrial production grew by more than a quarter. Whilst the service sector also expanded rapidly (by 4.6 per cent), agriculture and fisheries saw a much more limited growth of just 0.4 per cent annually, reflecting the process of economic and industrial modernisation which occurred in the 1980s (see Chapter 10). Projects such as 'Cartuja 93' – which utilises the site of Expo92 in Sevilla as a high tech science park and will provide the headquarters of the European Community Institute of Technological Research Studies – and the Málaga technology park, serve as the backbone of Andalucía's attempt to integrate with the modern world economy via a strong technological base (Chislett, 1994: 143).

Spanish regions are increasingly achieving a prominence outside the country comparable to that of their counterparts in France and Italy or the German *Länder*. In particular, Catalonia – whose president, Jordi Pujol, chairs the Assembly of European Regions – sees itself as leading the economic rebirth of southern Europe, along with Lombardy in Italy. Moves towards a 'Europe of the regions' are strongly supported throughout Spain, which – for the first time in its history – appears to have reached a reasonably successful compromise between the needs of the central state and the demands of the regions. The logic of European political integration, to which Spain is wholeheartedly committed, is that nation-states will gradually lose their political protagonism as internal European borders become more porous. Throughout the European Union, many nationalist groups support the emergence of a 'Europe of the regions' in which the concept of sovereign states becomes virtually meaningless. Pasqual Maragall, mayor of Barcelona and leader of the Socialist Party in Catalonia (PSC–PSOE), has an even more far-reaching vision of a Europe of cities. In 1989 he founded the Council of European Municipalities and Regions, a club for major European cities.

Somewhat ironically, as moves continue towards creating a united Europe in which regional units of government will assume ever-greater political significance, Spain is in some regards becoming more homogeneous. In spite of the emergence of distinctive regional identities throughout the country, the process of economic modernisation which Spain has experienced during the latter part of the twentieth century has ensured that regional disparities, although still great, are not so pronounced as in the past. Whilst the real impact of European integration should not be exaggerated – the EU budget still accounts for less than 1.5 per cent of the combined GDP of member states – the arrival of the 'Single Market' in Europe has already had a significant impact in terms of economic exchange and the free movement of citizens. Even if the single European state remains a distant federalist dream, a process of economic and cultural integration is already under way in Europe. Spain offers a microcosmic example of this process. Mass culture, mass production and mass media all contribute to a sense of shared experience in Spain, to an identity which is fashioned as much by the recent journey from dictatorship to democracy as by more historical legacies.

2

The 1978 Constitutional Settlement

The Spanish Constitution of 1978 represents a triumph of political compromise. Constitutional issues, it is true, rarely engage the passionate interest of citizens or even political analysts. However, in the Spanish case it is possible to talk of constitutional construction – as Miquel Roca i Junyent (1988: 10) has done – as the 'exciting' part of creating democracy which preceded the tedium of routine democratic administration. Two related reasons account for this alleged excitement.

First, after thirty-six years of Franco's brutal and repressive dictatorship, an important majority of the Spanish population looked expectantly to the possibility of establishing democracy (Gómez-Reino *et al.*, 1976: 1184). The death of the dictator opened up the opportunity to bring Spain back towards the mainstream of European political life. Secondly, though, there was an acute awareness of the dangers involved. Spain's previous twentieth-century experience of genuine democracy, the short-lived Second Republic, had degenerated into the Civil War which brought Franco to power in the first place. It had been precisely around constitutional issues that the various forces of the right coalesced in their opposition to all that the Second Republic represented. In particular, the constitutional provisions dealing with the Catholic Church and Spain's territorial organisation had provoked intense right-wing resistance (Carr, 1986; Preston, 1994). Thus, moves towards creating a new constitutional democracy gave rise to feelings of both hope and apprehension.

The Politics of Immolation: Using the Franco State Against Itself

One of the most noteworthy aspects of Spain's transition to democracy is that the entire process took place within the bounds of the Franco dictatorship's constitutional framework (see Exhibit 2.1). Although the dramatic collapse of communism following the revolutions of 1989 stimulated renewed scholarly interest in the success of Spain's democratic transition, little attention has been focused on the key factor of constitutional continuity. Unlike the

---

EXHIBIT 2.1

Key dates during the post-Franco transition to democracy, 1975–86

1975

20 November	General Francisco Franco dies
22 November	Juan Carlos assumes throne
11 December	First government under the monarchy sworn in with Carlos Arias Navarro as prime minister

1976

2 June	Juan Carlos announces to US Congress during first overseas visit as Head of State his intention to introduce democracy
10 June	Law of political association passed
1 July	Arias Navarro resigns; replaced as prime minister by Adolfo Suárez
6 July	Register of political parties established
15 December	Referendum on Political Reform Law

1977

9 April	PCE legalised, the result of personal decision by Suárez
28 April	Trade unions legalised
15 June	First general elections held; Juan Carlos nominates 41 senators
28 July	Spain applies formally for membership of EC
29 August	Catalan *Generalitat* reestablished
25 October	Moncloa Pacts signed

1978

4 January	General Council created in Basque Country
16 March	Galician *Xunta* established
21 July	Constitutional draft approved by lower house
31 October	Constitutional draft approved by both legislative chambers
6 December	Referendum on Constitution

1979

1 March	General elections held
3 April	Municipal elections held

9 May	Juan Carlos inaugurates first democratic legislature under terms of 1978 Constitution
28 September	Extraordinary Congress of PSOE, during which Felipe González is reinstated as party leader and Marxism is dropped from party's self-definition
25 October	Referenda on autonomy statutes in Catalonia and Basque Country

1980

9 March	First regional elections in Basque Country
23 March	First regional elections in Catalonia
24 April	Jordi Pujol becomes president of Catalan *Generalitat*
21 December	Referendum on autonomy statute in Galicia

1981

29 January	Suárez resigns as prime minister and as leader of UCD
23 February	Attempted *coup d'état*, led by Lieutenant-Colonel Antonio Tejero
25 February	Following collapse of *coup*, Leopoldo Calvo Sotelo invested as prime minister
2 December	Spain formally applies to join NATO

1982

30 May	NATO approves Spanish entry
27 August	Calvo Sotelo dissolves Parliament and calls general election
2 October	Three military leaders arrested for plotting a *coup*, due to take place on 27 October
28 October	General elections result in overwhelming victory for PSOE
1 December	Felipe González assumes office

1983

23 February	Government expropriates Rumasa holding company
8 May	Regional and municipal elections
5 August	Constitutional Tribunal declares 14 articles of LOAPA to be unconstitutional
5 December	First action by GAL (*Grupos Antiterroristas de Liberación*)

1984

26 February	Second regional elections in Basque Country
29 April	Second regional elections in Catalonia
9 October	Economic and Social Agreement (AES) signed between government, employers and unions

1985

| 12 June | Spain signs Treaty of Adhesion to European Economic Community |
| 24 November | Second regional elections in Galicia |

1986

1 January	Spain joins EC
12 March	Referendum on NATO membership: 52.5 per cent vote yes; 39.9 per cent no, with abstention rate of 40.6 per cent
22 June	General elections, resulting in second victory for PSOE

former communist regimes – which, in any case, crumbled for very different reasons – Franco's dictatorship dismantled itself voluntarily. In spite of a dramatic increase in the number of hours lost through strikes during the 1970s, and an upsurge in the violent activities of the Basque separatist group, *Euskadi Ta Askatasuna* (ETA), widespread popular mobilisation against the dictatorship always remained latent rather than actual. Whilst even a latent threat was able to act as a conditioning factor on the actions of many former Francoists, encouraging a prudent desire to salvage some form of political survival by anticipating what was seen as inevitable change, the fact remains that the transition to democracy was engineered from within the outgoing regime. This was to have a significant bearing on the nature and functioning of the new democracy.

Franco's death on 20 November 1975 provoked no constitutional crisis. By the terms of the 1969 Law of Succession, Prince Juan Carlos (son of Don Juan, the direct heir to the Bourbon throne) was to succeed as head of state (De Blaye, 1976: 526–31). It was widely expected that Juan Carlos – educated in Spain under Franco's supervision – would oversee some form of continuation of the regime, perhaps allowing modifications at the margins but unlikely to back wholesale change. Such a view found added support when Juan Carlos confirmed as prime minister the hapless Carlos Arias Navarro, a loyal Francoist who had inherited the post following ETA's assassination of Admiral Luis Carrero Blanco in December 1973. Arias Navarro's position reflected the dilemma affecting the entire regime. Whilst personally committed to the purpose and values of the reactionary Franco regime, Arias was none the less aware – in the light of growing pressure from an evermore confident opposition – of the need for some form of change. He was torn between the two main factions of the regime: those in the so-called 'bunker', Francoists resistant to any change, and the more numerous *aperturistas*, aware that some accommodation to opposition demands would have to be made if major social conflict were to be avoided. His weak concessions to political pluralism between 1974 and 1976 merely angered the former whilst signally failing to satisfy the latter (Preston, 1986: 53–90; Carr and Fusi, 1981: 195–217; Aparicio, 1988: 19–20, 22–3).

Contrary to contemporary expectations, Juan Carlos turned out to be in favour of genuine pluralism. In retrospect, this is hardly surprising. He would have been acutely conscious of the fate of both the Italian and the Greek monarchies in the aftermath of dictatorship, especially since his wife Sofia was the sister of the deposed King

Constantine.[1] Equally, he would have been all too conscious of the fact that the main opposition forces, especially the Communist Party, were strongly republican. His personal association with General Franco made him a particular target for the opposition, which was not only gaining in confidence but also seeking to take the initiative over political change. Thus, pragmatic political calculation demanded that he back reform. To this end, he was happy to accept Arias Navarro's resignation on 1 July 1976, having earlier apparently described his prime minister as a 'complete disaster' and 'flag-bearer of the bunker' whilst on a tour of the United States of America (*Newsweek*, 26 April 1976). However, his choice of successor to Arias provoked incredulous outrage from both within and without the regime. Adolfo Suárez, a 43-year-old apparatchik who had been Minister Secretary General of the Francoist single party, the *Movimiento*, hardly seemed an appropriate candidate to dismantle the regime. Leading *aperturistas* such as José María de Areilza and Manuel Fraga Iribarne were angered at being passed over in favour of someone they regarded as an inexperienced upstart; the opposition was appalled at the appointment of someone with seemingly faultless Francoist credentials. Indeed, the veteran Francoist historian, Ricardo de la Cierva, spoke for many when, in *El País* (8 July 1976), he described Suárez's appointment and first cabinet as 'A mistake! An immense mistake!'

Far from being a mistake, the choice of Suárez was inspired. His connections with the *Movimiento* enabled him to maintain the trust of many within the Franco regime, while his commitment to genuine reform soon impressed itself upon the opposition. The remarkable story of how Suárez engineered the dismantling of the Franco regime's institutions has been told elsewhere in considerable detail (Preston, 1986; Gilmour, 1985; Graham, 1984). Our concern here is with the specific question of constitutional construction. In September 1976, the Francoist Council of Ministers approved a projected Law of Political Reform. Not the least remarkable feature of the proposed new law was that it demanded respect for the legal provisions of the Franco regime in order that those very provisions could be undone. Thus, the new law was subject to ratification by both the National Council of the *Movimiento* and a two-thirds majority vote in the Francoist *Cortes*. An historic decision on 18 November 1976 saw 425 out of the 497 *procuradores* who voted agree to legislate their assembly out of existence.[2] A national referendum on 15 December 1976 provided overwhelming backing for the decision, with nearly 95 per cent of the 77 per cent turnout voting in favour of the Political Reform Law, thus providing strong legitimacy for the new arrangements. As a result, the first major institutional hurdle represented by the Franco regime had been overcome by exploiting the very mechanisms provided for in the constitutional structure of the dictatorship itself (Aparicio, 1988: 27–8).

Creating the Constitution: Process and Problems

The Law of Political Reform provided for the establishment of *Las Cortes Generales*, a two-house parliament comprised of the *Congreso de los Diputados* (Congress of Deputies) and the *Senado* (Senate), with members of the lower house to be elected by universal suffrage (see chapter 4). Although these changes were momentous, they represented *reform* of the existing system rather than the *rupture* which had been demanded by the democratic opposition (Sánchez Agesta, 1980: 41). Moreover, the five articles contained in the law allowed for considerable flexibility on the part of both the head of state and the government, who were in no sense bound by its somewhat ambiguous provisions. Accordingly, the opposition played little direct role in the constitutional steps towards democracy; instead, the government under Suárez reserved to itself considerable advantages over the process. For instance, it was to be allowed to draw up regulations for the first general elections and was not subject to any censure procedures. Equally, it could have recourse to a referendum at any stage, and was thus granted not only legislative, but also political initiative. The king, meanwhile, could invoke the provisions of the still extant Francoist *Ley Orgánica del Estado* to pass decree-laws – as happened on various occasions during the reform process.

The electoral system chosen for the lower house was deliberately designed to favour rural areas and large parties (see chapter 8). In the Senate, meanwhile, 40 seats were reserved for appointment by the king, while the territorial provision allowed for a highly distorted proportional factor in the remaining elected places. For example, the four senators from Soria represented around 100,000 voters each, compared with over 4.5mn voters per senator in Barcelona. In view of the fact that it was envisaged that the Senate would share legislative powers with the Congress, these provisions were of some significance in shaping Spain's new democracy. On 15 April 1977, a royal decree was published announcing general elections for exactly two months later. Given the short time which had elapsed since the death of Franco, little existed in the way of electoral infrastructure: political parties either had to come to terms with a return to legality after decades of clandestine existence (as in the case of the Communist and Socialist parties), or were of very recent origin, created with the June elections in mind (Heywood, 1995). A plethora of new political parties was registered, leading to considerable confusion amongst the overwhelmingly novice electorate. As expected, the party led by prime minister Adolfo Suárez, the *Unión de Centro Democrático* (UCD), won the most seats and was able to form the first democratically-elected government in Spain since February 1936.

The principal task facing the UCD government of Suárez was the drawing up of a democratic constitution (see Exhibition 2.2). The June general elections ensured that, although there now was a formalised opposition, all the major political parties operated according to broad agreement over this issue being given priority on the political agenda. Other issues, in particular the severe economic crisis facing Spain, were pushed onto a back-burner. Work on the new constitution commenced immediately. At the end of July it was agreed to set up within the lower house a constitutional committee (later known as the Committee on Constitutional Matters and Public Liberties), which, at the start of the following month, elected a 7-member *ponencia* charged with drawing up a draft agreement.[3]

The *ponencia* began negotiations on the basis of two agreements: first, a procedural accord that each member would submit a separate text to each session and one of these would then be chosen as a discussion document during the secret deliberations; second, a more significant general accord over certain minimum points, accepted by all, which would be reflected in the final document. This latter agreement lay behind the much vaunted 'consensus' which marked the discussions, and which came to influence the entire constitutional procedure. However, it should be noted that the composition of the *ponencia* excluded certain interests from direct involvement in the process. In particular, non-parliamentary groups such as trade unions and employers' federations were able to exert influence only through indirect means, a fact which naturally favoured the latter given the make-up of the *ponencia*. Equally, the private and secret nature of discussions, whilst enhancing the likelihood of achieving consensus, reduced still further the possibility of outside interests playing a role.

EXHIBIT 2.2

The Spanish Constitution of 27 December 1978

Preamble

Preliminary Title

Title I: **On fundamental rights and duties**
            Chapter 1: On Spaniards and foreigners
            Chapter 2: Rights and freedoms
                Section 1a.: On fundamental rights and public freedoms
                Section 1b: On citizens' rights and duties
            Chapter 3: On the guiding principles of social and economic policy
            Chapter 4: On guarantees of fundamental rights and freedoms
            Chapter 5: On the suspension of rights and freedoms

Title II: **On the Crown**

Title III: **On the *Cortes Generales***
            Chapter 1: On the Chambers
            Chapter 2: On the formulation of laws
            Chapter 3: On International Treaties

Title IV: **On government and administration**

Title V: **On relations between the government and the *Cortes Generales***

Title VI: **On the judiciary**

Title VII: **Economy and Treasury**

Title VIII: **On the territorial organisation of the state**
            Chapter 1: General principles
            Chapter 2: On local administration
            Chapter 3: On the Autonomous Communities

Title IX: **On the Constitutional Tribunal**

Title X: **On constitutional reform**

Two drafts by the *ponencia* were published on 5 January and 17 April 1978.[4] These were discussed by the Committee of Constitutional Matters and Public Liberties, which issued its favourable judgement on 1 July, and were approved by the Congress of Deputies on 21 July. Thereafter, the new text passed to the Senate's Constitutional Committee, which introduced some modifications before approval was granted on 9 October. Given the differences in the texts approved by Congress and Senate, a joint committee of the two houses met to reach a definitive draft version, which was issued on 28 October 1978. The final formal stage in the process was a public referendum, held on 6 December 1978, in which 88 per cent of those who voted granted approval to the constitutional draft. Although it is a commonplace to talk of the consensual nature of Spain's transition to democracy, as reflected in this overwhelming majority vote, it should be noted that the bare figure masks some important points. In particular, nearly 33 per cent of all eligible Spaniards abstained – leaving the overall vote in favour at 59 per cent of the electorate. Of far greater significance was the fact that abstention rates were much higher in some areas than in others – most particularly in the Basque Country, where in some provinces only a minority voted for the Constitution. Overall, 51.1 per cent of Basques abstained and, of those who participated, 23.5 per cent voted negatively (Clark, 1979: 361–3).

Basque discontent with the Constitution is of considerable importance. In spite of its general legitimacy, many in the Basque Country still feel the Constitution does not represent or reflect their interests. The issue of self-determination for the Basques remains very much alive, since a notable proportion of Basques believe that the constitutional provisions covering relations between the central state and the regions are unsatisfactory. Significantly, no representative of the *Partido Nacionalista Vasco* (PNV) – the historic Basque Nationalist Party – was included in the *ponencia*. In regard to the PNV's exclusion, it was argued that not all other parliamentary groups were included: Enrique Tierno Galván's tiny *Partido Socialista Popular* (PSP) was also denied representation – although in this case, because the main Socialist party insisted that no other Socialist group be admitted. Miguel Herrero de Miñón (1988: 67), one of the UCD's representatives on the *ponencia*, has suggested that the real reason for excluding the PNV lay in a shared belief between the UCD and the PSOE that they could marginalise nationalist forces in the Basque Country and divide control of the region's politics between themselves. Thus, it was important to deny the PNV any claim to political involvement.

Had the PNV been included in the *ponencia*, it is possible that its later attitude to the Constitution would have assumed a more positive tenor. As it was, the PNV abandoned the constitutional committee in May 1978 when it became known that secret deals were being made by the UCD and the PSOE on various clauses of the constitutional draft. Thereafter, the party adopted an oppositional stance. In all, the PNV presented slightly more than 100 amendments to the draft constitution, but was defeated on nearly every one in spite of a series of bilateral discussions with the UCD. In the parliamentary vote on the Constitution, the PNV abstained, controversially calling for a similar response by the electorate in the December national referendum (Clark, 1979: 352–66). The passage of time failed to bring about Basque reconciliation: as late as September 1994, Xabier Arzallus, president of the PNV, proclaimed 'We are not, and we will never be, loyal to the Constitution' (*El País internacional*, 3 October 1994).

Key Constitutional Issues

In spite of the general consensus within the *ponencia*, a number of critical constitutional issues required delicate negotiation. These centred on the nature and form of the new democratic state – whether it should be monarchical or republican, unitary or federal – and its relationship with leading interests amongst the so-called '*poderes fácticos*', such as the Catholic Church. Equally, the distribution of power between executive and legislature, as well as between head of state and head of government, were matters of some considerable debate. It has been argued that certain topics, such as the role of the military, were effectively removed from the agenda: they were considered simply too sensitive to be tackled head on in the immediate aftermath of the Franco dictatorship (Maravall and Santamaría, 1989: 297–8). All of these issues have their roots in the divisions which have characterised Spain's modern history. According to Jordi Solé-Tura (1988), a distinguished academic and politician who was a member of the *ponencia*, it is necessary to understand the nation's history in order fully to understand the process involved in instituting a new political order after the death of Franco.

In broad terms, divisions polarised around ideological position. Although the terms left and right are to some extent abstractions, hiding a multiplicity of conflicting stances, they none the less serve to outline essential differences between the main participants in the constitution-framing process. The right – that is, the *aperturista* reformers from within the Franco regime who were genuinely committed to the creation of a democratic constitution – wanted a short constitution specifying a highly centralised monarchy as the form of state, with checks against constitutional amendment in certain sensitive areas. The left – that is, the party political representatives of the anti-Francoist opposition – was in favour of a federal republic, with measures to protect 'progressive' constitutional provisions from amendment.

Monarchy versus Republic

Both the major parties of the left, the *Partido Socialista Obrero Español* (PSOE, Socialist Party) and the *Partido Comunista de España* (PCE, Communist Party), had been anti-monarchist throughout their history. Since its restoration in 1875 (after the abortive First Republic) the monarchy had been intimately associated with reactionary politics, and the PSOE's greatest moment prior to the post-Franco transition to democracy had come in 1931 when it had been a central participant in the founding of the Second Republic. Following the end of the Spanish Civil War in 1939, the Franco regime was forced into international isolation as a pariah state. As part of his effort to regain respectability, Franco formally restored the monarchy once more in 1947, although the dictator refused to allow anyone to accede to the throne while he remained alive, and arrogated to himself the right to appoint a royal successor (De Blaye, 1976: 167–8). Through an arrangement with the exiled Don Juan, son of Alfonso XIII, Franco was able to groom Juan Carlos as his successor, supervising the prince's education in Spain from an early age. It is hardly to be wondered at that, at the time of Franco's death, the leftist opposition should have been utterly opposed to the monarchy, and in particular to Juan Carlos. Santiago Carrillo, leader of the PCE, dismissed the new king as Franco's puppet, predicting that he would be known to history as '*Juan Carlos el breve*' (Juan Carlos the brief) (interview with Oriana Fallaci, *L'Europeo*, 10 October 1975; Carr and Fusi, 1981: 208).

However, the very fact that it was Juan Carlos himself who initiated proceedings in the transition to democracy ensured that there was never any real likelihood that the republican ambitions of the leftist opposition would be realised. The new king was sufficiently astute to appreciate that his own legitimacy remained in question when Franco died, and the most effective way to safeguard his position was to lead the process of political reform. This was a delicate act which was later to place him in some difficulty with Francoist die-hards. In the short term, however, the left appreciated that the real issue lay between dictatorship and democracy rather than monarchy and republic. Fear of unleashing a reactionary backlash, as had happened in both 1923 and 1936, served to temper the demands of the Socialist and Communist representatives on the *ponencia*. Thus, it could be argued that the new democracy effectively came with a monarchical pre-condition, with the role of the left reduced to that of trying to influence the nature of the post-Franco monarchy. None the less, leftist suspicion was betrayed at the formal constitution of the new parliament on 22 July 1977: Socialist deputies maintained an initial stony silence amidst the applause which greeted the entry to the chamber of King Juan Carlos and Queen Sofia (Peces-Barba, 1988: 16).

Unitary versus Decentralised State

Just as in the case of the monarchy, historical precedent ensured that the question of the state's structure would be highly sensitive. The issue of centralism versus regionalism has deep historical roots, reflected in the struggle between the notion of a single Spain as opposed to several Spains (see chapter 1). That it would be a critical issue in negotiations over the democratic constitution had been ensured by the scale of repression of regional demands under Franco: his death, to echo Fernando VII's final words, released the cork from the beer bottle. It is, therefore, unsurprising that the issue of the state's structure should have been the most contentious point of discussion during the *ponencia*'s deliberations over the new constitution.

In broad terms, the forces of the right – but most especially, the Franco regime – had always been associated with rigid centralism. The notions of *patria* and *Hispanidad* were cherished, particularly within the army, which had been inculcated during nearly forty years of dictatorship with the view that its principal role was to defend the territorial integrity of the Spanish nation. The greatest threats to Spain were seen as deriving not from overseas aggression, but from within the country's own national boundaries. The social and economic diversity of the Iberian mainland, reflecting the fact that Spain was created by the gradual unification of various distinct nations, had for centuries bedevilled attempts to establish a sense of Spanish national identity and had led in turn to the establishment of a series of highly centralised political structures. The idea that Spain could break up into distinct nationalities was anathema, a view which was shared across all shades of rightist opinion.

The desire of the right to maintain the integrity of the Spanish state was matched by no less an insistence from the opposition that some recognition of regional rights was a non-negotiable precondition of genuine pluralist democracy. For the left, however, the position was somewhat more complicated, as there was no unanimity over the preferred form of state structure. Options ranged from self-determination for all Spain's regions, fully-fledged federalism, some form of undefined political autonomy, to simple administrative decentralisation. Moreover, even within the main parties of the left there were contrasting opinions as to what was most desirable: while all accepted the need to recognise regional rights, there were widely divergent opinions as to how this should best be done.

In contrast to the position over the monarchy, where the left was obliged to accept that there was no realistic prospect of establishing a republic, the regional question generated deep divisions between the negotiating parties. The challenge facing the *ponencia*, therefore, was to create a state structure which moved away from the unitary conception of the Franco regime, but which did not provoke the ire of the army. The task was made even more difficult by the fact that those regions which most urgently demanded that their rights be recognised – the Basque Country and Catalonia – were precisely the most economically developed parts of the country. Further difficulties were created by the fact that the term 'autonomy' held different meanings for different people: while it was relatively simple to agree that some form of 'autonomy' was necessary and desirable, some saw it as remaining consistent with the notion of a unitary state, while others saw it as linked to the idea of federalism (González Encinar, 1983: 254). Moreover, the *ponencia*'s task was probably not helped by the fact that only Catalonia enjoyed real representation (through Miquel Roca of the Catalan Minority and, less directly, Jordi Solé-Tura). Catalan needs and desires in terms of regional autonomy, however, did not necessarily reflect those of Spain's sixteen other regions, as would become evident in later years (see chapter 7).

The Catholic Church

The centrality of the Catholic Church in the development of the modern Spanish state and, more particularly, its intimate connection with the Franco regime, meant that its constitutional position in the new democracy would inevitably be a delicate issue. In fact, the Church hierarchy was anxious to avoid political confrontation. Since

distancing itself from the Franco dictatorship after the Second
Vatican Council, the Spanish Church had consistently emphasised
the importance of compromise and national reconciliation (Pérez-
Díaz, 1993: 167). Exchanges between the Church and the democratic
opposition to Franco became commonplace, particularly amongst the
young and the working-class through such organisations as the
Juventud Obrera Católica (JOC, Catholic Workers' Youth Movement),
the *Hermandad Obrera de Acción Católica* (HOAC, Catholic Action
Workers' Brotherhood) and the *Frente de Liberación Popular* (FLP,
Peoples' Liberation Front) (Lannon, 1987: 232–5). As the Catholic
Church disengaged itself from the regime it had helped Franco
create, so sections of it came to be seen as part of the opposition to the
dictatorship.

Yet, neither the emergence of leftist influence amongst young
Catholics, nor the fluctuating relationship between the Catholic
hierarchy and Franco, altered the formal association between Church
and state during the dictatorship. Thus, the constitutional position of
the Catholic Church in the new democratic regime was bound to
raise considerable controversy. Vatican II had called unambiguously
for a separation between Church and state, but there were many in
the Catholic hierarchy who remained opposed to the loss of privilege
entailed by disestablishment. Critically, however, in Cardinal
Enrique Tarancón, Archbishop of Madrid and president of the
Episcopal Conference from 1971 until 1983, Spain's Catholics
possessed a leader of wisdom and pragmatic vision.

Tarancón led the Church with caution and realism during the
transition to democracy, providing strong support for reform –
particularly in his homily delivered at the king's coronation in
November 1975 (Pérez-Díaz, 1993: 167–8). King Juan Carlos also
took an important step when he unilaterally renounced the right to
nominate bishops, originally granted to Franco as head of state under
the terms of the 1953 Concordat. This opened the way to a partial
revision of the Concordat's terms, agreed upon in 1979. In the
meantime, Spain's 1978 Constitution significantly altered Church–
state relations, with the original draft document failing even to
mention the Catholic Church. Under considerable pressure from
bishops, reference was included in the final version to 'appropriate
relations of co-operation with the Catholic Church and the other
denominations'. However, in Article 16 the Constitution rejected an
official religion – an indication of how far the political position of the
Church had changed since the early years of the Franco regime.

Specific reference to the Catholic Church in the Constitution was seen as vital, as it implied that the state would be committed to respecting its structure even though the new regime supported religious pluralism. For the Church, formal mention in the Constitution invested added authority to its pronouncements on what it termed 'natural morality' – that sphere of interests which transcends any formal political arrangement. Of particular concern to Church leaders was that they should retain an influence in the field of education, as well as over decisions on such issues as abortion and divorce (Pérez-Díaz, 1993: 171).

The Constitutional Settlement: Artful Ambiguity

Given the complexity of the task facing the framers of the Constitution, it is unsurprising that the final result was a highly ambiguous document. In fact, there is a sense in which its prime virtue lies precisely in its ambiguity: in the best tradition of canonical texts, virtually all shades of political opinion can point to some detail to support their own viewpoint. However, in a number of instances, the constitutional document appears to be actually contradictory rather than just open to varying interpretations, and it has been argued that some of the main problems which have faced Spain's democratic functioning derive from this fact (Rubio Llorente and Aragón Reyes, 1979: 161–9). There are four main areas in which the Constitution is, to say the least, imprecise: the structure of the state, the position and role of the head of state, the duties of the armed forces, and the status of the Catholic Church. Each of these areas, it should be noted, has historically been a source of contention.

New constitutions, of course, are not created in a political vacuum. The framers of Spain's 1978 Constitution were able to look to precedents elsewhere and the final document shows the influence of various alternative models (Herrero de Miñón, 1979: 97–107). In regard to territorial organisation, the Spanish solution shows similarities to the Belgian model of institutionalised regionalism within a centralised state and to the Italian system of allowing varying degrees of governmental power by the regions within the framework of a unitary state. However, the constitutional arrangements for territorial organisation also demonstrate a profound sense of ambiguity, in one instance even within the same sentence. Thus, Article 2 states,

The Constitution is based on the indissoluble unity of the Spanish
Nation, common and indivisible country [*patria*] of all Spaniards,
and recognises and guarantees the right to autonomy of the nationalities and
regions of which it is comprised and solidarity amongst them (emphasis
added).

This extraordinary Article appears both to rule out regional
autonomy, as indicated in the first clause, and also specifically to
rule it in, as suggested by the italicised section.

Part of the problem resides in the fact that the definition of the state
in the Spanish Constitution is unclear: the term 'state' is used in
different places with various different meanings which are not always
reconcilable. According to a ruling by the Constitutional Tribunal in
July 1981, the term 'state' is sometimes used to mean the entire
juridico–political apparatus of the Spanish nation, including those
organisations which are specific to the nationalities and regions which
make up the nation (as in Articles 1, 56, 137 and the rubric of Title 8,
for example); on other occasions, 'state' refers only to the group of
general and central institutions and their peripheral organs,
specifically counterposing these to institutions which belong to the
Autonomous Communities (as in Articles 3.1, 149 and 150). An
attempt has been made – following a similar lack of definitional
clarity in the Italian Constitution – to draw a distinction between
'*Estado-ordenamiento*' (state-as-ordinance), meaning the totality of
elements within the ambit of the state, '*Estado-aparato*' (state-as-
apparatus), meaning the group of organisations which exercise
supreme power, and '*Estado-comunidad*' (state-as-community), meaning the group of subjects, distinct from the state-as-apparatus, which
have their own organisation for the exercise of those powers of
autonomy to which they are entitled. However, the distinction breaks
down, since the Constitution establishes a specific organic link in
Article 69.5 between the Autonomous Communities (state-as-
community) and the Senate (part of the state-as-apparatus) (López
Guerra, 1980).

The imprecision over the use of the term 'state' extends to the issue
of the *form* of state, and raises further confusion as to the precise
position and role of the monarchy and where sovereignty lies. Article
1.3 of the 1978 Constitution states that 'The political form of the
Spanish State is a parliamentary Monarchy', but the preceding
Article 1.2 says 'National sovereignty resides in the Spanish people,
from whom emanate the powers of the State'. The precise meaning of

this notion is hardly self-evident. According to Manuel Aragón (1980: 422), a distinction must be drawn between 'form of state' and *'political form of state'*: the latter formula describes the monarchy not in terms of the organ of headship of state, but rather as a symbol, referring to the 'latent functions, with no juridical relevance' that the crown can play. None the less, Article 56.1 states unambiguously that 'The King is the Head of State'. Article 64, on the other hand, ensures that the actions of the King are subject to endorsement (*'serán refrendados'*) by the prime minister, and where appropriate, by the relevant ministers. Effectively, the Spanish Constitution appears to establish a non-sovereign monarch whose formal position as head of state is fenced around with certain qualifications.

A further point of confusion derives from the clauses dealing with the duties of the armed forces, which Article 8 charges with the mission of guaranteeing Spain's sovereignty and independence, and defending both her territorial integrity and constitutional order. Article 62 describes the king as supreme commander of the armed forces. Article 97 states that the Government directs defence policy and military administration, and Article 149.1.4 gives 'the state' exclusive competence over defence and the armed forces. Such seemingly contradictory signals, compounded by the fact that the definition of the state and the role of the monarchy are in any case unclear, are not simply trivial semantic details. After the attempted military coup of February 1981, the conspirators arrogantly claimed during their trial that they were acting in accordance with their constitutional duty to protect the integrity of the Spanish state against the threats represented by regional demands. Equally, when the UCD and PSOE joined forces later in 1981 to pass the infamous *Ley Orgánica de Armonización del Proceso Autonómico* (LOAPA) – a measure to slow down the process of granting regional autonomy in response to the attempted coup – the law was successfully challenged in the Constitutional Tribunal for running counter to explicit provisions in the 1978 Constitution (see chapter 7).

Thus, if the Constitution's lack of precision is a virtue in some respects, allowing an apparently unlikely compromise on certain key issues, it has also served to fuel protest and discontent. Indeed, it has been suggested that the attempt to reach accommodation led in some cases to 'apocryphal compromises', reflecting the fact that it is easier to reach agreement over words than over ideas (Herrero de Miñón, 1988: 72). Apocryphal compromises resulted in articles with no juridical meaning. One example is Article 28.2, on the right to strike.

The PSOE and PCE–PSUC wanted the wording to read 'Workers have the right to strike', with no qualifications; parties of the centre and right wanted 'Workers have the right to strike in defence of their professional interests'. The final compromise reads 'Workers have the right to strike in defence of their interests', but the issue of whether 'their interests' has a narrow meaning relating only to professional matters or a wider meaning referring to general political well-being remains unresolved.

The 1978 Constitution and Democracy

For all the definitional imprecision which characterises it, Spain's 1978 Constitution situates the country firmly within the tradition of pluralist, liberal democracies. The task of the framers of the Constitution was to establish a legal framework for the emergence of parliamentary democracy. In this, they must be judged wholly successful. With regard to the democratic rights, liberties and guarantees enjoyed by its citizens, Spain stands comparison with any modern west European democracy. Indeed, this is only logical given that the inspiration for many of the provisions in the 1978 Constitution derived from European models. The main influences were Italy and the Federal Republic of Germany, largely on account of their own historical experiences of moving from dictatorship to democracy (Nieto, 1984: 29). Various specific features were taken from other countries.[5] Thus, for example, measures like the constructive motion of no-confidence, the creation of a constitutional tribunal and the establishment of an ombudsman were direct importations from alternative European models – so much so, that there have even been criticisms levelled against the Spanish document for its lack of originality (Aparicio, 1988: 51). Yet, it is precisely the particular mixture of 'borrowed' provisions which gives the Spanish Constitution its distinctive character. The 1978 document provides for a wide-ranging recognition of rights and liberties together with a complex system of guarantees – substantially derived from the Italian Constitution – which gives it a clearly 'progressive' feel. As a counterweight, though, there is a clear statement of the range of powers available, especially to the executive, which derives its inspiration from the French and German models.

This balance of progressive provisions within the context of a strong state reflects the weight of historical experience. On the one hand, there was a determination to guarantee those basic rights which had been in abeyance throughout the Franco dictatorship; on the other, there was a fear of creating a weak state, vulnerable to the challenges which had undermined the Second Republic. The single most important issue which motivated the political class of post-Franco Spain was to maintain the spirit of consensus which marked the transitional process. Thus, the 1978 Constitution contained a series of provisions designed to ensure a high level of political agreement, such as the requirement for specified majorities to pass organic laws, as well as the creation of numerous regulatory bodies to oversee the running of institutions such as universities, the broadcasting media and so on.

None the less, there has been considerable concern expressed in Spain over whether the constitutional provisions for democracy function effectively. The dominance of political power enjoyed by the PSOE since 1982, together with the scale of corruption in high places revealed during the early 1990s, has led some to question the efficacy of Spain's constitutional arrangements (Sinova and Tusell, 1990; Castellano, 1992). It is proper and necessary that vigilance should be practised: Spain's historical experience alone should warn against political complacency. However, the concern over Spain's democratic functioning may be to some extent misplaced.

There are certainly many political problems in Spain – some of them serious, and some of them derived from the country's constitutional provisions – as will be seen in the course of this book. Against this fact, though, must be placed the observation that *all* democracies suffer from varying degrees of deficit. It could even be argued that those which most vociferously laud their own democratic standing – the USA and Britain – suffer the most obvious drawbacks: in the former, non-participation has reached potentially damaging proportions, while the constitutional structure of the latter is arcane and electorally unrepresentative. In France, concern is routinely expressed over the power of the President, whilst the competing competencies of the German Chancellor and the leaders of the *Länder* also give rise to concern. Moreover, all these countries have seen a marked increase in debate over the issue of political corruption, with ministerial resignations becoming almost routine in the 1990s. Nowhere has this been more true, of course, than in Italy, where a situation of permanent crisis associated with the so-called *partitocrazia* had virtually been subsumed into political normality until the dramatic events of 1992.

The point of all this is to suggest that democracy is not some form of universal panacea. Nor does it correspond to a given model, against which it can be judged to see if it 'works' or not. That there are problems with Spain's democratic functioning is inevitable. Thus, while this study does not seek to downplay the need to be sober and vigilant, nor does it seek to be alarmist about any democratic deficit in Spain. Where critical comments about the functioning of Spanish democracy are made, these are not in any sense meant to be judgemental. Spain's achievement since the death of General Franco is quite remarkable: within a short space of time, it became and remains one of the most dynamic countries in Europe. For this reason, as much as any other, the formerly communist regimes of eastern Europe have looked to Spain for the elusive key to success. While such a search may ultimately prove to be misconceived, there is little to suggest that Spanish democracy is notably less secure than that of any other European country.

3

The Institutional Legacy of Francoism

Spain's 1978 Constitution and subsequent democratic functioning has been profoundly conditioned by the country's historical legacy. This can best be seen by analysing particular institutions, often referred to as *'poderes fácticos'* (a phrase which has no precise translation but roughly encompasses centres of power which enjoy major political influence). Given their significance under the Franco regime, the most important of these institutions are the military and the Catholic Church, both of which have played a critical role in the development of modern Spain.[1] However, they have had differing impacts on the political process in the post-Franco period. Whereas a large part of the former represented a real threat to the success of democratic transition – which it viewed with considerable mistrust – the latter deliberately distanced itself from active political engagement, a response in part to the virtual identification of Church and state in the early Franco years. More recently, however, whilst the military has effectively eradicated any residual *golpista* tendencies and fully accepts civilian authority, the Catholic Church – influenced by the theologically conservative pontiff, John Paul II – has become increasingly outspoken on political matters.

Also of considerable importance is the so-called fourth estate – the mass communications media. Strictly controlled under the Franco regime, it has undergone revolutionary developments since the return of democracy. The explosive impact of information technology has completely altered the face of Spain's mass media: deregulation of the press resulted in a veritable orgy of publications in the early post-Franco years, whilst broadcast media options have been steadily increased by both the advent of satellite and cable networks and by the impact of regional autonomy and privatisation. None the less, both the UCD and the PSOE governments have been accused of seeking to use national television for their own political ends, an echo of the years of media manipulation by the Francoist state. Indeed, it was only with seeming reluctance and after considerable delay that the Socialist government agreed to the granting of private television licences in 1989 (Cavero, 1990: 389–405).

The Military: from 'Poisoned Legacy' to Professional Force

The military, and in particular the Spanish army, has often been seen as the mainstay of Franco's 'poisoned legacy' (Preston, 1990: 165–202). The dictator deliberately sought to instil in the armed forces a narrow preoccupation with internal rather than external threats to Spain, thereby building upon a tradition of military intervention which has its roots in the early nineteenth century. There are perhaps three main elements which have shaped the nature of the military in modern Spain. First, the Spanish armed forces have traditionally suffered from macrocephaly: all the Spanish services have always had too many officers, who have in turn tended to be too old for their rank and responsibilities. In 1977 – in spite of a major reorganisation twelve years earlier which had slashed troop numbers in an effort to bring Spain into line with other European countries – the army still had one officer for every six to seven conscripts, and 340 generals (Treverton, 1986: 23). This top-heaviness derived from a rigid promotion structure, based on length of service rather than ability, which had often been jealously guarded against civilian interference. Second, the Spanish army frequently responded to a self-defined notion of patriotism, seen in terms of defending Spain from allegedly incompetent politicians. In large measure a result of the armed forces' failure since the early nineteenth century to achieve outright victory in any conflict against external enemies, this compensatory obsession with domestic politics was cultivated and deliberately used by Franco to repress internal opposition. Third, all the Spanish services have demonstrated an acute sensitivity to civilian criticism, intensified by widespread popular hostility to conscription and the regular use of the army to crush social agitation.

Although one-third of all the ministers appointed by Franco were military men, the armed forces were very much the poor relation of the dictatorship. Their low pay and antiquated equipment were compensated for, however, by social services: military stores, schools, and hospitals helped both to create a sense of privilege and to reinforce dependence on the regime. Moreover, a blind eye was turned to *pluriempleo*, the illegal practice of taking additional jobs outside the services in order to supplement income. Most important, great stress was laid on building up a feeling of pride within the armed forces for their role in the victory over the Second Republic. In the aftermath of the Civil War, the army's position on the far right of the political spectrum was consolidated by the systematic elimination of liberal officers, as well as by its complicity in the brutal repression of the 1940s. The combination of repression and association with the fascist regimes of Hitler and Mussolini led to Franco's diplomatic and commercial isolation following the Second World War (Preston, 1990: 131–62; Cardona, 1990: 181–208).

An international pariah, it is likely that Franco would not have been able to remain long in power but for the onset of the Cold War. In return for desperately needed political recognition and financial aid, in 1953 the Spanish dictator signed an agreement with the USA which allowed the Americans to construct three air bases – at Torrejón de Ardoz, near Madrid, Sanjurjo Valenzuela, near Zaragoza, and Morón de la Frontera, near Sevilla – as well as a naval base at Rota, near Cádiz, a sophisticated radar system, and an oil pipeline linking Rota with Zaragoza (Viñas, 1981; Vázquez Montalbán, 1984: 83–200). Beyond effectively mortgaging the construction of an independent Spanish defence policy to the USA, the 1953 Bases Pact obviated the need to modernise the armed forces which could now rely on American cast-offs as a main source of equipment.[2] From the early 1950s, Franco largely ignored the defence requirements of the air force and navy and concentrated instead on using the army in an explicitly political role. This was most clearly indicated by its territorial deployment: troops were concentrated near major cities, and the crack armoured mobile units, the *Fuerzas de Intervención Inmediata* (FII), were stationed outside Madrid, Sevilla and Valencia. The Parachute Brigade was in Alcalá de Henares near the capital, the Air-transportable Brigade was sent to La Coruña on the north-eastern coast, and the Cavalry Brigade to Salamanca, near the Portuguese border. In military terms, such deployment was senseless; in political terms, it accurately reflected Franco's threat perceptions.

By the time of Franco's death, a significant proportion of commanding officers had been thoroughly socialised into the anti-democratic values of his regime. Trained in the hermetic world of military academies, these officers – the so-called 'bunker' – upheld the Civil War mentality of victors and vanquished, of hierarchy, authority and discipline, patriotism and the fatherland. Military attitudes in the transition period were overwhelmingly conservative. A survey of 983 cadets from the *Academia General Militar* (AGM) conducted shortly after Franco died showed that over 40 per cent found 'irreligiousness' to be the most disagreeable feature of society at that time. In response to the question 'What is the most valuable factor in the efficiency of an army?', the most popular reply was 'The patriotism of its members', while only 6 per cent opted for 'The quality of its equipment and the technical proficiency of its regular soliders' (Hooper, 1986: 70–1; Paricio, 1983: ch.4).

Such narrow horizons were reinforced by limited contact with wider society: 50 per cent of officers married officers' daughters. It has been estimated that in 1981, 25 per cent of AGM cadets were from families that either belonged to, or sympathised with, the extreme right-wing party, *Fuerza Nueva*, or embraced other far right ideas (Aguilar, 1981). In short, the Spanish military represented an anachronism in a rapidly modernising society. Moreover, its suspicious attitude towards democracy several times threatened the success of Spain's political transformation.[3] The legalisation of the Communist Party two months prior to the general elections of June 1977 provoked fury amongst leading officers, and the bunker's subsequent unwillingness to respect the legitimacy of the first democratically elected post-Franco government of the UCD represented a constant threat to political stability (Bardavío, 1980; Preston, 1986: 97–107).

The UCD government took a number of measures aimed at reducing the military threat. Strategic promotions and an emphasis on fidelity to the monarch were intended to engender loyalty to the democratic regime. In addition, important structural reforms were enacted in 1977: a single Ministry of Defence was set up, thereby ending the inefficient system by which each branch of the armed forces had its own minister of state, and the *Junta de Jefes de Estado Mayor* (JUJEM), or Joint Chiefs of Staff, was established, modelled on British and American practice. Together, the Chiefs of Staff headed the chain of military command, although the precise role of the Prime Minister and the Defence Minister in the formulation of defence policy and their relationship to the military command was left unclear.

The UCD's basic strategy consisted of seeking to establish civilian supremacy over the armed forces in as short a time as possible. However, prime minister Suárez approached the military in a brusque, even confrontational, manner – in marked contrast to his dealings with the opponents to the Franco dictatorship. This high-handed approach, together with the fact that defence issues received relatively little attention during the immediate post-Franco years as Spain's politicians were primarily concerned with the construction of a new constitutional order, gave rise to uncertainty within military circles. It is thus perhaps unsurprising that the armed forces –the army in particular – should react negatively to seeming marginalisation within the political process. Moreover, resistance to innovation is a normal feature of any institution, and the armed forces were confronted by vast changes not only in their own structure, but also in the political structure of Spain as a whole. The UCD's failure to deal sympathetically with military sensibilities was emphasised by seemingly random and erratic reforms as a continuous redefinition of power relations took place.

A further factor which complicated the military equation was the ever-increasing threat from the Basque separatist group, ETA, which systematically targeted military personnel in its own struggle against the new democracy. The counterpoint of violence between the military and ETA claimed many victims and came close to destabilising Spanish politics in the crucial early stages of the transition. ETA-*Militar*, which emerged in the mid-1970s as the main operating wing alongside the more politically oriented ETA-*Político-Militar*, hoped to provoke revolution; in fact, its increasingly indiscriminate activities played into the hands of those ultra-rightists who shared – albeit from a very different perspective – its determination to prevent the 1978 Constitution taking effect (Clark, 1984: 87–119; Preston, 1986: ch.5 *passim*). Convinced by the late 1970s that the UCD government was failing in its duty to protect the unity and integrity of the Spanish state, members of the bunker started to conspire against democracy.

Between 1978 and 1981 military plotting, or *golpismo*, several times took Spain to the brink of catastrophe, and never more so than on 23 February 1981 when Lieutenant-Colonel Antonio Tejero Molina led the storming of the Cortes in what ultimately proved to be an abortive coup attempt.[4] Even though the leaders of the *Tejerazo*, as the attempted coup became known, represented a small, disaffected minority within the armed forces, their action served as a sobering reminder that military loyalty could not simply be assumed. One result of the attempted coup was to precipitate Spain's entry into NATO (see chapter 12), part of a belated attempt by the UCD government to modernise the armed forces.

The PSOE government of Felipe González, which assumed office at the end of 1982, continued and extended the modernisation of the armed forces, but was forced to tread warily. For the ultras of the reactionary right, the election of a Socialist government just seven years after Franco's death was anathema. Indeed, a further coup attempt had been planned for 27 October, the day before the general elections. Thoroughgoing plans for the coup, which was to involve the capture of the entire political class and the deposal of the king, were discovered in early October and military intelligence services acted swiftly to dismantle the plot (Preston, 1986: 224).

The threat of military intervention thus continued to loom menacingly over Spain's nascent democracy – even though the PSOE had received an overwhelming mandate from the Spanish electorate. That mandate, however, did allow the Socialists to move quickly on the issue of military reform. Under the guidance of Narcís Serra, Defence Minister from 1982 until 1991, the PSOE oversaw extensive and far-reaching reforms. Crucially, and in direct contrast to the UCD, the Socialist government sought to avoid political confrontation whilst consolidating civilian supremacy and systematically implementing modernisation measures.

Military bills in 1982 and 1984 provided for a significant increase in the budget to purchase the modern equipment necessary for a professional force (Ministerio de Defensa, 1986). In addition, far-reaching changes were made to the command structure and deployment of the armed forces. The position of the Prime Minister and Defence Minister in relation to defence policy was formalised, placing them in control of the decision-making process and clarifying the ambiguous relationship inherited from the 1977 reforms. Furthermore, the position of Chief of Defence Staff was created to facilitate collaboration between the armed forces and the Defence Minister. The PSOE government also put into effect the *Plan de Modernización del Ejército de Tierra* (META), originally drawn up in the late 1970s by the Army Chiefs of Staff. Its main provisions included a significant reduction in the number of officers and NCOs, which fell by 16 per cent in the army and 8 per cent in the navy and air force in the six years up to 1990. The total size of the armed forces in 1991 was 227,096, including 135,000 conscripts, compared to 373,005 (with 294,000 conscripts) in 1984.

Spain's military regions were re-drawn, and reduced from nine on the mainland to six, plus the Balearic and Canary Islands (Ministerio de Defensa, 1986: 111–14). The new deployment reflected a realistic assessment of defence requirements in terms of external, as opposed to internal, threats. Further reforms aimed at instilling a greater sense of professionalism within the armed forces. In particular, budgetary allocations under the Socialists continued the trend of shifting resources from ground forces to naval and air forces, a development which was strongly reinforced by the requirements of NATO membership. Thus, taking 1975 as an index of 100, the ratio of budgetary expenditure up to 1986 rose to 110 in the army compared with 160 in the navy and 180 in the air force. Overall during this period, in spite of the fact that it grew in real terms, military expenditure declined discreetly as a proportion of the state's central administrative budget, oscillating between 2.1 and 4 per cent of gross national product (GNP). In the same period, the civilian administrative budget rose from 11 per cent of GNP to over 20 per cent – notwithstanding the fact that central administration represented the very core of the Franco regime and might have been expected to swallow a larger share of the state budget than subsequent democratic regimes. The figures clearly demonstrate the shift in state expenditure patterns since the death of Franco away from the military towards social issues (Bañón Martínez, 1988: 339–45).

Nonetheless, the Socialist government invested extensive sums in technological modernisation, research and development, and arms procurement. Industrial and technological development of arms procurement, particularly within the framework of co-operation with Europe, served several objectives, including much-needed industrial restructuring (see chapter 10). With regard to the armed forces, it was hoped that modernisation of equipment would help to reinforce a professional outlook: the greater training requirements of advanced technological weapons systems and closer contact with other NATO forces were expected to instil professional values. By the same token, in terms of equipment modernisation, such a policy further bolstered the position of the navy and air force relative to the army, given their greater potential contribution to NATO requirements.

A wide-ranging and much amended Law on Military Personnel, passed in July 1989, represented a further critical step. Seen by some as putting a democratic seal on the reform process, its many provisions included fundamental changes to military career structures. Promotion patterns were altered to favour merit over seniority, salary scales were raised to match those of civilian officials, the structure of corps and promotion rosters was simplified, the average age of commands was tackled by limiting the period of active service to thirty-two years for those who do not reach the rank of general, and military education was reformed (González, 1990). Further changes were announced in mid-1991 aimed at bringing total numbers in the armed forces down to 180,000 (with 55 per cent professionals, compared with just 21 per cent in 1984) by the end of the century. These moves were facilitated by the significant changes to compulsory military service enacted during the 1980s. Legislation relating to conscientious objection came into force in late 1984, and the number of grounds for exemption from military service was increased – although a sharp increase in the number of conscientious objectors (68,000 took up the option of doing social work in 1993, compared with 42,400 a year earlier) led to stricter conditions being imposed from the start of 1994. A reduction in the length of military service from twelve to nine months was announced in 1990, and permission was granted for women to enter all sections of the professional armed forces.[5]

In December 1993 plans were approved to abolish Spain's military governorships (*gobiernos militares*), first established in 1841. A potent symbol of the Spanish army's traditional structure, military governors existed in each of Spain's fifty provinces to act as representatives of the Captain General in the given military region. By 1996, military governorships will be replaced by provincial defence delegations (*delegaciones provinciales de Defensa*), with their logistical and operational functions to be assumed by the newly-created figure of military commander (*comandante militar*).

Such developments reflect the determination to end irrevocably the tradition of military involvement in domestic politics. However, although it is widely believed that the military 'threat' has been effectively eliminated as a result of the 1980s reforms, controversy has continued to surface. In early 1991 it was revealed that there had been a coup planned in 1985, which would have involved assassinating the king and leading figures in the government. The conspirators apparently planned to bomb the official stand at the

Armed Forces Day military parade in La Coruña, and then blame the atrocity on ETA. The revelations, somewhat suspiciously timed to coincide with the tenth anniversary of the *Tejerazo*, elicited a muted response, an indication of the extent to which past rifts between military and society had healed (*El País*, 18 February 1991).

Spain's armed forces no longer command obsessive media attention. Where once reports on 'states of opinion' in the armed forces were a regular feature in all the major newspapers, now it is rare to see references to '*el poder militar*' – military power. The distant rattling of sabres may still be heard on occasion, but it elicits little reaction from the Spanish public. Thus, a 1989 study of military attitudes after a decade of democracy which showed that nostalgia for the Franco dictatorship remained remarkably high aroused no great concern. The survey indicated that while the military's political protagonism has declined, attitudes have remained highly conservative: although the armed forces in the late 1980s supported the democratic system in abstract terms, there remained considerable nostalgia for the authoritarian past. Of 302 active service members of the armed forces with a rank of officer interviewed in June 1988, 55.7 per cent saw democracy as preferable to any other political system, but fully 35.6 per cent believed that in some cases an authoritarian regime would be preferable and 3.4 per cent saw it as a favoured option in all circumstances. Equally, 39.4 per cent of high-ranking officers believed that Spain was better under Franco (Pérez Henares *et al.*, 1989: ch. 1).

Despite the study's findings (which were unsurprisingly rejected by the Ministry of Defence and military authorities) it is no longer possible to speak meaningfully of a 'military threat' in Spain. There has been undeniable advance along the road towards professionalisation within the armed forces, with the army in particular having undergone extensive organisational and cultural change. Although membership of NATO remains hedged with qualifications, the Spanish armed forces play a role which is now consistent with that of their counterparts in the rest of western Europe (see chapter 12). Indeed, the normalisation of relations between the civil and military estates, with the latter fully accepting the former's political authority, is one of the surest indicators that Spain's democracy is securely rooted.

A rather different source of controversy surrounds the very role and structure of the military in modern Spain. Towards the end of 1989 a serving army colonel, Amadeo Martínez Inglés, gave an interview in a national magazine in which he described the Spanish army as useless and called for the creation of a professional body, claiming that there was resistance to such a move from senior politicians and the military establishment (Martínez Inglés, 1989). Although he was immediately prosecuted – and subsequently expelled from the army – the interview raised important issues. Military modernisation, alongside dramatic changes in the world order following the collapse of communism, has prompted discussions on the future composition and purpose of Spain's armed forces. In marked contrast to the isolationism which has been a hallmark of defence policy throughout most of the twentieth century, Spain has become increasingly involved throughout the 1980s in western defence works (see chapter 12).

The Civil Guard and the Police

Under the Franco regime, policing was militarised. A wide range of offences fell under the auspices of military courts, including the spreading of ideas 'which threaten religion, the Fatherland, and its fundamental institutions' and verbal insults to the armed forces, including the police (Shubert, 1990: 249). Through their ubiquitous presence, two forces in particular – the *Guardia Civil* and the hated *Policía Armada* (Armed Police) – became virtual emblems of the dictatorship. Formed in 1844, the *Guardia Civil* has always been a highly disciplined and – despite its name – an essentially military force. Charged with patrolling the vast expanses of rural Spain, Civil Guards rarely came from the region to which they were posted, lived in barracks, and did not mix socially with the local population. Responsible under Franco to the Army Ministry, the Civil Guard recruited the bulk of its officers from the *Academia General Militar* (AGM). More so than the other militarised police forces, the Civil Guard found it difficult to assimilate Spain's transition to democracy, and it provided the main support for the *Tejerazo* of 1981.

Although Article 8 of the 1978 Constitution separated the armed forces from the police, the status of the Civil Guard has remained ambiguous. The 1980 National Defence Law contrived the device of making it responsible to the Interior Ministry in time of peace and to the Defence Ministry in time of war. Further confusion arose under the Socialist government, which – after some early debate as to the force's very future – in 1986 passed legislation affirming the military basis of Civil Guard regulations, and then appointed a civilian to command the force[6] (López Garrido, 1987). From a state security point of view, an efficient and reliable force was seen as offering considerable benefits, especially given the continued activities of terrorist organisations. The Civil Guard in contemporary Spain performs a major, if highly controversial, anti-terrorist intelligence role as well as more visible and routine functions such as stopping and searching traffic during terrorist alerts.

In contrast to the Civil Guard, reform of the police since the return of democracy has been more far-reaching. Under the 1978 Police Law, the *Policía Armada* was renamed the *Policía Nacional*, although it was not fully de-militarised. Military jurisdiction, however, was restricted and offences committed against members of the police and the Civil Guard were moved within the exclusive provenance of civilian courts. Membership of trade unions was sanctioned and two bodies soon emerged: the broadly right-wing *Asociación* (later *Sindicato*) *Profesional de Policía* (SPP) and the more leftist *Unión Sindical de Policías* (USP). However, after the PSOE assumed power in 1982 persistent stories emerged of corruption and of the existence of a police mafia within the plainclothes *Cuerpo Superior de Policía* (Higher Police Corps). In 1985, a damning report by Amnesty International (*Spain. The Question of Torture*) spoke of torture and ill-treatment by the National Police and the Civil Guard, as well as abuse of detainees' constitutional rights under the provisions of the 1980 anti-terrorist law.

Far more damaging were revelations about the activities of the *Grupo Antiterrorista de Liberación* (GAL), an anti-ETA group allegedly set up by two senior Spanish police officers. Operational between 1983 and 1986, the GAL – composed mainly of French and Portuguese mercenaries – was held responsible for a dirty war campaign involving 33 terrorist attacks (mostly in south-west France), 26 deaths and two unsolved kidnappings. Following a protracted investigation by Baltasar Garzón, a young judge at the National Court of Justice, the matter finally came to trial in June 1991 amidst widespread rumours that the GAL had been authorised and financed from within the Interior Ministry. The trial centred on the alleged activities of the two police suspects, José Amedo and Michel Domínguez, who were eventually sentenced to over 100 years in gaol, but the real issue surrounded the government's role. Testimony from over 100 witnesses, including written replies by the prime minister, Felipe González, and the Interior Minister, José Luis Corcuera, failed fully to allay strong suspicion of government involvement. In late 1994 the GAL affair resurfaced. A series of interviews with Amedo and Domínguez published in the newspaper *El Mundo,* which alleged high-level government involvement, led to the case being re-opened by Garzón. However, in January 1995 Garzón was temporarily suspended from the case following counter-allegations by a former member of the Interior Ministry that he was involved in an orchestrated campaign to undermine the government. His subsequent reinstatement as investigating magistrate promised to cause the government considerable embarrassment.

Partially in response to the Amnesty report and initial revelations about the GAL, the 1986 security forces law merged the National Police with the Higher Police Corps, creating the *Cuerpo Nacional de Policía* (National Police Corps), and allowed for the establishment of regional forces. Critics dismissed the reforms for failing to get to the roots of corruption and for strengthening the position of the Civil Guard as a frontline public order force. Nonetheless, between 1986 and 1990 over 800 inspectors and chief inspectors were relieved of their duties, and retirement ages were lowered as part of a policy to renovate and rejuvenate the police force.[7]

In addition to the above forces, there are the *Policía Municipal* (civic police), recruited and administered locally with the basic purpose of upholding local by-laws, and the *Policía Gubernativa* (government police), renowned for a heavy-handed approach to law enforcement. Furthermore, in 1989 regional police forces were established in the Autonomous Communities of Catalonia and the Basque Country, known respectively as the *Mosos d'Esquadra* and the *Ertzaintza.* Overall, there were some 160,000 police in Spain in 1989, a ratio of 3.15 per 1,000 inhabitants as compared with 4.27 in Italy, 3.9 in France, 3.57 in Portugal, and 3.78 in West Germany (Vera Fernández, 1989). However, figures vary considerably according to region. Thus, in the Basque Country, there are nearly 15,000 police in five different forces for a population of just over 2 million, a ratio of more than 6.5 police per 1,000 inhabitants.

The Catholic Church: Coming to Terms with Disestablishment

In few countries has the Catholic Church enjoyed so central a presence as in Spain. For 260 of the nearly 300 years since the

Bourbons took the Spanish throne in 1700, Catholicism has provided the state's official religion and established church. Through a holy alliance of throne and altar, the Catholic Church has been intimately associated with the emergence of modern Spain – even if the view of a homogeneous and all-pervasive religious identity owes more to caricature than reality. Throughout significant parts of rural Andalucía and Extremadura, for instance, Catholicism appears never to have re-established an effective institutional presence after the fifteenth-century expulsion of the Moors. Moreover, anti-clericalism has deep roots in Spain. Indeed, the struggle between anti-clericals and the Church has been one of the central dynamics of Spanish political development since the late nineteenth century.

The founders of the Second Republic (1931–6) ordered the separation of church and state, demolished many of the church's official privileges, and introduced a wide body of secularising legislation. In reaction, the Franco dictatorship established almost complete identity between Church and state. Backed during the Civil War by leading members of the hierarchy, General Franco rewarded the Church with unprecedented political influence in his New State. Freedom of worship for non-Catholics was abolished, the divorce law was rescinded and civil marriage ceased to exist, religious instruction was made compulsory, state funding of the Church was reinstated, and the religious orders expelled by the Second Republic were readmitted to Spain. A Concordat with the Vatican, signed in August 1953, set the seal on the symbiotic relationship between Church and state (Giménez y Martínez de Carvajal, 1984: 137–55). Of the myriad privileges granted the Church by the dictator, which included exemption from taxation and censorship as well as the right to ask for material it found offensive to be withdrawn from sale, the most important was control over all levels of education.

However, in marked contrast to the military – which in essence remained throughout a loyal bastion of the regime – the relationship between the Catholic Church and the state changed profoundly during the dictatorship. There were two main strands to the altered relationship, both of which contributed in significant measure to the success of Spain's transition to democracy. On the one hand, a somewhat unlikely dialogue developed between young Catholics – often connected with the Jesuits – and leftist opponents of the dictatorship. In the aftermath of the Second Vatican Council (1962–5), groups such as Christians for Socialism emerged, seeking to interpret Marxism from the viewpoint of a 'theology based on earthly reality' and accept class struggle. The opening of contacts between Catholics and leftists had a profound social impact, laying some of the groundwork for the pluralist co-operation which was to mark the Spanish transition to democracy (Pérez-Díaz, 1993: 169–71; Lannon, 1987: 224–57; Hermet, 1985: vol.1; Vincent, 1995).

On the other hand – and in almost direct opposition – members of Opus Dei gained political ascendancy and acted as a key force for economic modernisation. A secretive and somewhat mysterious Catholic organisation originally founded in 1928 by José María Escrivá de Balaguer y Albás, Opus Dei married a progressive belief in technocratic rationalisation as the key to Spain's economic development with a highly conservative theological, social and political outlook (Lannon, 1987: 225–30; De Blaye, 1976: 427–9; Walsh, 1989). Ministers associated with Opus Dei are widely credited with having persuaded General Franco at the end of the 1950s to introduce indicative planning, based on the French model, and to open up Spain's hitherto closely supervised economic borders to greater international penetration. These developments were crucial to the economic expansion enjoyed by Spain during the 1960s, and have been seen by some as contributing to the end of the Franco regime by creating an unsustainable disjuncture between economic modernisation and political repression (Preston, 1986: 1–52).

Opus Dei itself has consistently denied possessing a political agenda; none the less, struggles between so-called *Opusdeístas* and the Falange – the Franco regime's single party, which became deeply resentful of the technocrats' power and influence – were a constant feature of the dictatorship's final years. In 1969, Manuel Fraga Iribarne, Franco's Minister of Information and Tourism (who was to become a leading luminary of the right in democratic Spain), allowed the press to reveal details of a financial scandal surrounding the textile machinery firm, Matesa. Investigations implicated Opus Dei in a massive scandal involving the diversion of state funds, and spelled the end of the organisation's dominance of Franco's cabinet. Although Opus Dei has never recovered the political pre-eminence it enjoyed under the dictatorship, it retains extensive social and economic influence – particularly in the world of finance and the media. Indeed, under the benign gaze of Pope John Paul II, who granted it the status of a Personal Prelature in 1982, Opus Dei has flourished.

A central concern for the Catholic Church since the transition to democracy in Spain has been a continued decline in religious practice. The number of practising Catholics fell from 64.5 per cent in 1975 to 40.9 per cent in 1986. In 1990, the proportion of non-believers remained small – 13 per cent as opposed to 9 per cent in 1981 – and 86 per cent of Spaniards continued to describe themselves as 'Catholic'. Whilst an overwhleming majority (81 per cent) believe in God, for those between the ages of 18 and 24 the figure falls sharply to just 68 per cent. Only 55 to 60 per cent of Catholics go to church at all and, of those, a sizeable number go only very occasionally – sometimes just to perform their Easter duty. By 1990, the number of Catholics who went to church at least once a month was down to 43 per cent compared to 53 per cent in 1981. Attendance varies markedly according to region, being highest in the north – especially in the Basque Country and Castilla y León[8] – and lowest in the rural south (Villalaín Benito *et al.*, 1992: 40–7; Pérez-Díaz, 1993: 173–6).

However, more worrying to the Catholic hierarchy than the decline in church attendance has been the impact of the vocational crisis. A worldwide phenomenon since the 1960s, the crisis was reflected in Spain through a fall in the number of young men seeking to join the priesthood as well as an increase in the number of priests renouncing their vows. None the less, there remains a remarkably high number of Spaniards in Holy Orders: in 1984, there were 21,423 parish priests, 10,905 ordained monks, 7,695 unordained monks and 79,829 nuns (Hooper, 1986: 170). Equally, Spain's 918 enclosed convents represent 60 per cent of world's total. In spite of these high numbers, there are two related problems facing the Catholic Church in terms of falling numbers and secularisation. First, the age profile of Spain's clergy is distorted, with a notable bulge evident between the ages of mid to late thirties and early sixties. As the older clergy begin to retire and die, there are insufficient younger men coming through to take their place.

Second, the Church's ability to exercise moral and social influence will thus be hampered by the combined factors of fewer clergy and greater secularisation. This is likely to be of more concern to the political right than the left, since there is some evidence that political opinions are related to religious identity and that self-defined 'very good Catholics' tend to favour right-wing options. Yet, the link is far from clear-cut and, moreover, the most religious in terms of self-definition also tend to be the least politically active (Linz, 1980b: 262). In the 1982 general elections, more than half the country's practising Catholics voted for the Socialists. Furthermore, the absence of a christian democratic party in Spain – notwithstanding claims made since 1990 by the right-wing Popular Party's leader, José María Aznar, that his party represents the christian democratic option – has been taken as an indication of the Catholic Church's limited political power.[9]

Another key issue concerning the Catholic Church in post-Franco Spain has surrounded its funding. A two-stage agreement reached in 1979 to move towards total financial separation between Church and state was not properly implemented until the PSOE came to power. According to its terms, over a three-year period commencing in 1988, Spanish Catholics could opt to declare on their tax returns whether they wanted 0.52 per cent of their tax revenue to go to the Church, or else to other social ends (such as drug abuse treatment, or poverty relief) to be decided upon by the Minister of Social Affairs. During the three years up to 1991, the state guaranteed to make up the difference between the so-called 'religious tax' and the usual level of subsidy. Thereafter, the Church would have to be self-reliant for income generation. Initial returns indicated that just over 35 per cent took up the Church-funding option, with a further 12 per cent choosing to support social spending. Given the relatively low take-up of the 'religious tax', Church authorities expressed concern at the viability of the new funding system, and in 1992 a revised formula was agreed whereby the faithful could make direct donations which would be offset against income tax. The constitutionality of the 'religious tax' had in any case been called into question, since it appeared to conflict with the non-confessional nature of the state (*El País*, 12 October, 1992).

Whereas some dioceses – notably Barcelona and Madrid – have been strikingly successful in generating income, for the most part the Spanish Church suffers from a combination of high assets and low liquidity. In particular, the loss of tax privileges and the high-cost maintenance of Church treasures poses severe problems: since the 1960s, the Church has been forbidden to sell objects of historical or artistic value, yet must now find the means to protect and preserve them. None the less, Cardinal Angel Suquía, then president of the Episcopal Conference, confirmed in 1990 that it remained the Church's intention to achieve full financial independence from the state.

It would be a mistake to underplay the Church's social impact or to underestimate its desire or capacity to maintain a political presence in Spain. This much was implicitly recognised in 1990 by José Borrell, PSOE Junior Minister at the Treasury and later Minister of Public

Works, when he called on Church leaders to remind the faithful of the need to 'exercise moral exigence' and avoid fiscal fraud. A document published by the plenary assembly of Spanish bishops in November 1991, *Los cristianos laicos, la Iglesia en el mundo*, called on Catholics to participate actively in politics – although it avoided giving express support to any particular party. However, under the leadership from 1984 to 1993 of Cardinal Suquía, a noted admirer of Opus Dei, the Catholic Church in Spain became both more outspoken on political matters and more identified with reactionary stances.

Three issues in particular exercised the Church's concern: divorce, abortion and education. While legislation on divorce and abortion may perhaps be seen as belonging more properly to the sphere of social rather than political affairs, it continues to arouse controversy. A revision of Spain's Penal Code in 1992, which extended the legal grounds for abortion during the first three months of pregnancy, drew a furious response from some Church leaders, notably the archbishop of Toledo, Marcelo González Martín, and the bishop of San Sebastián, José María Setién. Education is also an intensely political issue. The 1984 *Ley Orgánica del Derecho a la Educación* (LODE), a radical step by the Socialist government to reform and rationalise Spain's somewhat chaotic educational provisions, provoked immense controversy (Sinova and Tusell, 1990: 185–7). The Church, in alliance with sectors of the middle class which were concerned at a perceived threat to the educational advantage enjoyed by their children, sought to block the legislation. Although the government's will eventually prevailed, the scale of protest contributed ultimately to the replacement in 1988 of the Education Minister, José María Maravall.

Even more controversial from the Church's point of view were the proposals contained in the 1990 education reform act, the *Ley de Ordenación General del Sistema Educativo* (LOGSE). At a plenary assembly of the Episcopal Conference in November 1990, Cardinal Suquía launched a bitter attack on the new law during a wide-ranging peroration which accused the government of – amongst other things – corruption, materialism and influence-peddling. The key issue for the Church concerned the status of religious education within the curriculum: the removal of academic recognition for religious instruction together with the offer of free periods of 'attended study' for those who chose not to take religion were seen as a direct governmental attack on the Church's influence within the educational system.

At the same assembly, a report on the moral state of Spaniards entitled 'Truth will set you free' was overwhelmingly endorsed. The document echoed Suquía's criticisms, and aimed further fire at the government for 'exercising power in its own interests' and for turning Spain into a 'huge casino' in which success was the only moral value recognised. In a move which marked the definitive end of the Church's self-imposed avoidance of political involvement, the Episcopal Conference called for a 'new crusade' aimed at penetrating the deepest roots of the country's social, economic and political institutions. The Church subsequently condemned a government campaign to increase the use of contraceptives by young people in response to the growth in the number of AIDS victims as well as unwanted teenage pregnancies. None the less, for all that the Catholic Church under Cardinal Suquía adopted more reactionary political stances, it is perhaps indicative of its reduced influence that government sources in general chose to avoid direct engagement with Church authorities over such matters. In any case, the Episcopal Conference itself delivered a sharp rebuff to Cardinal Suquía in 1993 when it failed to elect his chosen candidate as successor to the presidency, opting instead for the far more moderate Elías Yanes, archbishop of Zaragoza.

In addition to education and social legislation, a further source of tension surfaced between the Socialist government and the Catholic Church over the latter's private radio station, COPE (*Cadena de Ondas Populares Españolas*). During the early 1990s, when accusations of government corruption were rife, COPE gave considerable airtime on fashionable and seemingly never-ending *tertulias* (chat shows) to leading critics of the Socialist administration, such as Pablo Sebastián, Amando de Miguel and José Luis Gutiérrez. Alfonso Guerra, whose brother Juan stood at the centre of a major scandal over influence-peddling, was particularly critical of what he called the COPE's evangelical broadcasts, accusing them of engaging in calumnies, insults and outright lies. The Church has also been closely involved with the printed media, holding a controlling interest in the influential daily newspaper *Ya* until 1989, when the Episcopal Conference decided to give it up in order to raise funds. Opus Dei also has a significant presence through its close links to Europa Press, the main privately-owned news agency in Spain. In addition, Opus Dei controls an extensive series of publications with little ostensible relationship to Church concerns, including titles such as *Actualidad Económica*, *Nuestro Tiempo*, *Palabra* and a women's magazine, *Telva*.

The Mass Media: From State Instrument to Government Enemy

Some of the most profound changes which have marked Spain's emergence from dictatorship to democracy can be seen in the mass media, which have developed almost beyond recognition since the era of stultifying central state control. Paradoxically, however, one of the most persistent criticisms of Spain's democratic functioning has centred precisely on the perceived continuation of attempts by central political authorities to influence or control the news media (Sinova and Tusell, 1990: 203). In practice, the extent of involvement varies according to the political influence of the medium in question; thus it has been greatest – and most blatant – in regard to television, followed by radio and then newspapers, which have a very low readership (see Table 3.1).

Under the Franco dictatorship, the media were strictly controlled. Rigid censorship existed alongside a system of so-called *consignas* – items prepared by the government which newspapers were obliged to print. The 1966 Press Law, drafted by Manuel Fraga, has often been seen as paving the way towards a gradual relaxation of censorship during the dictatorship's final years. In fact, although relatively low-circulation oppositional journals such as *Cuadernos para el Diálago* and, from 1972, *Cambio 16*, were tolerated, state prosecutions for press infractions of the censorship laws actually increased following the so-called *Ley Fraga*. In general terms, the media under Franco was of execrable quality. Under the control of the *Movimiento*, a chain of over thirty newspapers, including national titles such as *Arriba*, *ABC* and *La Vanguardia*, served as little more than state mouthpieces or else dealt exclusively with sports and leisure interests. The situation was no better with regard to radio and television, both under monopoly state control. They were central pieces in what has been termed the

TABLE 3.1

Use of mass communications media in Spain

Percentage of Spaniards who:	Daily	Never
• watch television	81	1
• listen to radio	58	7
• read a newspaper	26	21

Source: CIS survey, quoted in Sinova and Tusell (1990: 212).

Franco regime's 'culture of evasion', offering a fare of banal and second-rate soap operas alongside sports transmissions and endless broadcasts of *zarzuelas*, stereotypical Spanish comic operettas (Carr and Fusi, 1981: 118–23).

State control of the media under General Franco left an insidious legacy to his democratic successors. Although the introduction of political pluralism was matched by an explosion of publications of every variety – books, newspapers and, above all, journals – the jewel in the communications crown from a governmental point of view was state television. Freedom of expression in the printed press, with all the potential for political criticism it implied, could be more easily granted while the state retained control of the most influential medium of all. As Adolfo Suárez must have appreciated, having been director-general of *Radio-Televisión Española* (RTVE) under the Franco regime, television held the key to reaching the eyes and ears of the Spanish population. Whereas newspaper readership has always been low in Spain, with a diffusion rate lower than any other EU country except Portugal (Rodríguez Lara, 1993: 191), television commands massive audiences.

Control of Spanish television has thus been particularly contentious since the return of democracy. Under the UCD, a new charter for RTVE in 1979 established a governing body composed of six deputies elected by the Congress, which naturally tended to favour the ruling party and was therefore fairly ineffectual as a watchdog. However, although the UCD government of Adolfo Suárez was regularly criticised for manipulating television news output, the true champions of this art have been the PSOE. Political manipulation of television was never more obvious than during the build-up to the referendum on NATO membership in March 1986. A propaganda campaign of unparalleled intensity saw the government use RTVE effectively as an extension of its own political resources (Cristóbal, 1989: 12–17). Such cynical manipulation represented a low point of political pluralism since the return of democracy. It is unlikely to be repeated following the concession, albeit reluctant, of licences to three private television channels which started broadcasting in early 1990.

Legislation on the introduction of private television, long delayed before its final passage in 1988, was marked by bitter controversy. Amongst the more contentious details of the new law was the restriction of private broadcasting licences to national stations, with regional and local transmitters having to remain in the public sector. Moreover, the government reserved the right to oblige the new private channels to transmit items deemed 'necessary'. There was fierce competition to win the three available concessions, granted only in late 1989, with accusations and counter-accusations amongst the competing parties (Cavero, 1990: 325ff.). Ultimately, although Socialist governments consistently sought to maintain a strong public sector presence within the media to act as a countervailing force to the private sector, its granting of private television licences contributed to the gradual emergence in Spain of major private sector media empires. For instance, Canal Plus España, one of the successful companies, reinforced the position of its principal share-holder, Prisa, which publishes the leading Spanish newspaper *El País*. Under the control of Jesús de Polanco, Prisa-El País has grown since its original creation in 1972 to become one of the dominant forces in the Spanish media.

El País was closely associated with leading figures in the Socialist party during the early years of the transition, and this fact contributed to the signal disquiet its success provoked amongst rival newspapers. The highly conservative *ABC*, one of the very few newspapers of the Franco era to have survived in democratic Spain, routinely referred to *El País* as 'the government's newspaper', while *El Independiente*, launched in 1988, described the Prisa-El País bid for a private television channel as representing '*el Régimen*' (a shorthand term originally used to described the Franco dictatorship). However, the Prisa empire holds no monopoly. Another of the successful private television licence bids came from the 'Godó empire', which linked the radio broadcasting company, Antena 3, the leading Catalan newspaper, *La Vanguardia*, the sports daily, *Mundo Deportivo* and the press agency, Prensa Lid, with a host of other regional titles as well as *ABC* and several major weeklies. Equally, one of the unsuccessful bids came from Zeta–Antonio Asensio, which owned over thirty publications covering a wide spectrum of interests.

Greater independence in the mass media has been matched by a deterioration of relations with the government, especially on the part of the press. Under the PSOE government open hostility has surfaced on several occasions, and never more so than during the so-called Juan Guerra scandal in 1990 and subsequent corruption scandals involving the Socialist Party. An unrelenting campaign, spearheaded by *El Independiente* and *El Mundo*, to force the resignation of deputy prime minister, Alfonso Guerra, saw virtual war declared between press and government. At one point during 1990, the prime minister, Felipe González, referred dismissively to '*los plumíferos de la democracia*' (democracy's hacks) and accused them of not knowing how to behave in a democratic society. Even the King was moved to comment in his 1990 end of year address on the need to maintain minimum standards in the press. Certainly, the lack of any effective libel law in Spain has allowed certain sectors of the press – in particular, weekly political magazines – to engage in sensationalist near-vendettas, disingenuously masquerading as investigative journalism, against particular individuals.[10]

Yet the press has been at the forefront of exposing a series of corruption scandals and cases of financial mismanagement by senior officials (Heywood, 1994a). For all the discomfort felt by a government unused to being challenged, such press revelations may have served a salutory purpose in guarding against further degradation of Spain's democracy. Badly damaged by the scandals, the PSOE government was obliged to introduce a series of anti-corruption measures in the summer of 1994. Although it is a clear duty of the mass communications media in any democratic society to investigate and inform, especially in cases of alleged political misconduct, such a duty also carries significant responsibilities. Equally, the defence of media independence and freedom from state intervention is a fundamental and legitimate goal. However, the media has the potential to exercise considerable political influence, and the argument has increasingly been made that its undoubted power should be matched by some form of codified legal accountability. Concern over press standards has grown markedly as Spain's democracy has moved from its infancy towards maturity. This is not to suggest that standards are universally poor; in *El País*, for example, Spain has a daily newspaper of ever-growing European standing and influence.[11]

The *poderes fácticos* and Spanish Democracy

All three of the institutional *poderes fácticos* discussed in this chapter have undergone profound changes as they have sought to identify a new role in democratic Spain. The armed forces have developed from a position of looming menace in the late 1970s and early 1980s, acting as a constant threat to the successful development of democratic stability, to one of full subordination to the civil estate. The key to this fundamental change has been modernisation and professionalisation, together with integration into international western defence works.

Whereas it was once necessary to talk in terms of 'the military threat', Spain's armed forces now play a role consistent with their democratic duty. This is not to argue that the Spanish military has become a bastion of political pluralism; indeed, residual suspicion of civic demands is a normal reaction in most military estates. The important point is that the armed forces *accept* pluralism as the constitutionally-defined political system, and see their role in terms of upholding that order in line with their orders from the civilian authorities.

The Catholic Church has had to come to terms with changes which have been equally profound, perhaps even more so. Whereas the relationship between civil and military estates in post-Franco Spain could be built upon lines which are well-identified within pluralist democracies, the disestablishment of the Church represented a move into far less certain waters. Thus, in contrast to the military, where there was little difficulty in identifying what its role *ought* to be, the Catholic Church had to define a new role for itself – as well as a new funding structure – in a period of major political upheaval. Unsurprisingly, perhaps, it has experienced some difficulty in adapting to its new position, not least on account of the secularisation of contemporary Spanish society. From a position in which it concerned itself fundamentally with pastoral issues, the Church since the mid-1980s began to adopt a more outspoken political profile. Under the leadership of Suquía, the Catholic Church in Spain attempted to recapture some of the political protagonism and influence it had enjoyed in earlier times. A striking example of this was the decision by three Catalan bishops in the aftermath of the collapse of communism in the Soviet Union to issue a pastoral letter, distributed in all churches of their dioceses, calling for Catalonia to be granted the right to self-determination. This move was given added significance by the fact that it coincided with the *Diada*, Catalonia's annual festival. However, for all that the Church has attempted to adopt a higher political profile, the enormous changes undergone in Spanish society since the death of Franco mean that its influence has waned significantly. Religion no longer polarises Spaniards (Pérez-Díaz, 1993: 176).

Whereas the Catholic Church has declined in political importance since the death of Franco, the mass media have continued to expand and prosper. Formerly under the strict control of the state and subject to heavy censorship, the media have seized upon political independence to claim an ever-more influential role. Indeed, it has been argued by some that the weakness of formal institutional checks on the political executive (see chapter 4) means that the function of control has been effectively devolved to the media (Cebrián, 1989). Some newspaper editors, such as Pedro J. Ramírez, editor of *El Mundo*, have become household names. However, real political influence is best exercised through television. Considerable controversy has attached to the control of television in democratic Spain. Greater independence in the media has been matched by growing concentration of power within so-called media 'empires', a potentially unhealthy development so long as much of the Spanish press remains obsessed with personalities rather than issues.

Part II

The Construction of a Democratic State

4

Central Government: Monarchy, Core Executive and Parliament

Spain is a parliamentary monarchy. Such a straightforward designation obscures the fact that, through a combination of constitutional design and political practice, neither parliament nor the monarchy wield effective power in Spain's democracy. The role of the monarchy was always meant to be mainly symbolic; in the case of parliament, however, its increasingly symbolic role was an unintended result of the core executive's particular structure.

The Very Model of a Modern Monarchy: Spain's Subject Sovereign

When Juan Carlos I de Borbón acceded to the throne on the death of General Franco in November 1975, the dynastic legitimacy of his title was questionable. The grandson rather than the son of the last reigning monarch, Juan Carlos had been designated legal successor to Franco only in 1969 (see Exhibition 4.1). In the aftermath of the 1946 Law on Succession, Don Juan, son of Alfonso XIII and first claimant to the throne, had with some reluctance acquiesced to Franco's demand that Juan Carlos be educated under the dictator's tutelage in Spain, rather than following a career which would have taken him to Sandhurst. It was not until May 1977 that Don Juan – who lived

83

EXHIBIT 4.1

King Juan Carlos I de Borbón

Born in Rome in 1938 to Juan de Borbón y Battenberg (1913–93) and María de Borbón-Nápoles, Juan Carlos acceded to the Spanish throne on the death of General Francisco Franco in November 1975. Franco's Succession Law of 1947 had defined Spain as a kingdom, but left the identity of any future king undecided. Though Juan Carlos's father, Don Juan, had been head of the Royal House since the death of Alfonso XIII in 1941, Franco was unwilling to see him become King of Spain. It was agreed, however, that Juan Carlos would be educated in Spain; to this end, the young prince went to Madrid in 1948 and served in the armed forces from 1957 to 1959. In 1961 he married Princess Sofía of Greece, by whom he had three children: Elena (1963), Cristina (1965), and Felipe (1968). Juan Carlos was formally designated heir to the throne and to General Franco as head of state only in 1969. However, Don Juan, who remained in exile in Portugal, refused to renounce his own claim to the throne until May 1977, although relations between father and son remained harmonious.

In 1975 Juan Carlos was widely expected to leave the basic structures of the Franco regime intact, but in fact the king moved quickly to dismantle the dictatorship. His first official speech affirmed his intention to rule over all Spaniards and return their liberties to them, thereby enabling the process of democratic transition to commence from within the constitutional framework of the dictatorship. In concert with Adolfo Suárez, whom he appointed prime minister in July 1976, Juan Carlos promoted the introduction of democracy under the rule of law. Under the terms of the 1978 Constitution, the king transferred sovereignty to the Spanish people.

Juan Carlos's enormous popularity in Spain stems in large measure from his decisive actions on 23 February 1981, following the attempted *coup d'état* by Lieutenant Colonel Antonio Tejero. After Tejero had attacked the *Cortes* during the investiture of Leopoldo Calvo Sotelo as prime minister, thereby taking hostage the entire political class, Juan Carlos made contact with various military authorities and demanded a return to barracks of all troops. After several hours of immense tension, the *coup* was successfully neutralised and its leaders arrested. Juan Carlos' instrumental role during the episode won him considerable admiration and respect, both in Spain and overseas. His reputation continued to grow thereafter as he performed his largely symbolic role as head of state with much dignity; in particular, Juan Carlos proved an outstanding ambassador for Spain on the international stage. He has been honoured throughout the world for his contribution to Spain's democratic transition.

---

until 1993 – formally renounced his own right to the throne, following the Political Reform Law of December 1976 (Cotarelo, 1991: 1–4).

During the reign of Juan Carlos, the monarchy has seen a dramatic increase in its prestige: the King has become a genuinely popular figure, widely credited with having been instrumental in ensuring the success of the transition to democracy. In particular, Juan Carlos is seen as the key figure in disarticulating the attempted coup of

23 February 1981 – and, perhaps unsurprisingly, he has been variously designated as 'the motor' or 'the pilot' of change (Areilza, 1977, 1983; Powell, 1991). In fact, such an emphasis on the role of one individual underplays the signal importance of both structural factors and other agents of change – such as the various anti-Franco opposition movements, reformists from within the regime, and international influences – in the success of Spain's transition to democracy (Morán 1991; Cotarelo, 1991: 4).

In practice, and somewhat ironically, the enhanced stature of the monarchy has occurred in parallel to a reduction in its real power. In constitutional terms, the Spanish monarchy has little political influence – certainly in comparison to its historic significance. The undoubted stature and authority enjoyed by Juan Carlos is predominantly personal rather than institutional – although the institution has clearly benefited from his reign.

The formal position of the monarchy is set out in Articles 56–65 (Title II) of the 1978 Constitution. The monarch is head of state, but remains at the margins politically: s/he acts as a moderating and arbitrating power, with the primary role of symbolising the Spanish state. The head of state has a right to be informed of political developments, and to this end holds a weekly audience with the prime minister. However, the monarch has neither executive nor discretional legislative power and is subject to judicial regulation. Political responsibility thus falls entirely on the government. None the less, the monarchy's symbolic functions are important in a double sense: they serve as a formal expression of the unity and continuity of the Spanish state, as well as facilitating the harmonious operation and interaction of the core executive's real organs of power.

The Constitution outlines a series of functions, as opposed to powers, attaching to the monarchy: the head of state sanctions and promulgates laws, issues decrees approved by the Council of Ministers, is supreme commander of the armed forces, represents Spain in its relations with other states, confers honours and distinctions, and is patron of the royal academies. These are all '*actos debidos*' (duty acts) in the sense that they are constitutionally required of the monarch, who is left no discretion over their fulfilment.

However, the head of state does enjoy discretion over certain other functions. For instance, the monarch may decide whether to accept an invitation by the prime minister to take the chair during a meeting of the Council of Ministers. Such invitations are generally offered at times of governmental difficulty in order to express symbolic backing, as occurred in early 1991 following the resignation of Alfonso Guerra as deputy prime minister. A refusal by the monarch to accept the premier's invitation would seriously undermine the prestige and authority of the sitting government. Of greater potential, but less actual, significance is the head of state's role in designating candidates for the post of premier. In the case of a clear-cut general election result, the monarch is politically obliged to name the leader of the largest party. In other circumstances, such as after close elections or when a prime minister has left office for whatever reason, the monarch can make suggestions but ultimately must accept parliament's recommendation. It was widely reported that King Juan Carlos urged Felipe González not to resign as premier at the end of the 1980s for fear that no other political figure could command similar support in the run-up to the introduction of the European Single Market.

Although the monarchy has virtually no specific powers, the significance of the institution lies in its political influence and authority. Through speeches, royal visits, attendance at public functions and so on, the head of state performs a crucial role in both representing and symbolising democratic Spain. Indeed, King Juan Carlos has assumed an ever more prominent role in his capacity as Spain's world ambassador – especially in Latin America, where he is held in great esteem. However, his readiness to comment on political matters has led, on occasion, to political controversy. In particular, Juan Carlos has been outspoken in his demands for a solution to the Gibraltar issue: in October 1991, during a speech to the General Assembly of the United Nations, he described it as 'an unresolved colonial problem which affects Spain's territorial integrity' (*El País internacional*, 14 October 1991). The King's accompanying the prime minister during an official visit to Morocco in July 1991, immediately followed by a further joint visit to the inaugural meeting of the Ibero-American Conference in Mexico, provoked opposition disquiet. A spokesperson for the *Partido Popular* argued that the King's presence on both occasions blurred the constitutional distinction between head of state and head of government.

King Juan Carlos has also provoked controversy through his comments on domestic politics. In his 1990 Christmas message, Juan Carlos called on the mass communications media to exercise self-discipline after a year in which accusations of corruption and influence-peddling by the PSOE government had reached unprecedented levels. Six months later, however, the King joined in the criticism, warning against public corruption, slovenliness and immobilism. It was suggested that Felipe González, with whom Juan Carlos had established close relations since 1982, approved the King's comments as the premier sought to impose discipline on his deeply divided party (*Cambio 16*, 8 June 1991). Other controversial political interventions include Juan Carlos's admonitory comments prior to the December 1988 general strike and his remark earlier in the same year that the Navarrese had made their choice over their own identity. This was seen as a direct criticism of those Basque nationalists who claim Navarra as part of the Basque Country. The monarch made further remarks on the regional issue in late 1992, prompted by renewed demands for greater autonomy in Catalonia and the Basque Country, when he insisted that Spain could accommodate different languages within its state boundaries. This was a clear example of how Juan Carlos has sought to represent the unity of Spain, whilst acknowledging the diversity which characterises the country (*El País internacional*, 2 November 1992; Cotarelo, 1991: 11).

One reason for Juan Carlos's great popularity is that he has been seen as an accessible monarch, in touch and in tune with the Spanish population. He is believed to have sought to identify with other citizens, often mingling with them in impromptu circumstances.[1] Equally, the lack of ostentation surrounding the house of Borbón (there is no extended civil list and no court) and the royal family's attempt to lead a relatively normal existence – the King pays taxes, just as all citizens are supposed to – have contributed to the positive image of Spain's first genuinely democratic monarch.

Monarchical succession follows the traditional formulation of primogeniture, with the heir being designated the Prince of Asturias. While not excluded from the order of succession, women are effectively relegated to a position of last resort, able to accede to the throne only if there are no male heirs amongst the monarch's siblings, children or grandchildren (Alvarez Conde, 1990: 325). In a further arcane reference, the marriage plans of the heir to the throne are subject to approval by both the monarch and the *Cortes*, although in practice this constitutional provision (Article 57.4) is likely to be interpreted in the sense of approval simply being assumed rather than formally granted.[2]

In short, the monarchy remains a largely symbolic institution whose continued prestige and influence remains dependent upon its lack of formal political power. The real centre of power in Spain resides in the executive office of the head of government rather than with the head of state.

The President's Power: Constitutional Arrangements

Although the Spanish head of government is routinely referred to as the prime minister, in formal constitutional terms the office of 'prime minister' does not exist in Spain (see Exhibit 4.2). The 1978 Constitution refers throughout to the 'President of the Government' and the 'President of the Council of Ministers'. While this may seem a trivial semantic point, the framers of the Constitution were very particular as to how they defined the position of the head of government. Historically, Spanish prime ministers have seen their authority easily undermined: the country's long tradition of authoritarian intervention has been reflected in the dominance of heads of state *vis-à-vis* heads of government. In the twenty years from

---

EXHIBIT 4.2

Spanish government leaders, 1975–94

	Dates	Party	
Carlos Arias Navarro	1974–5	(Appointed by General Franco)	
Carlos Arias Navarro	1975–6	(Appointed by King Juan Carlos)	
Adolfo Suárez González	1976–7	(Appointed by King Juan Carlos)	
Adolfo Suárez González	1977–9	*Unión de Centro Democrático*	E/M
Adolfo Suárez González	1979–81	*Unión de Centro Democrático*	E/M
Leopoldo Calvo Sotelo	1981–2	*Unión de Centro Democrático*	M
Felipe González Márquez	1982–6	*Partido Socialista Obrero Español*	E
Felipe González Márquez	1986–9	*Partido Socialista Obrero Español*	E
Felipe González Márquez	1989-93	*Partido Socialista Obrero Español*	E/M*
Felipe González Márquez	1993–	*Partido Socialista Obrero Español*	E/M

Key:
E: appointed following general election.
M: minority government.

Note:
* In the 1989 elections, the PSOE won exactly half the 350 seats in the Congress. The non-participation in Parliament of four Deputies from the Basque separatist party, *Herri Batasuna*, allowed the PSOE to function as if it still enjoyed an absolute majority.

1902 to 1922 there were thirty-three changes of prime minister, an average tenure of seven months, whilst the Second Republic suffered from the competing competencies of the offices of president and prime minister. General Franco, in contrast, held the position of both head of state and head of government – as well as leader of the single party and commander-in-chief of the armed forces – until 1973, when Admiral Luis Carrero Blanco was appointed to the post of prime minister (De Blaye, 1976: 526–31).

The 1978 Constitution was careful to avoid allowing any interpretation of the premier's position as being merely *primus inter pares*. The president of the government is vested with special authority and is specifically *not* responsible to the head of state, being instead technically responsible to the electorate through parliament. According to Gregorio Peces-Barba (1981: 52; 1988), a Socialist member of the constitutional drafting committee and President of the Congress between 1982 and 1986, the definition of the political form of the Spanish state as a parliamentary monarchy in Article 1.3 of the Constitution has a very particular and precise meaning: it serves to emphasise that national sovereignty lies with parliament rather than the monarchy. Parliament, or the *Cortes Generales*, is a bicameral body with a weak upper house (*Senado*) consisting of 257 members (208 directly elected and 49 appointed as regional representatives), and a lower house (*Congreso de los Diputados*) of 350 members elected by the d'Hondt system of proportional representation (see Exhibit 8.1).

Whereas in Italy the institutional framework of redemocratisation (1947/8) stressed popular sovereignty and proportional representation in an attempt to approach the ideal of balanced powers between executive and legislature within a system of parliamentary government, the Spanish model – in common with Portugal and Greece – placed major emphasis on strong and stable government. The provisional parliamentary standing orders of 1977 and 1982 have been described as 'the most pro-governmental in Europe' (Oscar Alzaga, quoted in Liebert, 1990: 11). Three points in the constitutional provisions relating to the core executive merit emphasis (Bar Cendón, 1983: 138–9):

● There is no clear separation of powers in Spain. Instead, there exists a deliberate integration of executive and legislature via the government, as defined in Articles 87 and 109–11. It could indeed be argued, notwithstanding Peces-Barba's observation, that parliamentary sovereignty has been something of a myth from the outset.

● The prime minister is encharged with the formation and leadership of the government as well as the co-ordination of its members, as outlined in Article 98.2. The premier has a virtually free hand over the structure of and appointments to cabinet, the number of vice-presidents, and so forth. Cabinet members do not have to be either deputies or members of the party in power.[3] While the premier has a free hand over how many ministers without portfolio to appoint, the number of ministerial departments may be changed only with the approval of the *Cortes* (Baena del Alcázar, 1988; 210–12).

● The government must have the confidence of the *Cortes* in order to govern, as expressed in a vote of investiture (a provision unknown in any previous Spanish constitution). Article 112 allows the president to demand a vote of support at any time, as happened for instance on 5 April 1990 when Felipe González, in spite of having won the general election six months earlier, submitted to a vote of confidence. Article 113 provides for a 'constructive censure motion' on the model of the Federal German Republic, which requires the nomination of an alternative candidate for the presidency.

The importance attached in the 1978 Constitution to a strong premier is further underlined by the nomination procedure. In particular, Article 99.2 specifies that the prime minister must present the political programme of the government to be formed and ask for the confidence of the chamber, which is given *only* to the premier and not to the entire government. According to Antonio Bar Cendón (1983:156), this personalisation is an important indicator of the pre-eminence specifically granted to the office of president in the 1978 Constitution. The manner of designating the head of government breaks with a long tradition in Spain of 'free' nomination by the head of state.

Monarchical intervention and authoritarian government meant that historically the position of the prime minister in Spain was considerably reduced in importance. Traditionally, therefore, the head of government has not been granted any special technical assistance or a large advisory staff; not until 1951 was a Ministry of the Presidency of the Government created. The 1978 Constitution, in contrast to previous practice, provides the office of president with an extensive support network. Formal presidential advisers as well as the *Gabinete de la Presidencia* (President's Office or Department) were established for the first time at the end of the 1970s, although the latter was not put into operation until the accession to power of Felipe

González in 1982.[4] Adolfo Suárez preferred to rely on a network of presidential advisers, who came to be known collectively as *'los fontaneros'* ('the plumbers', after Watergate). The President's Office, whose head is a close confidant of the premier, employs over thirty full-time staff, most of them from within the ranks of the civil service.

To sum up, then, the 1978 Constitution makes the President of the Council of Ministers the foremost figure in the political system. The position's pre-eminence is manifested in three clear respects: complete freedom of choice in the formation of the government; considerable incumbency insulation, with forcible removal from office possible only in very specific circumstances (which always entail the fall of the entire government); clear executive functions assigned by the Constitution specifically to the president. In practice, of course, in spite of these extensive powers, the political experiences between 1977 and 1994 of Spain's two elected presidents since the return of democracy could hardly have been more different. Adolfo Suárez, for many the principal architect of the successful transition from dictatorship to democracy, was so hamstrung by an inability to impose his will on the government that he eventually resigned in January 1981, to be replaced by Leopoldo Calvo Sotelo. On the other hand, Felipe González succeeded in becoming one of the most dominant figures in contemporary Spanish political history following his 1982 election victory. Clearly, between the constitutional theory of a strong executive and the political practice of government there is room for considerable variation.

Contingent Constraints on the Premier's Power

The most obvious variable which helps explain the different experiences of Suárez and González is the political context in which they held power. In relation to presidential power, political contexts, which are clearly contingent upon a variety of circumstances, may perhaps best be analysed by adopting a twin-level approach. At the first (or endogenous) level, relations between the president and the party in power need to be considered; at the second (exogenous) level, attention must be devoted to the principal political challenges facing a given president and the government. A crucial dimension to the relationship between the president and the party in power is security of governmental tenure: a president at the head of a government which enjoys an absolute majority of seats in parliament is likely to be in a far stronger position *vis-à-vis* the party than one who heads a minority or coalition government. Between 1977 and 1982, the *Unión de Centro Democrático* (UCD) was always a minority government and had, therefore, to rely on pacts with various forces (which differed according to the issue in question), whereas the *Partido Socialista Obrero Español* (PSOE) won convincing absolute majorities in 1982 and 1986. After the 1989 general election, in which disputed results and a re-run in one seat eventually cost the PSOE its absolute majority, there was a marked change in presidential tone and style, with far greater emphasis placed on inter-party accords. Subsequently, a reliance on pacts with other parties was made imperative by the 1993 general election results, in which the Socialist Party fell seventeen seats short of a majority.

The UCD and the PSOE were very different political animals. Whereas the PSOE has enjoyed a continuous, albeit fluctuating, history as an organised political party since 1879, the UCD represented less a coherent political party than an ad hoc group whose single rationale was to maintain some hold on the levers of power. This goes a considerable way towards explaining the eventual disintegration of the party in 1982. The UCD was never truly united. It emerged during the early months of 1977 as a broad coalition of divergent interests, mostly connected in some way with the defunct Franco regime, which sought to retain their privileged status. The new party opted for Suárez as leader mainly on account of the advantages which were deemed likely to accrue from his position as head of government since July 1976 (Preston, 1986: 108–13; Huneeus, 1985; Caciagli, 1989).

The divisions inherent in the UCD's structure were exacerbated by the party's lack of an overall majority and had a clear impact on Suárez's ability to govern effectively. The president soon found himself having to negotiate agreements not only with other parliamentary groups, but also with various factions within his own party. Suárez was careful to keep discussions between the government and the UCD's parliamentary group to a bare minimum in order to avoid latent differences of opinions from surfacing too obviously. None the less, tensions were all too apparent. Suárez increasingly surrounded himself with his group of presidential advisers, the *fontaneros*, much to the disgust of those outside this charmed circle. The *fontaneros* became the target of venomous resentment amongst leading UCD figures, which eventually culminated in barely concealed conspiracies against the president. Negotiations over a government reshuffle in May 1980 were described by *Cambio 16* as 'a macabre dance of the vampires'. Two months later, party barons discussed at length means of getting rid of Suárez; the president found himself isolated from his own cabinet, from the party, and from the general public. Without any unifying ideology or sense of political direction, the UCD began to collapse back into its constituent parts, a process hastened by the growing sense of '*desgobierno*' (literally, 'un-government') under a leader manifestly incapable of leading. By the end of the year Suárez had decided to resign.

Unsurprisingly, González enjoyed a marked advantage over Suárez in terms of governmental stability. This stability found its clearest reflection in the number of ministerial reshuffles under the UCD and PSOE respectively. During Suárez's first term in office, 1977–9, there was an important reshuffle in February 1978 and three other partial reshuffles; during his second term, 1979–81, there were major reshuffles in May and September 1980, as well as one partial reshuffle. His successor, Leopoldo Calvo Sotelo, presided over one partial reshuffle (September 1981) and one major reshuffle (December 1981) during his 20 months' tenure in office. The situation under the PSOE – at least until 1991 – could hardly provide a greater contrast. Between 1982 and 1991, there were a total of just 29 ministerial appointments to cover 18 portfolios, with only three ministries (Transport, Industry and the reorganised Ministry of Public Administration) experiencing more than one change of minister; another two (Defence and Agriculture) retained the same minister throughout. However, after the resignation of Alfonso Guerra as deputy prime minister in early 1991, González engaged in a major reshuffle, which involved the redesign of several portfolios. A further reshuffle in June 1992 was prompted by the resignation through ill-health of the foreign affairs minister, and the greater volatility of cabinet appointments during the PSOE's third administration reflected a more general decline in the party's dominance of parliament. The trend continued in González's fourth term, when reshuffles were forced on the prime minister in the spring and summer of 1994 by a spate of resignations connected with corruption cases.

In broad terms, though, the PSOE functioned until the early 1990s as a highly disciplined machine. Indeed, so much was this the case that the party leadership of González and Alfonso Guerra (who remained vice-secretary general of the PSOE after leaving the government) was often criticised for practising a form of democratic centralism. Guerra, in particular, was seen as a Machiavellian manipulator operating behind the scenes to ensure that the leadership's line prevailed. However, a greater distance developed between government and party following Guerra's resignation. Before then, the dominance enjoyed by González and Guerra was reinforced by the fact that no cabinet members were simultaneously members of the PSOE Executive Committee, which in turn was largely under Guerra's control. The PSOE leadership was not averse to suspending or even expelling members who refused to toe the party line; more generally, they were simply marginalised to such an extent that they left of their own volition, as happened in the case of Pablo Castellano. Very low party membership (hovering between 150,000 and 300,000 since 1982) also contributed to the leaders' strength. Individual deputies are in a very weak position, with little room for autonomous initiative; indeed, after 1982 the PSOE's parliamentary group played a limited role, being little more than a passive observer of the frosty relationship between executive and opposition.

Only during 1990 was the iron control exercised by Guerra seriously challenged from within the government, following the so-called 'Juan Guerra scandal' in which the deputy premier's brother was implicated in a number of shady business deals. In the meanwhile, speculation over a successor to González following the president's comment during the 1989 general election campaign that it would be his last (a comment he subsequently retracted), together with a growing sense of unease at the power exercised by Guerra, led a number of senior ministers to distance themselves from the so-called *guerristas* (supporters of Alfonso Guerra). Javier Solana, Narcís Serra and Carlos Solchaga, all seen at the time as possible future PSOE leaders, conspicuously failed to support Guerra during the early months of 1990 when the vice-president was under severe pressure to resign, and Solchaga later launched a stinging attack on the 'monolithic' leadership of the *guerristas*. Significantly, such criticisms were overwhelmingly directed at Guerra himself; in spite of overt and consistent support for his deputy until 1992, the prime minister, González, generally escaped the opprobrium of his colleagues. For all the misgivings at what were widely seen as abuses of governmental power, González retained sufficient authority to maintain his dominance of the PSOE. Unlike Suárez, he enjoyed the benefit of being manifestly the pre-eminent figure in the political firmament.

In part, such pre-eminence can be attributed to personality. Although it is difficult to quantify or systematise the importance of personality in core executive studies, it is clear that Suárez and González brought markedly different leadership styles to the Moncloa Palace. The former, for all his centrality to the transitional process, always remained uneasy with most of the political élite in Spain. Many of the key figures in the transition had distinguished academic track records, a fact which helped undermine the premier's surprisingly fragile self-confidence. Although a consummate performer when armed with a prepared script in front of a TV camera, Suárez was uncomfortable during parliamentary debates. Increasingly during his period in power, he came to avoid them – often going months without attending the *Cortes*, and even missing cabinet meetings. Instead, he preferred to retire to his office, 'cocooned by muzak and screened from the real political world' (Preston, 1986: 173). While González also had a tendency to go long periods without appearing in the *Cortes*, this had little to do with feeling uncomfortable there; on the contrary, his command of parliamentary debates was well-recognised.[5] The easy charm which marked his initial performances gave way over the years to a more sententious style, combined at times with witheringly dismissive contempt. Despite instances of verbal brutality, González has always been associated with charisma, a crucial political asset. His dominance as a political leader was reflected in the widespread references to '*Felipismo*', parallel in many respects to the notion of 'Thatcherism'.[6]

In terms of real power, however, probably more significant than personality were the different political challenges faced by Suárez and González as heads of government. The former assumed power amidst great uncertainty, facing enormous tasks. Principal amongst these was the elaboration of a new constitution, together with the need to confront economic recession and ever-growing demands for regional autonomy (see chapter 2). The constitutional issue dominated the proceedings of the first legislature, and its successful conclusion represented Suárez's greatest triumph. The other problems, however, proved far more intractable. Inflation in Spain in 1977 was running at 24.5 per cent, and heavy dependence on energy imports made the country particularly vulnerable to the escalating cost of oil. New-found political liberties gave rise to a massive wave of strikes as workers sought to flex their long-shackled economic muscle. Political uncertainties and international recession, meanwhile, militated against foreign investment in the nascent democracy. Equally serious was the growth of unemployment, which rose from 6 per cent of the active population in 1977 to 17 per cent in 1981.

In response, the Suárez administration put into effect a Programme for Rationalisation and Economic Reform, a six-point plan aimed at salvaging the ailing economy. In addition, the so-called Moncloa Pacts, a series of austerity measures, were agreed between the major political parties in October 1977. The rationalisation measures of the UCD government were vital to the eventual recuperation of the Spanish economy, but their impact could only be gradual and Suárez was unable to reap any political benefit from them. The UCD's main goals in terms of economic modernisation were in fact broadly retained by the PSOE when it assumed power in 1982. Suárez's discomfiture, however, was exacerbated by the internal disintegration of the UCD as the government found itself caught helplessly between the competing demands of regionalists and centralisers. The government's clumsy approach to the issue of regional autonomy (see chapter 7) merely fuelled general discontent. The emergence of a violent counterpoint between Basque separatists and military conspirators against democracy simply underlined the impossibility of the situation facing Suárez. By the time of his resignation in January 1981, it was already clear that the PSOE was effectively a government in waiting.

Ironically, when the PSOE came to power, much of the groundwork for its political success had already been carried out by the UCD. Moves towards membership of the European Community, achieved in January 1986 and heralded as a key success of the Socialist government, had been started in July 1977 when Spain formally applied for entry. The spectacular economic success which took place in Spain throughout the second half of the 1980s would have been impossible without many of the streamlining measures undertaken by UCD finance ministers. This fact may lend some support to a minimalistic interpretation of government response patterns, suggesting that political parties have limited impact on macro-economic policy objectives. Yet, the central point is that González, at least until the early 1990s, did not face a similar scale of political challenges to those confronting Suárez, and also enjoyed the cushion of economic success between 1985 and 1991. By the early 1990s, when world trade slowed and most European economies entered recession, the Socialist prime minister found his control subjected to far greater pressure as Spain struggled to meet the criteria for economic convergence agreed in the Maastricht Treaty. The twin challenges of the European Single Market and Maastricht led to a marked erosion in the dominance exercised by González.

Institutional and Structural Constraints on the Premier's Power

Beyond contingent political factors influencing the power of the Spanish premier, a series of institutional and structural constraints also need to be considered. Amongst the former, the most important are the military, the Catholic Church and the bureaucracy. After playing central roles during the Franco regime, all three have declined in influence in recent years – especially the military – but they continue to represent powerful interests (see chapters 3 and 6). However, as the influence of traditional institutional interests has declined in political importance, so new structural constraints on the power of the central executive have developed. The most significant of these is the growing importance of the Autonomous Communities (see chapter 7). Although the precise relationship between centre and periphery, together with the full extent of regional powers, remains to be resolved, the autonomous governments have steadily assumed a greater profile since the restoration of democracy.

National leaders in Spain increasingly face challenges from high-profile regional politicians. For instance Jordi Pujol, president of the *Generalitat*, the Catalan parliament, not only operates to some extent as the leader of a separate nation, but also enjoys high visibility throughout Spain; after the 1993 general elections, his party's support along with that of the PNV was critical to the PSOE government's survival in office. Other regional leaders with a strong national presence include the Basque *lehendakari* (president), José Antonio Ardanza, and Manuel Fraga, leader of the Galician *Xunta*. José María Aznar, leader of the main opposition party, the *Partido Popular*, came to political prominence as president of Castilla y León – a position he initially hoped to be able to retain in tandem with his new national-level responsibilities.

As the Autonomous Communities gain greater financial independence from the central state, so will their leaders and parliaments increase in importance. While the influence of regional leaders should not be exaggerated, especially given – as shown above – the very considerable powers granted to the national president, it is likely that they will represent an ever-more significant factor in the calculations of the core executive. Indeed, it could be argued that the failure to resolve the regional issue was a central element in the eventual fall of Adolfo Suárez. To utilise Richard Rose's typology of prime ministerships, the Spanish president will increasingly come to be seen as a 'bargainer' in terms of domestic politics (Rose, 1991: 18–19). However, Article 149 of the Constitution reserves to the central state exclusive competence over a large number of key policy areas, including foreign and defence policy, the administration of justice, customs regulations, the monetary system and general economic planning.

An altogether different level of structural constraint upon the power of the Spanish president derives from Spain's international treaty obligations and commitments. In this regard, two bodies are of particular importance: the European Union (EU) and NATO. The terms of Spain's accession to Europe in 1986, together with the introduction of the Single European Market in 1993 and the provisions of the Maastricht Treaty, have dictated legislation across a broad range of areas. Following entry to the EC, Spain was required to include 1,077 EC Directives in national legislation – although by the start of 1990, 235 of them were still pending legal transfer, with 134 having exceeded the time limit set by the European authorities. However, it is the NATO issue which provides perhaps the most instructive instance of an outside constraint on the power of the premier. Felipe González's abandonment of what appeared to be a clear anti-NATO stance prior to the 1982 general elections was in large measure a response to the fact that the Spanish government was left under no illusions by certain partners in the Atlantic Alliance – most notably, the USA and Britain – that withdrawal from NATO would incur considerable costs. Certainly, negotiations over the reduction of the American military presence in Spain, as well as any hope of a settlement of the Gibraltar dispute, were seen to be closely linked to continued membership of NATO. Equally, of course, some analysts have pointed to domestic factors, in particular the perceived link between defence expenditure and industrial restructuring, as providing the key to the Spanish government's change of heart (see chapter 10).

The PSOE government's success in the NATO referendum was attributed by some to a relentless propaganda campaign which involved cynical use of the communications media. However, the media – or at least its newspaper component – represents the final constraint on the premier's power to be considered here. According to Alejandro Muñoz Alonso (1988), the weakness of formal institutional checks on the executive means that the function of control has effectively been devolved to the media. During the Suárez administration, the press played an instrumental role in undermining the government's efficacy during 1980 by relentlessly using the term '*desencanto*' (disenchantment) to describe widespread disillusionment at the shortcomings of the UCD (Preston, 1986: 160). For military conspirators it was but a short step to read into such press comments disillusionment with democracy itself rather than merely the government in power, particularly as they were buttressed by an overt hostility towards democracy in extreme right-wing newspapers such as *El Alcázar*.

Some newspaper figures, such as Juan Luis Cebrián, formerly editor of *El País*, and Pedro J. Ramírez, have become virtually household names. Ramírez, who insists that his removal as editor of *Diario 16* in March 1989 was organised from within the PSOE government, used his new vehicle, *El Mundo*, as the spearhead of what developed into a relentless press investigation over the question of influence-peddling and corruption, initially sparked by revelations about the Guerra scandal. Indeed, after 1989, the press played a major part in helping to uncover so-called '*tráficos de influencia*' (influence-peddling) among the political class, contributing to the widespread sense of endemic corruption in Spanish politics. The sharp decline in support for the PSOE during the early 1990s was in large part due to the media's exposure of corruption scandals, although it cannot, of course, be divorced from other issues such as economic recession.

The Premier's Power and the Decline of Parliament

Perhaps the most central area of concern in regard to checks on the core executive surrounds the role of the Spanish parliament. The emphasis on moderation and negotiation which marked the transition to democracy in Spain paradoxically led to the creation of a weak parliament. As shown above, a central concern of the constitutional architects was to invest major strength in the position of the president; the function of parliament, meanwhile, was envisaged as being to facilitate negotiation between different political groups. The design of parliamentary rules was meant to encourage a 'pactist' style of decision-making: the minimum size of parliamentary groups was set at 15, and strict controls were placed on individual deputies – for instance, only parliamentary groups are allowed to introduce legislation, and deputies who wish to leave their own party may only switch to the 'Mixed Group' rather than to another party. The model, reinforced by the closed list system for elections, was intended to diminish traditional ideological conflicts as well as centre–periphery tensions. Parliament was designed to serve as a chamber in which negotiation between well-matched forces would act as a symbol of tolerance (Capo Giol *et al.*, 1990: 100–1). A well-balanced parliament would then serve as an effective check on a secure president, who would have to consider a wide range of interests.

The reality turned out very differently, for the prestige of Spain's parliament has been steadily eroded since the election of 1979. Under the UCD's second administration, parliament was criticised for its incapacity to stop agreements being reached without reference to parliamentary procedures. Thereafter, the PSOE's absolute majorities between 1982 and 1993 – an unanticipated electoral outcome when the Constitution was framed – further reduced the role of parliament in terms of policy-making. The search for consensus could be ignored by a government which enjoyed an overwhelming majority in both the Congress and the Senate. More than in any other European country, according to Muñoz Alonso (1988: 92–3), parliament follows government in a docile manner, unable to exercise its proper control functions. Investigative commissions are rarely established, and parliament has ceased to serve as a public forum in which the major national problems are debated. Indeed, the Spanish executive faces fewer formal limits on its power than does the President of the USA.

The Senate, initially intended as a chamber for territorial representation in central government, is widely seen as a useless body: it is granted just two months, and in urgent cases 20 days, to review bills passed to it by the Congress. However, a Senate debate on the Autonomous Communities in September 1994 concluded with the recommendation that the 1978 Constitution be amended in order to transform the upper house into a genuinely territorial chamber. To this end, a *ponencia* was established, with all-party support, to study the composition and functions of the Senate.[7] The revised Senate will be charged with representing the Autonomous Communities' interests in regard to financial transfers, co-operation with the central state, and their relations with the European Union (*El País internacional*, 3 October 1994). However, the structure of the Autonomous Communities as established in Title VIII of the Constitution will remain unchanged (see chapter 7).

The declining role of parliament was exacerbated between 1982 and 1993 by the lack of any strong or effective opposition party. After the collapse of the UCD, the PSOE went largely unchallenged within parliament for nearly a decade. Manuel Fraga, founder of the oft-renamed *Alianza Popular* (known since 1987 as the *Partido Popular*) was always seen as unelectable at national level on account of his associations with the Franco regime, under which he served as both a minister and an ambassador. The *Alianza*'s experiment in 1987 with a much younger leader, Antonio Hernández Mancha, turned out to be a disaster: a complete contrast to the belligerent Fraga, Hernández Mancha was clearly no match for the powerful PSOE machine. Fraga returned in 1988 to rescue a party which was threatening to disintegrate, before handing over the reins just prior to the 1989 general elections to another young protege, José María Aznar. Only after the emergence of a series of corruption scandals in the early 1990s did the *Partido Popular* begin to gain sufficient support to act as an effective opposition. With the loss of the PSOE's absolute majority in the 1993 elections, parliament was able to start regaining some of the initiative it had lost during the preceding fifteen years.

It is perhaps significant that González always manifested a far greater interest in the international arena than did Suárez, preferring to leave day-to-day domestic political matters to his ministers and to his deputy. In contrast to Suárez, whose domestic travails were such that he could probably never afford this luxury, the Socialist leader showed a readiness to adopt a 'hands-off' approach with regard to his cabinet – at least until the internal party divisions unleashed by the struggle over his succession (see chapter 9) – and a marked reluctance to engage in governmental reshuffles. González's behaviour in office was often seen as 'presidential' in a sense familiar from the French political context.

The resources at the disposal of the Spanish premier are immense. In constitutional terms, the president stands at the centre of Spain's political system, backed by an extensive staff of advisers and afforded considerable security of tenure. Formally, then, the Spanish president enjoys a very high degree of power. The extent to which this power can be translated into practice depends on a wide range of contingent political circumstances, most notably the nature of the government's majority, the relationship between the president and the party in power, and the nature of the political challenges to be faced. Although parliament's role as a regulatory body has been severely emasculated, a number of other institutional and structural constraints can act as checks on the president's power. In particular, Spain's seventeen Autonomous Communities have emerged as important political centres, whilst traditional interests, as represented by the military, the Church and the bureaucracy, retain significance.

The Spanish president is always likely to have a freer hand in foreign policy areas than in domestic politics: foreign affairs have traditionally been of little interest to most Spanish citizens, and also lie outside the competence of the Autonomous Communities. It is significant that the UCD government of Calvo Sotelo, despite major crises within the ruling party, was able to rush through NATO membership during 1981, in spite of opposition misgivings. The formal request to parliament for authorisation to sign the North Atlantic Treaty was made in late August 1981 and approval was granted by 26 November. The unpopularity of the move, however, was a key factor in the UCD's subsequent decimation in the October 1982 elections and the crushing victory of Felipe González and the PSOE. The later adherence by González to NATO, thus reversing his position at the general election, illustrates the political dominance of the Spanish president in foreign affairs. But his predominance depended on his retaining the support of his party. His power was contingent, dependent more on his political than on his constitutional resources.

5

The Judiciary and the 'State of Law'

After nearly four decades of dictatorship under General Franco, it was to be expected that the 1978 Constitution should place particular emphasis on legal accountability: the rule of law must underpin any democratic state's claim to political legitimacy. Of course, *all* regimes seek to assert their legal authority, and the Franco dictatorship was no exception in this regard. However, in contrast to the situation in a dictatorship, the declaration that the law is supreme in a democracy requires that citizens be able to enforce that law (Díaz, 1979: 11, 13–18). Thus, a central concern of Spain's new democracy was that it should be established as a 'state of law' (*estado de derecho*), in the sense of its constitutional arrangements being both legally accountable and enforceable. Yet, surprisingly, English-language texts on post-Franco Spanish politics have virtually ignored the legal dimension of the democratic state.[1]

The Spanish 'State of Law' (*estado de derecho*)

Towards the end of the Franco dictatorship, the judiciary ('*el poder judicial*') stood in a somewhat paradoxical position. On the one hand, the courts served as a bastion of the regime, imposing harsh sentences on critics of the dictator – notably journalists (Terrón Montero, 1981; Hollyman, 1974) – and even having recourse to the ultimate sanction in the case of some opponents, as occurred with the notorious executions of 27 September 1975. On the other hand, the principle of judicial independence served as a powerful point of reference for democratically-inclined members of the judiciary, and its occasional attempted translation into practice by defence lawyers, as occurred during the Burgos trials of ETA militants in 1970, helped undermine the dictatorship.[2] Although magistrates under the Franco regime were effectively beholden to the state, thus undermining any semblance of judicial independence, some members of the judiciary sought to support calls for democracy through small-scale organisations such as *Jueces para la Democracia* (Andrés Ibáñez and Pérez Mariño, 1991: 86–7). Ultimately, though, the judiciary under Franco operated as an arm of the state, masking its essentially arbitrary nature behind the façade of due legal process.

The notion of an '*estado de derecho*' is generally seen as deriving from the emergence of liberal states in Europe following the French Revolution (Díaz, 1963; 1979: 19–29). As such, it is a concept embedded in a European tradition of codified legality, based on Roman law, which is distinct from the Anglo–Saxon recourse to convention and precedent through common law. Conventionally, the 'state of law' – or *Rechtsstaat*, as it is sometimes known – entails four fundamental characteristics:

● the rule of law, which is seen as an expression of the popular will represented through the national assembly (or parliament)
● a division of powers between legislature, executive and judiciary[3]
● administrative legality, ensured through the law and appropriate judicial means of control
● fundamental rights and freedoms, formally guaranteed through the legal process and with effective translation into practice.

Clearly, the judiciary is required to play a pivotal role in invigilating the political estate. The existence of a Constitutional Tribunal, established under Title IX of the 1978 Constitution, ensures that the judiciary acts as ultimate arbiter of constitutional propriety in Spain.

The Judiciary in the 1978 Constitution

Title VI of the 1978 Constitution refers to 'the judiciary', a seemingly unremarkable observation were it not for the fact that the term had not been mentioned in any previous constitution since 1869 (Alvarez Conde, 1990: 501). Intervening constitutions had spoken instead of the 'administration of justice', suggesting that the judiciary stood in a subordinate position to the state's other powers, from which the definition of justice was seen to emanate. In fact, even after the 1978 Constitution came into force, Spain's legal system remained based on a provisional law on judicial organisation, originally passed in September 1870. Not until the *Ley Orgánica del Poder Judicial* (**LOPJ**) of 1 July 1985 was Spain's judicial system formally established on a revised footing. However, the 1978 Constitution did describe the general principles which govern the judiciary, as well as its organisational structure, and – significantly – expressly prohibited the creation of emergency courts. The key bodies outlined were the Constitutional Tribunal (*Tribunal Constitucional*), the Supreme Court (*Tribunal Supremo*), and the regional Higher Courts of Justice (*Tribunales Superiores de Justicia*), as well as the Attorney General's Office (*Ministerio Fiscal*). The Ombudsman (*Defensor del Pueblo*), although charged with defending the rights enshrined in Title One of the Constitution, is not formally a part of the judiciary. Regulation of the judicial system was charged to the General Council of the Judiciary (*Consejo General del Poder Judicial*, **CGPJ**).

The Constitutional Tribunal

The Constitutional Tribunal, described in Title IX of the 1978 Constitution and formally legislated into existence by the *Cortes* in October 1979, is the supreme interpreter of constitutionality in Spain. The Tribunal's authority effectively places it above the three classic powers of the state: executive, legislature and judiciary. Thus, it is not formally a part of the judiciary; instead, according to the 1979 law by which it was established, 'the Constitutional Tribunal is independent of all other constitutional bodies, and is subject only to the Constitution and to this law' (García de Enterría, 1981: pp. 35ff.). Intended strictly as a judicial, as opposed to political, body, the Constitutional Tribunal's authority extends over Spain's entire territory – including the Autonomous Communities – and there is no right of appeal against its decisions (Lucas Murillo de la Cueva, 1983: 210, 216).

Based in Madrid, the Constitutional Tribunal is composed of twelve members who must be of 'recognised standing' with at least fifteen years' professional legal experience.[4] Members are appointed for nine-year terms, with a third renewed every three years. In order to act as a counter-balance to the Tribunal's ultimate authority over them, the principal organs of the state are involved in selecting its members – although, in practice, the system entails political patronage, usually agreed upon between the major parties. The *Cortes* propose eight magistrates (four each by the Congress and the Senate), who must be approved by a majority vote of at least three-fifths of the respective houses. The government and the *Consejo General del Poder Judicial* each propose a further two names. Those elected to serve on the Constitutional Tribunal are debarred from holding any other representative office or public post, from playing a leading role in a political party or trade union, or from undertaking any other professional or commercial activity. The aim of such restrictions is to preserve the Tribunal's independence by supposedly freeing its members from any form of pressure which might affect their impartiality; to this end, they are also protected from dismissal during their term of office. The Constitutional Tribunal, funded by the state but with full authority over its own budget, is also empowered to decide on its own organisation and *modus operandi* (see Exhibit 5.1).

The Constitutional Tribunal can declare unconstitutional not only laws passed by the *Cortes* and the Autonomous Communities, but also executive measures such as decree-laws (*Decretos-leyes*). Issues can be referred to the Tribunal through direct appeal (*recurso de inconstitucionalidad*) or referral by a judge (*cuestión de inconstitucionalidad*). In the former case, the appeal must come either from the prime minister, the ombudsman, fifty deputies, fifty senators, or the assemblies of the Autonomous Community in cases where they are affected by legislation. In the latter, a judge may decide to refer legislation which is still at its drafting stage should there be concern over its constitutional implications. In addition, the Constitutional Tribunal can be called upon by the government or either house of parliament to pass judgement on the texts of international treaties. Finally, Spanish citizens can appeal to the Tribunal in cases where a public body is alleged to have contravened their constitutionally-protected rights. Naturally, decisions made by the Tribunal can have profound political consequences, as occurred for instance in 1983 when it declared significant parts of the LOAPA, a law which was designed to slow down the autonomy process, to be unconstitutional (see chapter 7). Of considerably more concern than the political consequences of its decisions, however, is the fear that the Constitutional Tribunal may be subject to direct political influence. In spite of the LOAPA ruling, various regional leaders – notably in Catalonia and the Basque Country – have argued that the Constitutional Tribunal's

The Judiciary and the 'State of Law' 107

EXHIBIT 5.1

The structure of the Constitutional Tribunal and the Higher Council of the Judiciary

Tribunal Constitucional

President
(elected for a period of three years by fellow members)

Plenary Assembly
(consisting of all twelve members, and encharged with making judgement on appeals, resolving disputes over areas of competence between the central state and the regions, and prior examination of constitutional matters, but empowered to take responsibility over any matter which falls within the Tribunal's ambit)

The Courts
(each one comprising six magistrates, and chaired respectively by the President and Vice-President of the Tribunal; encharged with deciding on appeals for assistance)

The Departments
(each one comprising three magistrates and encharged with deciding on admissibility of appeals and on routine settlements)

Consejo General del Poder Judicial (CGPJ)
Twenty elected members, of whom twelve are drawn from judges and magistrates with at least fifteen years' experience, and the remaining eight from lawyers and jurists of 'recognised prestige'. Members serve for a non-renewable term of five years, apart from the President who can be re-elected once only.

President
(nominated by the monarch and endorsed by the premier, following election by members of the CGPJ with a minimum of three-fifths majority vote)

Vice-President
(elected in the same manner as the President)

Plenary Assembly
(consisting of all members of the CGPJ, with a quorum of fourteen)

Permanent Commission
(consisting of President and four members of the CGPJ, elected by a three-fifths majority vote of the Plenary Assembly; two members of the Permanent Commission must be judicial figures)

Auxiliary Bodies
(General Secretariat, Disciplinary Committee, etc.)

judgements are excessively centralist (Cavero, 1990: 245–9). In particular, Jordi Pujol accused the Tribunal in 1989 of seeking to reduce the powers available to the Autonomous Communities following its refusal to sanction the transfer to the *Generalitat* of control in Catalonia over the central state's social security budget. The accusation was roundly rejected by the then vice-president of the Constitutional Tribunal, Francisco Rubio Llorente, who insisted that all cases were treated strictly on their merits.[5]

Yet it is widely believed that the Socialist government did seek to exercise influence over the Tribunal, especially in regard to the nomination of its members. The election in 1992 of Miguel Rodríguez-Piñero and Luis López Guerra as president and vice-president respectively of the Constitutional Tribunal certainly raised eyebrows: both had been government nominees to the Tribunal in 1986, and Rodríguez-Piñero was a close friend and former professor of the prime minister, Felipe González (*EIU Country Report, 4*, 1992: 17). In practice, there was little evidence of bias towards the government in some of the Tribunal's subsequent judgements: its overruling in 1993 of the provision to allow the police access to private homes without warrants – a key part of the highly-contested security law piloted through the *Cortes* by the interior minister, José Luis Corcuera – prompted the minister's resignation and represented a significant rebuff to the Socialist government (*El País internacional*, 22 November 1993). Nevertheless, many observers continued to believe that the Tribunal was routinely subjected to political pressure.

One of the key obstacles to the efficient functioning of the Constitutional Tribunal has been the sheer scale of its workload. The number of cases referred to the Tribunal has risen inexorably to reach unmanageable proportions: in the six years between July 1980 and June 1986, 730 cases were presented, of which 385 were resolved; in 1988 alone there were 2,268 cases and by 1993 the figure had reached 3,982, with 2,387 still outstanding (*Anuario El País*, 1987: 170; 1994: 176). Inevitably, serious delays in passing judgement became the norm: in the early 1990s, the average time taken to hear a case was more than two and a half years. The vast majority of cases concerned citizens protesting at infringements of their rights, but a highly significant number derived from the Autonomous Communities. However, after 1985 – in which 131 cases were referred to the Constitutional Tribunal by regional governments – there was a steady fall in the number of appeals made against central state laws,

FIGURE 5.1
Conflicts between central state and Autonomous Communities
referred to the Constitutional Tribunal, 1981–93

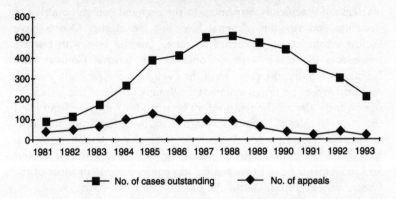

with just twelve cases presented in 1993 (see figure 5.1). In part, this fall reflected greater care by the government when drafting legislation, but also growing agreement at both national and regional level that political disputes should be resolved where possible without recourse to an already overloaded Constitutional Tribunal.

The Supreme Court

The Supreme Court (*Tribunal Supremo*) is the only centralised judicial body in Spain. Initially envisaged under the Cádiz Constitution of 1812, the Supreme Court was created in 1834. A major reorganisation in 1870 established the Court's basic structure which survived until the post-Franco transition to democracy (Alvarez Conde, 1990: 513). As was to be expected, the 1978 Constitution altered the formal position of the Supreme Court in a number of ways.[6] First, the creation of the Constitutional Tribunal provided an alternative source of supreme authority. Although there is no formal hierarchical relationship between the two bodies, the Constitutional Tribunal is generally seen as the court of last resort in Spain. In practice, although the Supreme Court is empowered to deal with all matters other than issues of constitutional interpretation (Article 123.1), and even though its judgements can play an important role in regard to defence of the Constitution, it is considerably less significant in political terms than the Constitutional Tribunal.

Secondly, the establishment of Higher Courts of Justice (see below) devolved significant elements of judicial authority to the Autonomous Communities. The Supreme Court maintains competence over all matters not specifically attributed to the regional courts, notably the cassation and revision of penal law, but the Higher Courts have exclusive competence in regard to '*fueros*' (special laws with historic precedents in certain regions, notably the Basque Country and Navarra). Finally, the creation of the *Consejo General del Poder Judicial*, responsible for the organisation and administration of the judiciary, significantly altered the relationship between the Supreme Court and the state. In spite of its formal designation, then, the Supreme Court in Spain's contemporary democratic state enjoys considerably less influence than it had under previous regimes. As a result, its actions and judgements have provoked far less controversy than those of the Constitutional Tribunal and the *Consejo General del Poder Judicial*.

The Higher Courts of Justice

The 1978 Constitution provided for the creation of regional higher courts, the *Tribunales Superiores de Justicia* (TSJs), to oversee judicial organisation in the seventeen Autonomous Communities (Article 152.1). It took more than a decade for the TSJs to be established, but their inauguration on 23 May 1989 provided for a separation of powers at regional level which mirrored the structure of government at national level. The TSJs are encharged with specific tasks, which include the hearing of appeals against laws passed at regional level and resolving electoral disputes. They are also empowered to pass judgement on regional politicians at all levels, from the president downwards, although they must bow to the authority of both the Supreme Court and the Constitutional Tribunal. Each of the TSJs is sub-divided into three chambers (*salas*), dealing respectively with administrative disputes, civil and penal cases, and social matters (Cavero, 1990: 230).

The seventeen presidents of the TSJs elected in 1989 were considered 'moderately progressive'; indeed, the conservative newspaper, *ABC*, stated that most of them had been 'vouched for' (*avalados*) by the PSOE. All were male, aged between 55 and 67, and twelve of them had formerly been elected presidents of *Audiencias territoriales* (the regional courts which the TSJs replaced) by the *Consejo Superior del Poder Judicial*. The TSJs achieved early prominence following the general elections of 29 October 1989 when they ruled that the elections in Murcia, Pontevedra (Galicia), and Melilla should be re-staged following investigations into electoral irregularities. In the event, the Constitutional Tribunal subsequently declared that only the Melilla election should be repeated – an intervention which was seen by some commentators as stepping beyond the bounds of its remit, since the judgements by the TSJs did not encompass any issue of constitutional interpretation (Cavero, 1990: 231–2).

More dramatic was the Cantabrian TSJ's sentencing in October 1994 of the regional president, Juan Hormaechea, to six years in gaol for abuse of trust and misappropriation of public funds (*El País internacional*, 31 October 1994). Hormaechea, the first regional leader to be convicted whilst in office, had long been under investigation.[7] Yet, in spite of his conviction, he was able technically to continue in office as regional president, pending ratification of the TSJ sentence by the Supreme Court; in practice, with some reluctance, he bowed to pressure and resigned the following month. The significance of the Hormaechea case – notwithstanding the Supreme Court's eventual judgement – lay in its demonstration of the effectiveness of the Cantabrian TSJ as a defender of the '*estado de derecho*' at regional level. Although the TSJs formally came into being only in 1989, there were early indications that they had the potential to become a highly significant element of the judiciary, particularly in regard to investigations into political corruption and financial irregularities.

The Attorney General's Office

The Attorney General's office (*Ministerio Fiscal*), outlined in Article 124 of the Constitution, was formally established under the terms of an organic law passed on 30 December 1981. Traditionally seen in Spain as providing a formal link between government and judiciary, the Attorney General's office no longer plays such a role – although the precise nature of its constitutional relationship to the government and the judiciary remains unclear (Alvarez Conde, 1990: 523–4). Formally, its principal functions are to promote the observation of justice and legality, to defend the rights of citizens, to defend the public interest in a manner consistent with the law, and to ensure the independence of the courts. In fact, several of these functions overlap with those of other state bodies, such as the General Council of the

Judiciary (CGPJ) and the Ombudsman. However, unlike members of the CGPJ, the attorney general is nominated by the government and can also be dismissed. Whilst the post does not confer cabinet membership (in contrast to some other countries, such as the USA), it has been seen by some observers as overly dependent on government patronage, in spite of the legal requirement that the attorney general should act independently and impartially.

Considerable debate was provoked in 1992 by the resignation of the attorney general (*Fiscal General*), Leopoldo Torres, who complained of being unable to perform his role effectively because of insufficient resources and too many limitations on his powers. The resignation derived particular significance from the fact that Torres had formerly been a member of the PSOE, and his appointment in 1990 was seen as consistent with those of his predecessors, Javier Moscoso and Burón Barba, both of whom had been accused of having close ties with the Socialists (Sinova and Tusell, 1990: 266–9). Yet, the selection of Eligio Hernández to replace Torres was once again widely interpreted as being designed to ensure that the attorney general's office would be sympathetic to the Socialist government (De la Cuadra, 1993: 134). In June 1994, the Supreme Court ruled that the nomination of Hernández had been illegal since the various legal posts he had held under the auspices of the government meant he had not served as a professional jurist for the requisite period of fifteen years (*El País internacional*, 20 June 1994).

The Ombudsman

The role of the Ombudsman (*Defensor del Pueblo*) is referred to at several points in the 1978 Constitution (Articles 54, 70.1 and 162.1), but the post was not formally legislated into existence until May 1981. Based on the conception originally established by the Swedish legislature of 1809, the institution of Ombudsman has been a source of some controversy in democratic Spain. In theory, the Ombudsman's functions are relatively straightforward: s/he is appointed for a period of five years by the *Cortes*, following a majority vote of at least three-fifths of each chamber, to supervise the activities of the Spanish administration and to investigate citizens' complaints against abuses of their rights. An annual report presented to the *Cortes* outlines the number and nature of complaints received, together with any action taken. The post is thus designed to be a central element in the upholding and protection of the '*estado de derecho*'. In practice, since the appointment on 28 December 1982 of Joaquín Ruíz Giménez as the first *Defensor del Pueblo*, the initial high hopes invested in the institution have been gradually replaced by disillusionment (Cavero, 1990: 145–98).

The creation of the post of *Defensor del Pueblo* entailed considerable overlap with the duties of the attorney general's office, leading various legal experts to express concern over the lack of any clear delimitation of spheres of responsibility (*El País*, 27 June 1982). Another major source of concern surrounded the budgetary provision for the new post, widely regarded as inadequate for the scale of its envisaged role. Indeed, the number of cases referred to the Ombudsman immediately assumed unforeseen proportions: in his first year in office, Ruíz Giménez received 30,763 complaints, the majority of them relating to work and social security issues. A third of these complaints fell outside the Ombudsman's ambit, and in subsequent years the number of cases presented fell, varying between a low of 12,256 in 1987 and a high of 29,396 in 1990. By 1993, most complaints centered on Spain's public administration, with the greatest proportion by far emanating from the Autonomous Community of Madrid.

As in the case of the Constitutional Tribunal and the attorney general's office, doubts have surfaced on occasion over whether a proper distance exists between the *Defensor del Pueblo* and the government. The influential newspaper, *El País*, accused Ruíz Giménez of submissive reverence towards the government – calling him '*el Defensor del Poder*' – after he refused to refer anti-terrorist legislation, which came into force in 1985, to the Constitutional Tribunal. In fact, a combination of insufficient resources and limited powers has undermined the capacity of the Spanish Ombudsman to act as an effective guardian of citizens' interests. Yet although widely dismissed as an ineffective institution, the continued political significance of the post of Ombudsman was demonstrated after the 1993 general elections: a bitter dispute over nominations for the post resulted in a stand off between the governing Socialists and the opposition, with each refusing the other's choice. Not until October 1994 was the dispute resolved when the 70–year-old Fernando Alvarez de Miranda, president of the *Congreso de los Diputados* following the first post-Franco elections of 1977, accepted the nomination.

The General Council of the Judiciary: Judicial Independence versus Political Interference

The critical issue surrounding the judiciary in Spain's new democracy was its independence. Indeed, independence of the judiciary has been judged one of the most advanced features of the 1978 Constitution, placing it on a par in this respect with France, Italy and Portugal (Sinova and Tusell, 1990: 248). Yet, in spite of unanimous agreement amongst the framers of the Constitution that the judiciary should be independent, Article 117.1 refers only to the independence of judges and magistrates, as opposed to the judiciary as a whole (Alvarez Conde, 1990: 504–5). Amongst the specific conditions designed to ensure that judges and magistrates are protected from executive interference is immunity from dismissal, transfer, suspension or enforced retirement other than for legally justified reasons. The *régimen de incompatibilidades* (rules of incompatibility), outlined in Article 127.2, meanwhile, forbids members of the judiciary from holding any other public post whilst they remain in active service.

More controversial is the injunction that judges and magistrates cannot belong to any political party or trade union (although no mention is made of any other form of associative body, such as business or religious groups). The measure provoked considerable debate during the drafting of the Constitution: whereas concern was expressed by the left that it represented an infringement of civil liberties, the right saw it as a means of reinforcing judicial impartiality. It has been argued (Alvarez Conde, 1990: 511) that the proscription on belonging to political parties is a pointless gesture, since judges and magistrates are unavoidably politicised in any democracy, and this fact influences how they interpret the law. Moreover, the rule could be seen as inconsistent: the provisions regarding the Consitutional Tribunal (Article 159.4) refer only to its members being debarred from holding leading posts in a political party or trade union, rather than belonging to one. Judges and magistrates are allowed to join professional associations, although according to the terms originally established in 1980 these were to betray no political connotation even in their title, and also had to encompass at least 15 per cent of all those eligible to be members.[8] The 1985 LOPJ eased these restrictions somewhat, but maintained the ban on any link with political parties or trade unions.

The most significant areas of dispute over the independence of the judiciary since the restoration of democracy have concerned the composition and activities of the General Council of the Judiciary (CGPJ, *Consejo General del Poder Judicial*). Based on the French and Italian constitutional models of 1946 and 1947 respectively, the CGPJ was conceived as an instrument to control and regulate the judiciary, thereby removing that function from the ministry of justice. The CGPJ was formally established in 1980 and, although seen by some as a 'revolutionary' innovation (Peces-Barba, 1981: 166), has been subject ever since to considerable criticism. In particular, the process through which its members are elected has given rise to extensive debate. According to the terms of the 1978 Constitution, the CGPJ was to consist of 20 elected members, twelve drawn from judges and magistrates, and four proposed and voted on by each of the two houses of parliament. In spite of widespread disquiet, the 1985 LOPJ established that all 20 members would be elected by parliament (ten by each chamber). Two rulings by the Constitutional Tribunal in 1986 confirmed the legality of this altered procedure, pointing out that whilst Article 122.3 states that twelve members will be *drawn* from judges and magistrates, it does not specify they will be *elected* by them. Nevertheless, the Tribunal also expressed the view that, although legal, the election procedure established in the LOPJ was not the most appropriate and that, at some future date, it should be restored to the original conception.[9]

In practice, in both 1985 and 1990 members of the CGPJ (who serve for five years) were elected by the *Cortes*, a fact which seriously undermined its independent status in the eyes of some critics (De la Cuadra, 1991: 132; Andrés Ibáñez and Pérez Mariño, 1991: 88). The suspicion became widespread that the Socialist government viewed the judiciary simply as state functionaries to be disciplined as necessary by a tame governing body. Judge Juan Alberto Belloch, subsequently appointed minister of justice in the Socialist government following the 1993 general elections, had warned in 1987 that the CGPJ should exist to defend judges rather than the core executive. Certainly, the CGPJ stood accused of being ineffectual in regard to such cases as the investigation into the activities of the GAL (*Grupos Antiterroristas de Liberación*), anti-ETA terrorist groups allegedly set up by two police officers using ministry of the interior reserve funds (see chapter 3). The investigating magistrate, Baltazar Garzón, was moved to comment in what was a clear reference to the government that some people appeared to confuse state security with the security of particular individuals (Sinova and Tusell, 1990: 254).

The independence of the CGPJ has also been called into question by the fact that it has no budgetary control. Whilst the government must ultimately decide on budgetary allocations, the CGPJ is apparently not even consulted by the ministry of justice during the annual negotiations over the state budget. It is widely acknowledged that Spain's judicial system is seriously under-resourced: the justice ministry's proportion of the state budget has never reached even 2 per cent of the total since the return of democracy (less than half the EU average) and under the Socialist government fell from 1.6 per cent of total state expenditure in 1983 to 0.8 per cent in 1994[10] (Hooper, 1986: 126; *Anuario El País*, 1984: 333; 1994: 424). Felipe González is reputed to have commented on his appointment of Juan Alberto Belloch to be minister of justice that 'now we have no money, we'll have to opt for imagination' (*Anuario El País*, 1994: 176). Certainly, on assuming office, Belloch moved quickly to initiate reforms, promising to revise the 1985 *Ley Orgánica del Poder Judicial* and to return responsibility for selecting judges from the executive to the judiciary, as had originally been established in 1980. It is significant that Belloch had himself been a member of the CGPJ from 1990 until his entry to government in July 1993; one of his first moves was to consult all Spain's professors of penal law over a controversial proposed revision of the Penal Code which had been interrupted in its passage through parliament by the 1993 general election.

Belloch's more open approach towards the judiciary probably also reflected the growing political protagonism of the judiciary in the 1990s, as well as concern over perceived government interference. In spite of criticisms that the CGPJ was a toothless organisation, the newly-elected General Council, under the leadership of Pascual Sala, delivered a sharp rebuff to the government in 1990 when it issued a highly unfavourable unanimous report on the draft security law (the so-called *Ley Corcuera*[11]). The interior minister's comment, following the law's eventual passage in 1992, that few judges merited his respect in turn provoked calls for his resignation by groups representing the judiciary. Controversy over the politicisation of the judiciary was further fuelled that summer by complaints made by José Luis Manzanares, vice-president of the CGPJ, about political interference in the Council, whose sphere of competence, he argued, had been reduced to a trivial level (Esteban, 1992: 303–6).

Defending the 'State of Law': The Judiciary and Political Corruption

The Spanish judiciary has been subject to unremitting criticism since the post-Franco restoration of democracy. Widely seen as inefficient and under-resourced, as well as being – when not harbouring innate conservative instincts – subject to political manipulation, the judiciary was once notoriously described by the Andalucían politician, Pedro Pacheco, as *'un cachondeo'* (a joke).[12] In spite of impeccable constitutional provisions for a fully independent judiciary, backed up by other institutions designed expressly to oversee the 'state of law', the administration of justice in democratic Spain has rarely been accorded plaudits. Indeed, the independence of the judiciary has regularly been questioned, with the Socialist government in particular accused of exercising improper influence through partisan appointments (Sinova and Tusell, 1990: 266–9; Andréz Ibáñez and Pérez Mariño, 1991: 86–90). Moreover, much of the legislation required to implement the terms of the 1978 Constitution reached the statute books only after considerable delay, whilst other much-needed reforms failed to materialise when promised.

Yet despite the generally poor regard in which Spain's judicial system had been held since the return of democracy, judges and magistrates began to assume an ever-more prominent political presence in the early 1990s. The catalyst to their emergence into the political spotlight was the revelation of a series of corruption scandals involving leading political figures. Fuelled by the remarkable revelations which began to surface in Italy in 1992, as well as by a number of high-profile cases in France, corruption became the dominant issue in Spanish politics; judges and magistrates in turn came to play the lead role in investigating the seemingly never-ending series of allegations which at times threatened to undermine the authority of the political class as a whole.

The upsurge of interest in political corruption was ignited by the emergence of the so-called 'Juan Guerra case' at the start of 1990, when it was alleged that the then deputy prime minister's brother had used official PSOE premises for private business purposes. An unprecedented year-long press campaign, presented as investigative journalism but often amounting to little more than vindictive personalism, culminated in the resignation from government of Alfonso Guerra in January 1991 (Martín de Pozuelo *et al.*, 1994:

119–26; Ramírez, 1990; Cavero, 1991). Guerra's resignation did little to stem the tide of accusations against the PSOE. A further series of corruption scandals emerged during the following three years, most of them centring on the issue of party financing. Two elected PSOE representatives – a deputy, Carlos Navarro, and a senator, José María Sala – were found to have run a group of front companies that paid bills for the party with money obtained by charging businesses and banks for fictitious consultancy work between 1989 and 1991.[13] Further scandals emerged in the early 1990s surrounding the payment of commissions in return for contracts to carry out work at the site of the Expo92 in Sevilla.[14]

That these scandals came to light was largely the result of judicial investigations, backed – and sometimes prompted – by the mass media, notably the newspaper *El Mundo*. By 1994, investigations were proceeding on several fronts, the most spectacular of which resulted in the imprisonment of the former governor of the Bank of Spain, Mariano Rubio, on suspicion of fraud, and the flight from justice of the former head of the Civil Guard, Luis Roldán, accused of a string of crimes including perversion of the course of justice, defrauding the public treasury, and embezzlement of public funds. Carlos Solchaga, minister of the economy from 1985 to 1993 and a central figure in the Socialist administration, and José Luis Corcuera, former minister of justice, both resigned as deputies over their failure to detect the alleged criminal activities. Roldán's escape into exile also prompted the resignation of the minister of the interior, Antoni Asunción, who had been appointed to replace Corcuera just five months earlier. Shortly beforehand, the minister of agriculture, Vicente Albero, had also resigned, the result of being implicated in a scam set up by Manuel de la Concha, Rubio's financial adviser, in the 1980s (*El País internacional*, 18 April, 2, 9 May 1994).

Widely seen as Spain's most serious political crisis since the attempted military coup of 1981, the explosion of corruption-related scandals firmly established the judiciary as central actors on the political stage. Through their investigations into the illegal funding of political parties, financial irregularities by government and business figures, false accounting by union federations, and fraud by public officials, some judges – such as Baltazar Garzón, Marino Barbero and Luis Manglano – became household names. Such prominence was hardly surprising. Given that one of the most corrosive side effects of political corruption is that it calls into question the functioning of the 'state of law', it could be seen as incumbent upon the judiciary to defend the liberties enshrined in Spain's constitutional provisions (Garzón, 1994: 11–26). Members of the judiciary became popular heroes: '*Super Garzón*' was a favourite tabloid sobriquet for the judge in charge of investigating the GAL affair.

Certainly, as in Italy, some members of the judiciary came to see themselves as protagonists fighting against the distortions of democracy perpetrated by the political class. Their need to do so reflected certain shortcomings in Spain's political structure. The extensive powers accorded to the core executive (see chapter 4) distorted the balance of its relationship with the legislature and judiciary, allowing it virtually to ignore some of the mechanisms of accountability established in the 1978 Constitution. The notorious inefficiency of Spain's public administration (see chapter 6) in turn compounded the lack of effective controls available to check an immensely powerful executive. Only when the Socialist Party lost the guaranteed political dominance afforded by a large parliamentary majority did it face serious calls to account; by then, however, the so-called '*cultura del pelotazo*' (sleaze culture, the vernacular term used to describe the scandal-ridden atmosphere) had become deeply ingrained in Spain.

Although the governing Socialist Party was far from alone in being implicated in political corruption, the judiciary's protagonism in investigating alleged cases naturally led to conflicts with political leaders. Fears were expressed that judicial independence would be even further compromised (De la Cuadra, 1993: 194). In a clear reference to investigations into some of the more notorious incidents of political corruption, the attorney general stated in August 1992 that public prosecutors should not initiate judicial proceedings in political cases which lacked foundation, and warned of a 'judicialistion of politics', rather than politicisation of the judiciary. Such comments were inevitably interpreted as offering the prospect of judicial immunity to politicians; in practice, however, investigations into corruption scandals continued apace, although magistrates regularly complained of obstruction in their pursuit of information.

The judiciary played a central role during the early 1990s in both investigating and prosecuting cases of political corruption. In a country like Spain, which saw democracy restored only recently, the political class can ill afford to alienate the population at large. The suspicion that that political power has been converted from a position of responsibilty into an instrument for obtaining fradulent profits carries with it the risk not just of undermining belief in the functioning of the 'state of law', but also of evoking memories of the intolerance and the lack of civil respect which has marked much of Spain's politics in the twentieth century. Although political corruption in Spain does not mirror the Italian experience, the opacity of party finances, the ambiguity of much of the major parties' public rhetoric, and the lack of transparency in dealings between politicians all suggest that the well-established networks and channels of influence which oil the wheels of governmental relations are unlikely to be dismantled simply through legislation. The ineffectiveness of Spain's system of ensuring political accountability has thus obliged the judiciary to become more actively involved in the political sphere than had been anticipated when the 1978 Constitution was drawn up. For all the criticisms to which it has been subjected, Spain's judiciary may prove one of the only effective means by which popular trust in the 'state of law' can be restored and maintained.

6

The Public Sector: Reform and Renewal

During the Franco regime, a cynical joke was often told to indicate the inefficiency of Spain's bureaucracy. A foreign tourist, so it went, called at an administrative office at 4p.m., but found the door locked. Coming across a doorman, he enquired, 'Do Spanish civil servants not work in the afternoon?,' only to be told, 'Oh no, it's in the mornings they don't work. The afternoons they spend at home.' As with many political jokes, the satire here barely masked an underlying truth. Public servants in Spain have never enjoyed a reputation for efficiency, a legacy which continues to inform popular attitudes to '*la administración*' in spite of a series of reforms enacted under the Socialist administrations of the 1980s.

The need for such reforms was unquestionable. The Spanish public sector has grown significantly during the post-war years, in line with all developed countries. Public intervention has multiplied through various forms of regulation, subsidies and controls, while the prosecution of some fundamental governmental tasks – such as defence, external relations and monetary policy – has become increasingly complex. Moreover, government has assumed ever-greater responsibility for urban development and environmental issues. As a result, public administration has acquired a preponderant weight in the social and economic activities of the country, with central responsibility for such issues as defence and security matters, external relations, transport and communications, education, and social security, and indirect involvement in many other areas, from heavy industry to culture. The two fundamental political changes which have taken place since the death of Franco – the transition from dictatorship to democracy and the establishment of seventeen autonomous regional governments – have had an immense impact on Spain's public sector. These changes have presupposed the most significant reforms in Spain's public administration since its emergence in a modern guise in the early nineteenth century. In fact, Spain's bureaucratic structure is still undergoing a highly confusing process of development, with some experts arguing that it is now possible to speak only of a constellation of different public administrations in Spain rather than a single entity (Beltrán Villalva, 1990: 316; Nieto García and Gutiérrez Reñón, 1991: 133). So complex is the current situation that it remains unclear precisely how many people work in the Spanish public sector.

Identifying the Public Sector

Taking as a baseline all those whose employment is dependent on the public purse, official figures in 1990 indicated a total of around 2 million. Of this figure, a little over a third were employed in the state's central administration (including the professional armed forces, the state security corps, legal administration, and social security staff), around 500,000 were employed by the seventeen Autonomous Communities,[1] a further 300,000 by provincial *diputaciones* (local councils) and *ayuntamientos* (municipal governments), and about 350,000 by public firms and state organisations (Beltrán Villalva, 1990; Nieto, 1984). In all, in 1993 public sector employees represented slightly over 20 per cent of the country's salaried workers (2.1 million out of a total of 8.6 million), a figure which looks relatively small when contrasted to the fact that public sector expenditure accounts for some 45 per cent of Spain's GDP. Compared to an EC average in 1983 of 69.9 public servants per 1,000 population, the equivalent Spanish figure stood at 44.4 (Nieto García and Gutiérrez Reñón, 1991: 143).

There has been a real shift of resources from the centre to the regions since the restoration of democracy. In 1977, compared to the then nine member states of the EC, Spain had by far the lowest number of permanent local officials: 19 per cent, as against 27 per cent in France and 57 per cent in Britain (Beltrán Villalva, 1990: 317). Since the promulgation of the 1978 Constitution, however, there has been a notable shift in the proportion of state budget expenditure from central to regional government, as shown in

TABLE 6.1

**Changing patterns of state expenditure between
central and regional government (Pta bn)**

	Central	Regional	Regional share (%)
1983	4.5	0.7	13.5
1985	6.1	1.7	21.8
1987	7.1	2.4	25.3
1990	12.6	4.4	34.9
1992	13.4	6.1	45.5
1994	16.5	7.3	44.2

Source: based on *El País* (25 April 1987); *Anuario El País, 1991, 1993, 1994.*

Table 6.1. During the last decade there has been a centre–periphery transformation in Spain, with the centre in Madrid becoming the economic metropolis for the first time in its history, while the regions have been granted significant political power. According to one analyst, the strongest regions now account for almost the entire public sector within their boundaries, apart from security forces and some nationalised industries, while the central ministries have been left with a 'moth-eaten blanket of responsibilities' (Hebbert, 1989).

In addition to administrative functions, the public sector is charged with responsibility for public enterprises. Although they remain difficult to define or classify precisely, public enterprises are among the most visible elements of the public sector through their involvement in a wide spectrum of Spain's economic activity (Salmon, 1991: 28). Essentially, public enterprises are those organisations which produce goods and services for the market in which the public administration either has over 50 per cent ownership or else enjoys significant managerial influence. In Spain, they have been prominent in many traditional industries, such as mining, iron and steel, ship-building, and the public utilities, as well as in transport and communications. In 1986, there were some 180 companies in which the state held a direct majority share-holding, alongside 300 subsidiaries and over 500 minority holdings (Fernández Rodríguez, 1989). Overall, they accounted for around 5 per cent of the total labour force, and 9 per cent of the industrial sector labour force.

There are three major state holding companies – the *Dirección General del Patrimonio del Estado* (DGPE), the *Instituto Nacional de*

Hidrocárburos (INH), and the *Instituto Nacional de Industria* (Grupo INI) – which are responsible for the co-ordination of most state-controlled companies. The oldest of these groupings is the DGPE, the State Assets Office, originally founded in 1874, which now supervises a loose grouping of companies within the Ministry of Economy and Finance. In 1989, it participated directly in 26 companies, holding between 50 per cent and 100 per cent of the capital in 22 of them. A diverse grouping, the DGPE is dominated by the telecommunications giant, Telefónica, and the tobacco company, Tabacalera. The INH (National Hydrocarbons Institute), by contrast, is of far more recent provenance, formed in 1981 under the direction of the Ministry of Industry and Energy to coordinate and restructure the state's dispersed interests in the hydrocarbon industry.

The major state holding company, however, is the Grupo INI, originally founded in 1941 as a direct replica of fascist Italy's IRI (Institute for Industrial Reconstruction). INI became a central force in the Spanish economy under Franco. Renamed Grupo INI in 1989, and further restructured in 1992 (see below), it employed some 150,000 workers in the early 1990s through its direct participation in over 50 companies – which in turn had total control over roughly a further 150 – and contributed around 10 per cent of Spain's GDP (Donaghy and Newton, 1987: 139). Given the ambit of its influence, it is unsurprising that the public sector should be the focus of major political attention. In all developed societies, the ever-increasing burden on the public purse has led to fundamental reviews of the role of the state in the administration of complex, modern economies. Public sector reform – linked most obviously in the 1980s to privatisation, deregulation and rationalisation initiatives – has become one of the central issues in the politics of administration. Regardless of ideological persuasion, all modern liberal democratic governments have had to confront the need to introduce stricter control over public expenditure within the context of achieving greater efficiency, a process which has been reinforced in the EU by the drive towards harmonising economic and monetary policy stances under the terms of the Maastricht Treaty of February 1992. In the Spanish case, such demands have served to intensify the already existing reform imperatives consequent upon the creation of a democratically accountable state. Although the question of administrative reform was widely seen as a key issue during the transition to democracy, demands for reform of the public administration have been a constant of Spain's political history for well over 150 years. In

1984, Alejandro Nieto published a polemical study with the telling title, *La organización del desgobierno* (The organisation of misgovernment), which depicted a hopelessly inefficient, demoralised, corrupt and self-serving bureaucracy which has always resisted any attempts at reform by the political authorities. Such resistance, argued Nieto, had been intensified over time through a marked loss of social and financial status for public officials, who have not only been badly treated by the state but also widely blamed for its various failings (Nieto, 1984; Albaladejo Campoy, 1980).

The Emergence of a Modern Public Sector

The modern Spanish bureaucracy was founded at the start of the nineteenth century, supposedly on the French Napoleonic model – a model which implied above all else centralisation and hierarchy. However, while Spain's bureaucracy shared certain structural similarities with the French example, in terms of administrative efficiency the two systems were far removed. According to Miguel Albaladejo Campoy (1980), the historic tension in Spain's public administration has been between the schemes proposed in various major reform attempts – Bravo Murillo's 1852 Royal Decree, Maura's 1918 Statute, and the 1964 Law on Public Servants – and the practice derived from them. That tension has been manifested in the reality of a chaotic, inefficient administration closely linked to the political powers that be, and their incapacity to engage in a real administrative reform whose objective would be to put the state's bureaucratic apparatus at the service of the whole society. In short, historically there has existed a division between an irresponsible political class and an incompetent administrative class – reflected in the ultimate failure of all reform efforts prior to the post-Franco transition to democracy.

Not until the death of Fernando VII in 1833 were traditional practices (in which professional bureaucratic posts were hereditary) superseded. The new constitutional regime introduced a different, but still rigidly hierarchical, administrative structure into which people entered while adolescents and then passed through a training process which lasted many years until they reached, generally well past the age of thirty, the status of *oficial* (officer). The political parties, meanwhile, looked upon the central administration as an instrument whose control had to be ensured through the ideological fidelity of its personnel. A spoils system was introduced whereby the victors at elections replaced existing officials with their own nominees. This in turn gave rise to the existence of two parallel bureaucracies: one in active service and the other awaiting the turn of the wheel of political destiny. '*Los cesantes*' (suspended civil servants) became typical Spanish figures, stock characters in the later novels of Benito Pérez Galdós (Brenan, 1963: 359).

The shortcomings of Spain's bureaucratic structure during the nineteenth century meant that major importance was devolved to other institutions of state consolidation – most notably the Catholic Church and the military. It was from the weakness of the central state administration that the pre-eminence of both Church and army derived: while the former has been 'intimately bound up with modern Spain's difficult search for political, social, and economic stability' (Callahan, 1990: 129–30), the latter 'became a leading political actor soon after the advent of modern liberalism, quickly supplanting weak civilian elites in helping to determine, sustain, or reverse fundamental political changes' (Payne, 1990: 40). Only with the heavily-bureaucratised Franco regime did Spain's administrative elite come to occupy a central role in the ordering of the state, although still backed by the army and legitimised – until the late 1960s – by the Church.

One of the most significant early attempts to reform Spain's administrative structure was Juan Bravo Murillo's Royal Decree of 1852, which sought to introduce criteria of rationality and efficiency as the organisational basis of a coherently structured bureaucracy. In practice, the reform measures failed to eradicate many of the administration's shortcomings, particularly patronage and immobilism. The establishment during the mid-nineteenth century of specialised elite corps ('*cuerpos*') reinforced these trends, and discontent amongst those outside the elite corps eventually led to more or less open confrontation between public officials and the state which employed them.

Following revolutionary stirrings which shook Spain during 1917, a further major reform of the country's administrative structure was introduced. Antonio Maura sought through his 1918 *Ley de Bases* to rationalise and professionalise the bureaucracy as a solution to endemic corruption. Revised structures, terms of entry, promotion procedures and job protection measures formed the basis of a statute which established formal administrative norms over the next fifty years. Once more, however, the best reforming intentions found little reflection in actual practice. Narrow corporative concerns came to replace wider political ones as an ever-greater number of specialised corps became established and sought to defend their elite privileges, once again reinforcing patronage and corruption.

Despite its shortcomings, the Maura system underwent no fundamental alteration until 1964. The Primo de Rivera Dictatorship (1923–30), for all the moralistic fervour of its claims to be 'cleansing' Spain of corrupt politics, left the country's administrative structure more or less untouched. In line with the Italian corporatist model, the period did see the creation of a number of autonomous associations – which gave rise to still more elite bodies – and the establishment of some important public service companies, such as the oil monopoly, Campsa, and Telefónica. However, it was during the short-lived, modernising Second Republic (1931–6) that the major opportunity for reform was squandered. Although attempts were made to confront the problem of state administration – for instance through the Committee to Study State Reform (established in 1934) – no fundamental reforms were ever enacted. Change was restricted to the abolition and recreation of autonomous agencies by governments of differing political persuasion (Subirats, 1990: 5–6). Indeed, the political divisions endemic to the Republic ensured that proposals for administrative reform were always unlikely to reach the statute books. Moreover, Spain's public servants achieved a certain immunity during the troubled Republic, whose politicians were dependent upon them in order to govern at all (Tuñón de Lara, 1985: 241–4).

The outbreak of civil war occasioned the effective dismantling of Spain's administrative structure. The war caused considerable loss of life amongst public officials, and this was followed after General Franco's victory in 1939 by a *'depuración'* (purge) of Republican sympathisers. Franco was uninterested in reform of the administration; instead, there was an avalanche of new appointments to the public sector in which the key criterion for selection was loyalty to the new regime: all state officials had to present a sworn declaration of their political background, and ministers took decisions on appointments with no right of appeal (Beltrán Villalva, 1990: 331). The bureaucracy was in fact to become a central linchpin of the highly centralised, backward-looking dictatorship and was accordingly well represented within the power elite of Franco's Spain (Alvarez Alvarez, 1984; Baena de Alcázar and Pizarro, 1982).

In addition to penetration of the political elite, perhaps the most notable feature of the bureaucracy under Franco was corruption.

Although Franco announced that his public administration would at last be 'moral', corruption became endemic throughout the regime (Nieto, 1984: 119–23; Payne, 1987: 399). Whilst large-scale financial corruption – with the exception of the notorious 1969 *Matesa* scandal (Ruedo Ibérico, 1972, vol.3: 41–109; Preston, 1993: 744–5) – was probably not particularly widespread within the administration under Franco, corrupt practices took other forms such as administrative nepotism, the adjustment of work output according to salary levels, moonlighting, favourable treatment for companies and firms offering outside work to bureaucrats, and the use of state facilities for private purposes (Nieto, 1984: 123). Nonetheless, for all the corruption, some reform and modernisation did occur. By the late 1950s, the Francoist model of economic protectionism, based on the subordination of civil society to a corporatist relationship with the state in which the bureaucracy acted as mediator, had reached the point of bankruptcy – in literal as well as metaphorical terms. A solution was proposed by 'technocrats' associated with the Opus Dei (a Catholic lay organisation), who sought to liberalise and rationalise the functioning of the capitalist market: the role of the state was changed to one in which it served as a promoter of economic development through indicative planning rather than as a producer or administrator. This entailed the need for a free labour market through the introduction of collective bargaining at factory-shop level, and a consequent reconstitution of civil society (Casanova, 1983: 955–9; Balfour, 1989). The main architects of the new technocratic state had two fundamental aims: legal institutionalisation and administrative rationalisation. The first of these was unsuccessful, since Franco's rule remained largely arbitrary, but adminstrative reform was to prove crucial in facilitating the eventual transition to democracy once Franco had died. Ultimately, the technocrats were responsible for radical change by positing instrumental rationality as the basic criterion for economic policy (Casanova, 1983: 963).

The technocrats' loyalty was thus to rational capitalist development rather than to the regime of General Franco as such. This fact set up an internal conflict in the regime which was central to its eventual undoing (alongside parallel civil–military and Church–state conflicts). Despite a backlash following the assassination of Admiral Luis Carrero Blanco in December 1973, a more rational, modern bureaucracy had by that stage gone some way towards displacing the traditional patrimonial one. Franco's post-1973 rejection of modernisation led various groups within the regime – the younger generation of Falangists, Catholics out of government, and younger technocrats, civil servants and administrators – to distance themselves from the dictatorship. They formed the nucleus of the *Unión de Centro Democrático* (UCD) under Adolfo Suárez, the former Falangist who was to oversee the transition to democracy (Preston, 1986).

The central administrative reforms sponsored by the Opus Dei technocrats opened with the 1957 Law on State Administration and closed with the 1965 Law on Payments to Functionaries. Between these dates the bureaucratic machinery of the Spanish state was renewed, as required by the commencement at the end of the 1950s of a stabilisation programme which had been assessed by the World Bank. Administrative reforms occurred within the context of an economic 'take-off' which was sustained through the 1960s and led to Spain becoming the tenth industrial power in the world (Beltrán Villalva, 1990: 322). The most important of the technocratic reforms is generally considered to have been the 1964 Law on Civil State Officials, which covered the creation of a central body with overall competence on questions of personnel, the organisational unification and reinforcement of the general corps, and the restructuring of the remuneration system (Albaladejo Campoy, 1980: 44). The practice of 'personal ranks', by which some civil servants were promoted to grades quite out of keeping with the actual job they performed, was scrapped, as was the payment of 'extra-budgetary' special rates for particular services (Beltrán Villalva, 1990: 324). The 1964 reform did not, however, reject the system of corps as the structural basis of Spanish public administration, but rather attempted to correct its tendency towards corporatism. Like its predecessors, the 1964 reform was never wholly effectively applied in practice. By 1970, the hopes engendered by the new provisions had been largely frustrated: of the 159 different bodies in the state's central administration, just four fell under the terms of the general statute (Albaladejo Campoy, 1980: 46; Beltrán Villava, 1990: 326). When Franco died in 1975, administrative reform remained a political priority.

Administrative Reforms and the Transition to Democracy

Even though the 1964 Reform was never properly implemented, sufficient rationalisation of Spain's bureaucratic structure had nonetheless taken place by the time of Franco's death to facilitate the subsequent transition from dictatorship to democracy. The nature of the transition, based on pacts and negotiations rather than a radical break with the past, ensured that there was no post-Franco purge of the bureaucracy. Indeed, Francoist personnel – most notably, Adolfo Suárez – were quickly incorporated into the civil administration of the emerging democratic state, although it is likely that those who had been involved in the more overt repression of democratic forces were moved to secondary posts. It seems that the first post-Franco democratic governments did not have to confront serious obstructive attitudes within the bureaucracy. Beltrán Villalva (1990: 335) argues that certain administrative sectors positively supported the change of regime, although the survey of attitudes he quotes to support this view was conducted well after democracy had become fact rather than aspiration. According to Juan Prat i Catalá, before 1982 such administrative reforms as took place were fragmentary, ad hoc adaptations to changes in the wider political sphere; against this view, José Luis Cádiz argues that there *was* an attempt to carry out systematic reform, but it failed on account of a lack of political support (see Subra de Bieusses, 1983: 78; Beltrán Villalva, 1990: 336).

The end of the Franco regime and subsequent transition to democracy in fact acted as a catalyst for the explosion of a whole series of tensions which had developed during the dictatorship. In particular, frustration over low rates of pay, the growth in the number of temporary contracts, and the arbitrary nature of promotion led to a generalised sense of demoralisation and even near paralysis within the administration. Moreover, little attention was devoted during the transition to administrative questions; there was no significant reform of Spain's public administration until 1984. Before then, democratic governments had concentrated on the more immediate issue of institutional and legislative renewal, leading to a discordance between the emerging democratic, pluralist political structure and a rigidly structured, hierarchical state administration (Nieto García and Gutiérrez Reñón, 1991: 135).

Furthermore, one of the central problems facing Spanish public administration – overstaffing – was exacerbated during the transition to democracy: administrative decentralisation consequent upon the gradual establishment of regional autonomy led to bureaucratic duplication. Whereas in theory the centralised civil service should have contracted as power was transferred to the regions, in practice government departments tended to expand – usually on the basis of claims that they were needed to improve co-ordination between the regions. Between 1982 and 1991 the number of civil servants working for the seventeen Autonomous Communities increased twelvefold to 565,460, yet the number working for the central government fell by only 23 per cent to 900,576 (Chislett, 1994: 27). This apparent confirmation of a Spanish version of Niskanen's bureaucratic oversupply model, according to which public bureaucracies use their monopoly of information on expenditure requirements to expand their budgets (Niskanen, 1973), emphasised the scale of the task which faced those who sought to modernise Spain's public administration.

The Reforms of the 1980s

Organisational Restructuring

When the Socialist Party (PSOE) came to power after its crushing victory in the elections of October 1982, the standing of Spain's bureaucrats had never been lower. At the PSOE's XXIX Congress in 1981, reform of the country's administrative structure had been identified as crucial to the consolidation of democracy. An ambitious four-point programme was outlined, seeking to:

● introduce professionalism by reinforcing the June 1982 'law of incompatibilities', which prevented state employees holding more than one post, and by altering promotion procedures
● introduce efficiency by reducing the number of specialised *cuerpos* and rationalising access to posts in public office
● improve social security benefits for state officials, and improve their morale by altering work patterns
● avoid unnecessary duplication of costs and personnel during the transfer of services to the newly-established Autonomous Communities.

In practice, the PSOE government's initial reform efforts were only partially successful. A law on administrative reform which came into effect in August 1983 was relatively modest, being restricted mainly to reorganisations in ministerial structures. The 1984 reform law on public office was more far-reaching, as it aimed to move away from the traditional *cuerpos* towards a new structure for public office, based around specific posts. In addition, the law removed frontiers between different tiers of public administration, allowing the interchange of personnel between state-level and Autonomous Community posts. The intention of the changes was to combat the corporativism of the *cuerpos*, which tended to promote the particularistic interests of their own members and engage in self-regulation. Considerable criticism resulted from the opening of all posts to public competition, which, it was argued, promoted a new spoils system by politicising appointments and distributing favours to PSOE sympathisers (Beltrán Villalva, 1990: 345–7). Moreover, the 1984 legislation was further criticised for its poor drafting, which led to difficulties in its practical application (Subirats, 1990: 11).

In recognition of the urgent need for overhaul of the public sector, the PSOE's second administration (elected in 1986) created a Ministry of Public Administrations. The first head of the new department, Joaquín Almunia, declared that thorough reform would take at least ten years, but as an initial step he launched a major inquiry into the structure of Spain's public administration. The results were published in a 1989 report, *Reflections on Modernising the Administration* (MAP, 1990), which served as the basis of a wide-ranging series of proposals subsequently presented in a *Plan to Modernise the State Administration* (MAP, 1992). In the meantime, however, significant steps towards reform had been taken in the 1987 Civil Service Act, which established formal channels of representation for public officials, together with their rights to participate in negotiations over working conditions and remuneration.

The 1989 report and 1992 proposals broke with long tradition by eschewing a legalistic approach, concerned above all with technical norms and hierarchical frameworks. Instead, they sought to separate politics from administration by promoting a new emphasis on modernity and efficiency. Thus, amongst the key reform measures proposed were:

● a change in administrative culture from a predominantly juridical model to a management-based model, concerned with results and serving 'the customer'
● a shift from the rigid structures of a 'mechanical bureaucracy' towards an organisational model based on grouping functional areas into self-contained units, budgeting according to policy objectives, and using audit-based methods of control

● the introduction of 'management-by-objectives', with greater mobility, streamlined procedures and increased use of new information and management technologies.

In addition, to combat excessively standardised treatment of personnel (which was held to be responsible for low levels of pay and motivation as well as limited training and promotion opportunities) the reports proposed improvements to recruitment, training and promotion procedures, and the creation of more rational salary scales.

One aim of the reports was to stimulate discussion within the administration itself, in order to build up a climate of consensus before initiating far-reaching changes. None the less, several preparatory reforms were introduced in parallel to the Ministry's investigation. The General Office of Public Administration Service Inspections (IGSAP) was established in 1986 to streamline bureaucratic procedures and working methods and introduce rationalisation measures. Set up as a private consulting operation, the IGSAP is responsible for conducting 'Operational Service Inspections' (OSIs), which are intended to improve the workings of public administration units and offer a means of evaluating Spanish bureaucracy and public services. In order to avoid being seen as an imposed control, OSIs are carried out only at the request of the agency involved, which is required to participate actively in the diagnosis of any operational problems. During 1987 and 1988, OSIs were conducted in fourteen ministries, affecting 40 executive departments and 150 service sections (Subirats, 1990: 14–19).

In addition to measures designed to assess the operation of the administration, there has been an increase since the mid-1980s in the number of autonomous agencies, private associations and other organisations taking charge of public activities formerly handled by the government. This development is aimed both at cutting through the red tape for which Spain's public administration has been notorious, and at ensuring more transparent management practices. In late 1992, the PSOE revealed plans to transfer the organisation of unemployment benefit, previously handled by the National Employment Institute (INEM), to an new agency under the control of employers and the unions. Although the new agency will have responsibility for fixing rates, collecting contributions and distributing benefits, it will remain under the ultimate control of Parliament and thus technically within the public sector. However, the reform will transfer direct responsibility for an annual budget of over Pta1 billion from the government to the new agency. INEM's primary role will be to organise professional training programmes for the unemployed.

The transfer of activities to autonomous agencies mirrors developments which have taken place throughout much of western Europe as governments have sought to improve efficiency whilst simultaneously reducing the financial burden on the public sector. As Spain's general government deficit threatened to spiral out of control at the start of the 1990s – largely, it should be noted, on account of expenditure by the Autonomous Communities and local authorities – the need to rein in public sector expansion has been identified as an urgent priority, particularly given the convergence terms established in the Maastricht Treaty for economic and monetary union (see chapter 10; EIU, *Country Report*, No.4, 1992).

Rationalisation and Privatisation

Since the mid-1980s, rationalisation and privatisation have been central to government policy on public sector reform. In addition to the internal restructuring of the public administration outlined above, the most significant rationalisation measures have included disinvestment (through liquidation of non-viable companies, closure of excess capacity, or privatisation), restructuring entire industrial sectors, forced mergers of public companies, selective investment, the reorientation of production in some companies, and the adoption of new technologies to improve efficiency (Salmon, 1991: 34). Of all these measures, privatisation has been the most controversial: critics have argued that it flies in the face of any government pretensions to represent democratic socialism.

In fact, privatisation initiatives in Spain under the PSOE have not been founded upon any ideological rationale. Unlike the UK economy, where an explicit market-centred ideology underlay the 1980s Conservative administrations' insistence on 'rolling back the state', Spanish privatisation measures have followed industrial logic rather than political belief (Aranzadi, 1989: Fernández Rodríguez, 1989 – quoted in Salmon, 1991). Until 1988, privatisation was aimed primarily at simplifying the portfolios of state-owned companies, and improving the efficiency of state control. Thereafter, the need to comply with EC requirements on deregulation and liberalisation in the run-up to the introduction of the European Single Market led to an acceleration in privatisations. Thus, although PSOE governments never officially operated a 'privatisation policy', they were active from the mid-1980s onwards in totally or partially selling state companies (see Table 6.2). In general, they opted for deregulation, the removal of protective legislation and private management of public companies as their preferred privatisation strategies (Subirats, 1990: 19–20).

In 1991 a General Secretariat of International Economy and Competition was established and the Competition Court – rarely called upon before 1990 – was given enhanced powers (Chislett,1994: 26). Plans to abolish restrictive practices formed a centrepiece of the Socialist government's 1992 convergence measures (see chapter 10), whilst in the same year Campsa's state oil monopoly was abolished. Since then, the government has been able to intervene only on issues related to safety conditions. In line with EU directives, prices of oil products were liberalised and in 1993, Iberia's monopoly on domestic flights was ended. However, the government was far more resistant to deregulating telephone services, in which competitive services will be allowed only from 1998.[2]

While some public firms have simply been sold to private companies – usually multinationals (as in the case of the sale of SEAT to Volkswagen and Enasa to Iveco, a division of Fiat, in 1986) – in many cases the rationale has been to introduce greater operating freedom and/or to eliminate state subsidies and special credits. Equally, there have been advantages identified in regard to improved access to technological, logistical and commercial expertise and facilities, economies of scale and industrial synergy (Salmon, 1991: 36). However, privatisation measures do not mean that state intervention is unimportant in the modern Spanish economy. Indeed, the government has often sought to maintain its controlling interest in public firms through partial privatisation whilst eliminating their privileged position in the market. In the words of the *Financial Times* (24 February, 1989), the PSOE controls its part-privatised companies 'like an imperious warlord'. Thus, to take the example of Repsol, which in 1989 was the PSOE's first major-scale partial privatisation and is now quoted on the stock market, the government insisted on maintaining a controlling interest and restricted market penetration to just two companies. Even though further privatisation, planned in 1994, may cut the government's stake to as little as 10 per cent, the state intends to retain a 'golden share' which will allow it to exercise a veto over company decisions (Chislett, 1994: 70).

TABLE 6.2

Principal Spanish privatisations, 1985–90

Year	Company	Seller	Purchasers	Capital sold (%)
1985	Textil Tarazona	INI	Cima Eursa (Entrecanales) (Spain)	69.6
1985	Secoinsa	INI	CTNE (Fujitsu) (Japan)	69.1
1985	SKF Española	INI	Aktiebogalet SKF (Sweden)	98.8
1985	Viajes Marsans	INI	Trapsa (Spain)	100.0
1986	Entursa	INI	Hoteles de Lujo (Spain)	100.0
1986	Cía Motores MDB	INI	Klockner Humboldt (Gemany)	60.0
1986	Pamesa	ENCE (INI)	Torras Hostench (Spain)	100.0
1986	SEAT	INI	Volkswagen (Germany)	75.0
1987	Acesa	Patrimonio	Stock market	100.0
1988	Telefónica	Patrimonio	Stock market	65.0
1988	ENDESA	INI	Stock market	25.0
1989	MTM	INI	GEC-Alsthom (France/UK)	85.0
1989	Ateinsa	INI	GEC-Alsthom (France/UK)	85.0
1989	Enfersa	INI	Ercros (Spain/Kuwait)	80.0
1989	ENASA	INI	FIAT-Iveco (Italy)	60.0
1989	Repsol	INH	Stock market	26.0
1989	Intelhorce	Patrimonio	Orecifi (Italy)	100.0
1990	Imepiel	Patrimonio	CFG Grupo Cusf (Spain)	100.0
1990	Hytasa	Patrimonio	Textil Guadiana (Spain)	100.0

Main Spanish state owned companies

Company	Shareholder	Capital controlled (%)
Repsol	INH	64.5
ENDES A	Teneo	75.0
Iberia	Teneo	99.0
CASA	Teneo	100.0
ENCE	Teneo	60.0
Inespal	Teneo	100.0
Babcock & Wilcox	Teneo	100.0
Trasatlántica	Teneo	100.0
Elcano	Teneo	100.0
Inisel-Cesela	Teneo	
Auxini	Teneo	100.0
Telefónica	Patrimonio	35.0
Tabacalera	Patrimonio	55.0
Trasmediterránea	Patrimonio	100.0
Argentaria	Patrimonio	100.0
Renfe	Ministerio de Transportes	100.0
Astilleros Españoles	INI	100.0
Ast ano	INI	100.0
Santa Bárbara	INI	100.0
Ensidesa	INI	100.0
Foarsa	INI	100.0
Hunosa	INI	100.0
Presur	INI	100.0

In the early 1990s, the government initiated a major reorganisation of state-controlled companies. The holding company, Grupo INI, was divided into two parts: Teneo, which encompassed its profitable and commercially attractive firms together with some from the DGPE, and a second company – based mainly on DGPE's holdings – which comprises those loss-making firms, such as the coal-mining concern Hunosa, with no chance of economic viability. Teneo will operate as a normal commercial company, with no guaranteed state aid, whilst companies in the second group will gradually be restructured and/or closed. A further state holding company, *Corporación de la Siderurgia Integral* (CSI, jointly owned by Grupo INI and DGPE), commenced operations in 1993 to oversee the reconversion of Spain's troubled steel sector.

The Challenges of the 1990s

Reform of the administration remained a key government objective ten years after the Socialists first came to power with a commitment to modernise Spain. Although significant progress had been made since 1982, particularly during the latter part of the 1980s, a number of factors explain the continued salience of administrative reform in the 1990s. At an obvious level, administrative efficiency is vital to the smooth functioning of any modern democracy. Public spending has grown as a proportion of GDP (from 27 per cent in 1978 to 42 per cent in 1988), but there has been no equivalent growth in the number of central state officials. Government tasks have become increasingly complex, reflecting the need to balance ever-more imposing budgetary constraints with improved managerial methods. Indeed, the emphasis placed in much of the developed world during the 1980s on values associated with the 'enterprise culture' – management, efficiency, risk-taking and individual success, as opposed to concern for the collective good and social security – has found its echo in Spain, in spite of a nominally Socialist government. Spain's traditionally ponderous and cumbersome bureaucratic structure has been seen as an obsolescent obstacle to progress, and the reforms of the late 1980s were thus but the first steps towards a root and branch overhaul.

Public perceptions of Spain's bureaucracy and the quality of service it provided remained negative after a decade of Socialist rule. Private provision of services, especially in the fields of health care and education, were widely seen as superior to their public counterparts. Given the centrality of 'modernisation' in the PSOE's political agenda, continued bureaucratic inefficiency was seen by many as an indictment of the government's reform efforts. On the occasion of a lengthy interview in late 1992 to mark ten years in office, Felipe González lamented the delays which continued to mark the operation of Spain's administrative apparatus, which he described as the greatest frustration of his premiership – a view echoed by several leading Socialists in commentaries on the PSOE's first decade in power (*El País internacional*, 26 Oct 1992; 3 November 1992). In August 1991, the Minister of Public Administrations had admitted that some public officials had no specific jobs to perform (*El País internacional*, 12 August 1991).

More important than its impact on governmental image, however, was the effect that administrative inefficiency could have on Spain's economic development. Of particular significance in this regard was the need to adapt to the demands of the European Single Market, which from 1 January 1993 exposed Spain to intense economic competition. The lack of a modern, technologically-advanced and efficient public administration was seen by the government as potentially highly damaging to Spain's competitive prospects; the country already suffered, in spite of very high levels of inward investment since the mid-1980s, from such a reputation for bureaucratic backwardness that an article in *The Economist* on business prospects in Spain suggested that it was easy to avoid paying tax. The existence of a sizeable 'black economy' has been identified as a major obstacle to economic efficiency in Spain: it not only deprives the government of significant tax revenues, but also artificially inflates official unemployment levels and leads to increased claims on the social security budget.

Administrative reform has clearly been beset by barriers in modern Spain, even under a government with an absolute majority and a popular mandate for change. Several reasons can be adduced for the apparent – if not entirely real – impermeability of traditional approaches within the public sector during the Socialists' period in power. Of particular importance was the fact that any reforms had to be enacted by the very bureaucracy which was the object of the proposed changes. Experience from other countries, notably the UK following the Fulton Committee report of 1964, suggests that bureaucrats are well-placed to frustrate reforms which are perceived as a threat to their power or influence (Kellner and Crowther-Hunt,

1980). Moreover, the initial response to Socialist reform proposals amongst Spanish civil servants was one of scepticism, borne of the belief that they represented 'yet another attempt' which was doomed to fail (Subirats, 1990: 24). This is not to suggest that there was necessarily active resistance to change; rather, a lack of positive enthusiasm may have militated against the effective implantation of reform measures.

Linked to such lukewarm attitudes towards change was a desire to preserve privileges. Civil service unions, such as *Confederación Sindical Independiente de Funcionarios* (CSIF), were concerned to protect their members against what was seen as a threatened erosion of status, reflected principally in declining salary levels. The flight of high-ranking public servants to the private sector became a source of governmental concern during the 1980s and was indicative not only of how remuneration of state officials failed to keep pace with private enterprise, but also of low morale within the public sector. Indeed, a significant obstacle to reform within the public administration was the lack of personnel at senior management level able and willing to act as agents for change. In turn, such a lack highlighted major problems in personnel selection and training evident at all levels within the public administration.

Recruitment procedures to the civil service have long been a contentious issue in Spain. In January 1990, the Ministry of Public Administrations announced a decree establishing guidelines to open up selection methods and bring them more in line with private sector practices. Although appointments since the end of the Franco regime have been formally neutral in party political terms, the notorious system of *oposiciones* (competitive examinations) for entry to public posts, alongside an unofficial brokerage system, has maintained powerful patronage networks. Gradually, however, more professional criteria for appointment have been introduced, linking training and qualifications more closely to the vacancies in question.

The stereotypical image of Spain's administrative officials as cantankerous, obstructive and lackadaisical has been rendered somewhat out of date by developments since the return of democracy. The average age of those working in the public sector at the end of the 1980s was just 40, in part a reflection of Spain's relatively young population profile. Just over a third of all public servants are women, compared to slightly under 30 per cent of employees in the private sector, and the proportion of women at higher levels is far greater than in equivalent private companies. The average level of formal qualifications on entry is notably high: more than half of all holders of university degrees among the active population work in the public sector (Nieto García and Gutiérrez Reñón, 1991: 144). None the less, the public administration has continued to suffer from a negative, even hostile, response among the general population – a view which has been exacerbated by the widespread sense of resistance to change or reform.

Conclusion

In practice, the perceived resistance to reform within the public sector is not supported by close analysis. After over 100 years of administrative stagnation, major refoms did begin to take place under the Socialist government first elected in 1982. Although such reforms were not always immediately visible to the general public – and in spite of continued dissatisfaction on the part of government officials even after ten years in power – a real change in Spain's public sector had by the start of the 1990s begun to bring it far more into line with that of its major European neighbours. Indeed, Spain's fully-fledged entry into western economic and political circuits, marked most obviously by membership of the EC and NATO, was a major stimulus to administrative renewal. The prospect of ever tougher international competition ensured that such renewal had to be far-reaching, affecting not only the country's decision-making capacity but also its ability to implement policy.

One of the most significant features of the 1980s' reforms was the shift from juridical concerns with the status of public servants to an explicitly non-juridical model which focused on administrative efficiency. Inevitably, such changes take a long time to permeate public consciousness, and it is undoubtedly the case that there remains a long road to travel. However, as has been seen, there have been far-reaching reforms in regard to the structure of Spain's public sector, in particular with regard to management changes and rationalisation procedures. Recruitment and training remain issues of central concern, but it seems likely that Spain's public sector will continue to modernise.

In fact, the main focus of demands for administrative reform will probably shift in the late 1990s from central government to the Autonomous Communities. As regional government assumes ever greater responsibility for administering its own affairs, the issue of administrative efficiency will come increasingly to the fore at regional level. In general, the Autonomous Communities followed the traditional central state model when establishing administrative structures in the late 1970s and early 1980s. Inefficient basic structures, together with jealous demarcation of areas of competence, have put a premium administrative collaboration – leading to pointless duplication of services and constant frictions between different administrative levels (see chapter 7). The major challenge facing Spain's public sector in the 1990s will be to extend the reforms which have started to take place at central level to the seventeen Autonomous Communities, ensuring that efficiency remains at the forefront of the drive towards modernisation.

7

The Autonomous Communities

Since the middle of the nineteenth century there have been various attempts to establish some form of de-centralised state structure in Spain. Most have ended in failure. The so-called '*sexenio revolucionario*', 1868–74, culminated in the short-lived First Republic which was profoundly influenced by the federalist ideas of the Catalan intellectual, Francesc Pi i Margall (1824–1901). Chaotic cantonalist uprisings provoked a military intervention, followed by the restoration of the monarchy in 1875 (Hennessy, 1962). For the next 46 years, Spanish politics was marked by a counterpoint between centralist rule and the regionalist demands of anti-monarchist groups. Occasional concessions to regional aspirations, such as the granting of a limited form of autonomy to Catalonia through the *Mancomunitat* (1913–23), were generally followed by further repression. Just as General Miguel Primo de Rivera refused to allow any regional autonomy during his dictatorial rule (1923–30), so General Franco's move against the Second Republic (1931–36) was motivated in large measure by his obsession with recreating a unified imperial state. The Republic's experiments with autonomy – the Statute of Catalonia (1932), which established the *Generalitat*, the Statute of the Basque Country (1936) and the putative Galician statute, which was approved but never enacted – were crushed under the centralising heel of Franco's repressive rule.

The Regional Issue: Compromise and Complexity

It is thus unsurprising that regionalism should have proved the single most contentious political issue during the post-Franco construction

142

of democracy; nearly one-tenth of the lengthy Constitution is devoted to regional matters. The constitutional settlement represented a compromise on the issue of territoriality: whereas leftist forces sought to establish a federal state structure, the right would not countenance any such proposal. The result was a hybrid formula which has often been seen not merely as confusing, but in fact quite contradictory (see chapter 2). In practice, the constitutional compromise entailed a recognition of regions' right to some form of autonomy, but with no statement on the definition of such autonomy, nor what powers it would entail. These issues were to be resolved through negotiation between the centre and the regions, an arrangement which would subsequently lead to considerable tension.

Prior to that, however, even the very identity of the regions had to be established. Whereas most were self-evident – such as the 'historic' regions of Catalonia, the Basque Country and Galicia, or the massive southern region of Andalucía – others posed problems. Some areas, like La Rioja, Cantabria or Murcia, had no distinctive, historic tradition of autonomous identity. Navarra, on the other hand, was claimed by many to be part of the Basque Country in spite of its former status as an independent kingdom. Yet whereas Navarra was accorded autonomous regional status, León, which likewise had once been a kingdom in its own right, was subsumed into a new region known as Castilla y León. Unlike the Italian Constitution, the Spanish document does not specify any territorial map. Instead, decisions on territorial identity were reached during the so-called 'pre-autonomies' process – which ran from September 1977 to October 1978 – when all intending autonomous regions were required to outline their claim to such status according to a complex set of legal requirements (Alvarez Conde, 1990: 609). Thereafter, the regions' specific route to autonomy followed the provisions set out in the 1978 Constitution.

The Constitution established three levels of autonomous community, distinguishing between privileged, grade one and grade two regions. Privileged status was reserved for the so-called 'historic' regions – Catalonia, the Basque Country and Galicia – which had been granted the right to autonomous government during the Second Republic. According to the terms of Transitional Disposition No.2, these regions would proceed automatically to autonomous status without the need to make any formal application to the central state. Moreover, they would enjoy full autonomous powers, entailing a 'high' level of responsibilities, from the moment of their formal creation. In contrast, the 'normal' (grade two) route to autonomy, outlined in Article 143 of the Constitution, required regions to follow a lengthy process of consultation before making a formal application for autonomy. Once granted, their autonomous status would be 'low' and subject to a transitional period of five years prior to their being granted the option of seeking a level of autonomy similar to that enjoyed by the privileged regions. Article 151, meanwhile, established a so-called 'exceptional' (grade one) route by which any region could apply to receive the same high level of autonomy as the privileged regions, provided that a stringent series of conditions was first satisfied and the draft autonomy statute was subsequently endorsed in a referendum.

In practice, the entire autonomous process was subject to considerable controversy. Indeed, following the approval in 1979 of autonomy statutes for Catalonia and the Basque Country, there was an outbreak of so-called '*fiebre autonómica*' (autonomy fever) as all the remaining regions sought to establish regional governments. The only region to follow the 'exceptional' route specified in Article 151 was Andalucía, but some regions – such as Valencia and the Canary Islands – were allowed an intermediate status between grades one and two, while Navarra was given its own special route in recognition of its historic 'foral' rights (*fueros*). Ultimately, just ten regions followed the 'normal', slow route via Article 143.

In the meantime, right wing discontent – especially in sectors of the military – at what was seen as the dissolution of Spain's national identity contributed to a growing sense of disillusion with the development of democracy during the late 1970s and early 1980s (see chapter 3). The confused regional picture, reflected in widespread perplexity over the formal structure of regional government, was a leading factor in the decision of some conspirators to plot against democratic government – especially since continued attacks by the Basque separatist group, ETA, kept tension high within the military (Preston, 1990: 175–202). One result of the attempted coup of 23 February 1981 – the most serious of a series of plots – was to place the regional question firmly at the top of the political agenda.

Fearful of continued military conspiracy, the ruling UCD government came to an agreement with the PSOE in the aftermath of the 23-F to slow down moves towards regional autonomy. Regions were warned not to make exaggerated demands and, in September 1981, the notorious and much debated LOAPA (*Ley Orgánica de Armonización del Proceso Autonómico*) was presented to the Cortes.

According to its terms – which were contested by the UCD's and the PSOE's political opponents on both left and right in the so-called *frente anti-LOAPA* – state law was always to prevail over regional law wherever there was a conflict, even in the privileged 'historic' regions. For the first time since the restoration of democracy, political compromise on a major issue was abandoned. Nationalists in both the Basque Country and Catalonia argued that the LOAPA's measures would be tantamount to reducing their status to that of grade two regions, and appealed against the law to the Constitutional Tribunal. In a shock judgement delivered in August 1983 (that is, after the PSOE had taken office) the Tribunal declared more than a third of the LOAPA to be unconstitutional (Alvarez Conde, 1990: 731–51). In effect, the judgement required that the entire regional autonomy process be reconsidered.

The PSOE's commanding majority in the 1982 general elections introduced a sense of stability to the political arena and allowed the regional issue to be confronted in a rather less tense atmosphere. The configuration of Spain's autonomous map was rapidly completed; by the end of February 1983, autonomy statutes had been approved for all seventeen regions (see Table 7.1). In May 1983, regional elections were held in thirteen communities, completing the process which had begun with elections in Catalonia and the Basque Country (March 1980), Galicia (October 1981) and Andalucía (May 1982). Overall, the results established the dominance of the PSOE at regional level, underlining the central government's political authority. This fact enabled the PSOE to embark upon the sensitive task of transferring powers to the Autonomous Communities without the need to seek alliances and agreements with other political forces. However, the Constitutional Tribunal's judgement on the LOAPA ensured that the new government would have to accommodate the demands of the politically significant regions, most notably the Basque Country and Catalonia.

The Structure of the Autonomous Communities

Asymmetrical Devolution

Each Statute of Autonomy defines the institutions of the region in question. All seventeen Autonomous Communities have a president, an executive and a unicameral parliament, together with their own

TABLE 7.1

Dates of Statutes of Self-government of Autonomous Communities

Date	Region	Official title of government
18 December 1979	Basque Country	Gobierno Vasco
	Catalonia	Generalitat de Cataluña
6 April 1981	Galicia	Xunta de Galicia
30 December 1981	Andalucía	Junta de Andalucía
	Asturias	Principado de Asturias
	Cantabria	Diputación Regional
9 June 1982	La Rioja	Consejo de Gobierno
	Murcia	Consejo de Gobierno
1 July 1982	Valencia	Generalitat Valenciana
10 August 1982	Aragón	Diputación General
	Castilla-La Mancha	Junta de Comunidades
	Canary Islands	Gobierno Canario
25 February 1983	Extremadura	Junta de Extremadura
	Balearic Islands	Gobierno Balear
	Madrid	Gobierno de la Comunidad
	Castilla y León	Junta de Castilla y León
10 August 1983	Navarra[a]	Diputación Foral

[a] Navarra was granted autonomy under the terms of an organic law on the rehabilitation and improvement of its Foral Regime.

administrative organisations and a High Court of Justice. However, in contrast to federal state structures in which the component states or regions of the federation enjoy clearly defined sovereignty, Spain's system of Autonomous Communities allows for variable competencies, not only between different regions, but also within the same region over time. The specific areas of competency assigned to the regions are established by a complex mechanism, dependent in the first instance on the particular route to autonomy (privileged, grade one or grade two) and, subsequently, on the basis of negotiation between the Community and the central state, subject to approval by the Constitutional Tribunal (Monreal, 1986).

The ultimate aim of this process was to establish virtual homogeneity in terms of the powers enjoyed by all seventeen Autonomous Communities. In 1992 it was agreed to transfer various central state responsibilities to the ten grade two communities and thus bring them into line with the seven remaining regions. However, in recognition of Catalan and Basque sensibilities, which had been heightened during 1991 by the emergence of newly independent states in the former communist bloc, the Minister of Public Administration, Juan Manuel Eguiagaray Ucelay, observed in early 1992 that 'equality does not equal identity. Some differences will continue to exist.' In particular, special bilateral relations between Catalonia and the Basque Country and the central state were maintained.

While ordinary laws passed at central and regional level have equal standing, the central government sets 'basic legislation' or 'basic norms', which rank above regional law, in such areas as education, health, law and order, and the civil service. Although the Constitution offers no *a priori* definition of basic legislation, the formula is intended to provide 'a common normative denominator from which each Autonomous Community can develop its own competency' (Monreal, 1986: 69). Several areas, such as defence, foreign affairs, economic stabilisation measures, pensions and unemployment legislation, remain the exclusive preserve of central government, as defined in Articles 149 and 150 of the Constitution (see Exhibit 7.1).

In regard to regional responsibilities, the Constitution refers to exclusive, shared and concurrent powers, which can be either legislative or executive. Regional powers denominated 'exclusive' are seen as such only insofar as they do not conflict with the constitutional provisions which granted exclusivity to the powers of the central state. Moreover, ambiguity exists over the scope of shared and concurrent functions, and the extent to which the powers of an Autonomous Community can oscillate between state and region. The very framework of regional government in Spain is deliberately indeterminate, allowing for fluctuations in decision-making power. Such indeterminacy invests the Constitutional Tribunal with considerable significance, since its decisions over conflicts between centre and regions are both binding and final. Moreover, the Tribunal is not constrained in its judgements by the text of any given Statute of Autonomy, which it can override or amend as it deems appropriate (Monreal, 1986).

Between 1981 and 1991, the central government appealed to the Constitutional Tribunal against 120 of more than 1,500 laws approved by regional governments; by contrast, in the same period, regional governments appealed against 127 of 528 laws approved by the state. The vast majority of these disputes have involved the historic regions, with the LOAPA being by far the most contentious issue. After 1989, the number of cases brought before the Constitutional Tribunal fell sharply, suggesting that a more

EXHIBIT 7.1
**Distribution of powers between central state
and Autonomous Communities**

1 Powers explicitly reserved to the central state (Article 149):

- nationality, immigration, emigration, aliens and right to asylum
- international relations
- defence and armed forces
- administration of justice
- customs and excise, foreign trade
- monetary system, exchange control, currency convertibility
- control of credit, banking, insurance
- inland revenue and state budget
- merchant navy and registration of ships
- ports and airports of national importance
- control of airspace, air transit and transport
- meteorological service and registration of aircraft
- train and road transport travelling through more than one Autonomous Community
- control of communications, traffic and motor vehicles, mail and telecommunications, cables, submarine and radio communications
- public works of national importance or which involve more than one Autonomous Community
- control of production, commerce, possession and use of arms and explosives
- regulation of academic qualifications
- statistics for state use
- authorisation of referenda

2 Powers shared between central state and Autonomous Communities (Article 149.1)

- areas in which state provides 'general framework' (e.g. basic legislation on environment)
- areas in which state shares general legislative powers, with specific elements left to Autonomous Communities (e.g. public security)
- areas in which the state retains the planning powers or determines the basic administrative policy of the sector (e.g. the economy)
- areas in which the state is given a co-ordinating role over the Autonomous Communities
- areas in which the state determines the economic parameters for public service management
- areas in which the state retains certain managerial responsibilities, allowing the rest to be undertaken by the Autonomous Communities
- areas in which the state retains responsibility for public service, but not its management

Article 149.3 stipulates that powers in all areas not expressly attributed to the state under the terms of the Constitution may be taken over by the Autonomous Communities, in accordance with the provisions of their respective statutes. Any powers not specifically taken over remain within the remit of the state. Article 148 lists specific powers that the Autonomous Communities may take over.

harmonious modus vivendi, with developed channels of communication, was becoming established between centre and regions (Eguiagaray Ucelay, 1992: 341–3). However, the issue of demarcation between central government and the Autonomous Communities acquired renewed political significance in September 1992, when the Catalan president, Jordi Pujol, created the post of commissar for foreign relations, with an official rank within the *Generalitat*. Although the action was formally within constitutional bounds, some leading politicians in Madrid saw it as both deliberately provocative and a potential threat to Spain's Constitution.

Seven other Communities also had foreign affairs departments, but none had been given such prominence as the Catalan post: most were established specifically to defend regional interests within the EC. The Catalan case encompassed a more wide-ranging international profile, and followed closely on the attempt by Pujol to claim the triumph of the 1992 Barcelona Olympic Games for the 'nation' of Catalonia. The Catalan president insisted that he was not seeking independence, but during his visit to Slovakia in the aftermath of its separation from the Czech Republic, he was treated as a head of state and the Catalan rather than the Spanish anthem was played.

Further disquiet was provoked when it emerged that, during 1992, the presidents of the seventeen Autonomous Communities had been on 124 official, but unco-ordinated, foreign visits. These visits created confusion not just within the Ministry of Foreign Affairs, which was rarely informed of their occurrence, but also in the receiving countries, which on occasion found themselves host to both an official Spanish state visit and one from an Autonomous Community. Moreover, the commercial policies promoted by some Communities did not always coincide with those of the central government – or, indeed, with those of other Communities. By 1993, when the European Single Market came into force, ten Communities had established offices in Brussels. These are required to operate only as lobbying organisations and are forbidden from carrying out representative functions. The central government introduced proposals in early 1993 aimed at ensuring that these various organisations would co-ordinate their activities.

The Financial Structure

The Statutes of Autonomy, individually negotiated for each region, outlined basic responsibilities and tax-raising powers: seven Autonomous Communities were granted a high level of responsibilities, defined in terms of control over expenditure functions, while the remaining ten had a low level. The main differences in expenditure centred on the areas of education and health. In February 1992, agreement was reached to transfer most remaining responsibilities – with the important exception of health and social security expenditure, which was seen as being too great a financial burden – to the low level communities, thereby bringing them more or less into line with the remainder. The transfer was to take place over a four-year period (Eguiagaray Ucelay, 1992: 346–9).

The only taxes specifically allocated to central government in the Constitution are customs duties; all remaining tax fields can be assigned to any level of government. However, regional and local powers to levy a particular tax have to be transferred by central government, which means that specific tax assignments are dependent upon decisions taken in Madrid. Central government has in practice retained the most important tax bases (Solé-Vilanova, 1989: 217). 'Ceded' taxes are those which are set at central level, but collected at regional level; they include death and gift duties, wealth tax, property transfer tax, stamp duties and gambling taxes. Whereas fifteen Communities have the same limited powers to levy a surcharge on ceded taxes and on personal income tax, the Basque Country and Navarra were granted special charters in recognition of their 'foral' traditions. Although these charters allow the two regions to collect so-called 'contracted' taxes (personal income tax, corporation tax, and, in the Basque Country, valued-added tax) as well as ceded taxes, out of which they pay an annual quota to the government, they have little real flexibility given that contracted taxes must be levied at the same rate as in the rest of Spain, while customs duties and taxes on petroleum products are excluded from regional control (see Exhibit 7.2).

The principal sources of revenue for the fifteen Communities without special charters are tax-sharing grants from the central budget. The size of these grants (or budget transfers) was initially dependent upon the expenditure incurred by the Communities in respect of the specific services transferred from the central state. However, in 1985 the Organic Law on Financing of Autonomous Regions established a new 'definitive' formula for the transfer of resources. This was based on a series of variables which included population, area, migratory balance, population spread, insularity, relative poverty and relative tax revenues (Alonso Zaldívar and

EXHIBIT 7.2

Selected Political Features of Regional Governments

Autonomous Community	Senators: (a) Directly elected	Senators: (b) Regional	Provinces	Municipalities (1986)	Level of powers assigned under the Constitution[a]	System of finance[b]
Andalucía	32	7	8	764	A	C
Aragón	12	2	3	727	B	C
Asturias	4	2	1	78	B	C-P
Balearic Islands	5	1	1	66	B	C
Canary Islands	11	1	2	87	A	C
Cantabria	4	1	1	102	B	C-P
Castilla y León	36	3	9	2,248	B	C
Castilla-La Mancha	20	2	5	916	B	C
Catalonia	16	6	4	940	A	C
Extremadura	8	3	2	380	B	C
Galicia	16	3	4	312	A	C
Madrid	4	5	1	178	B	C-P
Murcia	4	2	1	45	B	C-P
Rioja	4	1	1	174	B	C-P
Valencia	12	4	3	536	A	C
Navarra	4	1	1	265	A	F-P
Basque Country	12	3	3	236	A	F
Ceuta and Melilla	4			2	A	F

[a] A: high level of powers (Article 151); B: low level of powers (Article 143).
[b] C: standard system (*régimen común*); F: foral provisions; P: provincial resources.
Source: adapted from Solé-Vilanova (1989: 212).

Castells, 1992: 146). The new formula – which provoked controversy over the relative weighting given to each component factor – was subject to revision every five years, a time period which was intended to allow for a degree of stability in financial planning by regional governments.

In practice, the vagaries of the general economic climate have undermined such aspirations. In late 1992, the proposed transfer by the central government of 15 per cent of its income tax receipts to the Autonomous Communities was put on ice – officially because of the failure by the Communities to reach agreement over its distribution, but in reality more likely to have been the result of the central state budget deficit.[1] However, following the Socialist government's loss of its absolute majority in the June 1993 general elections, and its consequent reliance on support from Jordi Pujol's Catalan nationalists to remain in power, an agreement was finally reached on fiscal co-responsibility. In October 1993, the 15 per cent transfer was approved in spite of opposition from Galicia, the Balearic Islands and Extremadura.[2] Even so, according to one study, Spain's regions remain dependent on central government transfers and debt instruments for 86 per cent of their revenue, compared with equivalent figures of 72 per cent in Germany and 54 per cent in the United States (Chislett, 1994: 136).

One central aim of the system of Autonomous Communities was to ameliorate the sharp regional disparities which historically have characterised Spain. Since the end of the nineteenth century, Catalonia, the Basque County and Madrid have enjoyed economic predominance over the rest of the country, and the contrasts between the income levels of these three regions and those of Extremadura, for example, remain pronounced (see Table 1.4). Less developed regions account for 76 per cent of Spain's geographical area and contain 58 per cent of the population (European Commission DG XVI, 1992). In recognition of this fact, Article 2 of the 1978 Constitution specifically refers to 'solidarity' amongst the regions, thus seeking to establish the principle of levelling out regional disparities. To this end, the Constitution established an Inter-Territorial Compensation Fund (FCI) – the only source of regional revenue specifically regulated by the Constitution – with the purpose of transferring resources from richer to poorer regions.

The FCI's budget, which is revised annually, has been limited since 1986 to 30 per cent of the state's total public investment. It provides grants for capital investment, and was initially distributed according to a formula based upon relative levels of income, migration, and unemployment rates. The formula had to be recalculated in 1990 after it became evident that the migration factor had resulted in the Basque Country and Catalonia enjoying major increases in their share of the FCI during the 1986–9 legislature, whilst some of the poorer regions, such as Extremadura and Andalucía, suffered marked reductions (Ministerio de Economía y Hacienda, 1989). With the onset of economic recession in the early 1990s, many of the richer regions began to express disquiet at the level of their contribution to the FCI. Catalonia, for instance, got back only Pta68 for every Pta100 it paid to Madrid in 1992.

In fact, the scale of migration from poorer to wealthier regions since the 1960s has contributed to a relative diminution of income disparity in Spain over recent decades – although the positive trend evident between 1960 and the mid-1980s has levelled out since 1985. Contrary to widespread assumptions, regional inequality in Spain is no greater than in other European countries; indeed, according to some calculations, it is considerably better than in Germany, Portugal and, above all, Italy (Alonso Zaldívar and Castells, 1992: 154). However, the relative poverty of nearly all Spain's regions compared to the European average leaves its poorest regions in an acutely disadvantaged position. In 1991, GDP per capita was above the EC average in just three regions (Madrid, Catalonia and the Balearic Islands), while others (notably Andalucía and Extremadura) remained at around 50 per cent of the European average, and below 80 per cent of the Spanish average figure.

In addition to budget transfers and the Inter-Territorial Compensation Fund, a third main source of regional finance has been the EU's Structural Funds – the European Regional Development Fund (ERDF), the European Agricultural Guidance and Guarantee Fund (EAGGF) and the European Social Fund (ESF) – from which Spain has benefited enormously since joining the EU in 1986. The EU's Structural Funds – reformed with an increased budget in 1989 – are distributed according to five priority objectives, of which Spain qualifies for three (see Exhibit 7.3): Objective 1 (regions where per capita GDP is less than 75 per cent of the EU average), Objective 2 (regions which are undergoing industrial decline, whose percentage share of industrial employment and average rate of unemployment both exceed the EU average), and Objective 5b (rural areas in need of economic diversification, which are dependent on vulnerable agricultural activities). In addition,

Spain is the main beneficiary of the Cohesion Fund which was established in 1993 under the terms of the Maastricht Treaty.

Structural funds are allocated according to a Community Support Framework (CSF), drawn up for each priority objective by the central government in negotiation with the regions in question and the European Commission. It has been calculated that the 1989–93 CSFs, which were co-financed by the European Commission and the central government, contributed an extra 1.5 per cent to GDP in 1993 and helped create between 80,000 and 105,000 jobs (European Commission DG XVI, 1992). In the 1989–93 period, Spain received some 12 billion ecu in structural funds, about 23 per cent of the EU's total structural aid expenditure. The distribution of Objective 1 funds for the 1994–9 period again saw Spain emerge as the major beneficiary with 26.3 billion ecu.

One of the regions which benefited most was Andalucía, which received almost a third of ERDF assistance under the Objective 1 CSF, and 3 billion ecu from the Structural Funds as a whole. In 1987, the *Instituto de Fomento de Andalucía* (IFA) was set up, with EC financial assistance, to promote the region's productive resources, industrial competitiveness, technological progress and access to financial markets. Amongst its major initiatives have been the Cartuja 93 project for the partial re-use of the hugely successful Expo92 site, and the completion of the AVE high-speed rail network linking Sevilla and Madrid (Chislett, 1994: 142–4).

Control over public spending serves as a graphic indicator of the extent of decentralisation in Spain since the creation of the Autonomous Communities. In 1979, central government was in control of 84.5 per cent of public expenditure, a figure which had fallen to 65.5 per cent by 1990. It can be anticipated that, before the end of the 1990s, most public spending will be in the hands of regional and local administrations.

The Bureaucratic Structure

Under the dictatorship of General Franco, bureaucracy was used as an instrument of central control over the periphery. The central government delegated administrative, but not political, autonomy to various bodies established at provincial level under the general co-ordination of the Ministry of the Interior. Essentially, Spain's provinces, established in 1833, acted as agents of central government and, until 1925, as controllers of the municipalities (Solé-Vilanova,

EXHIBIT 7.3
Community support frameworks, 1989–93

- Objective 1

  Andalucía, Asturias, the Canary Islands, Castilla-La Mancha, Castilla y León, Extremadura, Galicia, Murcia, Valencia, Ceuta and Melilla.

- Priorities:

  1 Basic infrastructure: transport and telecommunications
  2 Promotion of production in industry, craft industries and services
  3 Development of tourism, in particular in qualitative terms
  4 Assistance for agriculture and rural development, stabilisation of the agricultural population
  5 Infrastructure to support economic activity: water, energy, environmental protection, research and innovation, training infrastructure
  6 Development of human resources, occupational integration, fight against long-term unemployment.

- Objective 2

  All or part of:
  Zaragoza (Aragón); Cantabria; Barcelona, Gerona and Tarragona (Catalonia); Madrid; Navarra; La Rioja; Alava, Guipúzcoa and Vizcaya (Basque Country).

- Priorities:

  1 Establishment and development of productive activities, access for small and medium-sized enterprises (SMEs) to financial markets and inter-mediaries, business service centres
  2 Protection of the environment via urban and industrial waste processing and the reclamation of derelict sites
  3 Support for research and the provision of university-level and technical training facilities
  4 Improvement in the communications network
  5 Preparatory, assessment and back-up measures.

  All of these priorities include complementary training activities.

- Objective 5b

  Partially covers:
  Huesca, Teruel and Zaragoza (Aragón); the Balearic Islands; Cantabria; Madrid; Gerona, Tarragona and Lérida (Catalonia); Navarra; La Rioja; Alava (Basque Country).

- Priorities:

  1 Improvement of structures and diversification of the agricultural sector
  2 Protection and improvement of the natural environment
  3 Economic diversification and infrastructure improvement
  4 Development of human resources.

1989: 207). The system as a whole was known as the *administración periférica*, and it burgeoned under the Franco regime. The key figure in the whole structure was the Provincial Governor (*gobernador civil*), equivalent to the French Prefect. Appointed by Franco on strictly political criteria, Provincial Governors were charged with ensuring the smooth running of the *administración periférica*. In practice, the actual functioning of the *administración periférica* became exceedingly complex (Medhurst, 1973: 128–9, 182), but the crucial point about territorial administration under the Franco regime is that local authorities were organs of the central state, with no meaningful autonomy.

Since the return of democracy, many of the functions assigned to the *administración periférica* have been transferred to the Autonomous Communities' own bureaucracies. However, the overall pattern of administrative organisation in Spain has become, if anything, even more confused (see chapter 6). More than 360,000 civil servants, formerly in the employ of central government, changed masters during the peak years of transfer (1982–6), whilst a further 40,000 were recruited directly at regional level (Hebbert, 1989). By February 1992, a total of some 432,186 posts had been transferred from central to regional government, the majority of them going to Andalucía, Catalonia, Valencia, Galicia and the Basque Country (Eguiagaray Ucelay, 1992: 326). In spite of these transfers, central government has retained more administrative staff than its remaining powers warrant, leading to a marked increase in the total number of public service personnel since the establishment of the Autonomous Communities (Alonso Zaldívar and Castells 1992: 165).

A law of May 1983 incorporated what remained of the central state's provincial delegations into the civil governor's office of each province. However, the central government maintains a regional presence through the figure of the government delegate (*delegado del gobierno*), who is appointed by the Council of Ministers. Government delegates are the central government's highest representatives at Autonomous Community level and, at official functions, take precedence over all local dignitaries except the regional president.

Civil governors are the provincial equivalent of the government delegate. Generally political appointees, they have a much more specific role than government delegates, reflecting the historical importance attaching to the post. Specifically, they are in charge of maintaining 'public safety and the defence of citizens' rights and liberties', with responsibility for security forces at provincial level.

They also perform an important co-ordinating role between provincial level administration and the state. In single province regions, such as La Rioja, government delegates perform all the roles which would normally attach to the civil governor, thereby obviating the need to appoint one.

Provincial and Municipal Government

Beyond identifying provinces and municipalities as the two tiers of local government, the 1978 Constitution did not specify any reform of Spain's already existing local administrative structure (Solé-Vilanova, 1989: 213). Reforms since the return of democracy have been mainly initiated by regional governments, although the 1985 Local Government Act sought to regulate basic aspects of local administration. Formally, Spain's seventeen Autonomous Communities are further divided into 50 separate provinces (although the seven single-province regions effectively erased the distinction by absorbing their provincial institutions) and over 8,000 municipalities.[3] The precise number of municipalities has varied as a result of regional initiatives: most Autonomous Communities have the power to create both supra- and infra-municipal units of government, leading to the creation of 63 new municipalities between 1981 and 1992.

In fact, as the Spanish state was being decentralised through the establishment of the Autonomous Communities, local government was effectively being re-centralised (Alonso Zaldívar and Castells 1992: 165). Under the terms of the Constitution, control over the municipalities passed largely to regional governments, which in practice have often been reluctant to cede powers to the local level. Indeed, the Catalan *Generalitat*, which never completely accepted the provincial division, dismantled the Barcelona Metropolitan Corporation in 1987 as part of a plan to substitute the county tier for the provincial tier in the medium term, while the Autonomous Community of Madrid was regularly involved in disputes with the Madrid City Council – even though both were under Socialist control – throughout most of the 1980s.

The real reason for such developments has been political: regional governments have sought to maximise their control over local administration for fear of ceding any of the political initiative gained through the establishment of the Autonomous Communities. Indeed, municipal leaders in both Barcelona and Madrid have achieved national prominence since the return of democracy, sometimes to the chagrin of their respective regional presidents. Narcís Serra, defence minister between 1982 and 1991 and deputy prime minister thereafter, sprang to notice as the first democratically-elected mayor of Barcelona in 1979. His successor, Pasqual Maragall, maintained the Catalan Socialist Party's high visibility in a region dominated politically by Jordi Pujol's *Convergència i Unió* (CiU): his was the initiative behind Barcelona winning the 1992 Olympic Games, and gestures such as cycling around the car-choked city to demonstrate his ecological credentials have helped maintain his popularity. In Madrid, Enrique Tierno Galván – mayor between 1979 and 1986 – won a special place in the heart of many *madrileños*, both for his imaginative leadership as mayor and for his earlier trenchant opposition to the Franco regime. Tierno was credited with transforming the spirit of Spain's capital, opening it to the influences of youth culture which generated the so-called '*movida*'. His funeral in 1986 was attended in vast numbers.

The 1985 Local Government Act, in keeping with the system of asymmetrical devolution, was quite flexible about the allocation of responsibilities to the municipalities. The level of compulsory responsibilities is a function of the size of the municipality (those with under 5,000 inhabitants have a minimum level), but the law was deliberately ambiguous as to the additional areas in which municipalities could become involved (Solé-Vilanova, 1989: 216). This has naturally compounded the problem of administrative duplication which has been one of the *bêtes noires* of devolved government in Spain.

Provincial finance is highly complex. Different structures have contributed to the confused picture: whereas the single-province Autonomous Communities have absorbed the provincial administration, in the Basque Country provinces remain highly significant, in Catalonia the regional government has emasculated the provincial level, in the island Communities provincial administration is run by the island councils, and in the remaining six Communities provincial governments sometimes rival their regional government (Solé-Vilanova, 1989: 221). Until 1986, provincial government was financed by a turnover tax, but this was abolished with the introduction of VAT on Spain's entry to the EC. Thereafter, provinces received two different unconditional grants, which were merged into one under the terms of the 1988 Law on Local Finance. Provinces also receive capital grants, distributed to municipalities as project grants. Since 1990 provinces have in addition been able to levy a discretionary surcharge on the municipal business tax.

Municipal finance derives from taxes on property, local business taxes, fees and charges, an unconditional grant, and project grants. Fees and charges are an important source of municipal revenue, being levied on such services as refuse collection, water, and sewerage. The level of the unconditional grant is decided upon by the central parliament in Madrid, and since 1990 has been indexed on the same basis as regional tax-sharing grants. Project grants, which are generally transferred by provincial governments, are of particular relevance to municipalities with fewer than 20,000 inhabitants. The metropolitan city of Barcelona has its own system of financing, comprising an unconditional grant from central government and a share in the revenues of its municipalities and the province to which it belongs.

Overall, provincial and municipal governments in Spain are financially highly dependent. A lack of horizontal equity (in contrast to the situation in all the Autonomous Communities except Catalonia and the Basque Country) has been identified as a key problem in municipal financing, along with inefficient financial management in the 7,000 smaller municipalities (82 per cent) which have fewer than 5,000 inhabitants (Solé-Vilanova, 1989: 222). This has led to significant variations in the fiscal capacities and revenues of municipal governments, reflected in turn by marked disparities in the provision of basic services. Achieving a balance between decentralisation of service provision and managerial efficiency in the smaller municipalities has proved difficult, but the asymmetrical structure of Spain's system of devolved government should allow for continued flexibility in administrative arrangements. Different regions will adopt different solutions to universal problems.

Areas of Tension between Regions and the Centre

It would be absurd to argue that the system of Autonomous Communities has fully resolved the regional issue in Spain. Although regional government has operated since the early 1980s more successfully than many would have dared predict in the aftermath of the Franco dictatorship, there remain significant areas of tension between the regions and the centre. Perhaps the most obvious concerns the issue of finance. In spite of the cumulative transfer of control over expenditure from central to regional government since the establishment of the Autonomous Communities, several regions – most notably, Catalonia and the Basque Country – continue to seek greater fiscal responsibility and financial independence. In particular, there have been calls for a change in the existing arrangements whereby the major component of regional finance is dependent upon transfers from the central state.

It has been pointed out that the Autonomous Communities control a smaller percentage of national GDP than do the regions in France, which – until President Mitterrand's 1991 regional reform proposals – has been far more centralised (Sinova and Tusell, 1990: 234). However, it is equally the case that regional governments were granted extensive powers to raise funds through borrowing; indeed, until 1992, decentralisation extended to regional treasurers being free to engage in deficit financing which was unregulated by the central state (Hebbert, 1989). Between 1984 and June 1991, regional government debt rose by over 570 per cent, from Pta196.6 bn to Pta1.3 trillion, with just three regions – Andalucía, Catalonia and Madrid – responsible for 59 per cent of total borrowing. Meanwhile, local authority borrowing grew at an even more vertiginous rate, rising from Pta551 bn in 1984 to over Pta2.4 trillion in 1991 (Alonso Zaldívar and Castells, 1992: 164).

The competing requirements of granting genuine autonomy to regional and local government whilst at the same time seeking to keep the overall public sector deficit within manageable proportions highlights one of the key areas of tension between the central government and the Autonomous Communities. In this respect, Spain faces a problem common to all governments in western democracies: public sector spending has risen to levels which make it impossible to balance budgets in periods of slow economic growth without engaging in measures which entail high political costs. The solution to this problem, which is likely to be exacerbated by the restrictions on budget deficits contained in the Maastricht Treaty's convergence terms for economic and monetary union (EMU), is far from obvious. It represents perhaps the most substantial obstacle to the smooth functioning of relations between the centre and the regions.

More emotive, but probably less significant in political terms, is the residual desire for independence amongst some nationalists in the Basque Country and Catalonia. In spite of the continued (if increasingly sporadic) activities of ETA, and the bedrock of around 15 per cent support in elections for its political wing, *Herri Batasuna*, Basque separatism remains a minority aspiration which shows little sign of achieving its goal. More threatening to the unity of Spain is the potential emergence of Catalan demands for independence. Although formal demands for Catalan separatism are effectively restricted to the *Esquerra Republicana de Catalunya* (ERC), which remains marginal in spite of an increase in its support to 8 per cent at the 1992 regional elections, fears have been expressed that Jordi Pujol's ever-more assertive political protagonism after four consecutive regional election victories betokens a move towards independence.

Pujol himself has consistently denied that he has any interest in independence, stressing instead his aim of 'defending Catalonia within the framework of the Spanish state', and appealing to the constitutionally-defended right of 'self-determination' (*autodeterminación*). A large part of the problem lies in the lack of clarity over what 'self-determination' means in practice. However, it is certainly the case that any significant move towards Catalan independence would prompt a sharp riposte from the central government; in the unlikely event that independence were to be achieved, it can be safely assumed that the Spanish state would adopt a highly obstructive attitude towards Catalonia's integration into the international community.

In fact, there is little evidence to suggest that separatism has significant support in any Spanish region. A regionalism index, measuring the extent to which the Spanish population was in favour of a state which was neither centralist nor broken up into independent units, was constructed by Alvira Martín and García López on the basis of opinion surveys covering the 1976–87 period. It showed that after an initial upsurge of regionalist feeling when democracy was first established – particularly in the historic regions, as well as Valencia and Andalucía – a plateau was reached by the early 1980s. Although regionalist sentiments continued to grow in Catalonia, they fell in the Basque Country, Galicia and Andalucía. Moreover, stated support for independence in Catalonia fell from 15 per cent of those surveyed in 1979 to just 8 per cent in 1987, while in the Basque Country it fell from 32 per cent to 17 per cent over the same period (Alvira Martín and García López, 1988). Fears of an irresistable demand for Catalan or Basque independence appear somewhat exaggerated.

The Spanish Model: Moving towards Federalism?

For all its imperfections, the Spanish system of Autonomous Communities appears to enjoy widespread support. However, a system which is distinguished by its fluidity must continue to develop and evolve. In the late 1980s and early 1990s, the issue of federalism returned to the political agenda – prompted by the unanimous decision of the PSC (the Catalan branch of the Socialist Party) at its 1987 Congress to call for Spain's system of regional government to adopt a federal structure. The precise nature of the PSC's vision of federalism was unclear: its call responded primarily to a fear that central government was slowing down the process of devolving power to the regions. However, the demand for federalism stimulated a political debate which continues to have a wide resonance (Brassloff, 1989).

According to one definition, what distinguishes regionalism from federalism is that the centre remains intact, with no transfer of state sovereignty. Regional governments are set up alongside the institutions of the unitary state, but do not participate in its decision-making processes, which continue to be constructed on a basis of national majority (Hebbert, 1987: 248). In this respect, the Spanish democratic state is clearly not federal. Indeed, Spain's lack of any effective mechanism for collegiate representation of regional governments in national decision-making represents one of the key challenges which still confronts the country's territorial structure.

Some analysts see federalism as the most likely ultimate destination for Spain's system of devolved government. Whereas regionalism is held to promote centrifugal tendencies, since regional elites have little to gain from cooperation with the centre and can make much political play of their grievances, federalism gives the regions some form of co-responsibility for national policy. Federalism has been openly discussed within the PSOE since its 1988 Congress, even though, officially, the Socialist government does not support such an option. None the less, there is widespread recognition that the Autonomous Communities should be more closely involved in central state decision-making, particularly on matters which have an impact on the regions.

There is disagreement over whether the 1978 Constitution presents any impediment to the introduction of a federal structure in Spain: at the very least, the composition of the Senate would have to be revised to allow it to operate in a fully representative regional capacity.[4]

Equally, it would be impractical to introduce federalism while deep disparities continue to exist in the regions' economic strength. It is thus highly unlikely that there will be any formal move towards such an outcome in the short term. Instead, the system of Autonomous Communities will continue to evolve in its rather idiosyncratic manner. The greatest obstacle to a uniform regional structure is the insistence by the historic regions – particularly Catalonia and the Basque Country – that they should retain a distinctive level of autonomy over and above that enjoyed by the other Communities. However, the current system could develop into a more clearly delineated mixed model, referred to by some as 'federo–regional' (Brassloff, 1989: 44). Such a model would involve the historic regions enjoying what would amount to formal federal status, while the remainder continued with more limited powers.

The EU Dimension: towards a Europe of the Regions?

The federal argument may in fact be superseded by events beyond the control of the central state. Moves towards European union are changing ideas about what it means to be an independent state. Whereas in the early 1980s many Basque and Catalan nationalists declared outright independence to be their ultimate aim, in the 1990s they have tended to adopt a rather more vague attitude. Xabier Arzallus, leader of the Basque nationalist PNV, has predicted that regions will become more concerned with avoiding economic marginalisation than gaining independent statehood (The Economist, 1992). In a 'Europe of the regions' the role of national states would become secondary as decision-making power moved both upwards to the supra-national European level and downwards to the regional level.

The European Commission already encompasses a variety of consultative mechanisms to co-ordinate with the regions. All Spain's Autonomous Communities, except Navarra and Castilla-La Mancha, are members of the Assembly of European Regions (ARE), a putative precursor of a Europe of the regions. Catalonia and the Basque Country are also represented in the Consultative Council of Regional and Local Authorities. In addition, European local authorities have their own associations – the Council of European Municipalities (CEM) and the International Union of Local Authorities (IULA) – in which Spanish municipalities participate. Although only the

(West) German *Länder* are allowed an observer in the European Council of Ministers, the EU Commission encourages direct contact with the regions, especially in regard to its Structural Funds. Indeed, the administration of the Structural Funds has created a new role for regional government, especially at the application and implementation stage (Kellas, 1991: 235).

As in the case of Spain's Autonomous Communities, the future development of the EU's political structure is uncertain. In both Spain and Europe, strong advocates of some form of federalism are faced by equally adamant opponents. However, whereas in Spain, federalism is feared by some because of its supposed risk of breaking up the state, at a European level opponents of federalism see it as a highly centralising development. The force of political developments since the mid-1980s appears to point towards the emergence of some form of federal structure at both Spanish and European level, under which national states will have a much reduced role. However, as the collapse of communism demonstrated, political events can not only take place with bewildering speed, but can also have wholly unexpected consequences. As has been seen, the post-communist emergence of nationalist movements in Eastern Europe and the former Soviet Union had a profound impact on the political aspirations of some Spanish regions. Indeed, the confidence over the future direction of Europe which surrounded the signing of the Single European Act in 1987 and the Maastricht Treaty in 1992 quickly began to evaporate as the harsh realities of recession took hold throughout the EU.

8

The Electoral and Party Systems

A country's electoral system influences its party political structure in two obvious and related ways. On the one hand, the electoral system has an important bearing on the number of parties able to attain parliamentary representation; on the other, any electoral system tends to favour the interests of some parties – generally those involved in its elaboration – at the expense of others. In Spain, the current electoral system remains in essence that which was developed for the first post-Franco elections of June 1977, which had the specific purpose of electing a constituent assembly. Thus, many of its features reflect the exigencies of the earliest stages of Spain's transition to democracy, most notably the negotiations between Adolfo Suárez and other key protagonists between September 1976 and March 1977 (Esteban and López Guerra, 1982: 55–6; Gunther, Sani and Shabad, 1986: 43–53).

The Electoral System

The success of Spain's transition depended on a series of compromises over its constitutional design (see chapter 2). In regard to the electoral system, the outgoing Francoist *Cortes* demanded a number of concessions from Suárez in return for voting itself out of existence under the terms of the Political Reform Law of November 1976. First, a bicameral system was sought, with the second chamber (the Senate) designed to favour conservative interests through its system of recruitment, in order to protect against the lower house (the

Congress of Deputies) adopting radical measures during the constituent process. Secondly, universal suffrage was to be restricted to those over the age of 21, for fear of the impact of more radical younger voters on the political composition of the constituent parliament. Thirdly, a majoritarian ('first-past-the-post') system of voting – believed to favour conservative parties – should be adopted. The first two demands were granted (the voting age was subsequently lowered to 18 prior to the 1979 general elections), but on the third it was decided to restrict the majoritarian system to elections for the Senate and adopt proportional representation for the Congress of Deputies.

The final document on electoral norms was promulgated on 18 March 1977 (and subsequently revised in 1985). According to its provisions, the Congress was to be composed of 350 deputies, elected according to a proportional system based on the d'Hondt model (see Exhibit 8.1).

The system, which protects against strict one-to-one proportionality (especially in cases where electoral districts have fewer than six representatives), tends to favour larger parties at the expense of smaller ones (Montero, 1992: 280–1). In Spain, there exists a 3 per cent threshold requirement, applicable in each constituency rather than nationally, which was designed to protect against extremist groups gaining representation. A challenge to the 3 per cent rule was rejected in 1985 by the Constitutional Tribunal, which argued that it was non-discriminatory since it applied to all parties – a decision which was ratified in two further judgements issued in 1989. In practice, larger parties have benefited considerably in those provinces with a small number of deputies (that is, fewer than five), and in rural areas. Equally, small parties with highly concentrated support, such as regional ones, tend to be favoured over those whose support is widely dispersed: this trend is most notable in Catalonia and the Basque Country (see Table 8.1).

Electoral Districts and Party Lists

Spain's fifty provinces were adopted as electoral districts, a move clearly intended to under-represent the left; half of the entire Spanish electorate is concentrated in just sixteen provinces (the regions of Andalucía, Catalonia, Madrid, and Valencia) and supporters of the left were expected to be found mainly in industrial, urban areas. However, the decision avoided the potentially conflictive need to

EXHIBIT 8.1

The d'Hondt electoral system

Spain's electoral system is based on the d'Hondt model, named after the Belgian mathematician and jurist. Its method of calculating the distribution of seats is fairly complex: seats are assigned to parties on the basis of the 'highest average', obtained by dividing the number of votes received by a party by the number of seats already received plus one. Initially no seats have been assigned, so the denominator is one and the highest average is equal to the total number of votes received by each party. Thus, the party with the highest average (i.e., the highest number of votes) is awarded the first seat, and its vote is then divided by two (one seat plus one) for the second seat, and so on. If its vote, after being divided by two, remains the highest, it is awarded the second seat, and then its vote is divided by three (two seats plus one) for the next seat. However, if the first party's vote, after having been divided by two, is lower than that of the second party, then the second party wins seat number two and *its* vote is divided by two (one seat plus one) for the next seat. The distributive calculations continue until all seats have been assigned.

The Spanish model introduces a variation, in that the denominator increases by one for each seat available, with seats distributed in accordance with the highest resultant totals. Thus, in the hypothetical case of an election contested by six parties, with eight seats at stake and at which 480 000 valid votes have been cast, the distribution of seats might work as follows (this is adapted from the example used in the Spanish decree-law of 18 March 1977):

	1	2	3	4	5	6	7	8
A	*168 000*	*84 000*	*56 000*	*42 000*	33 600	28 000	24 000	21 000
B	*104 000*	*52 000*	34 600	26 000	20 080	17 333	14 857	13 000
C	*72 000*	36 000	24 000	18 000	14 400	12 000	10 285	9 000
D	*64 000*	32 000	21 333	16 000	12 800	10 666	9 142	8 000
E	40 000	20 000	13 333	10 000	8 000	6 666	5 714	5 000
F	32 000	16 000	10 666	8 000	6 400	5 333	4 571	4 000
Total:	480 000							

Party *A* would win 4 seats, Party *B* would win 2, Party *C* 1 seat and Party *D* 1 seat. Party *E* would have won a ninth seat had it been available.

In practice, the proportionality of the d'Hondt system is dependent upon a number of variables. In smaller constituencies, with few seats to distribute, large parties are strongly favoured, most particularly if there is a low level of fractionalisation of the vote (i.e., if it is not widely shared between different parties). The system is most proportional in large constituencies with a high degree of fractionalisation, such as occurs in Catalonia. In Spain it is possible to identify three distinct patterns: provinces in which one party is dominant (such as Soria or Pontevedra), provinces in which there is a two-party balance (Alicante or Ciudad Real, for example), and provinces in which there is a high level of fractionalisation (Barcelona, Vizcaya).

TABLE 8.1

Index of disproportionality[a] in Spanish electoral districts, 1993

	% of national population	Number of seats in *Congreso de los Diputados*	% of total number of seats	Index of disproportionality
Andalucía:				
Almería	1.17	5	1.43	1.22
Cádiz	2.77	9	2.57	0.93
Córdoba	1.94	7	2.00	1.03
Granada	2.03	7	2.00	0.98
Jaén	1.64	6	1.71	1.05
Huelva	1.14	5	1.43	1.25
Málaga	2.99	10	2.86	0.96
Sevilla	4.17	12	3.43	0.82
Aragón:				
Huesca	0.53	3	0.86	1.60
Teruel	0.37	3	0.86	2.32
Zaragoza	2.15	7	2.00	0.93
Asturias	2.81	9	2.57	0.91
Baleares	1.82	7	2.00	1.10
Canarias:				
Las Palmas	1.98	7	2.00	1.01
S.C. Tenerife	1.87	7	2.00	1.07
Cantabria	1.35	5	1.43	1.22
Castilla y León:				
Avila	0.45	3	0.86	1.91
Burgos	0.91	4	1.14	1.26
León	1.35	5	1.43	1.06
Palencia	0.48	3	0.86	1.80
Salamanca	0.92	4	1.14	1.24
Segovia	0.38	3	0.86	2.26
Soria	0.24	3	0.86	3.52
Valladolid	1.27	5	1.43	1.12
Zamora	0.55	3	0.86	1.56
Castilla-La Mancha:				
Albacete	0.88	4	1.14	1.30
Ciudad Real	1.22	5	1.43	1.17
Cuenca	0.53	3	0.86	1.62
Guadalajara	0.37	3	0.86	2.29
Toledo	1.26	5	1.43	1.13
Cataluña				
Barcelona	11.97	32	9.14	0.76
Gerona	1.31	5	1.43	1.09
Lérida	0.91	4	1.14	1.26
Tarragona	1.39	6	1.71	1.23

Extremadura

Badajoz	1.67	6	1.71	1.02
Cáceres	1.06	5	1.43	1.35

Galicia

La Coruña	2.82	9	2.57	0.91
Lugo	0.99	5	1.43	1.44
Orense	0.91	4	1.14	1.26
Pontevedra	2.31	8	2.29	0.99

Madrid	12.73	34	9.71	0.76
Murcia	2.69	9	2.57	0.96
Navarra	1.34	5	1.43	1.44

Valencia:

Alicante	3.33	10	2.86	0.86
Castellón	1.15	5	1.43	1.24
Valencia	5.45	16	4.57	0.84

Basque country:

Alava	0.70	4	1.14	1.63
Guipúzcoa	1.74	6	1.71	0.99
Vizcaya	2.97	9	2.57	0.87

La Rioja	0.68	4	1.14	1.69
Ceuta	0.17	2	0.57	1.64
Melilla	0.15	2	0.57	1.96

[a] The index of disproportionality is calculated by dividing the percentage of seats in each electoral district (the 50 provinces, plus Ceuta and Melilla) by the percentage of the population living there. The closer the resulting figure is to 1, the more proportional the allocation of seats. The most over-represented provinces are Soria (by 252 per cent), Teruel (132 per cent), Guadalajara (129 per cent) and Segovia (126 per cent). The most under-represented provinces are Madrid (by 24 per cent), Barcelona (24 per cent) and Valencia (16 per cent).

Source: based on Vidal Prado and Iglesia (1994: 82–4).

create new boundaries, even if it did undermine the principle of equal weight for all votes (Esteban et al, 1977: 374). Each province has a minimum of two deputies, with an extra seat granted for every 144 500 head of population above 70 000. This measure naturally led to severe distortions in representation, which ranged from the 34 639 votes needed to elect a deputy in Soria to the 136 422 required in Madrid.

Parties (or coalitions), which have been registered at the Interior Ministry, present lists of candidates for each electoral district, containing as many names as there are seats available. The lists must be 'closed and fixed' (*cerradas y bloqueadas*), meaning that once they have been presented no alterations can be made to the number of names, nor the order in which they appear. Potential criticisms of such a system are familiar: the closed list means that candidates are chosen by party bureaucrats rather than by constituents, or even party members. Nor do candidates have to be members of the party on whose list they are included: in the 1993 general election, the PSOE sparked controversy by naming an independent – the judge, Baltazar Garzón – as number two on its Madrid list, behind Felipe González.[1]

In practice, political careers depend more upon party officials – who determine which deputies will be reselected – than the voters. Given deputies' dependence on their party, political conformism tends to be the norm, which in turn leads to the devaluation of parliament as a debating chamber (see chapter 4). The system also creates large, multi-member constituencies, in which there is little direct relation between individual citizens and their representatives. Against these criticisms, it has been argued that Spain's civic and political culture – as evidenced by low levels of party membership and trade union affiliation – has not yet been sufficiently well-established to allow for an open list system to operate effectively: party control serves to guarantee a certain stability (Alvarez Conde, 1990: 357–8).

The Senate initially comprised 207 elected representatives – four from each mainland province, plus one more for each island province (Las Palmas, Tenerife and the Balearics) and two each for the north African enclaves of Ceuta and Melilla – together with a further number, no greater than a fifth of those elected, appointed directly by the king. Given the fixed number of senators per province, the distortion between the number of electors and representatives in different provinces was extreme, ranging from over a million voters per senator in Madrid and Barcelona to under 40 000 in Guadalajara, Segovia, Soria and Teruel.

The 1978 Constitution, which defined the Senate as a chamber for territorial representation, introduced some amendments, but failed to address the anomaly of provincial distortions. The royal prerogative to appoint senators was rescinded and replaced by a system whereby the Autonomous Communities could nominate representatives. Each Community was designated at least one senator as of right, together with an extra one per million inhabitants (or fraction thereof above 500 000). The 46 'Community senators' thus have a different relationship to the electorate than do their directly elected colleagues (indeed, they are not necessarily bound by the same length of term in office), but are unable to perform a function equivalent to that of the German *Bundesrat* in relation to the *Länder*.

The composition of the Senate reflects an unsatisfactory compromise between the desire to secure the defence of regional interests and to maintain the political influence of conservative forces. In fact, neither intention has been well served: the 'Community senators' have little influence, whilst rural provinces have since 1982 regularly returned Socialist majorities. In contrast to the list system for elections to the Congress, voters are required to choose up to a maximum of three names from all those presented on Senate ballot papers (although parties can present lists if they so decide). The restriction to three choices was intended to introduce some element of proportionality and allow for the representation of minority groups (Esteban *et al.*, 1977: 374). In practice, however, the Senate's odd structure and limited powers have seriously undermined its effectiveness as a second chamber (Alvarez Conde, 1990: 379). In September 1994, it was agreed to reform the Senate and convert it into a chamber to represent regional interests (see chapter 4).

Voting and Campaigns

There is no requirement for prior registration to vote in Spain: all those whose names appear in census lists and are in full possession of their civil and political rights are entitled to take part in elections. Electoral administration is charged to various independent councils, which operate at three levels: the *Junta Electoral Central* (Electoral Board Headquarters) based in Madrid, *Juntas Provinciales* in each of the provinces, and *Juntas de Zona* based at the headquarters of each of the parties. The *Junta Electoral Central* is responsible for the electoral register, with technical support from a government body, the *Instituto Nacional de Estadísticas* (INE, National Statistics Institute). Nonetheless, concern has been expressed as to the reliability of official lists (*Anuario El País 1990*: 60–1). Votes are scrutinised by electoral colleges which are composed of citizens chosen by lot, who receive no formal training. The system appeared to work effectively until the general elections of 1989, when there were widespread accusations of electoral fraud. Results released by the Ministry of the Interior differed by nearly a million votes in total from those issued by the *Junta Electoral Central*; in some districts there were more votes registered than members of the electorate. Re-runs were eventually ordered in three seats, but a generalised air of suspicion over the contest as a whole remained – a harbinger of what would develop into relentless attacks on the probity of the third Socialist administration.

Electoral campaigns officially last a fortnight (reduced in March 1994 from three weeks in order to keep down costs), with a propaganda-free 'day of reflection' (*jornada de reflexión*) immediately preceding the vote. Although mass rallies remain a strategem favoured by all parties, they no longer attract the vast numbers which attended opposition meetings in the aftermath of Franco's death. Instead, in common with all western liberal democracies, campaigns are dominated by the battle to win access to the mass media. Television air-time during elections is apportioned according to the results of the preceding elections, giving governing parties a marked advantage. Moreover, the state television network, RTVE, has often been seen as a tool of the government – most notably under the Socialist administrations of the 1980s, which were regularly accused of making cynical use of the television news (see chapter 3).

Figures for the late 1980s showed that of nearly 29 million Spaniards over the age of 14, around 80 per cent were regular watchers of TVE-1 (the main national network), with up to 40 per cent of these watching one of the three daily transmissions of the news programme, *Telediario*. This stands in marked contrast to the 30 per cent who read daily newspapers and highlights the importance of television coverage during elections (*Anuario El País 1989*; Heywood, 1989: 326). The establishment of a limited number of private television stations in the early 1990s, together with the growth of regional networks, altered the picture in some degree: the 1993 general election for the first time saw the main contenders – Felipe González and José María Aznar – engage in televised debates, which were broadcast on two of the new private channels, *Antena 3* and *Tele 5*. However, in spite of this significant innovation, access to the state-run network remains critical.

Early campaigns in the post-Franco era, if not exactly tame, were nevertheless marked by a certain air of respect between political opponents, promoted in part by a shared determination to avoid any actions which might destabilise the democratic experiment. In contrast, since the PSOE's overwhelming victory of 1982, electoral campaigns have become increasingly aggressive and acrimonious. The June 1989 European elections represented a turning point in regard to the virulence with which anti-PSOE sentiments were expressed. Widely seen as improperly manipulating state resources, the PSOE was accused of practising high-tech *neo-caciquismo* through its use of the media – a reference to the corrupt electoral practices which marked Spanish politics at the end of the nineteenth and start of the twentieth century. The general elections of June 1993, conducted against the background of judicial investigations into a series of corruption scandals involving the PSOE, plumbed new depths of hostility. Personal attacks proliferated, with the Socialists accused by their opponents of 'Italianising' Spanish politics.[2] In turn, the PSOE sought to summon up the spectre of the Franco regime in the shape of the opposition *Partido Popular*, which it accused of harbouring unreconstructed right-wing attitudes.

Violence during election campaigns has been virtually non-existent. In the early post-Franco years, Manuel Fraga showed a proclivity for rhetorical excess – he threatened on one occasion to smash pro-amnesty demonstrators to pulp (Preston, 1986: 86–7) – and also achieved a certain notoriety for physically squaring up to hecklers on the hustings. However, serious threats to the electoral process have occurred only in the Basque Country, where ETA's presence serves as a menacing reminder of the need to guard against complacency. It is widely believed that *Herri Batasuna*, ETA's political wing, garners at least some of its votes through intimidation. In general, though, Spanish election campaigns resemble those of most other European democracies, generating heat rather than light, but increasingly leaving the electorate cold.

In the early 1990s, Spanish voters manifested a low level of interest in political affairs, with 74 per cent declaring themselves in a 1990 survey to be indifferent to or bored with politics (Villalaín Benito *et al.*, 1992: 53). In a major survey of political and social values conducted in 1991 by the Times Mirror Group Center, 55 per cent of Spanish respondents agreed with the proposition 'I am losing interest in politics', a lower figure than Italy (73 per cent) or France (72 per cent), but higher than Britain (50 per cent) and Germany (23 per cent). Cynicism over the political process appeared widespread in the early 1990s, but more or less in line with European trends.

The Party System: The Difficulties of Definition

Political parties are of course synonymous with liberal democracy. Indeed, parties have been the prime actors in twentieth-century politics, serving as channels of popular expression, aggregators of interests, implementers of collective goals, and agents of elite recruitment. It is thus unsurprising that much attention should have been devoted in political science literature to the analysis of parties and party systems. Since the pioneering work of Maurice Duverger (1957), the study of how party systems influence democratic stability has been a central concern of political scientists (Sartori, 1976; Mair, 1990). More recently, emphasis has been placed on the critical role played by political parties during the southern European transitions from dictatorship to democracy: parties guided, shaped and helped legitimise democratic establishment (Pridham, 1990).

Since the post-Franco instauration of democracy there has been no shortage of attempts to categorise the Spanish party system. The endeavour has, in part, derived its stimulus from the belief that the nature of the party system has a crucial bearing on the prospects for democratic consolidation: it is conventionally held that 'predominant' and 'two-party' systems tend to produce strong government, whilst 'multi-party' systems promote coalitions which are inherently less stable. However, while the number of parties can be a good indicator of political fragmentation, it is probably less important to system stability than the degree of polarisation which exists between parties. Prospects for political stability in multi-party systems depend in large measure on whether they are moderate (centripetal) or polarised (centrifugal).

Between the general elections of 1977 and those of 1986, the Spanish party system was variously defined as: 'two-party' (Martínez Cuadrado, 1980), 'imperfect two-party' (Morodo, 1984), 'two-party-plus' (Gunther, Sani and Shabad, 1986), 'polarised pluralism' (Maravall, 1979; Rodríguez Aramberri, 1980), 'segmented pluralism' (Linz, 1980a), 'fluctuating' (Capo Giol, 1981), 'predominant party' (Caciagli, 1984), 'limited multi-party with a tendency towards bi-polarity of options' (Ramírez, 1982), and 'non-crystallised, non-stabilised' (Bar Cendón, 1984). This very diversity of definitions highlights a conceptual drawback to party systems analyses: even if it can be demonstrated that some systems are more conducive to political stability than others, the approach can do no more than describe a given system at a particular moment in time. An emphasis on taxonomic rigour cannot easily encompass the political fluidity which is characteristic of nascent democracies; indeed, party systems approaches are inevitably static, more or less focused snapshots of political structures frozen in time. The identification of a particular party system offers few clues as to its dynamics: how and why it emerged, and under what circumstances it can be transformed.

In the Spanish case, these issues are compounded by two further complications. First, since a key to the definition of party systems is the number of parties involved – usually distinguished according to whether they are system-supportive (generally 'catch-all') or anti-system (often radical or single-issue) – no significant ontological distinction can be drawn between them. To qualify as a 'party', a political group simply has to present itself for public office at elections candidates identified by an official label (Sartori, 1976). However, the history, internal operation, and specific aims of parties not only differ greatly, but also affect their adaptabilty and survival prospects. This can be seen most clearly in the Spanish case with regard to the *Unión de Centro Democrático* (UCD), led by Adolfo Suárez.

Created in early 1977, the UCD won the general elections of that year, as well as those of 1979, only to suffer a dramatic collapse in the 1982 elections: it plummeted from 168 seats in the *Cortes* to just twelve. In early 1983 the party was disbanded. The key to this collapse lies in the internal structure of the UCD. In reality, the UCD was less a coherent political party than an electoral coalition whose principal rationale was to maintain some hold on the levers of power (Martín Villa, 1984: 83; Muñoz Alonso, 1984: 25). It encompassed divergent interests – most connected in some way with the Franco regime – which sought to retain their privileged status. Five principal groups, each in turn comprised of several others, made up the UCD: conservative christian democrats, state officials associated with the *Tácito* group (reformists who came to prominence during the latter stages of the Franco regime), social democrats under Francisco Fernández Ordóñez, various liberal parties under Joaquín Garrigues, and former *Movimiento* bureaucrats, such as Adolfo Suárez himself (Huneeus, 1985; Caciagli, 1989; Preston, 1986: 108–14).

Once the UCD had achieved its primary purpose of overseeing the creation of a new democratic constitution, it began to break up. With neither unifying ideology nor organisational coherence, the UCD rapidly disintegrated, its symbolic *coup de grâce* delivered by the resignation of Suárez in early 1981. Yet, in all analyses of the Spanish party system prior to 1982, the UCD was counted as if it were just one more national party, analogous to any other. For this reason, its dramatic collapse caught many analysts unawares and prompted unwarranted speculation as to the volatility of Spanish political parties. Definitions of the party system were inevitably rendered inaccurate by the sudden disappearance of the hitherto governing party.

The second complication in regard to defining the Spanish party system concerns the structure of government. The system of Autonomous Communities makes it necessary to distinguish between national and regional party systems (Montero, 1992: 265; Botella, 1989). Although such a distinction is a standard feature of many west European polities, the Spanish model is characterised by the strength of regional parties at the national level. Thus, the Catalan coalition, *Convergència i Unió* (CiU), emerged as the third largest party at national level after the 1989 general elections, even though it presented candidates only in Catalonia. The Basque Nationalist Party (PNV) has also regularly won a significant number of seats (never fewer than five between 1977 and 1993) in the Madrid parliament. After the 1993 general elections, the Socialist Party, which had fallen short of a majority by 17 seats, was forced to rely on CiU and PNV support in order to continue in office. The Spanish party system is thus multi-layered and complex, with developments at regional level – most notably in Catalonia and the Basque Country, where autonomous systems are well-established – having a marked impact on the national scene.[3]

Moreover, the Spanish party system is not just diverse, but is still evolving. From 1977–1982 it could be seen at national level as an 'imperfect two-party' system or 'moderate pluralism', followed by a 'predominant party' system in the period 1982–93 (Blas Guerrero, 1992), after which it assumed the characteristics of a 'two-party plus' system. At regional level, Catalonia is best characterised as a 'predominant party' system, whilst the Basque Country could be seen as an example of 'polarised pluralism'. Such definitions, however, give few clues as to the dynamics of party development, ideology, competition and support. In order to understand the nature of party politics in Spain, attention must be devoted to the history, detailed aims and internal functioning of the major parties, as well as the political context in which they operate (see Table 8.2 and chapter 9).

Political Parties and the Decline of Ideological Distance

In Spain, the national level parties of the left – the *Partido Socialista Obrero Español* (PSOE) and the *Partido Comunista de España* (PCE) –

TABLE 8.2

Evolution of party system indicators, 1977–93

	1977	1979	1982	1986	1988	1993
Distance between first and second parties (index of electoral competitiveness)	5.1 (UCD–PSOE)	4.5 (UCD–PSOE)	22.2 (PSOE–AP)	18.2 (PSOE–AP)	13.8 (PSOE–PP)	4.0 (PSOE–PP)
Percentage of vote for first two parties (central bi-partyism)	63.9 (UCD–PSOE)	65.5 (UCD–PSOE)	74.6 (PSOE–AP)	70.4 (PSOE–AP)	65.0 (PSOE–PP)	73.6 (PSOE–PP)
Percentage of vote for second two parties (collateral bi-partyism)	17.3 (PCE–AP)	16.8 (PCE–AP)	11.2 (UCD–PCE)	13.9 (CDS–PCE)	17.0 (IU–CDS)	14.2 (IU–GiU)
Percentage of vote for regional and nationalist parties	8.3	10.7	9.3	11.4	12.3	12.2

Source: based on Tezanos (1992: 52) and author's calculations.

have a long history, which pre-dated the Franco regime. In contrast, the remaining national parties, whether of the centre or the right, have all been established since the post-Franco return of democracy. Historical continuity has been of immense significance to the PSOE and the PCE: both have sought to claim added legitimacy from their longevity and past struggles, most notably against the Franco dictatorship. Moreover, it has been argued that there was a remarkable continuity in the geographical distribution of leftist loyalties before and after the Franco dictatorship, explained by 'the intergenerational transmission of ideological orientations' (Maravall, 1984: 203–9).

In reality, both the PSOE and PCE have undergone profound transformations since the transition to democracy, reflecting the electorate's rejection of maximalist political options – whether of the right or left (see chapter 9). According to survey data, the ideological self-positioning of the Spanish electorate between 1976 and 1990 on a scale of 1 (far left) to 10 (far right) has fluctuated between a maximum of 5.5 (1977) and a minimum of 4.5 (1980 and 1983). The period average was 4.8, suggesting that Spanish voters have tended to see themslves as marginally centre-left (Moreno, 1990: 306; Villalaín Benito *et al.*, 1992: 56). This assessment is confirmed in studies conducted by the Centro de Investigaciones Sociológicas (CIS), which show that only once since 1980 have fewer than 50 per cent of the electorate identified themselves as either 'left' or 'centre' (see Table 8.3).

Catch-all parties have thus been obliged to seek the centre-ground, while parties of the extreme left and right have generally fared badly

TABLE 8.3

Ideological self-positioning of Spanish electorate, 1981-91, percentage of respondents placing themselves on scale of 1 (far left) to 10 (far right)

Position	1981	1983	1985	1987	1989	1991
Far Left	0.9	1.1	4.4	7.0	7.8	9.6
Left	34.6	41.3	33.7	31.2	25.9	31.0
Centre	22.9	15.1	29.8	25.4	22.1	25.1
Right	12.0	14.1	9.9	8.7	9.4	12.3
Far Right	0.2	0.7	1.0	2.5	3.1	3.9
Average on scale of 1–10	4.8	4.5	4.6	4.7	4.5	4.8

Sources: based on Tezanos (1992: 47); Alonso Zaldívar and Castells (1992: 393–4)

in national elections. Indeed, political polarisation in Spain, especially since 1982, has been much lower than in other European countries (Maravall and Santamaría, 1989: 228–9). Only at the regional level, under the specific political circumstances of the Basque Country, have anti-system parties prospered: *Herri Batasuna*, in particular, has maintained a solid bedrock of around 15 per cent support in elections. Even so, the dominant parties in Basque elections, just as in Catalonia, have been centrist and the ideological self-positioning of Basque and Catalan voters mirrors that of Spaniards in general.

Alongside moderation, Spanish voters have manifested a low level of party identification, with nearly half the electorate claiming not to feel close to any party. A poll conducted in 1990, less than a year after the previous general elections, indicated that fully 40 per cent of the electorate refused to express support for any party (Villalaín Benito *et al.*, 1992: 58). Consistent with these findings has been the high degree of electoral volatility evident in Spain, especially between 1979 and 1982. Parties of the extreme left and right which contested the elections of 1977 and 1979 had largely disappeared by 1982; moreover, after major internal divisions, the UCD and PCE were effectively different parties in 1982 compared to three years earlier, whilst AP had broadened its ambit via coalitions. However, although there were thus very marked shifts in voting patterns at the 1982 election, volatility *between* left and right, as opposed to *within* each sector (especially the latter), remained relatively low at under 6 per cent (Maravall and Santamaría, 1989: 239–40). The evidence suggests that, at national level, the Spanish electorate can be broadly divided into two reasonably well-defined areas of political identity, situated left and right of centre, which relatively few have been prepared to cross.

In regard to the sociological and geographical distribution of party support, the combination of electoral volatility and a short time-scale since the return of democracy means that any generalisations must remain tentative. However, while support for the main national-level parties in terms of occupational structure broadly reflects the electorate as a whole, it is possible to discern some clear patterns. Support for the PSOE across the six general elections between 1977 and 1993 tended to over-represent workers (both employed and unemployed), pensioners and housewives compared to their presence in the electorate as a whole – an average of 83 per cent PSOE support compared to 79 per cent distribution in the electorate. On the other hand, there was much lower support for the socialists amongst young people in search of their first job, the self-employed and students, who together accounted on average for 15 per cent of the PSOE vote, around 5 per cent less than their presence in the electorate[4] (Maravall, 1992: 18).

Young voters between the ages of 18 and 24 are the least decided in terms of electoral preference, but show a marginal – and perhaps somewhat surprising – bias towards the right. Support for the *Partido Popular* is lowest, by contrast, in the age group 25–34, but increases, as one would expect, amongst older voters and the wealthiest sectors of society. *Izquierda Unida*, the left-wing coalition built around the Communist Party, finds its greatest levels of support from within the 25 to 44 age group, notably amongst the unemployed (Villalaín Benito *et al.*, 1992: 57–8).

In the first post-Franco elections, held in June 1977, Socialist support was concentrated mainly in the regions of Andalucía, Valencia and Asturias, especially in large conurbations. Over time, however, the electoral map has changed: in the 1980s, the sparsely-populated regions of Extremadura and Castilla-La Mancha joined Andalucía and Murcia as strongholds of the PSOE vote, which also made inroads into the rural north-west. The highest levels of PSOE support were in population centres of between 2000 and 50000, whilst those with more than 300000 shifted to the right. Strong PSOE support in the cities fell away sharply during the 1980s, dropping by 19 points in Madrid between 1982 and 1989, and registering significant losses in Barcelona, Valencia, Valladolid, Vitoria, Bilbao, Alicante, Cádiz and Málaga (Maravall, 1992: 18). By the end of the 1980s, electoral support for the Socialists was highest in Extremadura (54 per cent), Andalucía (53 per cent), Castilla-La Mancha (48 per cent), Murcia and Valencia. The *Partido Popular*, meanwhile, enjoyed its greatest support in Castilla y León, La Rioja, Navarra, Galicia and Madrid, where José María Aznar outpolled Felipe González in both 1989 and 1993.

Prior to the 1993 general elections, which sharply polarised support between the PSOE and the PP, there had been a marked rise in support for regional parties in several Autonomous Communities with no previous history of strong nationalism, such as Aragón, Valencia, and Andalucía. Equally, disaffection amongst young voters in particular was reflected in growing levels of abstention, up from just under 20 per cent in 1982 to nearly 30 per cent in 1989. By the early 1990s, voting patterns in Spain had become considerably more fragmented than had been the case in preceding elections. However, the 1993 general election and the European elections of June 1994 saw a significant alteration in patterns of voting in Spain.

It was not until 1993, nearly twenty years after the death of Franco, that the *Partido Popular* (PP) was able to capitalise on the decline in support for the PSOE which began in the latter part of the 1980s, prompted by a combination of economic recession, corruption scandals, and boredom with the same party remaining so long in power. Yet, the 1993 general elections saw the number of votes received by the PSOE *increase* by over a million compared with 1989, even though its percentage share of the overall vote fell from 40.3 per cent to 38.8 per cent. Faced with a resurgent right-wing challenge, the Socialist Party deliberately sought to play on fears of a residual association between the PP and the Franco regime. Although the tactic served to ensure a fourth election victory for González, the PP none the less saw its vote expand by nearly 3 million, rising from 26.3 per cent of the overall total in 1989 to 34.8 per cent in 1993. It is noteworthy that the PP breakthrough came after a sustained campaign by its leader, José María Aznar, to present the party as part of the mainstream christian democratic right in Europe, in marked contrast to the hardline position of its early years.

Aznar's adoption of a moderate mantle achieved a major reward in the 1994 European elections, in which the PP won over 40 per cent of the vote and took 28 seats compared with the 15 seats it has won in 1989. The PP won in 59 of Spain's 72 cities and towns with populations of more than 100 000, including Barcelona, where the PSOE was beaten into second place. Of equal significance, the *Partido Popular* also saw its share of the vote in regional elections in Andalucía, held at the same time as the European elections, increase from 22 per cent to 34 per cent. A further advance in the Basque regional elections of October 1994, in which the PP saw both its vote and seats won nearly double (albeit, from a low base), confirmed José María Aznar as a serious challenger to the hitherto unassailable Felipe González (see Figure 8.1).

Party Finances: Catalyst to Corruption?

The financing of political parties became a central issue in Spanish politics during the early 1990s. In theory, parties are bound by a series of laws on funding which restrict them to the proceeds of public

FIGURE 8.1
**Percentage share of votes by national parties
in general elections, 1977–93**

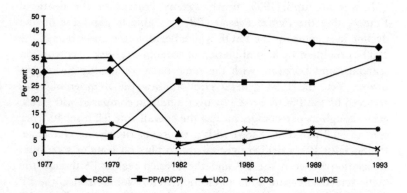

Key:
PSOE   Partido Socialista Obrero Español
PP(AP/CP)   Partido Popular (Alianza Popular/Coalición Popular)
UCD   Unión de Centro Democrático
CDS   Centro Democrático y Social
IU/PCE   Izquierda Unida/Partido Comunista de España

subsidies, members' dues and strictly limited donations. According to
the terms of the decree-law on electoral organisation of March 1977,
the state defrays expenses incurred by parties during electoral
campaigns according to their results, measured primarily in terms
of seats won. Such an *a posteriori* system clearly has an in-built
tendency to favour larger parties, as well as those whose close
relations with the financial world allows them to seek credit advances
(Cotarelo, 1992: 306–7). Critics have also argued that it undermines
the principle of all votes being of equal worth, since the electoral
system has a crucial impact on which parties are able to win seats
(Alvarez Conde, 1990: 74–5). Subsequent legislation – the 1978 Law
on Political Parties, the 1985 Electoral Law and the 1987 Law on the
Financing of Political Parties – sought to ensure clearer guidelines
and, above all, transparency. In particular, the 1987 law distinguished between public and private sources of finance and charged
the independent *Tribunal de Cuentas* (Audit Commission) with
auditing party accounts.

In practice, political parties have systematically by-passed the legal restrictions on funding. In spite of the introduction of official audits – a response to concern over unexplained sources of income – the *Cortes* is ultimately responsible for enforcing the law; until the early 1990s, audits were rubber-stamped even if they indicated clear financial irregularities. It took a series of major scandals in the late 1980s and early 1990s to reveal that the leading parties not only ran up huge debts, but increasingly engaged in what has been termed 'parallel financing'.[5] In essence, parallel financing involves a trade-off between money and favours. Whilst the full scale of its existence in Spain remains unclear, the issue of political corruption became an almost incessant theme of political reportage after 1989. Particular attention was focused on the ruling PSOE, which stood accused of engaging in systematic abuse of its hold on power and distorting the democratic process through the use of what might be termed 'bureaucratic clientelism' (Lyrintzis, 1984) – that is, the handing out of favours and sinecures to party members as well as influence-trafficking.

Though such accusations had simmered in inchoate fashion since the PSOE administration first took power in 1982, they only gained significant momentum after the 1989 general elections; by 1994, the government was widely perceived even by supporters as badly tainted by corruption. Opposition parties – most notably the *Partido Popular* – seized upon the scandals to attack the Socialists' moral integrity. However, the PP had itself been implicated in a corruption probe – the so-called 'Naseiro case' – in April 1990, when two of its leading members in Valencia were accused of raising money for the party through bribery over property development and local government contracts (Martín de Pozuelo *et al.*, 1994: 77–83). Those involved were obliged to resign from the PP, although they were acquitted on a technicality when the case came to trial in 1992.[6]

During the early 1990s, the financing of political parties became a source of major controversy in Spanish politics and the probity of politicians and political parties – especially the Socialists – was repeatedly called into question as the issue of corruption became virtually the only focus of political debate and analysis. After much prevarication, the Socialist government launched a series of anti-corruption initiatives in the summer of 1994. These included the creation of a special prosecutor's office, increased powers for the *Tribunal de Cuentas*, and the introduction of tougher penalties for malfeasance in office. In addition, after staving off opposition calls for an inquiry into the allegations against the PSOE, the government agreed to set up a parliamentary commission to investigate the financing of *all* political parties.

One of the principal reasons for corrupt practices is that political parties are unable to meet the ever-greater financial costs imposed by the electoral process. Since the return of democracy, referenda and/or general, regional, local or European elections have taken place every year, imposing a massive burden on party resources (see Exhibit 8.2). In addition, the major parties maintain local headquarters throughout Spain, staffed by paid officials, in spite of the fact that they have very low memberships (see chapter 9). With advertising and access to the mass media central to political success, parties find themselves waging ever-more costly battles to maintain their profile even between elections. In short, political parties are over-extended and under-resourced, which leads to the search for funds from any available source (Esteban, 1992: 79–88). As is universally the case, those parties in power (whether at national, regional or local level) and able to peddle influence are the ones faced by both temptation and opportunity.

However, claims by political opponents, prominent journalists, and Church leaders that corruption had plumbed new depths in Spain under the PSOE were decidedly exaggerated. Both the Franco regime and the UCD government of Adolfo Suárez were notoriously involved in corrupt practices; indeed, systematic corruption was one of the central pillars of the dictatorship, ranging from the all-pervasive black market of its early years to massive financial scandals such as the *Matesa* case in 1969. Urban and real estate developments were also a highly profitable source of backhanders and kickbacks for local officials and favoured companies. None the less, the *Filesa* case and other scandals involving the PSOE thoroughly undermined the Socialists' oft-repeated claims to moral integrity and promoted justified cynicism on the part of much of the electorate. Ironically enough, the PSOE itself was responsible for the 1987 legislation under which its affairs were subsequently scrutinised by the *Tribunal de Cuentas*.

New Social Movements and the Crisis of Representation

Throughout the established European democracies, political parties are facing increasing difficulties in their efforts to act as representative organisations (Lawson and Merkl, 1988). On the one hand, there is

EXHIBIT 8.2

Electoral consultations in Spain, 1976–94

Year	Referenda	General elections	Regional elections	Municipal elections	European elections
1976	* Political Reform				
1977		*			
1978	* Constitution				
1979	Autonomy Statutes: Euskadi Cataluña	*		*	
1980	Autonomy Statute: Galicia Autonomy initiative: Andalucía		Euskadi Cataluña		
1981	Autonomy Statute: Andalucía				
1982		*	Andalucía		
1983			13 CC.AA.[a]	*	
1984			Euskadi Cataluña		
1985			Galicia		
1986	* NATO	*	Andalucía Euskadi	*	
1987			13 CC.AA.[a]	*	*
1988			Cataluña		
1989		*	Galicia		*
1990			Andalucía Euskadi		
1991			13 CC.AA.[a]	*	
1992			Cataluña		
1993		*	Galicia		
1994			Andalucía Euskadi		*

* denotes election was nationwide.
[a] CC.AA. = *Comunidades Autónomas* (Autonomous Communities)

evidence that young voters in particular are disillusioned with party politics, preferring to abstain at elections; on the other, there has been a rise of so-called 'new social movements', whose political concerns find no outlet in the traditional structures of parliamentary politics. New social movements first emerged in the USA during the 1960s, associated with such single-issue campaigns as the anti-Vietnam protest movement and the struggle for black civil rights. In Europe, they have encompassed peace movements and environmental concerns, as well as feminism.

In Spain, of course, the anti-Franco struggle dominated the radical politics of the late 1960s and early 1970s. Democracy had first to be established before it could be found wanting, and new social movements emerged rather later in the Iberian peninsula than in northern Europe. However, the later 1980s and early 1990s saw peace campaigners and environmental groups begin to make an impact on Spanish politics (although women's groups remained more marginal in a society where *machista* attitudes ran deep). The catalyst to this development was the anti-NATO campaign of the mid-1980s, a key issue in the disillusionment felt by many on the left with the Socialist administration of Felipe González. From out of the anti-NATO protest movement grew the coalition *Izquierda Unida* (United Left), which sought to provide a political focus for a wide variety of voluntarist movements which did not necessarily identify with Spain's established social and political forces.

However, *Izquierda Unida* has been faced since its inception by a conundrum over its central political purpose. Dominated by the Communist Party, it has remained committed to participation in the electoral process, seeking to compete with traditional parties on their own political ground. Yet, for all its protestations that it is not a political party in the traditional sense, such 'conventional' involvement runs the risk of alienating precisely those new social movements whose members it is trying to attract (Heywood, 1994a). The challenge posed to traditional parties by new social movements is less one of ideology than of political purpose: they have arisen in response to a perceived decline in the parties' ability to perform their functions effectively. Single-issue movements and special interest groups have sought to intervene where parties have failed in their traditional role of providing linkage, in terms of either participation, policy responsiveness, resource allocation and/or control.

Indeed, it could be argued that political parties and the electoral process no longer play the dominant role in democratic systems they once did. Primary responsibility for major areas of policy-making has increasingly been devolved or abandoned to interest groups, bureaucratic planners or specialised agencies. Concurrently, much of the parties' traditional function of political communication and agenda-setting has been taken over by the mass media. Protest against traditional political parties stems to a large extent from their manifest inability to perform effectively the central role they once did. The problem is compounded when party officials are seen to be unaccountable or corrupt.

In the face of such perceived shortcomings on the part of mainstream political parties, there has been a growth in organisations with more narrowly-defined concerns, as well as single-issue groups. The rise of regional parties can also be seen in part as a response to the failure of national parties to persuade the electorate of their continued effectiveness. Similarly, environmental groups have been able to identify a central issue of concern to many citizens, although the impact of such groups has tended to be limited on account of their fissiparous nature. Prior to the 1993 general elections, nineteen such organisations – including groups of anarchist, marxist and nationalist provenance – came together to establish *Los Verdes* (The Greens). Modelled on a confederal structure, *Los Verdes* claimed the inheritance of emancipatory movements which included 'ecologism, pacifism, feminism and alternative movements in general', arguing that 'traditional parties are bureaucratic machines which represent very few people' (*El País international*, 1 February 1993).

Another manifestation of the crisis of representation facing mainstream parties has been the emergence of maverick individuals on the political stage. At the 1989 European elections, José María Ruiz-Mateos won two seats with over 600 000 votes for his eponymous political grouping. A right-wing financier, the colourful though sinister Ruiz-Mateos had been on the run from Spanish justice since the PSOE's sequestration of his massive *Rumasa* business empire in early 1983. Faced with various corruption charges, Ruiz-Mateos had finally been extradited to Spain after more than two years abroad, but had several times given the police the run-around by escaping custody in bizarre circumstances – on one occasion he strolled out of the High Court having donned dark glasses and a false moustache.

In the 1989 Euro-elections, in which Ruiz-Mateos sought by winning a seat to obtain immunity from prosecution, his most effective campaigning stratagem turned out to be punching in the face, in front of television cameras, the former minister responsible for expropriating *Rumasa*, Miguel Boyer. This somewhat unconventional move was supported by his daughter, Belén, who threw a cream pie in the face of Boyer's wife, Isabel Preysler (Heywood, 1989: 326). During the 1993 general elections, in which Ruiz-Mateos stood in Madrid as part of his tireless campaign to win back the companies of which he claimed he was robbed, he went into hiding after it was reported by his team that he had been shot at.

Rather more serious than the obsessive Ruiz-Mateos was the political protagonism of Jesús Gil y Gil. A hugely controversial self-publicist, the corpulent Gil – property developer, former convict, and chairman of *Atlético Madrid* football club – launched his rise to prominence from the platform of local politics in Marbella, of which he became mayor in 1991. His unconventional, and somewhat simplistic, approach to politics was in a similar vein to that of other self-made tycoons, such as Ross Perot in the USA. With a party named GIL (*Grupo Independiente Liberal*), Jesús Gil based his campaigns on tirades against Socialist profligacy, the big banks, corruption and prostitution, and promised to wage war against criminals and drug dealers. The message had a clear resonance in the recession-hit resort of Marbella, where the GIL astonished even themselves at the 1991 municipal elections by taking 21 seats out of 25. However, prior to the 1993 general elections – at which the GIL put up candidates throughout Andalucía – the autocratic Gil was again convicted of fraud and debarred from standing for office.

Although the rise of single-issue campaigns and maverick individualists does not presage the disintegration of the party system, it does undermine to some extent the seriousness of Spain's political process. Populists like Jesús Gil can mask the complexity of modern political administration, as shown in his remark that 'I have shown that politics is common sense. Ideology has collapsed – the traditional parties have failed. Populism is to return democracy to the people it's been stolen from'. In reality, populism is often an insidious precursor to the derogation of democracy, particularly in countries where a democratic civic culture has not been well-established. In Spain, democracy is sufficiently secure to withstand the periodic emergence of characters like Gil and Ruiz-Mateos, but the support they enjoy reflects real disillusion with mainstream political parties. The danger lies in the risk of political fragmentation if the support-base of national parties continues to shrink, in contrast to that of regional parties and single-issue groups.

9

Political Parties: Devalued Defenders of Democracy

During nearly forty years of dictatorship under General Franco, party political activity was illegal. Inevitably, this fact had a significant impact on the nature of the political parties which emerged in the post-Franco democracy. Even those parties which could claim some form of continuous existence through the dark years of dictatorship – the *Partido Comunista de España* (PCE) and the *Partido Socialista Obrero Español* (PSOE) – had, effectively, to be recreated under the conditions of democracy.

The Peculiarity of Political Parties in Spain

In broad terms, Spanish political parties are characterised by three distinctive features: low levels of membership reflecting a lack of rootedness in society, a high degree of personalism, and a tendency towards ideological imprecision. To a greater or lesser extent, all of these features are related to the legacy of the Franco regime: forty years of dictatorship had inhibited the assumption of individual responsibility, the taking of organisational initiatives, and collective action. In short, there existed neither the tradition nor the experience of associative mechanisms which are central to the functioning of a democratic party system. Not only did democracy have to be established, but the civic culture necessary to sustain it had also to be nurtured.

Political parties thus faced a double challenge in post-Franco Spain: they had both to support the establishment of a democratic culture and to forge their own identity within it. However, there was little time to sink roots in society: parties were legalised just months – or even weeks, in the case of the Communist Party – before the first elections of June 1977. Electoral success inevitably became a more immediate priority than the development of a mass membership. Votes were the first objective; party structures could develop later. Unsurprisingly, there was an explosion of new political parties seeking to capitalise on the new political freedoms: over 300 parties contested the 1977 elections. Even though the number of significant national-level parties was soon reduced to just three or four, in 1986 there still remained over 200 officially-registered parties nationally and a further 300 at regional level (*Anuario El País 1987*: 97–103).[1]

In practice, mass affiliation to the new parties never took place. Compared to a European average figure in the early 1980s of 15 per cent overall party membership, Spain barely reached 6 per cent (Bar Cendón, 1985; Cotarelo, 1992: 304). When the Socialist Party took over 10mn votes (48.4 per cent) in the 1982 elections, it had a membership of just 116,514 (Tezanos, 1992: 46). By the same token, levels of party identification have remained low. It has been argued that Spanish parties went from being elite parties (*partidos de notables*) to vote-maximising parties (*partidos de electores*) without ever being mass-membership parties (*partidos de masas*) (Esteban and López Guerra, 1982: 14; Amodia, 1990). Alternatively, following Lawson and Merkl, it could be said that Spanish parties offer electoral and clientelistic, rather than participatory, linkage to their supporters: party leaders dominate and offer 'favours' in return for votes (Lawson and Merkl, 1988: 13–38).

In Spain, as throughout the developed world, political leaders increasingly appeal directly to voters via television, thereby under-cutting some of the traditional functions of party organisations (Linz and Montero, 1986: 343). Indeed, François-Henry de Virieu has spoken of the emergence of a 'mediacracy', taking over from conventionally defined democracy (Esteban, 1992: 13). The public image of party leaders has in turn assumed an ever greater significance. Adolfo Suárez and Felipe González, the two dominant figures in post-Franco politics, were both consummate television performers. Political parties have become almost exclusively identified with their leading figures, both in popular perception and in media coverage. Concentration on personalities, rather than issues and party programmes, has been a marked feature of much political reportage and commentary in Spain.

The importance accorded party leaders is reflected in the internal organisation of the major political parties. In spite of a Constitutional injunction (Article 6) that parties must be internally democratic, strictly regulated hierarchical command structures are the norm, with little room for independent initiatives by the rank and file membership (Esteban, 1992: 75–8). The attempt to impose 'discipline' and party unity is common to all the parties, though it has met with varying degrees of success. In general, control can be most effectively exercised via electoral success (at both national and regional level), both through the manipulation of party lists and appointments to party-nominated posts. Thus, a combination of political power and small party memberships allows the leaders of successful parties to dispense patronage to loyal backers. The reverse side of this coin, however, is that excluded aspirants to positions of influence are apt to engage in damaging intrigue.

Most Spanish parties conform to Roberto Michels' 'iron law of oligarchy', according to which organisational structures inevitably concentrate power in the hands of a small leading group. Unsurprisingly, changes of party leadership in Spain have usually provoked a sense of crisis rather than continuity. The suggestion by Felipe González that he would stand down from the PSOE leadership after the 1989 general elections unleashed such a disruptive struggle within the party over the succession that he was obliged to rescind his decision. The right-wing PP was similarly plunged into disarray following the resignation of its founder and leader, Manuel Fraga Iribarne, in December 1986. Just over a year later, he was requested to resume control and restore order. The contrast with both the Conservative Party in Britain and the Labour Party in Australia in the late 1980s – when the replacement of Margaret Thatcher and Bob Hawke respectively whilst in their third terms as prime minister was swift and clinical – could hardly be more stark.

Personal tensions and rivalries abound within all the main parties. Again, whilst such developments are hardly unique to Spain, the striking feature of the Spanish case is the scale on which they have occurred. The tendency of support networks to develop around leading figures is reflected in references to party 'barons' and 'caliphs', often associated with particular regions. In the PSOE, for example, Andalucía has been seen almost as the personal fiefdom of the deputy leader, Alfonso Guerra, whose rivals – such as Joaquín

Leguina in Madrid, Joan Lerma in Valencia or Raimon Obiols in Catalonia – have far smaller power bases.

The *Partido Popular* has been no less riven by personalistic tensions involving rival aspirants to positions of influence. The very founders of the party in 1976, all ex-Francoist dignitaries, were known collectively as the '*siete magníficos*' (magnificent seven); within months, however, deep divisions had become apparent, and by 1979 only Manuel Fraga remained of the original seven (Preston, 1986: 108; Esteban and López Guerra, 1982: 160–71). The party's subsequent development was punctuated by a succession of leadership crises, resignations and power struggles. Other parties, at both national and regional level, have been similarly affected. The importance which continues to attach to individual leaders might be seen as vaguely redolent of Spain's *caciquista* heritage, in which patronage networks underlay the political organisation of the state.

Linked to this dominance of individuals within party organisations has been a somewhat cavalier attitude towards ideological consistency. A number of leading political figures have engaged in spectacular political shifts in their search for a springboard to political influence. The political trajectory of Adolfo Suárez, for instance, was extraordinarily erratic. Suárez's gradual disillusionment with factionalism in the ruling *Unión de Centro Democrático* (UCD) led to his establishing a new party, the *Centro Democrático y Social* (CDS) in 1982. In its first five years of existence, the CDS tried to carve out a distinctive centre-left identity, then allied in municipal elections with Fraga's right-wing *Alianza Popular* against the Socialists, before claiming to stand to the left of the PSOE at the 1987 European elections. Thereafter, in 1990, Suárez – elected a year earlier as president of the Liberal and Progressive International – entered an informal pact with the Socialists, together with the Basque and Catalan nationalist parties, before resigning as party leader two years later and abandoning politics altogether (Sarasqueta, 1991). Not for nothing was Suárez referred to as '*un chusquero de la política*' (political foot-soldier).

Similarly, Francisco Fernández Ordóñez – foreign affairs minister in the Socialist government until shortly before his death in 1992 and one of the most widely respected of Felipe González's cabinet members – had served under both the Franco regime and as a minister in Adolfo Suárez's UCD government before creating the *Partido de Acción Democrática* (PAD) and subsequently joining the PSOE in 1982. Ramón Tamames, a noted economist and academic, was a leading figure in the Communist Party until his expulsion in the early 1980s, whereafter he joined various organisations en route to Suárez's ideologically indeterminate CDS. Jorge Verstrynge, one time secretary-general of the *Alianza Popular* who had entertained ambitions in the mid-1980s of succeeding Fraga as its leader, was to be found by the end of the decade seeking to join the Socialist Party. Such instances of what might be termed 'ideological slippage' may have led to confusion on the part of the electorate, but they reflect the attempt by all mainstream political forces to colonise the centre-ground.

Whilst individuals and political parties may have engaged in labyrinthine ideological maneouvrings, the Spanish electorate has remained steadfastly in the centre. Moderation has been the ideological watchword of Spanish party politics since the transition to democracy (see chapter 8). Yet, when the first post-Franco democratic elections were held in June 1977, the PSOE defined itself as Marxist and was seen as one of the most radical Socialist parties in Europe, the PCE was widely expected to win considerable support, Fraga's *Alianza Popular* was seen by most voters as quasi-Francoist, and only the confused amalgam which made up the UCD explicitly claimed centrist credentials. By 1982, however, parties of both left and right had moved to fill the gap created by the UCD's impending disintegration. The origins and details of this ideological repositioning can best be analysed by considering more closely each of the major parties in turn. Although the left-right continuum is a somewhat artificial device – and is arguably of declining relevance in an age of ideological uncertainty – it remains a useful framework for analysis (Toharia, 1989: 85); for all the evidence that ideological distinctions are becoming increasingly blurred, the major parties still tend to see themselves in terms of their location on left or right of the political spectrum.

The 'Historic' Parties of the Left

The Partido Socialista Obrero Español: from Marxism to Modernisation

The PSOE dominated Spanish politics for over a decade after its crushing victory in the 1982 general elections. Under the leadership of Felipe González, it oversaw Spain's re-emergence onto the international stage under the leitmotiv of modernisation (see Exhibit 9.1). The party itself, though, was far from a modern creation. Under the leadership of its founding father, Pablo Iglesias, a dour socialist ascetic who dominated the party from 1879 until his death in 1925, the PSOE was hampered by both organisational inflexibility and theoretical poverty. A tension between revolutionary rhetoric and reformist political practice, divorced from any effective analysis of the socio-economic situation through which Spain was passing, continued to characterise the party up until the Civil War (1936–9) (Heywood, 1990). Divided and outmanoeuvred during the conflict, the PSOE was left broken and defeated by the time General Franco marched into Madrid (Graham, 1991).

Obsessed by the idea that the only way to remove Franco was through concerted international pressure, the PSOE seemed caught in a time warp and drifted ever further into self-absorbed stasis (Gillespie, 1989; Mateos, 1993). From the early 1960s onwards, the PSOE leadership – based in Toulouse since 1947 – found itself increasingly isolated from party militants in Spain. During that decade a number of socialist groups emerged, all of which expressed concern at the failure of the Toulouse-based party to adjust its policies in accordance with the changes occurring in Spanish society. From these new groups, particularly those attached to the so-called Seville–Bilbao–Asturias triangle, emerged most of the leaders who would eventually challenge the exile leadership.

Following a split within the party in 1972, official recognition was granted by the Socialist International to the 'young Turks' of the interior; in October 1974 at Suresnes, Felipe González was elected, after some negotiation, to the post of first secretary (later renamed secretary general). The PSOE's XXVII Congress in December 1976 adopted a radical posture, rejecting 'any accommodation to capitalism or simple reform of the system.' The vision of a classless society, in which the state apparatus would be replaced by self-management, thus appeared fixed in the party's long-term horizon. There were two principal reasons for the PSOE adopting such a stance. First, the explicit embrace of Marxism as a feature of the party's identity allowed PSOE leaders to present an image of radical opposition to Francoism which would match that of their rivals in the Communist Party. In 1976, the PCE was expected to dominate the left, in a manner similar to the Communist Party in Italy. By espousing the doctrine of Marxism, the PSOE sought to negotiate with the PCE on equal terms and to avoid the inferiority complex

EXHIBIT 9.1

Felipe González

Felipe González Márquez, Spanish prime minister since his crushing victory in the general elections of October 1982, is one of the country's leading political figures in the twentieth century.

Born in Sevilla (Andalucía) on 5 March, 1942, he first joined the PSOE in 1964, after having been a member of the Socialist Youth movement. Having studied economy and law at Sevilla, and later at Louvain in Belgium, in 1968 González set up a labour law practice in the Andalucían capital. Together with his friend and subsequent first lieutenant, Alfonso Guerra, González began writing for the PSOE's newspaper, *El Socialista*, and the pair soon established a reputation for trenchant arguments and a highly critical attitude towards the party leadership. Repeated interference and pressure from the exiled executive led to their resignations, followed in 1974 by a successful assault on the existing leadership.

Once established in the new executive, González and Guerra consolidated their position. Guerra became editor of *El Socialista*, and González moved to Madrid in 1975, where he largely bypassed the existing PSOE organisation and set up his own party machinery, aided by Miguel Boyer (later to become economy minister in the first González administration). One key to their success was unity and discipline. González was able to attract loyalty and support on the basis of his undoubted political talents. Possessed of great intelligence, he was also highly articulate and charismatic – all vital attributes for an aspiring democratic leader. Equally important, in Alfonso Guerra he had the perfect partner. A meticulous organiser, Guerra operated behind the scenes to set up and run a dynamic party machine.

As prime minister, González dominated Spanish politics; his command of parliamentary debates was often magisterial. His first period in office saw the consolidation of Spanish democracy and the full incorporation of the country into the international community, as Spain joined the EC and confirmed its membership of NATO. His second administration (1986–9) reaped the economic rewards of these developments and saw Spain enjoy dramatic levels of growth. However, González appeared to become disillusioned with the burdens of office in this period. His presence in the Spanish parliament became increasingly infrequent, and he concentrated ever more on international affairs, apparently seeking to assume a role similar to that of the French president.

Often looking weary, or even bored, with domestic political matters, González announced that the 1989 general election would be the last in which he led the Socialist Party. He was forced to retract this remark as a major struggle developed within the party over the succession. Indeed, his third administration (1989–93) was marked by internal party strife, exacerbated by growing evidence of corruption. After the enforced resignation of Alfonso Guerra – implicated in a scandal involving his brother, Juan – as deputy prime minister in 1991, relations between the two PSOE leaders deteriorated sharply. González associated himself ever more closely with the liberal market-oriented version of social democracy espoused by his controversial economy minister, Carlos Solchaga, against the more populist leftist rhetoric of Guerra and his followers. As the boom of the mid- to late 1980s was replaced by recession in the early 1990s, arguments within the PSOE became increasingly bitter. González remained identified, however, as the party's greatest electoral asset. This was dramatically demonstrated in the 1993 general election, in which he took full charge of the PSOE campaign and defied opinion polls to pull off an unexpected victory.

Following the 1993 elections, González came under fire for presiding over a government which seemed mired in corruption. An escape route seemed to open as the Spanish premier was widely tipped to succeed Jacques Delors as President of the European Commission in 1995, especially after the British veto of Jean Luc Dehaene. However, González refused all approaches, insisting that his duty lay in rooting out corruption and in steering Spain through the challenge of meeting the convergence terms for European economic and monetary union.

which might derive from its less visible role in opposing the Franco dictatorship (Juliá, 1990).

Second, Marxism represented almost a badge of identity for the left-wing, anti-Franco opposition: it implied a wholesale rejection not only of the Francoist political system, but also of the capitalist values which underlay it. Moreover, Marxism chimed with the ideological tenor of the time, reflected in the prominence accorded in progressive circles to vogue 'neo-Marxist' thinkers such as Gramsci, Lukács, Althusser, and members of the Frankfurt School. This was a period in which capitalism was held to be on the verge of collapse, whether through legitimation or fiscal crises. The PSOE's adoption of an explicit Marxist self-image was thus seen at the time as neither particularly noteworthy nor surprising. It also helped fix the PSOE as the central focus of the myriad socialist groups and parties which sought to challenge the PCE's anticipated hegemony on the left.

The 1977 election results, however, in which the PSOE won 28.5 per cent of the vote, ended the Socialists' marginal status. Equally, by establishing the party's dominance on the left, they removed a major element of the rationale for its having embraced Marxism in such an explicit manner. In the aftermath of the 1977 elections, a shift in the PSOE leadership's political line started to become apparent: emphasis was now placed on consolidating the new democratic system and the party's self-definition as Marxist came to be seen as an obstacle to further electoral progress. By 1981, the need to defend and deepen Spain's fragile democracy against threats posed by both separatists and the military had become a key feature of Socialist thought. To defend democracy, the Socialists had to win power; to win power, they required sufficient electoral support. It was this simple calculation which lay at the heart of the move away from Marxism.

For all his radical reputation at the start of the 1970s, in May 1978 González shocked party activists by casually announcing to a group of journalists in a Barcelona restaurant that he would propose dropping the party's Marxist label at its next congress. The PSOE's XXVIII Congress in May 1979, which followed modest gains in the general elections of March, proved critical to the party's future development. True to his promise, González proposed removing Marxism from the party statutes, but met with considerable opposition from radical party activists. Defeated in a vote, the PSOE leader stunned followers and opponents alike by resigning, supported by the entire executive. Not expecting such an outcome, the so-called *sector crítico* (which would become *Izquierda Socialista* in late 1980) had no candidate to replace González, and the party was left in the control of a *comisión gestora* (steering committee) pending an Extraordinary Congress scheduled for September 1979.

In the intervening period, González toured Spain arguing the merits of his position. His diligence was rewarded at the September congress, when he was returned as PSOE secretary-general with overwhelming support. One key to his success was an organisational change, masterminded by Alfonso Guerra at the XXVIII Congress, which dramatically reduced the number of delegations (50 as opposed to 1,000) and introduced a form of block vote. Guerra had control over the largest delegation, the Andalucían, which controlled 25 per cent of the total vote. The manner in which González was returned immensely increased his stature within the party. Organisational control and strict party discipline were central to the PSOE's success during the 1980s – but, in return for the rewards of political success, the leadership demanded uncritical support from party members.

However, the iron control exercised by the PSOE leadership and the refusal to brook internal dissent provoked ever-greater criticism from disaffected militants, several of whom – such as Pablo Castellano and Ricardo García Damborenea – eventually left the party. Nevertheless, the disaffection of a critical minority was easily outweighed by the loyalty of the majority of party members. Such loyalty was the more easily ensured by the small size of party membership and the ample opportunities for political rewards afforded by electoral victory after 1982 (see Table 9.1). Patronage became a basic practice in the hold of PSOE leaders over militants: it has been estimated that about 50,000 public posts were given to PSOE members between 1982 and 1984, during which time the party's total membership reached only just over 150,000 (Pérez-Díaz, 1987). In addition, the speed with which the PSOE achieved its national pre-eminence ensured that local and provincial networks were established only after the centre had become firmly entrenched, making it easier for the leadership to impose its decisions and guarantee discipline (Juliá, 1990).

The PSOE's formal adoption and subsequent abandonment of Marxism must be seen in terms of an electoral strategy designed to win power.[2] Having established itself as the hegemonic force on the left, the party targeted the centre ground of Spanish politics and sought to displace the crumbling *Unión de Centro Democrático* (UCD), which had held power in Spain since 1977. To do so, the PSOE eschewed its recently rediscovered Marxist heritage and set about presenting a moderate, centrist image. Party membership and support reflected the changes in society which had taken place in the 1960s and 1970s: just 19 per cent of the PSOE's 10mn votes in the 1982 election came from the manual working-class, while 32 per cent of new party members in 1983 were professionals, office workers and technicians. All vestiges of radicalism were jettisoned as the PSOE became a modern, catch-all political party in which ideology was secondary to pragmatic management of the economy. The success of this strategy – at least up until the early 1990s – was demonstrated by the PSOE's dominance of Spanish political life.

However, after the PSOE's third consecutive electoral triumph in 1989, the party's air of invulnerability faded rapidly. A breakdown in its relationship with the union movement (most notably the *Unión General de Trabajadores* (UGT), which had been created by the PSOE in 1888), internal divisions over economic policy between market-oriented liberals and proponents of a more populist leftist stance, and the emergence of major corruption scandals, all contributed to a sense that the party had lost its sense of direction. As the benefits of the boom years were replaced in the early 1990s by the ravages of recession, the PSOE's internal discipline began to break down. After his resignation from government in 1991, Guerra and his supporters engaged in bitter attacks on the economy minister, Carlos Solchaga, who continued to enjoy the full backing of Felipe González. Collaboration between González and Guerra was gradually displaced by confrontation, and support for the PSOE fell markedly. Although the PSOE leadership attempted to present a united front during the 1993 election campaign, González immediately asserted his authority after winning the election by proposing Solchaga as parliamentary leader and spokesperson.[3] As a result, bitter division ensued within the party between '*guerristas*' and '*renovadores*', according to whether they backed the leftist rhetoric of the deputy leader or the market-oriented policies favoured by Felipe González – a far cry from the organisational unity and discipline which had characterised the PSOE during the 1980s.

Partido Comunista de España: Refusing to Die

The collapse of communism at the end of the 1980s had a profound impact on all west European communist parties, prompting several of

TABLE 9.1

Evolution of membership, PSOE and UGT

Year	Groups	Membership[a]	UGT membership
1888 (I Congress)	16		3,355
1890 (II Congress)	23		3,896
1892 (III Congress)	37		7,170
1894 (IV Congress)	42		8,555
1899 (V Congress)	55		15,264
1902 (VI Congress)	78	4,288	40,087
1905 (VII Congress)	144	6,155[b]	46,485
1908 (VIII Congress)	115	6,000	39,668
1912 (IX Congress)	198	13,000	128,914
1915 (X Congress)	238	14,332	112,194
1918 (XI Congress)	233	14,588[c]	89,601
1919 (Extraordinary Congress)	338	42,113	–
1920 (Extraordinary Congress)	536	52,897	211,342
1921 (Extraordinary Congress)	480	45,477	208,170
1927 (Extraordinary Congress)	221	8,083	223,349
1928 (Extraordinary Congress)	219	9,001	230,279
1931 (Extraordinary Congress)	953	25,000	958,451
1932 (Extraordinary Congress)	981	75,133	1,041,599
1976 (XXVII Congress)[d]	150	9,141	6,974
1979 (XXVIII Congress)	2,402	101,082	1,459,793
1981 (XXIX Congress)	2,473	97,320	1,375,000
1984 (XXX Congress)	3,538	153,076	600,853
1988 (XXXI Congress)	3,962	213,028	665,920
1990 (XXXII Congress)	4,375	273,535	–
1994 (XXXIII Congress)			

Notes:

[a] Accurate membership figures for the PSOE's early years are impossible to ascertain.

[b] 1904 figures from Instituto de Reformas Sociales, *Estadística de la asociación obrera* (Madrid, 1907).

[c] Tezanos gives figures of 223 groups and 30,630 members. The figures used here follow Juan José Morato, *El Partido Socialista Obrero* (Madrid, 1981, p. 301; first published, 1918).

[d] Figures for the Congresses held in exile (13 in total) have not been included, since they are of limited value or practical relevance.

Source: adapted from Tezanos (1989: 438–9) and (1992: 46)

them to abandon the very name and relaunch as socialist organisations (Bull and Heywood, 1994). In Spain, however, the *Partido Comunista de España* (PCE) had already undergone a near fatal crisis in the late 1970s and early 1980s. The PCE reached its electoral nadir in 1982 when it failed to muster even 4 per cent of the vote. Thereafter, its gradual re-emergence as a significant player on the political stage was intimately linked with the launch of a wide-ranging alliance of left-oriented groups, *Izquierda Unida* (IU, United Left), which owed its origins to an anti-NATO platform first established at time of the 1986 referendum. As the dominant organisation within IU, the PCE discovered a much-needed new political impetus.

In fact, it had been widely anticipated that the PCE would assume a rather more imposing dominance on the Spanish left after the death of General Franco. The PCE leadership had stressed both the party's opposition to Franco and its links to an emerging west European communist order which claimed ever greater distance from the CPSU in Moscow. Santiago Carrillo, secretary-general of the PCE since 1960, was a leading exponent of 'eurocommunism', hosting a summit with colleagues from Italy and France in March 1977. As the June elections approached, confidence within the PCE was riding high: the party looked first to establish itself as the cornerstone of democracy and then lead a steady advance towards socialism.

The dream was cruelly shattered. The PCE fared badly in the elections, winning just under 10 per cent of the vote, well below its Socialist rivals. Almost immediately, the party began to break up. By the time of the 1982 elections, acrimonious internecine struggles within the leadership, a collapse in membership, and a loss of prestige amongst the intellectual elite which had been drawn to the PCE by its opposition to Franco, had all combined to leave the party on the verge of extinction (Morán, 1985).

Three main reasons explain the PCE's precipitous collapse. The first two relate less to the PCE itself than to the context of Spain's transition to democracy. In terms of image, the PCE leadership – associated principally with the Civil War veterans Carrillo and the legendary '*Pasionaria*' (Dolores Ibárruri) – looked out of touch compared to the youthful and telegenic Felipe González and Adolfo Suárez. In a period when consensus and moderation were the watchwords of democratic progress, the PCE leadership provided an uncomfortable reminder for many of bitter division.

Secondly, the party's freedom of political manoeuvre was severely circumscribed by the need to avoid antagonising the *poderes fácticos*, especially the military. The PCE's legalisation in April 1977 was made possible only by Carrillo's promise of extensive compromise: effectively, the party allowed the terms of its role in the transition to be dictated by former Franco regime apparatchiks such as Suárez. Although it could be argued that the PCE had little option over this, it is equally the case that many communist militants felt betrayed by the scale of accommodation.

The third reason relates more directly to developments within the PCE. Eurocommunism became a double-edged sword: on the one hand, it appalled those traditional militants for whom communism derived its identity by reference to '*la lucha*' (the struggle) and to Moscow; on the other, it promised an exciting avenue for progress to younger militants, many of whom had been involved in the opposition to Franco within Spain. In practice, however, Carrillo was never prepared to relax the rules of democratic centralism. Relations between the PCE in Madrid and its Catalan and Basque

TABLE 9.2

Membership, PCE, 1977–91[a]

1977	201,757
April 1978 (IX Congress)	240,000
July 1981	132,069
December 1983 (XI Congress)	84,652
December 1987	62,342
October 1991	55,000

[a] Reliable figures are virtually impossible to ascertain. The figures given above are those claimed by the PCE, although they have been disputed by some observers. Botella, for instance, believes that the figure for 1978 should be reduced to around 175,000.

In terms of the profile of PCE membership, figures are again difficult to obtain. A report on the delegates who attended the PCE's IX Congress, published in *Nuestra Bandera* 93 (1978), indicated: (i) there was a clear imbalance between men (87 per cent) and women (13 per cent); (ii) that 45 per cent of delegates had joined the party between 1971 and 1978, compared with 32 per cent between 1961 and 1970, 14 per cent between 1940 and 1960, and 9 per cent before 1939; (iii) that occupational categories were industrial workers (39 per cent), non-manual workers (15 per cent), professionals (32 per cent), small businessmen and self-employed (3 per cent), agrarian workers (3 per cent), students (4 per cent) and 'others' (4 per cent).

Source: based on Botella, (1988: 70); Amodia, (1993: 103, 108, 119).

counterparts became particularly acrimonious as Carrillo, for whom discipline and loyalty were not negotiable, sought to impose his will on the party. Ironically, his attempts to foster an image of moderation and pluralism – for instance by dropping Leninism from the PCE statutes in 1978 – were imposed in a heavy-handed manner. In the context of unrestricted political activity under the new Spanish democracy, a growing number of PCE militants began to question their loyalty. A major haemorrhaging of support had become clear as early as 1978 as membership fell from 201,757 in 1977 to 171,332 a year later. By the start of 1982, it had fallen to under 100,000 (see Table 9.2).

The PCE's electoral performances were no less devastating: in the March 1982 regional elections in Andalucía, a traditional PCE stronghold, the party won just 8 out of 109 seats and saw its vote fall by more than 150,000 from 1979 figures. Similarly, in the general elections of October, the PCE saw its level of support fall by over 1 million votes to just 865,267 (3.9 per cent), leaving it with just four deputies compared with 22 in the outgoing parliament. Carrillo's subsequent resignation caused little surprise, but acrimony and divisions continued under his chosen successor, Gerardo Iglesias. Eventually, Carrillo was expelled and set up his own rival party. By the end of 1985, the PCE appeared in terminal crisis, gaining just over 1 per cent of the votes cast in the Galician regional elections of December.

The issue which proved to be the PCE's salvation was the referendum on NATO membership. Delayed by the PSOE government until the last possible moment in March 1986, the referendum served as a catalyst for an alliance of leftist forces which sought to represent the anti-NATO views of peace campaigners, green groups and feminists. Although the government eventually secured a narrow success on the NATO issue, the alliance remained intact for the general elections of June 1986. A marginal improvement on the PCE's 1982 results, however, was less important than the new sense of direction provided by the initiative. *Izquierda Unida* was officially launched in early 1987, composed of the PCE, the *Pasoc* (a small socialist group which claimed continuity from that sector of the PSOE which had been defeated in 1974), the *Partido Comunista de los Pueblos de España* (established in 1984 by the veteran communist Ignacio Gallego), the tiny Progressive Federation (also established in 1984 by another former PCE member, Ramón Tamames), and various independents. Together they claimed a combined membership of around 100 000, of which the PCE accounted for roughly two-thirds.

Under the leadership of the charismatic Julio Anguita, who replaced Iglesias in 1988, *Izquierda Unida* made steady headway in public opinion polls. In the two major elections of 1989 – European in June and general in October – IU emerged as the only force which could point unequivocally to tangible advances. Ironically, just as communism in Spain seemed to be emerging from a protracted period of crisis, so communism in eastern Europe entered its death throes. IU was severely disconcerted by the changes in eastern Europe, and major divisions soon emerged over the organisation's future direction and the PCE's role within it (Heywood, 1994a). Although overlain by complex regional issues, essentially these divisions crystallised around the question of whether the PCE should continue as an independent entity, relaunch itself as a social democratic party in the manner of the PCI under Achille Occhetto, or dissolve itself into a new political organisation based on IU.

Divisions were further complicated by policy disagreements, most notably over Europe. Whilst support for European union remained high, the IU leadership's opposition to the terms of the Maastricht Treaty did not meet with wholehearted support within the organisation. Anguita, though, as co-ordinator of IU and secretary-general of the PCE, was able to exercise a predominant influence over both of them. His determination that the PCE continue to maintain both its communist and Marxist identity ensured the party's survival, even if its long-term organisational structure and relationship to IU remained unresolved.

The Born-again (and Again) 'New' Right

Partido Popular: Right Back to the Centre

The *Partido Popular* (PP) – founded in 1977 as the *Alianza Popular* (AP), and briefly reconstituted as the *Coalición Democrática*, then the *Coalición Popular*, between 1979 and 1986, before its relaunch in 1988 under its current name – only began to emerge fully from the shadow of its founder and *eminence grise*, Manuel Fraga Iribarne, in the early 1990s. Under the intellectually accomplished but politically volatile Fraga, it was widely held that the AP would remain unelectable. Just as the Communist leader, Santiago Carrillo, prompted unwelcome memories of the Civil War, so Fraga was intimately associated with the Franco regime. Indeed, in 1977–8, fully 69 per cent of the electorate (and 73 per cent of its own voters) saw the AP as a Francoist party, whilst just 33 per cent believed it to be democratic (Montero, 1989: 500). Between the elections of 1977 and 1979 the party saw its support fall from 7.9 per cent to just 6 per cent, a drop of some 400,000 (in spite of a lowering of the voting age to 18) – nearly a million votes fewer than the Communists.

The AP engaged upon a major process of renewal after its III National Congress of December 1979. In a bid to relaunch itself as a catch-all organisation, the party took the strategic decision to refer to itself as 'liberal–conservative', rather than right-wing, adding that it was 'reformist, popular and democratic'. Its political language, however, remained in tune with the traditional values of the Spanish right, with an emphasis on authority, public order, and religion. Moreover, Manuel Fraga's personal dominance was enhanced as the party bolstered the role of its president and relegated the post of secretary general to a position of secondary importance (López Nieto, 1988). Nevertheless, the AP was to capitalise upon the disintegration of the UCD as right-leaning former supporters of the centrist coalition flocked towards Fraga's new model party. The 1982 elections (which the AP contested in collaboration with various regional parties) saw a spectacular rise in the AP's support: it won nearly 5.5 million votes (26 per cent) and 107 deputies. Between 40 and 48 per cent of UCD voters at the 1979 election switched to the AP, which was now able to present itself as the main opposition to the dominant PSOE.

In the aftermath of the elections, there was widespread confidence within the AP that it would soon capture what it believed was the 'natural majority' of centre-right voters in Spain (Fraga, 1983). Instead, however, the AP's failure to make further gains at the 1986 general elections, as well as during various regional elections in the intervening period, prompted speculation that it would never be able to breach its so-called electoral 'ceiling' of 25 per cent of the popular vote. Although precise figures are not available, membership also struggled to reach an estimated maximum level of 200,000 (Colomé and López Nieto, 1989; Amodia, 1990). The party's confused stance over the NATO referendum in March 1986 – when its call for 'active abstention', even though it supported continued membership, was ignored by its own voters – further contributed to a growing sense of stagnation, both political and intellectual.

Fraga himself was identified as the principal obstacle to progress: the apocalyptic tone with which he opposed the PSOE's reform measures struck a discordant note with a large part of the electorate. The small Liberal Party and the christian democrat *Partido Democrático Popular* (PDP), which had contested the 1986 election in coalition with the AP, soon broke their pact with Fraga's party as dissension and division took hold. Moreover, the AP's organisational structure, which elevated its leader's status, allowed few outlets for constructive internal opposition. The introduction at the VII National Congress in 1986 of an open list system for elections to the Executive Committee further promoted discord. Personal disputes and factionalism became rife as would-be leaders manoeuvred to oust the party's founding father from his post. With the party deeply divided and on the verge of financial bankruptcy, Fraga eventually stood down in December 1986 in favour of a youthful lawyer, Antonio Hernández Mancha.

A complete contrast to the belligerent Fraga, the inexperienced and unprepossessing Hernández Mancha attempted to relaunch the AP as part of the 'modern European right'. The new leader proved no match for the PSOE machine, however, and following the disappointment of the 1987 European elections – in which the AP's vote remained stuck at just under 25 per cent – serious splits developed once more within the party. Fraga returned to the helm in 1988, still convinced that the AP could aspire to a 'natural majority' provided it enticed Adolfo Suárez's small liberal party, the *Centro Democrático y Social* (CDS), to join a new partnership. In a bid to construct a broad coalition of conservative, liberal and christian democrat forces, the AP once again relaunched itself – this time as the *Partido Popular*. Suárez, though, remained unimpressed.

An experiment with twin leadership during the European election campaign of June 1989, when the christian democrat former UCD minister, Marcelino Oreja Aguirre, was brought in alongside Fraga to front the PP's campaign with a more moderate image, proved a disappointment. However, regional elections in Galicia in December 1989 offered Manuel Fraga the opportunity to win power in his homeland: a native of Villalba in Lugo, he stood as PP candidate for president of the *Xunta* (regional parliament) and won a comfortable majority (Gibbons, 1990). It is deeply ironic that a man whose entire political career had been spent in the service of a highly centralist right-wing should finally achieve democratic legitimacy through the auspice of a regional election. Nevertheless, Fraga proved to be a dynamic and effective regional leader, able to utilise his high profile and vast political experience to promote the interests of this often overlooked region.

The new leader of the PP was José María Aznar, president of the Castilla y León Autonomous Community. Ratified as party president at the X National Congress in April 1990, Aznar brought into the party's central executive many of his Castilian colleagues, the so-called 'Valladolid clan' – a move which upset several leading party figures. Defeated rivals for the PP leadership, such as Miguel Herrero de Miñón and Isabel Tocino, were vocal in their criticism of Aznar's leadership style, whilst accusations of a lack of internal party democracy and executive dominance echoed criticisms made of the ruling PSOE. Yet Aznar gradually imposed his authority on the party. One of his primary purposes was to distance the PP from its association with the traditional right in Spain, still redolent of intolerance and authoritarianism. In 1990, Aznar sought to claim a christian democratic identity for the PP and announced the party's formal application to join the European Popular Party (PPE) – much to the disquiet of another Spanish member of the PPE, the *Partido Nacionalista Vasco* (PNV), which expressed doubts over the PP's sudden conversion. However, Aznar's credibility was initially undermined by Felipe González's tactic of continuing to deal with Manuel Fraga, a move which the former PP leader did not discourage.

In a bid both to raise his own profile and to capitalise on the growing unpopularity of the Socialist government, Aznar engaged in an unremitting series of media offensives throughout the early 1990s. The PP president continued to stress his liberal and modernising inclinations, expressing antipathy towards the *'derechona clásica'* (traditional far-right) whilst lambasting the PSOE's involvement in corruption scandals. The tactic appeared to reap dividends as the PP, following notable gains in the municipal elections of May 1991, made steady headway in public opinion polls. By 1993, Aznar was widely seen as a likely victor at the general elections, although in the event he was narrowly defeated by Felipe González. However, a clear victory in the June 1994 European elections suggested that the PP could look confidently towards the next general elections in Spain. For the *Partido Popular*, the fundamental achievement of Aznar's leadership was to dissociate the party from its Francoist heritage. Just 22 years old when Franco died in 1975, Aznar escaped the opprobrium reserved for those members of the right who had been more closely involved in the dictatorship.

The Centre: Squeezed into Submission

Following the dramatic collapse of the UCD, the successful colonisation of the centre-ground by the PSOE and, albeit several years later, the PP, placed a premium on new national-level centrist groupings. Former prime minister Adolfo Suárez set up the *Centro Democrático y Social* (CDS) in 1982, but the party failed to take-off in spite of promising briefly to do so in the mid-1980s. The fundamental problem facing the CDS was one shared by all parties which have sought to establish an independent centrist presence: the lack of sufficient available political space (Esteban and López Guerra, 1982: 210).

The problem was reflected in the CDS's remarkable peregrinations during the 1980s. Regional pacts with the right during 1989 to keep out the PSOE followed earlier claims that the party stood to the left of the Socialists. The CDS subsequently entered the so-called 'constitutional bloc' at national level with the Socialist government, in spite of explicit denials that it would do so. In the face of such confusion, several leading party members – concerned at the impression being given of opportunism – left to seek safer shores. By the early 1990s voters had evidently become equally disillusioned with the CDS's constant shifts in political orientation and, after disastrous results in the May 1991 regional elections, Suárez resigned as party leader.

Other centrist parties which emerged from the wreckage of the UCD during 1982 fared even worse. A series of 'liberal clubs' set up during 1981 by members of the UCD formed the basis of the *Partido Democrático Popular* (PDP), which was founded by Oscar Alzaga the following year and subsequently collaborated closely, but briefly, with the *Alianza Popular*. A rival liberal party, the *Partido Democrático Liberal* (PDL), was relaunched in 1982 by Antonio Garrigues Walker, having originally been established by his late brother, Joaquín, but similarly had no significant success. Instead, it made the fatal error of joining the *Partido Reformista Democrático* (PRD), masterminded by Miquel Roca. Both the PDP (renamed *Democracia Cristiana*) and the PDL formally joined the *Partido Popular* in early 1989.

Roca's Reformist Party represented the most ambitious (and most spectacularly unsuccessful) attempt to capture the centre-ground. First conceived in 1984, the so-called '*operación Roca*' was intended to bring together all centrist forces in a new, national-level, organisation. Roca had been a member of the committee which had drafted the 1978 Constitution, and had ever since harboured ambitions of political prominence. Overshadowed in his home region of Catalonia by his more illustrious colleague, Jordi Pujol, Roca saw the PRD – officially launched in November 1984 – as a potential replacement for the defunct UCD. However, in spite of a blaze of publicity, in the general elections of June 1986 the new party failed to capture even 1 per cent of the vote and won no seats: a 'most splendid disaster' (*esplendoroso desastre*) in the sardonic words of Garrigues Walker.

Roca – whose project had been heavily backed by various Spanish banks – was personally unaffected. Having never formally joined the PRD, he was elected in Barcelona as head of the list for Pujol's Catalan nationalist coalition, *Convergència i Unió* (CiU). Conservative by instinct, he had conducted his vicarious campaign for the PRD almost entirely in the Catalan capital, and mainly in the vernacular. Such tactics reflected Roca's realisation that a centrist christian democratic option was unlikely to prosper at national level. Indeed, it is really only at regional level that explicitly centrist political forces have been able to establish a solid presence. Roca's attempt to reproduce the achievement of the CiU at national level simply demonstrated how effectively the major parties have colonised the centre ground in spite of their formal ideological designation.

Regional Parties

One of the clearest trends in Spanish politics since the return to democracy has been the growing importance of regional parties and legislatures. From a peak of 84 per cent of the vote cast in the 1979 and 1982 general elections, national parties saw their share of the vote fall to 78 per cent in 1986 and 74 per cent in 1989. This fall in the national vote can be most clearly seen in the two regions with the strongest sense of national identity, Catalonia and the Basque Country. Whereas in the 1977 general elections, national-level parties took 67.7 per cent of the vote in Catalonia and 51.4 per cent in the Basque Country, by 1989 these figures had fallen to 52.3 per cent and 39.5 per cent respectively (see Table 9.3).

In recognition of this development, most national parties have granted their regional branches considerable autonomy, as in the case of the *Partit del Socialistes de Catalunya* (PSC-PSOE) which, while organically linked to the Madrid-based PSOE according to the terms

TABLE 9.3

**Percentage breakdown of votes in Catalonia and
the Basque Country at General Elections, 1971–93**

	1977	1979	1982	1986	1989	1993
Basque Country						
Regional Parties						
PNV	30.0	27.6	32.9	25.7	20.3	21.2
EE	6.5	8.0	7.9	9.1	9.0	–[a]
HB	–	15.0	15.1	17.0	16.2	14.1
EA	–	–	–	–	11.4	10.0
Total	36.5	50.6	55.9	51.8	56.9	45.3[b]
National Parties	51.4	44.1	44.1	45.8	39.5	47.3
Catalonia						
Regional Parties						
CiU/PDC	17.0	16.4	22.2	3 7.2	38.3	36.1
ERC	4.7	4.1	4.0	2.9	3.2	6.8
Total	21.7	20.5	26.2	40.1	41.5	42.9
National Parties	67.7	69.3	66.4	56.2	52.3	54.3

Key: PNV – *Partido Nacionalista Vasco* (Basque National Party); EE – *Euskadiko Ezkerra* (Basque Left); HB – *Herri Batasuna* (People's Unity, political wing of ETA); EA – *Eusko Ta Alkartasuna* (breakaway from PNV); CiU/PDC – *Convergència i Unió* (Convergence and Unity); ERC – *Esquerra Republicana de Catalunya* (Republic Left of Catalonia).

[a] EE merged with the Basque Socialist Party (PSOE–PSE) in March 1993.

[b] The percentages do not always add up to 100 because only the more important parties have been included in the calculations.

Source: based on Gunther, Sani and Shabad (1989: 311); *Anuario El País 1987, 1990, 1994*; Fundación Friedrich Ebert (1983: 72–3); author's calculations.

of a Unity Protocol (1978), has full sovereignty within Catalonia (Colomé, 1992). A similar arrangement pertains in regard to *Izquierda Unida*: the Catalan version is known as *Iniciativa per Catalunya*, in which the fully independent *Partit Socialista Unificat de Catalunya* (PSUC) – the Catalan Communist Party – plays the leading role. Indeed, in contrast to IU, *Iniciativa per Catalunya* followed the example of Achille Occhetto's Italian Communist Party and in April 1990 formally relaunched itself as a socialist party.

Catalonia: Convergència i Unió

Dominant in Catalan politics since the first autonomous elections of March 1980, the CiU is a conservative coalition made up of the *Convergència Democrática de Catalunya* (CDC), set up in 1974 initially as a social democratic nationalist party, and *Unió Democrática de Catalunya* (UDC), whose origins go back the Second Republic. Headed by Jordi Pujol and Joan Rigol i Roig respectively, the CDC and UDC first came together in 1979 and have maintained a stable, if occasionally tempestuous, political partnership ever since (Walker, 1991). Dominated by Pujol, CiU has strong connections with the Catalan financial centre, and stands primarily for the defence of business interests. For all Pujol's rhetoric about the Catalan nation, it has no pretensions to full independence. Pragmatic to the last, Pujol is mainly interested in ensuring that Catalonia derives the maximum benefit from Spain's system of regional government.

The CiU has managed to appeal successfully in regional elections to a broad cross-section of Catalan voters, winning an absolute majority in all but the first of the four contests held between 1980 and 1992. At national elections, it has steadily closed the gap since 1982 to the PSC–PSOE; by 1989, when CiU won the city of Barcelona for the first time, the two parties were separated in Catalonia by just 90 000 votes and two deputies. Four years later, the PSC–PSOE obtained just one more seat than the CiU in Catalonia.

The only other nationalist force of any significance in Catalonia is the historic *Esquerra Republicana de Catalunya* (ERC), founded in 1931. The political home of Josep Taradellas, the exiled leader of the largely symbolic *Generalitat* during the Franco dictatorship who became a Catalan folk hero, the ERC has consistently adopted a radical nationalist stance. In 1992, it adopted the call for outright Catalan independence and was joined by the remnants of *Terra Lliure*, a former terrorist organisation which had earlier renounced the use of violence.

The Basque Country: Partido Nacionalista Vasco

The *Partido Nacionalista Vasco* (PNV) was founded in 1895 by the ardently nationalist Sabino Arana, and subsequently played an important role in the politics of the Second Republic before being reduced to impotence by the repression of the Franco dictatorship.

Since the post-Franco transition to democracy, the PNV's ideology has developed along christian democratic and centre-right lines; it is similar to that of CiU, although the PNV adopted a more radical stance towards autonomy in the early years of the transition. In 1978, it called on voters to abstain in the referendum on the Constitution, in protest at the document's treatment of the Basque Country's historic 'foral' rights.

The modern PNV has been divided between a traditionalist sector, which claims to represent the legacy of Arana in its concerns with the Basque Country's cultural heritage, and a more aggressively nationalist, but still socially conservative, sector. The party split in 1986, leading to the creation of a rival, non-confessional social democratic centrist grouping, *Eusko Alkartasuna* (EA), under the leadership of Carlos Garaikoetxea, a former president of the Basque regional government. In the regional elections of 1986 – called early on account of the PNV's internal crisis – EA took 16 per cent of the vote and 13 seats, depriving the historic nationalist party of victory for the first time since the establishment of the Basque regional government.

Since then, however, the PNV has again consolidated its position as the leading nationalist force in Basque politics. Obliged to confront the fact that the recreation of a traditional Euskadi was inappropriate to the region's political needs at the end of the twentieth century, the PNV sought to rationalise its ideological position. Appeals to the Basques in exclusively ethnic and cultural terms gave way to more conventional political concerns over the economic regeneration of a region in deep industrial crisis. The PNV sought to develop its relations with bankers, business leaders, and trade unions, and established an effective partnership with the PSOE, with whom it has governed in the Basque Country (with a short break during 1990) since 1986.

Extremist and Anti-System Parties

Given the studied moderation of the Spanish electorate, it is hardly surprising that extremist parties have not prospered since the return of democracy. The extreme right is still too closely associated with the memory of the Franco dictatorship to develop an effective presence in democratic Spain, and has been restricted to such marginal groups as Blas Piñar's *Fuerza Nueva*, an ultra right-wing Catholic organisation created in 1966 but disbanded in 1983, and the neo-fascist *Frente Nacional*, which developed out of *Fuerza Nueva*'s remnants. However, the extreme right in the early 1990s has been associated more with skinhead groups in Spain's major cities than with serious political parties (Ellwood, 1992).

Any success enjoyed by the extreme left has effectively been restricted to the Basque Country, where *Herri Batasuna* (HB, Popular Unity) – widely seen as the political arm of ETA – has won consistent support. Indeed, in contrast to the rest of Spain, the number of Basque voters placing themselves near the centre of the political spectrum fell from 39 per cent in 1976 to 20 per cent just two years later (Gunther, 1992: 79) – a development explained by the intensity of the political struggle in the region, where left–right divisions are overlain by cleavages over centralism–independence and democracy–violence.

HB was created in 1978 by the veteran nationalist, Telesforo Monzón (who had been expelled from the PNV a year earlier), as an electoral coalition which brought together various parties associated with ETA (Sullivan, 1988). An unlikely admixture of seemingly incompatible groups, HB prospered nevertheless: its support rose steadily from 150 000 votes in 1979 to nearly 220 000 in 1989, before falling back slightly in the 1993 general elections. HB draws its membership from family members of the more than 500 imprisoned ETA members and those who remain at large (estimated at a further 500), nationalist deserters from the PNV, the children of immigrants seeking admission to the world of nationalism, middle class groups distrustful of conventional political parties, and self-styled radicals (Alonso Zaldívar and Castells, 1992: 171).

In every national election since 1979, HB has secured enough votes to send at least two deputies (five in 1986) to the Madrid parliament. However, HB deputies have never taken up their seats; after the 1989 election, when it was decided that their four representatives would do so, one of them was assassinated by a right-wing gunman in a Madrid restaurant on the day before the opening of parliament. Thereafter, the remaining deputies were expelled from the *Cortes* for adding the phrase 'by legal imperative' to their oath of loyalty to the Constitution.

Concluding Remarks: Political Parties and the Danger of Democratic Decay

Political parties remain synonymous with liberal democracy. Once a democracy has been established and begins to take root, parties are its most identifiable political actors. Yet the *way* in which parties operate in a given democracy is dependent on a host of factors, not least the institutional design of the core executive. It has been argued by Linz (1990) that parliamentary systems are more conducive to successful transition than presidential ones, since they spread the costs and benefits of change more widely. However, a system's formal designation is not necessarily a good indicator of how it operates in practice. As has been argued above, the *nature* of Spain's political parties was crucially affected by the transitional process itself. Rather than open, interactive organisations responsive to their members' concerns and aspirations, Spanish parties developed into oligarchic bodies demanding unquestioning loyalty from their small memberships. One unsurprising result was that many of these parties became weaker, rather than stronger, as Spain's democracy developed. The UCD was a case apart and collapsed under the weight of its internal divisions. However, other parties – most notably the PCE and the historic Basque Nationalist Party (PNV) – were also subject to acrimonious internal divisions, resignations and expulsions. The early history of the far-right Popular Alliance (AP, later PP) was similarly marked by personal rivalries and tensions.

The one exception to this general pattern was the PSOE. No less oligarchic than any other party, the PSOE nevertheless benefited from a sense of cohesion and direction under a highly charismatic leader. By early 1980, as the UCD began to break up, it had become clear that the PSOE would almost certainly form the next government. The promise of power had an agglutinative impact, serving to mask any internal divisions and to attract new members. Indeed, loyalty was the more easily ensured by the ample opportunities for political rewards afforded by the PSOE's electoral victory of October 1982. Such was the dominance that the PSOE established over political life that some analysts spoke of a blurring of the distinction between government and state: Socialist governments after 1982 were able almost 'to become' the state (Heywood, 1992). Yet by the early 1990s even the PSOE had fallen victim to bitter internal divisions, precipitated both by corruption scandals and the struggle for the eventual succession to González.

Thus, in spite of the undoubted contribution of political parties to the successful establishment of democracy in Spain, it is also possible to draw the somewhat paradoxical conclusion that their actions could represent a potential threat to democratic stability in contemporary Spain. Four trends in particular point towards the risk of democratic distortion and the entrenchment of a clientelistic style of politics (Pérez-Díaz, 1993: 43–9). First, political parties have tended to become increasingly oligarchic, with a growing divorce between leaders and members and little effort expended on recruitment. Second, the public discourse of major parties often bears little relation to their actual behaviour.[4] Third, parties have tended to ignore public opinion in their policy formulation, preferring to deal directly with powerful economic interest groups whilst parliamentary debates are reduced to a banal and trivial level. Fourth, and most important, the revelation of widespread influence-peddling (what the French term *pantouflage*) and corruption within the major parties, together with the opacity of their financial arrangements, has engendered deep cynicism over the probity of the political class as a whole.

None of these features should be exaggerated. However, taken together, these developments in party political activity may contribute to an insidious undermining of civil society, replacing trust in democratic procedures with suspicion and doubts. The failure of political parties to sink deep roots in society and act as genuine participatory linkage organisations (as opposed to clientelistic ones) is a major contributory factor to this risk. Political parties are central to any representative democracy, but they can also serve to undermine the very survival of the open and free discourse and exchange upon which democratic institutions depend.

Part III

The Emergence of a Modern Democratic Power

10

Economic Modernisation

Spain's transition to democracy took place against the backdrop of a deeply unfavourable economic climate. Inflation was running at high rates throughout the developed world in the mid-1970s, the petroleum price shocks imposed by OPEC in 1973 and 1979 dealt hammer blows to an economy highly dependent on imported oil, and Spain's export markets were hard hit by two world recessions. Moreover, after years of repressive dictatorship, the labour movement was naturally eager to make up for lost time by exercising its new-found political rights. Investors, meanwhile, held back from committing funds to a country faced with a highly uncertain economic and political outlook (Allard and Bolorinos, 1992: 14).

The Roots of Economic Modernisation

Although the challenge which faced Spain in the mid-1970s of democratising in the midst of economic crisis superficially looks similar to that which confronted the former communist regimes nearly twenty years later, there is a crucial difference between the two experiences. In Spain, full integration into the western, market-based, capitalist economic system had already taken place under the Franco dictatorship. Thus, whilst the economic panorama during Spain's transition to democracy was grim, no fundamental reorganisation of basic economic principles was necessary. Such a development had already occurred during the 1960s, albeit from a markedly dissimilar starting point to that of the Eastern bloc countries: the Franco regime abandoned autarky, originally modelled on the planned economies of Fascist Italy and Germany, rather than state-controlled communism.

217

The roots of Spain's integration into the western capitalist framework lay in the rise to political influence during the 1950s of technocrats associated with Opus Dei (see Chapters 3 and 6). By the winter of 1956–7, when the US aid which had been instrumental in sustaining the dictatorship began to fall off, Spain's various protectionist policies had come to be seen increasingly as counter-productive. With economic stagnation threatening to undermine his regime, a reluctant Franco was persuaded to seek salvation in the international capitalist order which he had repeatedly denounced since 1936. Stabilisation and development plans – based on the French model of indicative planning – were introduced, setting Spain on the road to the so-called 'economic miracle' of the 1960s.

The rapid industrialisation of the 1960s brought about radical changes in the occupational and territorial distribution of the labour force (see Table 10.1). As industry and the service sector came to dominate GDP, there were major migratory shifts from rural to urban centres: whereas in 1950 around 70 per cent of Spain's population lived in settlements of under 50,000 inhabitants, by 1970 the proportion had fallen to 55 per cent. A second consequence of rapid development was that the system of industrial relations saw significant changes, with the introduction of collective bargaining and limited representation for workers in state-controlled syndicates. In part the result of pressure from industrialists, bankers and business leaders who saw the Franco regime's labour policies as a hindrance to economic progress, these changes ultimately led to a sharp rise in labour disputes which helped undermine the dictatorship (Balfour, 1989: 63–109; Maravall and Santamaría, 1989: 189–90; Preston, 1986: 18–52; Fishman, 1990).

TABLE 10.1

Distribution of workforce, 1950–90

Year	Agriculture	Industry	Services
1950	47.6	26.5	25.9
1960	36.6	29.6	33.2
1970	22.8	37.6	39.6
1980	15.7	34.7	43.8
1990	11.8	33.4	54.8

Source: based on Alonso Zaldívar and Castells (1992: 279).

Furthermore, the apparently outstanding performance of the Spanish economy during the 1960s masked some important weaknesses. The industrial sector was dominated by small- to medium-sized firms with underdeveloped financial, economic and technological structures. Import and price controls, together with the use of cartels, provided short-term protection from external competition, but again left the Spanish economy poorly equipped to deal with the impact of the oil crises (Galy *et al.*, 1993: 3–6). The financial system, dominated by banks, was closely regulated and, in spite of a small public sector, the government was strongly interventionist. Inevitably, the first oil crisis of 1973 was exacerbated by the political context within which it occurred. The disarticulation of the Franco regime and the uncertainties surrounding the transition to democracy restricted the capacity of successive governments to deal with the crisis. Between 1973 and 1977, inflation rose from 11.4 to 24.5 per cent, the exchange rate fell into deficit, and the current account surplus was wiped out. Spain's first post-Franco democratic government was thus confronted not only by major political challenges, but also by deep-rooted economic crisis.

Adolfo Suárez's UCD government, elected to office in June 1977, sought to confront the crisis through consensus and to this end in October 1977 an agreement was signed by all major political parties to deal with the major disequilibria afflicting the Spanish economy. Known as the Moncloa Pacts, the agreement included five major adjustment measures: a 20 per cent devaluation of the peseta against the US dollar, extensive price and wage controls, a limited relaxation of job-protection legislation, fiscal reform, and reform of the monetary and financial system. Although the Pacts eased the immediate economic pressure, they were short-lived and one-sided in their impact, demanding considerable sacrifices from the workforce in return for pledges which ultimately remained largely unfulfilled. Moreover, they instilled a lasting suspicion within Spain's union federations of government-sponsored economic accords. Most important of all, the Moncloa Pacts maintained intact the broad parameters of an essentially inefficient economic structure (Salmon, 1991: 9).

By 1979, when OPEC announced the second major oil price rise, the Spanish economy remained, in structural terms, extremely vulnerable. Monetary restraint and incomes policies were not only unable to prevent a massive increase in unemployment, which continued to rise until the mid-1980s, but also accelerated the obsolescence of the capital stock. As had been the case in 1973, the new rise in energy costs came during a period of high political uncertainty: regular government reshuffles, reflecting the unravelling of the UCD into its various constituent parts, culminated in the resignation of Suárez, swiftly followed by the attempted coup of 23 February 1981. Once more, economic issues were eclipsed by the severity of the political situation. Nevertheless, the Industrial Reconversion Act of 1981 paved the way for fundamental economic reforms which gathered momentum once the Socialist Party had been elected to office in October 1982.

Economic Restructuring during the 1980s: The European Imperative

When the PSOE assumed office in 1982, the major structural weaknesses of Spain's economy had remained largely unattended for nearly a decade, even though some positive measures had been enacted in regard to reform of the financial system, the labour market and industrial policy (García Delgado, 1990: xxiii). The new administration was confronted by an economy in need of major overhaul: GDP growth had virtually stagnated over the previous four years, productive investment was falling, the public deficit had reached 5.4 per cent of GDP compared to 1.8 per cent in 1978, inflation remained at around 15 per cent, and the unemployment rate had risen to 16.5 per cent from 7.4 per cent in 1978 (Segura, 1990: 59–60) (see Table 10.2). The scale of these disequilibria would largely determine the macroeconomic policy priorities of the incoming government: harsh adjustment measures were a necessary, if painful, response to a situation which had already been confronted in most other OECD countries after the first oil price shock of 1973.

The Socialist government was faced with the daunting challenge of reconciling the promotion of social justice with competitive expansion in order to prepare Spain for entry to the European Community (EC). The principal economic targets outlined in Felipe González's 1982 election manifesto had been tax reform, regulation of savings banks, and – as a centrepiece – the creation of 800 000 new jobs within four years. In practice, the promise on jobs was soon dropped as the new government confronted the true scale of restructuring which was necessary to make Spain economically competitive. The

TABLE 10.2
Evolution of the economy, 1973–94

Year	GDP growth		GDP per capita (EU12=100)	Inflation level		Unemployment (% of active population)	Budget deficit (% of GDP)
	Spain	EU12 avge		Spain	EU12 avge		
1973	7.7	6.2	78.1	11.8		2.3	−1.1
1974	5.3	2.0	80.4	15.7		2.6	−0.2
1975	0.5	−1.0	81.1	17.0		3.8	0
1976	3.3	4.9	79.3	17.7		4.7	0.3
1977	3.0	2.4	78.7	24.5		5.7	0.6
1978	1.4	3.1	76.8	19.8		7.6	1.7
1979	−0.1	3.2	73.7	15.7		9.4	1.6
1980	1.2	1.2	73.4	15.5		12.4	2.6
1981	−0.2	−0.1	72.7	14.6		15.1	3.9
1982	1.2	0.6	72.7	14.4		16.8	5.6
1983	1.8	1.2	72.6	12.2		18.1	4.7
1984	1.8	2.0	72.1	11.3		21.3	5.4
1985	2.3	2.4	71.8	8.8		21.7	6.9
1986	3.3	2.6	72.8	8.8	3.5	20.9	6.0
1987	5.6	3.0	74.7	5.3	2.9	19.9	3.2
1988	5.2	3.8	75.7	4.8	3.5	18.4	3.3
1989	4.8	3.4	76.9	6.6	5.1	16.8	2.7
1990	3.7	2.9	77.8	6.7	5.7	16.1	4.0
1991	2.3	1.5	79.2	5.9	5.1	17.0	5.0
1992	0.8	1.1		5.9	4.3	20.1	4.5
1993	−1.0	−0.4		4.6	3.4	22.7	7.3
1994	2.0	1.9		4.4	3.3	24.7	7.1

Source: based on Banco de España, *Informe Anual* (selected years); *Anuario El País 1993, 1994*; García Delgado (1990: 536); Alonso Zaldívar and Castells (1992: 73, 289, 292); Salman (1991: 8); *Eurostat* (selected years).

PSOE thus decided to place major emphasis on 'modernisation', which became virtually a leitmotif of the government. To this end, the Socialists reinforced the measures begun in 1981, with the 1984 Law on Reconversion and Industrialisation representing the first comprehensive attempt to co-ordinate industrial programmes and integrate their financial support through the state budget. The central aims of the new law, which covered mainly the steel, shipbuilding and textile sectors, were to liberalise the economy, increase labour market flexibility and adopt international economic practices (Galy *et al.*, 1993: 5; Salmon, 1991: 9). Other austerity measures adopted by the Socialist government included immediate devaluation of the currency on assuming office, a reduction in the money supply, a limit on wage increases, a phased reduction of the budget deficit and legislation to reduce labour market rigidities (Maravall, 1992: 24). In addition, an energy plan was adopted, seeking to reduce the proportion of imported energy in Spain from the 70 per cent of the early 1970s to 52 per cent by 1992.

Although it entailed high social costs, mainly involving heavy job-losses, the PSOE's economic restructuring programme was relatively successful if judged in terms of conventional macroeconomic indicators: GDP growth rose from 1.4 per cent in 1982 to 3 per cent in 1986, the rate of inflation was halved over the same period, and labour productivity grew faster than real wages by an average of nearly 2 per cent. The principal justification for economic restructuring was the need to compete effectively once Spain joined the EC on 1 January, 1986. Entry to the EC – applied for in the late 1970s by the government of Adolfo Suárez, but negotiated by the PSOE under González – was immensely popular in Spain, as the move was seen as situating the country firmly and irrevocably within the First World. By joining the EC, Spain gained virtually unrestricted access to a market fifteen times larger than its own in terms of purchasing power.

In spite of fears in some quarters that EC membership would have a devastating impact on Spain's economy (Preston and Smyth, 1984), economic development was better than predicted by even the most zealous pro-Europeans. From 1986 to 1991, Spain enjoyed the highest, investment-led, output growth in the OECD area. In this period, GDP per capita rose from 72.8 per cent of the EC average to 79.2 per cent (Alonso Zaldívar and Castells, 1992: 74–5; OECD, 1991). Whilst membership of the EC was largely responsible for the dramatic post-1986 upturn in Spain's economic fortunes, the foundations for the upturn were laid in the restructuring policies initiated in the early 1980s. Before joining the EC, the Spanish economy was one of the most protected in OECD Europe. Subsequently, there was rapid progress in liberalising foreign trade flows, harmonising the regulatory framework within which the economy operates and directing external transactions towards the EC (Salmon, 1992; Almarcha Barbado, 1993: Part I).

It was not until the advent of the PSOE government in 1982 that major measures were instituted to tackle structural problems in the Spanish economy, following what Alonso Zaldívar and Castells (1992: 75) have termed the 'missed adjustment' of 1979–82, when the political demands of the transition to democracy precluded effective economic reforms. The industrial reconversion programme, implemented in 1983, and the introduction in 1984 of fixed-term employment contracts, were instrumental in promoting employment flexibility, investment recovery and productivity growth. In particular, foreign direct investments, especially from EC countries, increased dramatically. In 1986, inflows exceeded those for the whole period 1970–9, and were 50 per cent higher than for the period 1980–5. After 1986, foreign investment in Spain grew substantially year on year, reaching 3.7 per cent of GDP in 1990 (Salmon, 1991: 19–21; *Anuario El País, 1991*). The investment boom, efficiency gains and a stronger labour supply boosted output growth from the mid-1980s. Foreign investment also played an important role in the rationalisation and efficiency gains which derived from modernisation of the capital stock.

Overall, it is clear that Spain's accession to the EC led to a number of major qualitative benefits (Almarcha Barbado, 1993; OECD, 1991). EC membership provided a significant stimulus to aggregate demand, as well as to both actual and potential real GDP (mainly through greater investment activity and technical progress). The opening of domestic markets to foreign competition, together with supply-side improvements, helped reduce Spain's tendency to high inflation. Moreover, the opening of domestic markets to foreign investors and improved rates of return on capital made Spain an attractive country for capital inflows. Integration into the EC also favoured specialisation and economies of scale and Spain has in addition benefited enormously from EC membership through direct financial transfers via the Community's Structural Funds (see Chapter 6). In short, there has been a profound structural transformation of the Spanish economy since entry to the EC.

Given these undoubted achievements, it is unsurprising that the Socialist government should have remained deeply committed to ever closer European integration. EC membership was a key elememt in the government's goal of modernisation, a process which, in the wake of the 1992 Maastricht Treaty, remained firmly at the top of the economic agenda (see Exhibit 10.1). Yet, in spite of its unquestionable benefits, membership of the EC also entailed significant economic and political costs. Vertiginous growth in the period 1980–9, during which GDP increased by an average 5 per cent a year, unleashed the economy's major disequilibria: high inflationary pressures, aggravated by excess domestic demand, and – in the early 1990s – a growing current account deficit. Of particular significance was a sharp increase in import penetration ratios, reflecting the reduction of tariff barriers, real exchange rate appreciation of the peseta and a change in the composition of trade. Spain's pattern of trade has been marked by a dramatic shift towards Europe as a result of liberalisation measures. In 1980 trade with the EC accounted for 31 per cent of imports and 52 per cent of exports; by 1991, these figures had increased to 60 and 71 per cent respectively (Salmon, 1992).

Such a shift in trade patterns is a natural consequence of EC membership. However, the performance of imports and exports after EC entry diverged sharply: the former expanded by 40 per cent in

---

EXHIBIT 10.1

Maastricht Treaty convergence criteria

The convergence criteria for participation in EMU, as set out in the Maastricht Treaty, were as follows:

- Inflation over 12 months prior to EMU must not exceed the average rate of the three lowest-inflation EU countries by more than 1.5 percentage points
- Long-term nominal interest rates over 12 months must not exceed by more than two percentage points the average for the same three lowest inflation countries
- The currency must remain in the narrow band of the Exchange Rate Mechanism (ERM) for at least two years without a devaluation
- The budget deficit should not exceed 3 per cent of GDP
- Total public debt should not exceed 60 per cent of GDP

The latter two criteria in fact allow some room for flexibility if progress is deemed to be being made.

real peseta terms between 1986 and 1990, compared to a rise in the latter of 20 per cent during the same period. Spain's current account went from a surplus of 1.6 per cent of GDP in 1986 to a deficit of 3.4 per cent of GDP in 1990. The worsening trade deficit reflected an overheating domestic market, sucking in imports made more competitive by the removal of tariff barriers and the strength of the peseta. So severe were the disequilibria that the government was obliged to take a series of measures in 1989 and 1990 to cool the economy and try to engineer a 'soft landing' in preparation for the 1993 Single Market. These included bringing the peseta into the Exchange Rate Mechanism (ERM) of the European Monetary System (EMS) in June 1989, a restrictive monetary policy combined with a tightening of fiscal policy, which up to 1990 had been moderately expansive, and a proposed 'competitiveness pact' (later renamed a Progress Pact) which was ultimately rejected by the labour unions. The measures were blown off course, however, as a result of two factors: the short-term impact of the Gulf crisis in 1991 and the longer-term impact of a marked slowdown in world trade. Thereafter, the government found itself further constrained by the need to meet the convergence terms for economic and monetary union set out in the Maastricht Treaty, negotiated in late 1991 and signed early the following year.

The PSOE in Power: Socialists or Neo-Liberals?

The PSOE government consistently defended its economic policies on the grounds that they were ineluctably driven by the twin imperatives of modernisation and European integration. Indeed, the decision to use integration into Europe as a strategic option for modernising the country, broadly backed by all the democratic forces, became the key policy of Socialist governments after 1982. Such an option entailed economic and foreign policy implications which inevitably clashed with some of the traditional principles defended by the political left, a fact which contributed significantly to divisions between what might be termed technocrats and ideologues within the PSOE.

Not long after the PSOE assumed power under Felipe González in 1982 it became a commonplace to refer to the government's economic policy as 'neo-liberal', basically a replica of the policy stances of Ronald Reagan and Margaret Thatcher (Aumente, 1985; Share,

1988: 412, 1989: ch.5; Holman, 1989; Petras, 1990, 1993). At first sight, the charge of neo-liberalism looks understandable. Austerity measures under Miguel Boyer – aimed at reducing inflation, the public sector deficit and the balance of payments deficit, as well as encouraging foreign investment and beginning a process of industrial streamlining to ease negotiations over EC membership – bore similarities to the restrictive policies being carried out by right-wing governments influenced by the monetarist creed of Milton Friedman. Moreover, they entailed severe job losses and cuts in public services. Equally, once the Spanish economic turnaround began after 1985, it was accompanied by many elements which sat uncomfortably with supposed socialism. For instance, there was a marked decline in the solidaristic ties between the PSOE and the union movement, prompted in large measure by unemployment levels and the massive increase in temporary contracts as a result of 1984 legislation to introduce greater flexibility in the labour market (Santillán, 1993). By June 1991, over 32 per cent of the wage-earning population was on fixed-term contracts. The unions argued that this ran the risk of segmenting the labour market and rendering it precarious. Equally, privatisation measures seemed to fly in the face of traditional socialist nostrums on state ownership, whilst an emphasis on consumerism, with economic growth being demand-led, created the impression that private accumulation mattered more than social welfare. A 1992 decree on labour market and benefit reforms and a proposed new strike law, confirmed for many that the PSOE government was indistinguishable from its right-wing neighbours in Europe.

However, for all the failure of successive Socialist governments to oversee any radical redistribution of wealth in Spain, a more nuanced view of their economic policy is needed. The *locus classicus* of neo-liberalism in western Europe was the UK under the Conservative administrations of Margaret Thatcher, with whose policies those of the PSOE governments have been explicitly compared (Redondo, quoted in Sánchez and Santos, 1990; Redondo, 1992). The neo-liberalism of the Thatcher governments was principally associated with supply-side policies premised upon a political philosophy of minimal state interference in the working of the free market system, together with the economic belief that the free play of market forces would lead to an improvement in economic performance. Individuals, in this view, were seen as rational actors, with well-formed, transitive preferences which they sought to satisfy at minimum cost in order to maximise their personal utility functions. Reductions in direct taxation, major reform of trade unions aimed at reducing their influence, and extensive privatisation (involving not just de-nationalisation, but also contracting out and de-regulation) became the central pillars of this approach. Both the rhetoric and the reality of economic policy under the Thatcher governments was that of 'rolling back the state'.

It is a caricature to construe the economic policy stances of the PSOE governments in quite these terms. In fact, the role of the state was one of the key features of differentiation between the economic policy of the PSOE government and that of its UK counterpart. Far from rolling back the state, the PSOE government consistently used it as a leading player in its attempt to 'make Spain work'. Indeed, in direct contrast to one of the principal nostrums of neo-liberalism, the Spanish Socialists engaged in what has sometimes been termed neo-corporatism (Martínez Alier and Roca, 1985, 1988). In two areas of critical importance to Spain's economic structure – the banking sector and the energy utilities – the government was consistently interventionist. From at least 1986, Socialist administrations exerted considerable pressure for banking mergers, ultimately using the public sector as a lever against the private sector when all the state-owned banks were merged into the Corporación Bancaria de España in April 1991. As the *Financial Times* commented at the time, 'the Socialists have become more and not less interventionist'. With the energy utilities, the government initially resisted EC requirements for the entry of European multinationals to its petroleum distribution monopoly, and then ensured that the state-controlled Repsol retained the lion's share of the network, effectively restricting market penetration to just two companies (Elf Aquitaine and British Petroleum). Even more direct was the government's refusal to sanction the sale of the electricity utility, Unión Fenosa, to the German RWE in 1989. Again, the PSOE government sought to concentrate utilities via a policy of mergers (Alario, 1991: 7–25).

The government was also interventionist in terms of committing vast state resources to infrastructural modernisation. Expenditure on public works was massive, much of it stimulated by the events of 1992 – especially the Olympic Games in Barcelona and Expo92 in Sevilla. Public investment in roads, railways, ports, airports and hydraulic engineering between 1986 and 1989 grew from Pta270.5 bn to Pta617.4 bn, a rise of 128 per cent. Such a scale of spending on state-sponsored projects would be anathema to neo-liberal regimes which favour the provision of public goods via unfettered market forces, brokered through the private sector. Equally, the use of credit ceilings to contain demand (as applied in July 1989) and increases in personal income tax rates (as in the rise of the lowest marginal rate from 8 to 25 per cent and the extension of withholding tax on investment income), fly in the face of neo-liberal orthodoxy. Even though the increase in the *overall* tax burden from 28.1 per cent in 1982 to 35 per cent in 1990 can be seen as being in line with neo-liberal practice, the *direct* tax burden on family income also increased during the same period, rising from 9.7 per cent to 11.8 per cent in 1990. Between 1980 and 1988 the overall tax burden in Spain increased by 36 per cent (compared to 6.7 per cent in the UK), the highest rise in the EC.

It is certainly the case that if socialism is defined in terms of nationalisation, then the PSOE governments were hardly socialist at all: only the electric high tension network was nationalised.[1] One former Socialist minister (Maravall, 1992: 25–7) has argued that the PSOE had to confront the fact that inequalities in Spain were far deeper than in most west European societies and that welfare policies were more limited. In spite of a substantial increase in welfare expenditure between 1975 and 1982 (social spending grew by 47.9 per cent in real terms, rising as a share of GDP from 9.9 to 14.6 per cent), the Socialist administration had to improve the competitiveness and performance of the economy whilst at the same time responding to the demands for social equity which had contributed to its electoral victory in 1982. The PSOE thus sought to balance economic efficiency with redistribution, allowing for a greater role for the market in the economy yet expanding the state's role in social policies. In the period 1982–9, public social expenditure grew by 94 per cent in real terms, accounting for 17.8 per cent of GDP by 1989 – an increase which was mainly financed by larger tax revenues. Nevertheless, for all that welfare provision was improved through the introduction of universal entitlement, the PSOE was widely criticised – especially by the union movement – for seeming to favour rampant consumerism and private accumulation at the expense of social welfare (Heywood, 1992). More important, the government stood accused of indifference towards the level of unemployment: although it fell gradually from over 21.5 per cent in 1985 to 15.9 per cent in 1990 (before starting to rise again), this remained nearly double the EC average of 8.4 per cent. Of equal concern was the disproportionate impact of unemployment on the young, with 30.5 per cent of Spaniards between the ages of 16 and 24 unable to find a job in 1991 (Allard and Bolorinos, 1992: 25)[2].

What has been strikingly absent in discussions of the Socialists' economic policy – with the exception of Maravall (1992) – are analyses which situate the PSOE's experience within a wider literature on the dilemmas facing social democratic parties in the 'post-material' world. On the one hand, as Przeworksi and Sprague (1986) have argued, working-class based parties must choose between appealing to their traditional base (thereby consistently losing elections, since this base has shrunk) or chasing voters from other social groups (thereby losing their character as working-class parties). On the other hand, social democratic parties face a series of policy dilemmas which overlap with their electoral strategy problems: do they remain faithful to traditional expansionist, welfare-oriented policies, or else seek to widen their appeal to encompass new social groups, including white-collar workers, professionals and so-called 'post-materialist' voters. Policy choices, the party's institutional structures, its relationships to the trade union movement, and the demands of coalition-building will all have an impact on how a given party seeks to resolve these dilemmas.

Merkel (1992) has spoken of the end of the 'golden age' of social democracy which ran from the end of the Second World War to the early 1970s. The failure of Keynesian mechanisms – the result of such factors as internationalisation of the world economy, a marked shift to service sector employment and increased differentiation within a declining blue-collar workforce, the rise of new social demands, and the loss of intellectual ascendancy on the Left – effectively removed the most obvious social democratic model. Without a working blueprint, the practical realisation of 'socialism' was pushed to some future date as a utopian ambition which could be achieved only through the foundation of economic 'modernisation' via European integration. In common with social democratic parties throughout Europe, the PSOE was faced with the inescapable fact that traditional egalitarian tools – national demand management, state ownership, mass public provision – had to varying degrees grown rusty. The language of social reform, justice and opportunity was always easy to articulate; its translation into practical politics turned out to be less straightforward.

Ironically, perhaps, EC membership was itself of particular significance in this regard. Widely seen as one of most important achievements of the first González administration, integration into the EC had a notable impact on both the design and capacity for action of Spanish macroeconomic policy. The original terms of entry and the subsequent moves towards ever-greater economic and political union under the terms of the 1987 Single European Act and two inter-governmental conferences – including entry to the exchange rate mechanism of the EMS in 1989 – considerably reduced the government's margin for manoeuvre on macroeconomic policy, a trend which was, of course, sharply intensified by the terms of the Maastricht agreement.

The Challenges of the 1990s: The Single Market, Convergence and Cohesion

Although there was no realistic alternative to seeking full integration into Europe, it could be argued that the Socialist government thereby surrendered economic – and to some extent political – initiative to wider forces. Foreign penetration of the Spanish economy since the mid-1980s is deemed by some to have entailed a significant transfer of control to multinational companies, with a concomitant reorganisation of trade. According to a 1991 World Bank survey (based on 1988 figures), foreign companies generate half of Spanish production and employ 43 per cent of the occupied population. Critics of multinational penetration talk of Spain becoming a 'branch plant economy', dedicated to assembling imported goods, and point to the fact that many foreign investors are more concerned with expanding market share than improving productive profitability. The lack of major multinational companies with headquarters in Spain is seen as working against the country's long-term interests, 'since it is at headquarters that a complex of high value added activities develop, including marketing, finance, legal, research and engineering' (Salmon, 1992).

Of considerably greater significance, the logic of European integration ties Spain into a macroeconomic process over which it inevitably has limited control. Economic and monetary union (EMU), the central pillar of the Maastricht Treaty, has major implications for Spanish – and, of course, European – economic policy-making. If ultimately implemented as envisaged, the Maastricht terms mean there will be a single currency and one monetary policy set by the European Central Bank. Interest rates on similar assets will be the same in all member states, and short-term rates will be under the control of the central bank. There will also be a Europe-wide definition of the money supply for which the central bank will set a target (Britton and Mayes, 1992).

The creation of an integrated EU necessarily involves increasing 'convergence' of economic behaviour in a number of respects, including policy, structure and behaviour. Economic integration has already involved reducing the regulation and intervention capacity of individual states in various ways. Decision-making over certain activities – such as commercial, agricultural and fishing policies – has been transferred to EU institutions (a process which under the terms of the Maastricht accords will be expanded to encompass industrial, environmental, consumer protection, R&D, public health, education and cultural policies). The introduction of common regulations through EU directives adopted by majority vote will necessarily lead to uniform provisions and standards being adopted through the principle of reciprocal recognition. The power of domestic governments to provide grants and financial assistance to companies is being reduced in order to eliminate unfair competition. Finally, EU members have for several years been engaged in co-ordinating their macroeconomic policies, most notably in the field of monetary policy through the European Monetary System (EMS) (González Fernández, 1993a; Alonso Zaldívar and Castells, 1992).

Nevertheless, European economic integration has been viewed positively in Spain: a Times Mirror Center survey on attitudes throughout Europe, conducted by Gallup in September 1991, found that 53 per cent of Spanish respondents thought that the overall community would be strengthened by economic integration, compared to equivalent figures of 45 per cent in Germany, 44 per cent in the UK, 43 per cent in Italy and just 31 per cent in France. Equally, 70 per cent of Spanish respondents viewed the post-1992 Single Market as a good idea, second only to Italy (77 per cent) and well ahead of France (66 per cent), Germany (64 per cent) and the UK (58 per cent). Spanish respondents were also reasonably optimistic about the prospects for agriculture, manufacturing, high technology industry and tourism under the conditions of the single market, a majority believing that each sector would do 'very well' or 'fairly well' (Times Mirror Center, 1991).

Support for Europe derives in large measure from the belief that it is only through membership of the EU that Spain can escape the traditional isolationism which has left it lagging behind its competitors and marginal to international developments. If Spain is to realise its ambition of being one of the core economies at the forefront of an integrated Europe, it has no option but to seek convergence with its major EU competitors. On the other hand, if Spain's economy is not brought into line with others in Europe, the country could not only suffer damaging consequences, but would also be consigned to long-term second division status within the EU. It is for this reason that convergence is seen as being so vital.

Three main characteristics clearly differentiate the Spanish economy from those of its major EU partners: a high rate of unemployment, a deficient development of some basic infrastructural and social service provisions, and a low level of productivity per person employed. Spain's welfare level is below the EU average level, the country employs proportionately fewer people than the leading EU nations, and they produce less (see Table 10.3). Spain's GDP per capita is 65 per cent of the UK and Italian level, and 49 per cent of the German level, while productivity per person employed stands at 70 per cent of the German level and 85 per cent of the UK and Italian levels.

Spain's deficit in terms of infrastructural provision is still considered serious: despite massive investment throughout the 1980s, by 1991 it remained 37 per cent below the EU average in terms of roads, 43 per cent in railways and 26 per cent in telecommunications (González Fernández, 1993b). In particular, Spain's existing transport infrastructure is poor. Out of a total of

TABLE 10.3

Efficiency and equity in Europe, 1990

	Spain	Germany	France	Britain	Italy
GDP per capita ($ purchasing power parity)	11,792	18,291	17,431	15,720	16,021
Relative GDP compared to EC average (%)[a]	79.3	113.8	108.9	101.3	103.6
Rate of activity or occupation of population (%)	31.0	43.3	39.3	47.0	40.7
GDP per employed person (Pta mn)	3.6	5.3	5.2	3.7	4.3
Share of wages and other income in GDP (%)[b]	63.2	66.1	70.5	73.6	72.8
Share of profits in GDP (%)[b]	36.8	33.9	29.5	26.4	27.2

[a] 1991 figures.
[b] 1988 figures.
Source: Based on De la Dehesa (1990: 360) and Alonso Olea *et al.* (1992: 278).

90 000 km of national roads, only 7 000 km will be motorway by 1999 (the same level as France and Italy had in 1990). In 1989, the projected cost of this road-building plan was Pta3 trillion. Plans announced in 1989 for investment in railways were Pta2 trillion up to the year 2000, mainly directed towards the development of a high speed network linking the major cities. In addition, a further Pta1 trillion was projected in order to adjust the Spanish track gauge to match the European norm. Including expenditure on ports, coasts and hydraulics, the total expenditure necessary at 1989 prices to bring Spain's infrastructure up to the level of the major EC economies was Pta15 trillion, with perhaps half as much again to be spent on energy and telecommunications.

These indicators highlight the scale of the challenge faced by the Spanish economy if it is to converge with its leading European partners. Convergence, however, necessarily entails the adoption of a macroeconomic policy stance which will increasingly be determined by the wider needs of the EU, rather than the specific needs of Spain, and which therefore may entail significant political costs. For instance, the need to defend the peseta within the ERM against currency speculators meant that the Bank of Spain was forced to resist demands to reduce interest rates in the spring of 1993, even after the Bundesbank had finally brought its own rates down. Supporters of full European integration may argue that there is no contradiction between Spain's needs and those of the EU: as a fully-fledged member of the Union, Spain will automatically benefit from the anticipated greater coherence of EU economic policy formation under the terms of EMU.

Yet, the approach to economic policy expressed in the Maastricht Treaty is very different from the philosophy which guided economic policy in the late 1950s when the EEC was founded; different, too, from the views of policy-makers in most industrialised countries during the 1960s and 1970s. The Maastricht approach is ultimately based on classical economics and the liberal tradition of political thought, but also owes much to the re-assertion (and re-interpretation) of that tradition in the USA and Europe during the 1970s and 1980s (Britton and Mayes, 1992). Of central importance to the entire conception is the role of free markets and open competition, the very antithesis of state intervention or central planning (Elliott, 1992). Traditional Keynesian policies depended, amongst other things, upon the capacity of a national government to establish its own fiscal and monetary policy, to decide upon the main parameters of its own economic development, and to negotiate about these with social partners at a national level. Economic planning required that a national economy could be sufficiently insulated from the surrounding world economy to allow governmental controls to have some effect. However, the ever greater globalisation of world markets has undermined the independence of national economies. The Maastricht model recognises and reinforces this reality. In some senses, Maastricht mirrors the neo-liberal conception of placing economic limits on democracy: the economic sphere will increasingly be protected from immediate control by the *demos* (Pierson, 1992).

The Maastricht Treaty set out specific convergence criteria for the implementation of EMU. By 1993 it had become clear that the terms agreed at Maastricht were highly unlikely to be implemented in unamended form: reservations on the part of various member states, as well as the unexpected length and depth of recession in the early 1990s, presaged some reconsideration of its key features as convergence deadlines approached. However, even if the Maastricht Treaty were to collapse, the likelihood is that some form of EMU – possibly involving just the core European economies – will take place by the end of the century. Moreover, the Spanish government insisted that it drew a distinction between 'nominal' convergence, which related specifically to the Maastricht criteria, and 'real' convergence, which referred to Spain's ability to compete on even terms with the leading European economies. Achieving nominal convergence would imply that the economy was well run, but would not mean necessarily that Spain had achieved real convergence in regard to living standards, productivity, the quality of goods and services, the strength of Spanish companies or competitiveness. Real convergence with European partners was thus identified as a central priority of the Socialist administration, even if the Maastricht Treaty does collapse.

All EU governments were required to indicate what measures they proposed to take in order to meet the Maastricht terms. In April 1992, the PSOE government set out the framework for Spanish economic policy to 1996 in its controversial *Programa de Convergencia, 1992–96* (see Table 10.4). The plans established in the document, which was updated in July 1994,[3] were intended both to dictate and to justify economic policy over the following years, and represented an impressive commitment to ensuring that Spain would take its place in any initial establishment of EMU. One of the principal assumptions upon which the plan rested was that the Spanish economy would maintain an annual rate of growth of around 1 per

TABLE 10.4

The Convergence Plan: Government's macroeconomic projections, 1991-7

	1991	1992	1993	1994	1995	1996	1997
GDP and components (% real change)							
Private consumption	3.0	3.2	3.0	3.0	3.0	2.9	
Public consumption	4.4	3.5	2.0	2.0	2.0	2.0	
Fixed investment	1.6	3.2	5.1	6.2	5.8	5.4	
construction	4.3	2.7	4.0	5.0	5.0	4.5	
equipment	-2.5	4.0	7.0	8.0	7.0	6.7	
Domestic demand	2.9	3.3	3.4	3.6	3.6	3.4	
Exports of goods and services	8.4	7.9	7.9	8.0	8.1	8.1	
Imports of goods and services	9.4	8.0	7.1	7.0	6.8	6.6	
GDP	**2.4**	**3.0**	**3.3**	**3.6**	**3.6**	**3.5**	
				[1.3][a]	**[2.6]**	**[3.5]**	**[4.3]**
Prices and labour costs (% change)							
GDP deflator	6.9	6.0	4.7	3.8	3.3	3.1	
				[4.2]	[3.8]	[3.5]	[3.5]
Wages	8.5	6.5	5.3	4.5	4.0	4.0	
Productivity per worker	2.1	2.3	1.7	1.7	1.7	1.7	
Unit labour costs	6.3	4.1	3.6	2.7	2.3	2.3	
Labour market							
Population: % change	0.4	0.6	1.0	1.0	0.9	0.9	
Employment: % change	0.2	0.6	1.6	1.9	1.9	1.8	
				['light']	[1.5]	[2.6]	[2.6]
actual change (000)	30	76	203	245	250	241	
Unemployment: % of active population	16.3	16.3	15.8	15.1	14.3	13.5	
actual (000)	2,464	2,478	2,427	2,335	2,225	2,125	
Current payments account							
Balance (Pta bn)	-1.59	-1.71	-1.83	-1.75	-1.78	-1.81	
% of GDP	-2.9	-2.9	-2.8	-2.5	-2.4	-2.3	
Public administration							
Revenue: % change	10.4	11.4	8.8	9.6	8.1	7.8	
Expenditure: % change	11.5	10.0	7.6	7.4	5.9	5.9	
Deficit (Pta bn)	-2.43	-2.37	-2.25	-1.84	-1.32	-0.79	
% of GDP	-4.4	-4.0	-3.5	-2.7	-1.8	-1.0	
				[-6.7]	[-5.9]	[-4.7]	[-3.4]
Total public debt: % of GDP	**45.6**	**45.8**	**45.8**	**45.3**	**44.1**	**42.3**	
				[60.7]	**[63.9]**	**[65.5]**	**[65.2]**

[a] Figures in square brackets indicate July 1994 revisions.

Source: Ministerio de Economía y Hacienda, *Programa de Convergencia* (Madrid, 1992); *El País internacional* (4, 11 July 1994).

cent above that of the European average up to the end of 1996, a feat which it had achieved comfortably over the five years up to 1991. However, this latter period had been exceptional, reflecting the investment and consumer boom that resulted from Spain's entry into the EC. Significantly, it was also a period of strong public expenditure growth. The particular problem facing the government in the run-up to EMU was the need to maintain above average economic growth in the context of a deflationary policy.

The convergence plan, to which the Socialist government remained strongly committed in spite of its unpopularity, stated that the only sustainable way for the economy to achieve the required above-average growth was by developing and implementing a series of structural reforms. These structural reforms involved labour market changes (including the elimination of the corporatist *ordenanzas laborales* – established under the Franco regime to provide job protection – and enhanced geographical mobility), economic deregulation (aimed primarily at the service sector and, in particular, restrictive practices in the professions), liberalisation (implementing EU competition policy in areas such as telecommunications and transport), a reduction in the number of public agencies, a freeze on subsidies to the public sector (together with management reforms), defence of consumer rights in the financial sector, and extensive reforms of the health service, including devolved management of budgets to hospitals and increased co-operation between central, regional and local administrations.

The reforms represented a coherent policy framework. However, they were widely criticised for their lack of specific detail and for the scale of their ambition. Economic projections are always, of course, notoriously fickle. Indeed, within months of publishing the *Programa de Convergencia*, the government had been forced to announce further adjustment measures as a result of developments beyond its control. The failure of the US economy to emerge from recession as anticipated, combined with the continued impact of the Bundesbank's policy on interest rates, undermined hopes of an early recovery of economic activity in Spain. The government was then dealt a further severe blow by the impact of the ERM crisis of September 1992 on its economic projections: the need to devalue the peseta by 5 per cent, followed by the temporary reimposition of exchange rate controls, dented confidence in the health of the Spanish economy. By the time the 1993 state budget proposals were approved by Parliament, the details originally outlined in the convergence programme just six months earlier looked decidedly unrealistic (and appeared even more so following a further 5 per cent devaluation later in November 1992). Yet, the feasibility of the plans was of rather less significance than what they meant for Spain's commitment to real convergence with the EU.

Critical to the convergence plan's possibility of success was the establishment of a 'cohesion fund', provided for in the Maastricht Treaty. According to the policy on cohesion, it was agreed that a fund should be set up to help create an infrastructure in both physical and human capital which would give the less advantaged regions an equal opportunity to compete with the rest of the EU in the single market. None the less, considerable controversy soon emerged both as to the size of such cohesion funds, and as to their efficacy. In the view of some, income transfers to disadvantaged regions achieve relatively little and may actually reinforce the causes of disparity by creating a culture of dependence in the receiving regions; equally, the need for such transfers can create resentment in the providing regions (Britton and Mayes, 1992). It is for this reason that the focus of the cohesion policy is on fostering sources of indigenous growth by providing necessary resources to develop them through investment in infrastructure, communications, training and so forth.

The initial sum proposed for the cohesion fund was relatively small (a total of Pta1.3 bn over the period 1993–7), but the Maastricht protocol recognised that it would be revised during the negotiations over the Community budget for 1993–8. In practice, negotiations on cohesion soon stalled. The Germans, stung by the costs of unification with the former GDR, were reluctant even to discuss implementing the Maastricht protocol on cohesion. Moreover, the Portuguese presidency of the Community during the first half of 1992 refused to call a special meeting of EU leaders to discuss the issue: since direct flows of EU funds account for about 5 per cent of Portugal's GDP (compared to less than 1 per cent of Spain's), Lisbon was not anxious to open a discussion which could alter that balance. Ultimately, a compromise was reached at the Edinburgh summit in December 1992 after Felipe González adopted Thatcher-like negotiating tactics to ensure that his European partners agreed to the establishment of a cohesion fund.

The new fund was formally established by the EU Council in May 1994 for 'projects in the fields of environment and trans-European networks', and applies to less favoured regions in member states whose average GDP per head was below 90 per cent of the EU average figure. Its initial budget of 15.15bn ecu over seven years was lower than the Spanish government had hoped, even though Spain receives the lion's share. In June 1994, the European Commission approved six major schemes concerning the environment in Spain at a cost of 18.8mn ecus. These involved 162 environmental projects related to the production of olive oil, 54 projects in the management of industrial residues, eight projects for the management of used oils, four projects for the recycling of water used to clean containers and ships' holds, three projects for the restoration of soils damaged by industrial and mining activities, and the construction of a bypass at Lardero in La Rioja leading to the A68 motorway as part of the trans-European road network. However, even with cohesion fund support, the convergence plans remained immensely ambitious.

Conclusion: The Costs of Convergence

Developments in the Spanish economy since accession to the EC/EU highlight the extent to which it has been integrated into the global economy and is ever more shaped by evolving international factors: indeed, the 'internationalisation of activity represented by the growth of capital markets and corporate production systems severely limits the degree to which national governments can shelter their domestic economies and citizens from the impact of external developments' (Wallace quoted in Salmon, 1992; Velarde *et al.*, 1991). Loukas Tsoukalis (1991) has referred to the emergence of the 'European economy', describing prevailing and future links between EC/EU countries and their European neighbours. These links are seen as being halfway between the full integration of territorial units in a national economy and the interdependence of the world's leading domestic economies. Thus, EU countries are less closely linked in economic terms than are, for instance, Spain's autonomous regions or the German *Länder*, but their economies are more integrated than Germany's economy is with that of Japan, or Japan's with that of the USA.

Spain's Socialist government found itself caught in a classic Catch-22 in the early 1990s. An unquestioned commitment to Europe meant that it was obliged to continue on a journey to a destination which was always liable to change the closer it approached. In the wake of the Maastricht Treaty, the destination was EMU by the end of the century, yet by 1993 major doubts had begun to emerge over the

entire project. Nevertheless, the Spanish governent gambled on a bid
to ensure that Spain joins the European elite in time to pass the
economic fitness test agreed upon at Maastricht. The convergence
plan appeared draconian, and was always likely to lead to social
clashes as public spending was reduced, and interest rates remained
high in an attempt to squeeze out inflation. Spain has been strike-
prone since the mid-1980s (see Table 10.5), and relations between the
government and unions had plumbed new depths even before the
convergence plan was announced.

In regard to convergence, the government remained in a virtually
impossible position. The attempt to achieve convergence ('real' *or*
'nominal') was almost bound to provoke some degree of social unrest
and therefore carry significant political costs as the government laid
itself open to the charge of making workers bear the brunt of the
effort. Abandoning the attempt would condemn Spain to second
division status within the EU and would also carry significant
political costs, leaving the government open to the charge of having
'failed' Spain. Meanwhile success – should it be achieved – would
leave the government open to the charge that it had abandoned any
vestige of social democratic principles and would once again carry
significant political costs as it wrestled to square the circle of moving
towards socialism within the context of a free market Europe.

By committing itself wholeheartedly to Europe, the PSOE
government surrendered a substantial degree of autonomy over the
elaboration of economic policy. Antoni Zabalza, secretary of state at
the Treasury, recognised as much when he commented in Brussels in
late July 1992 that 'we are at a stage in which there are fewer
economic policy instruments to which we can turn, and more
obligations which are not easy to comply with' (*El País internacional*,

TABLE 10.5

**Working days lost through strikes,
per 1,000 employees, annual average, 1986–90**

Greece	887	France	75
Spain	647	Denmark	40
Italy	271	Holland	8
Ireland	244	Luxembourg	7
Britain	136	Germany	5
Portugal	84		

Source: European Commission.

27 July 1992). This is a process which is likely to intensify. Under the Maastricht terms, once EMU has taken place the European System of Central Banks (ESCB) – composed of the national central banks and the European Central Bank (ECB) – will be charged with maintaining price stability within a clear framework of free market principles. In order to do so, it will be responsible for defining and implementing monetary policy, conducting foreign exchange policy, and managing foreign exchange reserves. The ECB will act as an executive organ within the ESCB, and both bodies will operate independently from national governments and other Community institutions (Britton and Mayes, 1992). The fact that the ECB will be run by a six member executive board appointed for a non-renewable term of eight years, and that its voting structure will be based on member states' population and GDP, inevitably highlights the thorny issue of both equity and political accountability.

The PSOE government's dominance of the Spanish political scene was severely dented by the results of the June 1993 general elections. A large part of the reason for its sharp decline in popularity during the early 1990s can be attributed to the economic difficulties consequent upon its commitment to convergence with Spain's major EU competitors. After the heady years of economic growth in the latter part of the 1980s, austerity measures and recession – exacerbated in Europe by the Bundesbank's response to the costs of German unification – hit hard. One result was the emergence of a certain scepticism amongst the Spanish population about the benefits of European integration. Whereas entry to the EC in 1986 enjoyed virtually unanimous support, the enthusiasm for all things European had started to wane by 1993 as the costs of the Maastricht Treaty gradually began to emerge. By the summer of 1994, the Socialist government appeared to have little prospect of long-term survival.

11

The Policy Process

The policy-making process is one of the least researched aspects of contemporary Spanish politics. Although competitive pluralism is enshrined in constitutional provisions as the model of representation, it is difficult to locate policy-making in Spain within analytical categories familiar from the study of other west European polities, such as incrementalism, rational choice, systems analysis and so forth, or the more recent 'power-dependence' model[1] (Furlong, 1994: 20–3). At present, there is insufficient detailed information available to identify the existence of policy communities, issue networks or pressure group activity.

In Search of the Policy Process

It is clear that executive dominance, combined with strong clientelist relations within political parties and low levels of associational membership, has facilitated the continued primacy of the state in the policy process. In contrast to the high degree of institutional co-ordination characteristic of policy communities, in which a professional public administration acts to marshal and regulate competitive interests within a bureaucratic market place, the policy process in Spain appears to favour dominant elites – notably the party of government, which is able to utilise the resources of the state to control access to the policy arena.

241

The unequal distribution of resources which characterises the Spanish policy process is reinforced by low – and declining – levels of associational activity (Stoetzel, 1982: 337; Orizo, 1983: 22). In 1981, 31 per cent of the population was involved in voluntary organisations, such as political parties, religious groups, artistic or professional bodies and so forth. By 1990, the figure had fallen to 22 per cent, indicating a widespread unwillingness to participate in the organisational structures of civil society (Keating, 1993: 343). The lack of powerful interest groups in Spain and the weakness of the bureaucracy has further skewed the real distribution of power within the political system. Party elites, unencumbered by mass member-ships which might call them to account, have therefore tended to dominate formal decision-making processes, at both national and regional level.

Yet, in spite of the considerable authority which continues to attach to the central state, Spain after the return of democracy was pitched into the European-wide crisis of the post-war Keynesian consensus which undermined activist governmental management of the economy through the use of so-called 'big levers' of monetary and fiscal policy (Heidenheimer *et al.*, 1983: 125ff.). The traditional function of state intervention as a means of managing the macro-economic constraints within which the economy operates (Furlong, 1994: 196) had been weakened long before the Socialist Party assumed power in 1982. Although Spain had not participated in the post-war construction of social welfare states which took place throughout much of the rest of Europe, it was not immune from the generalised failure of industrialised states to meet the ever-growing scale of demands placed on them by the 1970s, a situation exacerbated by the two oil-price shocks which marked that decade.[2] Thus, for all the resources at the government's command and in spite of much-vaunted promises to introduce major social welfare reforms, the Socialist administration immediately found itself obliged to adopt market-led policies of economic restructuring. As had been demonstrated by the examples of Socialist administrations elected in 1981 in both France and Greece, radical redistribution premised on Keynesian-style reflationary measures were simply not an option in a hostile international environment (Machin and Wright, 1985; Spourdalakis, 1985/86: 249–67). Subsequently, full integration into the EU – particularly after the signing of the Maastricht Treaty in 1992 – compounded the government's loss of autonomy over significant areas of policy-making (see chapter 10).

Policy Styles: From Neo-Corporatism to Euro-Conformity

The primacy of the state over civil society in modern Spanish politics significantly influenced the nature of the policy process after the transition to democracy. The historic weakness of civil society in Spain – which militated against the development of a participative, democratic culture – had been sharply exacerbated by the experience of General Franco's rule: nearly forty years of dictatorship inhibited the taking of initiatives and the assumption of individual responsibility, as well as the organisation of mechanisms of participation and collective action (Mella Márquez, 1992: 327–8). Whilst the post-Franco restoration of democracy provided the constitutional framework for a political process based on pluralist decision-making, it could not guarantee its translation into effective practice. The lack of a well-developed civil society was reflected in the small number of interest groups, most of which were in any case weak. Moreover, the provision for a highly powerful executive in Spain's new democracy (see chapter 4) reinforced the centrality of the state and militated against the diffusion of policy initiatives to autonomous institutions.

Spain's political structure in the late 1970s and early 1980s has been referred to both as 'corporatist' and 'neo-corporatist', an indication of the emphasis placed on pacts and agreements between government, employers and unions (Giner and Sevilla, 1984; Pérez-Díaz, 1993: 220–30). That tripartite agreements should have become a central feature of policy-making in the post-Franco years was in turn a reflection of the much-vaunted consensus and accommodation which characterised the Spanish transition. In particular, negotiations between elite actors, essential for the establishment of inter-class solidarity, facilitated the development of stable corporatist arrangements (Pérez-Díaz, 1993: 190; Gunther, 1992). The most well-known of these agreements was the Moncloa Pact, signed in October 1977 by the major political parties (see chapter 10). The Moncloa accord prefigured the basis upon which economic and social policy would be organised until the mid-1980s, a period which saw a wide-ranging series of contracts and pacts between government and social partners (see Exhibit 11.1).

Under the premiership of Adolfo Suárez (1977–81), agreements with leading social partners were a necessary recourse for a minority government forced to rely upon building coalitions of support in order to implement policy. The Socialist government, first elected in 1982 with an overwhelming majority, chose to continue the adoption

EXHIBIT 11.1

Pacts and agreements between government and social partners, 1977–86

Date	Agreement	Partners	Main issues covered
October 1977	*Pactos de la Moncloa*	All political parties represented in the *Congreso de los Diputados*[a]	Wage increases Inflation target Fiscal reform Public spending Social security Agricultural policy Energy policy
January 1980 (original agreement between CEOE and UGT, July 1979; revised 1981)	*Acuerdo Marco Interconfederal* (AMI, Interconfederal Framework Agreement)	UGT and CEOE initially; later joined by USO	Wage increases Working hours Job creation Recognition of union committees Productivity agreements Mediation, conciliation and arbitration
July 1981	*Acuerdo Nacional de Empleo* (ANE, National Agreement on Employment)	Government, CEOE, UGT, CC.OO.	Wage increases Pensions Job creation Overtime Unemployment cover Social security contributions Compensation for lost union assets
February 1983	*Acuerdo Interconfederal* (AI, Interconfederal Agreement)	CEOE, CEPYME, UGT and CC.OO.	Wage increases Working hours Retirement age Collective bargaining
October 1984 (renewed 1985 and 1986)	*Acuerdo Económico y Social* (AES, Economic and Social Agreement)	Government, CEOE, CEPYME, and UGT	Wage increases Pensions Investment Job creation Unemployment cover Social security Union assets Health and safety Productivity Collective bargaining

Key:
Trade unions: UGT (General Workers' Union), CC.OO. (Workers' Commissions), USO (Workers' Syndical Union).
Employers' organisations: CEOE (Spanish Confederation of Employers' Organisations), CEPYME (Spanish Confederation of Small and Medium-Sized Firms).
[a] The Moncloa Pacts entailed two documents, covering economic and political reforms respectively. All parties signed the first, but the Popular Alliance did not sign the second.
Sources: based on Pérez-Díaz (1993: 219–20); Keating (1993: 342); Alonso Zaldívar and Castells (1992: 293–5).

of corporatist-style agreements for rather different reasons. On the one hand, given the traditional suspicion of socialism among leading economic interests, the government sought to garner support for its policies through an emphasis on dialogue and cooperation with bankers, industrialists and employers' organisations. On the other, it was able to rely on its historic links with the *Unión General de Trabajadores* (UGT, General Workers' Union) to defuse potential opposition to its policies of economic restructuring during the early 1980s, which involved considerable sacrifice from the workforce and extensive job losses. In parliamentary terms, however, the Socialist government was able to adopt a majoritarian style of policy-making between 1982 and 1989: opposition parties regularly complained that the PSOE was using its absolute majority to steamroll legislation through the *Cortes*, thereby precluding effective legislative oversight of the executive. After 1989, Socialist governments were forced to bargain with other parties, notably the mainstream Catalan and Basque nationalists, for legislative support; indeed, such was the Socialists' reliance on the backing of *Convergència i Unió* in the 1993 legislature that the Catalan president, Jordi Pujol, was often referred to as *de facto* vice-president of the government.

The (neo-)corporatist approach to policy-making began to come under strain in the mid-1980s as the unions became increasingly disillusioned at what they judged to be unfair demands by a government which seemed more concerned to appease business and financial interests. The UGT leadership was compromised by its support for a Socialist government which continued to impose unpopular economic reforms aimed at preparing Spain for the challenge of competing within the EC. Broad agreement on entry to Europe, with its promise of a brighter future in which workers would be rewarded for the short-term pain of economic adjustment, initially helped keep conflict between government and unions to a minimum. However, once Spain had become a member of the EC on 1 January 1986 the broad outlines of economic policy remained unchanged, and relationships between the Socialist government and the UGT soured rapidly (Gillespie, 1990b). A serious rupture occurred in October 1987 when Nicolás Redondo, a long-time close associate of Felipe González, resigned as deputy for Vizcaya over the 1988 budget proposals.[3] In December 1988 a one-day general strike – the first to be called in Spain since the 1930s – won massive support, resulting in a formal break between the Socialist Party and the union federation it had created one hundred years earlier (Juliá, 1988a). Two further general strikes followed in 1992, and another in January 1994, although none had the same impact as the 1988 stoppage.

The Socialist government argued that it had no option but to continue enacting liberalisation and deregulation measures as part of its drive to make the Spanish economy competitive. Yet, in spite of the collapse in relations with the UGT which effectively ended neo-corporatist arrangements in Spain, the government continued to seek accords over policy-making: in 1990, it proposed the establishment of a 'Competitiveness Pact', aimed primarily at stemming labour costs through improved productivity – but negotiations with the unions soon foundered. A revised version, referred to as a 'Social Pact for Progress', was presented to the *Cortes* in June 1991, covering wages, anti-inflation measures, and labour market reforms. Yet, the government's apparent desire to promote consensus amongst social partners and mend relations with the union movement was undermined by the tone in which the measures were presented: the minister of the economy threatened that if agreement were not forthcoming, the proposals would be imposed on unions and employers (EIU Country Report, 3, 1991: 11–13). Agreement was reached the following year, however, to set up the *Consejo Económico y Social* (CES, Social and Economic Council), intended as a tripartite consultative body with no governmental presence. The CES, based on a model designed by the UGT, comprised 61 members: 20 each from the unions, employers' groups and consumer groups (including a number of government-proposed economic experts), together with an elected president. The CES commenced operations in 1992, but was widely seen as lacking real influence.

After the mid-1980s, the UGT began increasingly to co-ordinate its actions with its former rival federation, the *Comisiones Obreras* (CC.OO., Workers' Commissions), which had historically been linked to the Communist Party (Soto Carmona, 1993: 516–21). Regular joint actions by the two main unions led to a series of hostile confrontations with the government, particularly over the issue of labour market reforms. Union attacks on the government's economic policy were mirrored by criticism from the business and financial interests that the policy supposedly favoured. Any prospect of reviving a neo-corporatist policy style was further undermined in the early 1990s by the increasingly hostile posture towards the government adopted by employers' organisations. The combination of economic recession and the real prospect of a pro-business right-wing government following a sharp fall in popular support for the

Socialists led to hardening of attitudes by industrialists and financiers, who wanted to see further labour market reforms and deregulation measures.

In practice, the prospect of establishing a genuinely neo-corporatist policy style – involving an effective system of interest mediation and participation in the definition and execution of economic policy – was always remote in Spain (Keating, 1993: 342). Organised interest groups tend to be small and weak, unable to negotiate authoritatively on behalf of their members, whose support they are anyhow unable to commit with any certainty. More significant, however, has been Spain's integration into the EU. The signing of the Single European Act in 1987 and of the Maastricht Treaty in 1992 committed EU members to the adoption of broadly similar macroeconomic policy orientations, as well as opening up internal markets to trade and capital flows (Allard and Bolorinos, 1992: 72). European limitations on government intervention in industry, and the adoption of legal and regulatory frameworks according to EU standards, transformed the Spanish economy, exposing it to the shock of open competition after decades of state-sponsored protection. Yet, such developments also constrained the government's policy-making capacity. Increasingly, Spain has been forced to comply with policy orientations designed beyond its borders. Neo-corporatist arrangements ceased to offer a realistic basis for policy formulation, although the search for consensus amongst social partners over policy implementation remained a priority.

Between Association and Antagonism: Social Partners in the Policy Process

For all that analysts have referred to the persistence of corporatist arrangements in contemporary Spain, the relationship between the major social partners since the return of democracy has been far from smooth. Although the early years of the transition were marked by consensus and accommodation, mutual suspicion – when not outright hostility – has often characterised dealings between government, unions and employers. After assuming power in 1982, the Socialist government sought to tread a cautious line between, on the one hand, overcoming the historic fears of Spanish socialism amongst financiers, industrialists and the business class and, on the other, maintaining a close relationship with its allies in the union movement. The first of these objectives was achieved in spectacular fashion, but only at the expense of complete failure in the second. Spain's private banks, which own large slices of the economy and are generally controlled by limited oligarchies, wield considerable power (Graham, 1984: 90). Felipe González's concern to demonstrate that a Socialist administration would not harm the interests of the business community had led him even in the late 1970s to cultivate good relations with leading bankers and financiers (Rivases, 1988: 26–7), thereby laying the basis for the subsequent emergence of '*los beautiful*' – a closely interconnected group of wealthy individuals who occupied key posts in government and the private financial sector. During the 1980s, PSOE administrations under Felipe González came to be seen as pro-business and anti-worker, a remarkable turnaround for a socialist party which had been seen as one of the most radical in Europe in the late 1970s.

The Government: Ministries and Technocrats in the Policy Process

Given the primacy of the state in Spain's political structure, alongside a powerful core executive and correspondingly weak parliament (see chapter 4), it is understandable that policy initiatives should emanate mainly from government departments. A similar situation pertains at regional level, within the confines of the competencies granted to the Autonomous Communities. The structure of government in Spain in based on the French model: in constitutional terms, it is a unified entity with no formal separation of roles between government, cabinet and ministers (Alvarez Conde, 1990: 472–3). The 1978 Constitution allows the premier almost total freedom over ministerial appointments, but it does specify a number of departments which *must* be established.

Most Spanish ministries have a *gabinete del ministro* (minister's cabinet), again similar to the French model. Composed of politically-appointed advisers recruited mainly (but by no means exclusively) from within the civil service, the *gabinetes* exist to provide help with policy formulation, liaisons with other departments, and relations with the outside world (Keating, 1993: 336). In 1994, the government was composed of sixteen ministries, of which all but five had a *gabinete del ministro*; the exceptions, however, were the major portfolios of Foreign Affairs, Defence, Economy, Health, and Public Works, Transport and the Environment, which between them accounted for more than a third of state expenditure in the budget.

The real centre of decision-making power is the Ministry of the Economy and Finance (*Economía y Hacienda*). Known as a 'super-ministry', it groups together in one department responsibility for the Treasury, elaboration of the state budget, fiscal policy and foreign trade and investment policy (De la Dehesa, 1993: 12). Under the PSOE administrations of Felipe González, the Ministry of the Economy and Finance served as the hub of government policy, particularly after Spain joined the EC: it not only established broad macroeconomic priorities, but also had control over budget allocations to other government departments.

Miguel Boyer, minister of the economy from 1982 until 1985, was an orthodox economist from the Bank of Spain, who played a key role in moderating the more radical ambitions of several ministerial colleagues, including González himself. One of the most controversial figures in the Socialist administration, Boyer came to symbolise virtually everything left-wing critics of the government opposed. A leading moderate, who had briefly left the PSOE to join the short-lived Social Democratic Party of Francisco Fernández Ordóñez (himself later to be a minister in the Socialist administration), Boyer's frequent clashes with Alfonso Guerra ultimately led to his resignation. He subsequently gave up his parliamentary seat, citing boredom as the reason – although his appointment to head the Banco Exterior de España shortly after leaving government provoked much criticism for its potential conflict of interests. Boyer's considerable personal wealth and close involvement with '*los beautiful*'[4] provoked the ire of many on the left who saw his lifestyle as incompatible with membership of a Socialist party (Company and Arroyo, 1989: 155–7). Boyer's successor, Carlos Solchaga (who remained in post until 1993) was another former Bank of Spain economist. Trained at the Massachusetts Institute of Technology (MIT), Solchaga continued Boyer's line of moderation, leading to serious tensions within the PSOE between the so-called reformists and the backers of the more populist Alfonso Guerra, deputy premier from 1982 until 1991 (see chapter 9). It is a measure of the central importance of the Ministry of the Economy that Guerra was never able to force a change of policy direction, in spite of his close control of the party apparatus.[5]

Indeed, economic technocrats have exercised a major influence on the policy process in contemporary Spain (Fuentes Quintana, 1991). Even under the dictatorship of General Franco, the economic reforms of the 1960s were primarily sponsored by '*Técnicos Comerciales y Economistas del Estado*' – high-level civil servants trained in economics.

Starting at the Ministry of Commerce and then later in other ministries such as Finance, Industry and Energy, Agriculture, and Labour, these top government advisers helped ensure that economic rationality underpinned political decision-making. Several became ministers or secretaries of state, or even vice-presidents – as in the cases of Enrique Fuentes Quintana and Juan Antonio García Díez under the premiership of Adolfo Suárez. The research department of the Bank of Spain has also been a rich source of high-level appointees, including both Boyer and Solchaga as well as governors of the central bank, such as Mariano Rubio and Angel Rojo (De la Dehesa, 1993: 27).

The Labour Movement: Power, Partnership and Political Marginalisation

On the basis of membership figures alone, the Spanish labour movement might be considered one of the weakest in Europe. In 1994, around 10 per cent of salaried workers belonged to the *Unión General de Trabajadores* (UGT, General Workers' Union), the *Comisiones Obreras* (CC. OO., Workers' Commissions), or to one of the other, much smaller, unions.[6] This figure represented a dramatic fall from 57.8 per cent membership in 1978, which reflected the rush to join the newly legalised unions in the aftermath of the Franco dictatorship. The decline in union membership was not only steep, but also rapid: by 1980, the level of affiliation had fallen to 33.8 per cent and by 1984 stood at 23 per cent, a drop of some 60 per cent from the 1978 figure (Pérez-Díaz, 1993: 267). By the late 1980s, the UGT and CC. OO. each had about 800 000 affiliates, a figure which continued to decline annually.

Although overall membership of unions is low, some 80 per cent of salaried workers vote in union elections, which are open to all those in the workforce (Chislett, 1994: 36). In the initial stages of the transition to democracy, the CC. OO. enjoyed a larger following than the UGT, largely on account of their activities against the Franco dictatorship since the early 1960s (Ruiz, 1993). Results of works' council elections, held every two years between 1978 and 1982 and every four years thereafter, indicate how support gradually shifted to the UGT, which took a majority of votes for the first time in 1982 (see Table 11.1). Support for the CC. OO. was based mainly in the industrial sector and in large factories, whereas the UGT fared better · in small and medium-sized firms – a factor which worked to the latter's advantage given the structural changes in the Spanish

TABLE 11.1

Works' council election results, 1978–90, per cent of vote received

	1978[a]	1980	1982	1986	1990
CC.OO.	34.5	31.8	34.5	34.4	37.0
UGT	21.7	31.7	39.9	41.0	42.0
USO	3.9	9.0	4.9	3.6	2.9
Others[b]	40.0	27.5	20.7	21.0	18.1

Key:
CC.OO.: *Comisiones Obreras* (Workers' Commissions, associated with the Communist Party).
UGT: *Unión General de Trabajadores* (General Workers' Union, historically linked to the Socialist Party).
USO: *Unión Sindical Obrera* (Workers' Syndicate, an independent centrist union)
[a] The official 1978 results released by Labour Ministry and reproduced here were disputed by the CC OO and UGT, which gave both organisations a higher overall percentage.
[b] Independent and small unions, of which the most important are the ELA–STV (*Eusko Langileen Alkartasuna - Solidaridad de Trabajadores Vascos*, a left-leaning Basque union), the INTG (*Intersindical Galega*, a moderate Galician union) and the CSIF (*Confederación de Sindicatos Independientes de Funcionarios*, an independent union of government employees).
Sources: based on Soto Carmona (1993: 515), Allard and Bolorinos (1992: 8): *EIU Country Report*, 1 (1991: 12).

economy during the 1980s. Yet, despite the erosion of membership, Spain's unions have on occasion been able to exert considerable political influence, as demonstrated most notably by the success of the December 1988 general strike. Government consultation with unions on major policy issues during the transition to democracy set an important precedent: even though relations between the PSOE administration and the UGT broke down during the course of the 1980s, ministers continued to seek union support for most major economic policy decisions – albeit, often with little success.

The unions' real influence since the return of democracy has derived from their involvement in wage bargaining, established under the terms of the 1980 Workers' Statute and the 1985 Organic Law on Trade Union Freedom. The Workers' Statute provided for an annual minimum wage to be fixed by the government and outlined both worker representation and collective bargaining procedures. In firms with between 10 and 50 employees, workers were to be represented by up to three delegates (*delegados de personal*). In firms with more than 50 employees, works' councils (*comités de empresa*) were to be established, their size to be governed by the number of workers (see Table 11.2). Unions which obtained 10 per cent or more of members of the works' councils were granted the status of 'most representative union', regardless of formal membership levels, which automatically entitled them to form part of a negotiating committee for collective agreements and to nominate representatives to the boards of public bodies.

In May 1994, in the face of fierce opposition from the unions, the *Cortes* passed a far-reaching package of labour market reforms, which entailed significant changes to the Workers' Statute. The reforms were primarily concerned with dismantling those elements of employment protection which remained from the Franco dictatorship in the form of *ordenanzas laborales*, paternalist measures which regulated working conditions, job categories, promotions, and terms of dismissal. Under the terms of the 1994 reforms, which sought to reduce the role of the state as a regulator of labour norms, wage bargaining negotiations were partially decentralised (CES, 1994: 108–9). Individual companies unable to support a wage increase for a given sector would no longer be obliged to follow legally-established guidelines, and greater flexibility was introduced in regard to the length of the working day (although the maximum weekly total was to remain at 40 hours), holiday provisions and overtime pay.

The 1994 legislation, primarily motivated by the very high level of unemployment and escalating labour costs, also introduced far greater flexibility in regard to hiring and firing, and provided incentives for part-time contracts, as well as apprenticeships and

TABLE 11.2

Representation on Works' Councils

No. of employees in company	No. of members on Works' Council
50–100	5
101–250	9
251–500	13
501–750	17
751–1,000	21
1,000+	21
	+2 per 1,000 employees up to a maxmimum of 75 members

Source: Donaghy and Newton (1987: 182).

vocational training schemes. Although the unions were under-standably opposed to the reforms, which sponsored the creation of more temporary and lower-paid jobs, their response did not reflect a dogmatic refusal to countenance change in the labour market. In 1993, they had entered a four-year tripartite agreement with the government and employers' organisations to promote a better match between supply and demand for professional qualifications through the creation of a National Programme for Vocational Training. The new programme, designed on the German model, placed emphasis on greater co-ordination between the ministries of labour and education, together with the involvement of chambers of commerce (Chislett, 1994: 23).

Yet, the unions were undoubtedly marginalised from the policy process during the 1980s, forced to respond to government proposals rather than sponsor new inititiatives. Attempts to influence the economic policy agenda – such as through the demand in the early 1990s for a *'giro social'* (social policy shift) which went beyond increased spending on social welfare provisions to encompass wage increases, redistribution of wealth and a reduction in the number of temporary contracts – met with little success. Similarly, the unions' Priority Platform (1990) and Initiative for Progress (1991) were ignored by a government which insisted on the need to push ahead with its European-oriented policies of deregulation and liberalisation. Opposition to the government's emphasis on wage restraint and productivity increases was linked: the unions argued that workers deserved a larger share in Spain's growing prosperity, and that banks and employers should restrain profits in order to allow for a greater transfer of wealth.

That such arguments made little impact on the government was graphically demonstrated in early 1992, when the PSOE adminis-tration issued a decree-law as part of its Convergence Plan (see chapter 10) limiting unemployment benefit entitlement to those who had previously been in employment for a full year. In the event, the threat of industrial action, as well as a revolt within the PSOE, forced the government to abandon the decree and present its measures in the form of a parliamentary bill, subject to amendments by the *Cortes*. The episode demonstrated the extent to which the government was prepared to impose economic policy, even at the expense of generating intense union opposition, rather than to develop a 'social partnership' along the lines familiar from the policy process in Germany. Miguel Boyer apparently told the UGT leader, Nicolás

Redondo, that 'the norm in democracies is that the government takes decisions and afterwards informs the social agents' (Petras, 1993: 120).

The unions could be so easily ignored because of their declining capacity to exert significant political influence. In 1976, Spanish labour was the most militant in Europe, with 150 million working hours lost in disputes, many of them politically inspired; thereafter, following a peak of activity in 1979, the number of working hours lost showed a discernible downward trend in the 1980s, punctuated by occasional eruptions of strike activity, such as in 1984 and 1988 (Camiller, 1994: 235; Allard and Bolorinos, 1992: 8–9). For some analysts, the decline in union power resulted from a concerted attack on workers' rights by the Socialist government, which – under the guise of restructuring and modernising the economy – sought to consolidate the power of the state over civil society and to shift the balance of power decisively from labour to capital. By marginalising the unions, working-class solidarity would be destroyed, thereby enabling Socialist-connected entrepreneurs and bankers to enter the upper echelons of the ruling class (Petras, 1993). A more measured assessment might attribute the decline of union influence less to the demonic purposes of the Socialist administration than to a combination of structural changes in the economy, which eroded traditional working-class communities, and a 'crisis of representation' amongst an increasingly *moderate* union membership, which often came to resent the actions of more militant radicals (Fishman, 1990; Pérez-Díaz, 1993: 281–312). In an era of reduced class antagonism, workers saw unions as organisations which could best defend their interests through direct negotiation with firms, rather than through mass action (Mella Márquez, 1992: 334).

The Employers: From Partnership to Partisan Politics

The view that the labour movement had lost influence as a result of its gradual marginalisation from the policy process was not one shared by the Spanish employers' organisation, the CEOE (*Confederación Española de Organizaciones Empresariales*). On the contrary, the CEOE charged in 1991 that the Socialist government was standing by passively whilst the unions accumulated a degree of social and political power not anticipated in the 1978 Constitution (Allard and Bolorinos, 1992: 9). Such an interpretation reflected a marked shift in the CEOE's stance, which in the early stages of the transition to democracy had been strongly committed to a policy of corporate agreements with government and unions (Pérez-Díaz, 1993: 209–10). In the latter part of the 1980s, however, the CEOE began to assume more overtly right-wing stances which stressed economic liberalism and deregulation, the promotion of domestic private enterprise (in opposition to the infiltration of foreign capital), wage restraint and sharply reduced public spending.

The CEOE had been founded in late 1977 and expanded rapidly. Under the leadership of its first president, Carlos Ferrer Salat, the CEOE soon developed a close working relationship with the UGT.[7] A strongly committed Europeanist and supporter of the UCD government of Adolfo Suárez, Ferrer negotiated a basic agreement with the UGT in July 1979 which culminated in the *Acuerdo Marco Interconfederal* (AMI, Interconfederal Framework Agreement), the first in a series of accords between the CEOE and the unions. Ferrer's successor as president of the CEOE, José María Cuevas, was far less sympathetic to the consensus-seeking approach; an overt backer of the right-wing *Alianza* (later *Partido*) *Popular*, he adopted from the early 1980s onwards a much more confrontational stance towards both the unions and the Socialist government. Even before the UCD started to collapse, leading figures in the CEOE were seeking to help establish '*la gran derecha*', a right-wing alternative to the Socialists (Mella Márquez, 1992: 340–1).

Yet although by the late 1980s the CEOE had established a *de facto* monopoly over the representation of employers' interests, the organisation lacked the negotiating authority that might have been expected to follow from this fact. A number of reasons account for the CEOE's reduced influence. First, like the unions, the employers' organisation found it difficult to gain access to the process of policy formulation under the Socialist administration, dominated increasingly after the mid-1980s by the drive for competitiveness within Europe. Secondly, the CEOE's own organisational structure hampered its effectiveness: business firms can affiliate to the CEOE through joining either sectoral or territorial groups, which then represent their interests at central level. Sectoral groups, such as those in metals (CONFEMETAL, *Confederación de Organizaciones Empresariales del Metal*) and construction (CNC, *Confederación Nacional de la Construcción*), wielded considerable influence compared to territorially-based groups – with the exception of *Confederación Empresarial Independiente de Madrid* (CEIM) and the *Fomento del Trabajo Nacional*

(FTN) in Catalonia. This imbalance gave rise on occasion to tensions, as well as making it difficult for the CEOE to represent its members' diverse interests. Thirdly, the high level of foreign ownership of Spanish businesses – foreign capital controlled about 50 per cent of Spain's industrial production capacity at the end of the 1980s – and the ability of multinationals to deal directly at governmental level has militated against the development of a homogeneous and powerfully organised entrepreneurial class in Spain (Keating, 1993: 340).

The real centre of influence amongst Spanish employers has been the banking world, which controls substantial commercial and industrial interests (Salmon, 1991: 151) and is represented in the CEOE through the *Asociación Española de Banca Privada* (AEB, Spanish Banking Association). Spanish banks have historically been powerful institutions; since the turn of the century, when the bulk of Spain's major banks took shape, they have been at the core of the country's modern industrial development (Graham, 1984: 73). Even before the transition to democracy was under way, the presidents of Spain's leading banks met each month to hold informal discussions on a wide range of issues; known as the '*Club de los Siete*', the meetings brought together the heads of Banesto, Central, Hispano-Americano, Bilbao, Vizcaya, Santander and Popular. The banks' direct involvement in the economy, reinforced by a 1962 reorganisation to create specialised commercial and industrial banks, ensured that their presidents wielded enormous influence. Secretive and patriarchal, the banks organised intricate networks of interests which were often tied to a select group of closely-related families.

Yet, in spite of the close inter-connections which characterised the Spanish banking world, the banks have not worked in concert to promote particular policies. Even under the Franco regime, there is little evidence that the banks acted together to try to influence or alter economic policy. That the transition to democracy coincided with a generational shift in the management of several of the leading banks helped ensure that, in the early stages of the post-Franco reforms, the 'big seven' remained preoccupied with their own rivalries rather than elaborating a unified or coherent policy stance. In July 1977, the minister of the economy, Enrique Fuentes Quintana, introduced reforms to the financial system which represented the first attempt at liberalisation ever seen in the Spanish banking and finance system (Graham, 1984: 99). The reforms acted as the catalyst of far-reaching changes in the banking world, the need for which had been exacerbated by the impact of the severe recession which gripped the Spanish economy in the aftermath of the dictatorship (see chapter 10). Between 1977 and 1983, over fifty banking institutions (more than half the total in existence in 1977) were affected by a prolonged crisis which accounted for over a quarter of all employees in the sector (Chislett, 1994: 106). The crisis culminated in the 1983 expropriation of the *Rumasa* group, which forced restructuring on the financial sector (Salmon, 1991: 149).

Three of the 'big seven' – Bilbao, Hispano-Americano and Vizcaya –had become alarmed at the increasingly close identification of the CEOE in the early 1980s with Manuel Fraga's right-wing *Alianza Popular*. Although not PSOE sympathisers, José Angel Sánchez Asiaín and Pedro Toledo, presidents respectively of the Bilbao and Vizcaya banks, developed close relationships with Felipe González and Carlos Solchaga, minister of the economy between 1985 and 1993. They were even sometimes referred to as 'Socialist bankers' and Sánchez Asiaín has been seen as a key figure behind the PSOE government's policy towards the banks. The views of the president of the Banco de Bilbao chimed with those of the Socialist administration in two crucial respects: he was a strong supporter of Spain's progressive integration into the Single European Market, and he also backed the policy of bank mergers in order to create institutions which could compete internationally (Sánchez Asiaín, 1992: 123–4).

The Bilbao and Vizcaya banks joined forced in January 1988 to create Spain's largest bank, the BBV, after an unsuccessful attempt a few months earlier by Sánchez Asiaín – with top-level government support – to take over Banesto. There then followed an extraordinary period of merger activity, culminating in the Bank of Spain's intervention in Banesto at the end of 1993 and its subsequent purchase by Banco de Santander. A constant feature of this period was the opposition between the European-oriented vision of the Socialist-backed BBV and the more nationalistic stance of Mario Conde, president of Banesto (Cacho, 1988). Conde, one of Spain's most prominent financial figures who carefully cultivated his public image, became an outspoken critic of the PSOE's European project.[8] He argued for the strengthening of civil society against the state in order to promote an entrepreneurial class which would stimulate the Spanish economy at the micro level, and repeatedly denounced the Socialists' preoccupation with European policy – in particular, the peseta's 'premature' and over-valued entry into the Exchange Rate Mechanism (ERM) of the European Monetary System (EMS) in

1989 and the government's acceptance of the Maastricht Treaty two years later.

Conde had nevertheless attempted to bring about the merger of Banesto and Banco Central in 1988, a bizarre and ultimately unsuccessful episode in which he was opposed by the former minister of the economy, Miguel Boyer (Cacho, 1994).[9] In June 1990, two Catalan savings banks were merged, followed in May 1991 by the grouping together of six public banks into the Corporación Bancaria de España (CBE), later renamed Argentaria. Two days after the establishment of the CBE, another major merger was announced, this time between the Banco Hispano-Americano and the Banco Central. The creation of the Banco Central Hispanoamericano (BCH) represented a highly significant step in the government's policy of concentration in the banking world: four of the five largest banks were now in the control of presidents closely connected to the world of '*los beautiful*'. The one exception was Conde's Banesto, which was thereby excluded from any policy-making influence within the banking sector.

In bid to compete with the newly merged banks, Banesto – which retained extensive industrial interests – over-extended its loan book, leaving it highly vulnerable to the recession which hit the Spanish economy in the early 1990s. Insufficient provision against loan losses obliged the state-run Deposit Guarantee Fund to intervene and plug the gap created by Banesto's massive losses. Conde was dismissed and subsequently subjected to a fraud investigation; in the meanwhile, the purchase of Banesto by the Banco de Santander created Spain's largest banking group.[10] Thus, the Spanish banking world underwent a process of radical restructuring between 1987 and 1994, with the 'big seven' becoming four large and one smaller group (see Exhibit 11.2).

In contrast to Spain's banks, which have played a central role in the country's economic development, farming organisations have been unable to exercise significant policy influence since the return of democracy. The importance of agriculture in the Spanish economy is substantially less in the mid-1990s than it was even a decade earlier when Spain joined the EC, and massively less than it was under the Franco regime. The numbers employed in agriculture, forestry and fishing have fallen from 4.9 million in 1960 (around 40 per cent of the active population) to 3.7 million in 1970, 2.3 million in 1980 and just 1.8 million in 1990 – in part the result of mechanisation replacing labour-intensive production methods (Salmon, 1991: 42, 67). By

EXHIBIT 11.2

Major bank groups in Spain, 1994

	Assets (Pta bn)	Employees	Branches
Santander/Banesto	15,366	45,000	4,000
Banco Central Hispano	12,950	34,400	3,450
Banco Bilbao Vizcaya	11,635	28,700	2,900
Argentaria	11,192	17,600	1,500
Banco Popular	2,865	12,000	1,800

Source: adapted from Chislett (1994: 107).

1994, agriculture employed roughly 10 per cent of the labour force and accounted for less than 5 per cent of GDP.

Moreover, agricultural lobbies have been divided, reflecting the diverse nature of Spain's agrarian structure: the country has the widest range of agricultural produce in the EU. Thus, the demands of wheat-growers in Castile do not necessarily coincide with those of fruit growers in Valencia, olive producers in Andalucía, or milk farmers in Galicia and so forth (Keating, 1993: 340). In any case, the government's available range of policy options in regard to agriculture is constrained by Spain's membership of the EU. The extensive web of state intervention and product protection which characterised the agrarian system under Franco has been unravelled as significant parts of the agricultural policy-making process have been transferred to Brussels (Salmon, 1991: 54). Rationalisation, together with the transfer to the regions of many functions previously carried out by the Ministry of Agriculture, has further reduced the role of central govenment, which has concentrated instead on sponsoring modernisation and restructuring. The terms of the Common Agricultural Policy (CAP), which are widely regarded as highly unfavourable to Spain, have also set limits on protection and state intervention in agriculture, thereby exposing Spanish producers to substantially increased competition.

It is measure of the sheer scale of the transformation that has occurred in Spain's economic structure that agrarian issues are no longer central to the concerns of policy-makers. Agrarian conflict had been endemic for centuries in Spain. It became chronic during the course of the Second Republic (1931–6) and was one of the most critical confrontations in the build up to the Civil War (Preston,

1984: 159). Under the Franco dictatorship, *latifundistas* – the owners of great estates concentrated in Spain's arid central and southern regions – maintained political power until well into the 1950s. Only with the economic growth and industrialisation of the 1960s did agrarian predominance begin to recede, a process which continued and accelerated following the post-Franco transition to democracy. In parallel with developments in other sectors since the mid-1980s, agricultural production has been subsumed into the international economy, regulated by the EU, and subject to the discipline of international markets. The policy process has in turn reflected Spain's changed economic and political circumstances: although the state retains its central role, it has been forced to cede ever more areas of influence to the interests and demands of the international community of which it now forms a part.

12

Spain as an International Power

Spain's emergence as an international power is of very recent origin. It was only after democracy had been securely established that Spanish leaders were really able to confront the issue of defining an international profile. Under the dictatorship, Spain's foreign policy had been subordinated to the domestic demands of the regime, leading to a lack of any overall coherence. The main purpose of Franco's foreign policy was simply to secure international recognition in order to bolster his hold on power (Armero, 1978; Espadas Burgos, 1988). Franco's attempts to escape isolation did see some successes: the Concordat with the Vatican and the military pacts with the USA in 1953, membership of the United Nations in 1955, and in 1970 a preferential trade agreement with the European Community (EC). However, the nature of his regime denied Franco a significant voice in international affairs and, by 1975, even these meagre achievements were under threat. The return to repression which marked the dictatorship's last years severely compromised Spain's international standing and saw a serious deterioration in relations with Europe, the USA and the Vatican.

Democratic Spain: Rediscovering an International Role

Spain's first post-Franco prime minister, Carlos Arias Navarro, sponsored no new initiatives in foreign affairs, preferring – as in his domestic policies – to follow the broad outlines established by the dictator. Not until Adolfo Suárez became premier in mid-1976 did foreign policy concerns emerge as a focus of government attention. However, Suárez's attention was primarily fixed on the more immediate domestic demands of democratic construction. The establishment of a coherent foreign policy orientation thus took considerably longer than the formal establishment of democracy. Although Suárez and King Juan Carlos made significant early moves to develop a sound basis for Spain's international relations, it was only after the election of Felipe González's Socialist government in 1982 that a clear sense of direction began to emerge (Arenal, 1991: 46–50).

There have been two key changes in Spain's foreign policy orientation since the return of democracy: the decision-making process has been reorganised on democratic grounds, in line with the 1978 Constitution, and a focus for action has emerged through the elaboration of a clear set of principles, based on the rhetorical commitment to support peace, solidarity and a reduction of international tensions. These changes evolved over a period of several years, during which four distinct phases can be identified (Arenal, 1991). The first runs from the appointment of Suárez in July 1976 until the decision, announced in 1980, to seek membership of NATO. During these four years, there was consensus amongst the main political forces over the broad lines of foreign policy and polemical issues were largely avoided (Aldecoa Luzarraga, 1994: 162–3). Indeed, a shared commitment to seeking membership of the EC was virtually the sole foreign policy objective, and the 1978 Constitution lacks a distinct international dimension.

Amongst the most significant international issues facing Spain during this first period were the need to achieve full integration into international fora (particularly within the European context), the definition of a location and role within a western defence framework, the question of decolonisation and the Mahgreb (notably in regard to Morocco), and relations with Portugal following the coup of 25 April 1974. Suárez, rather than foreign affairs minister Marcelino Oreja, took the initiative on most international matters, but failed to elaborate a coherent and clearly defined perspective. Although Suárez referred on occasion to seeking a rather vague 'third way' between North and South[1] – stressing Spain's role as a mediator between Latin America and Europe, its deep friendship ties with the Arab nations, and its special interests in Northern Africa – the UCD's general policy orientation was European, western and democratic. Diplomatic relations were established with most countries in the world, with the exception of Israel, Albania and North Korea. Of particular note was the establishment of relations with the Soviet Union (9 February 1977) and Mexico (28 March 1977), two countries which had continued to support the defeated Second Republic after the Spanish Civil War.

In July 1977 a formal application was made to join the EC. Later in the year, on 24 November, Spain became a member of The Council of Europe and adopted the European Convention for the Protection of Human Rights and Fundamental Freedoms. Whilst membership of Europe was an aspiration embraced by all leading political forces in Spain, a further initiative undertaken by the Suárez government led to a collapse of the consensus which had characterised foreign policy developments during the early years of democracy. On 15 June 1980, Marcelino Oreja announced in the *Cortes* that Spain would seek to join the Atlantic Alliance, a move which met with trenchant opposition from parties of the left (Rodríguez, 1988: 62–3). For the first time since the restoration of democracy, foreign affairs became a highly politicised issue.

The second period in the redefinition of Spain's foreign policy stance runs from the breakdown of consensus in 1980 to the referendum on NATO membership of March 1986. Dominated by the debate over Spain's relationship with the Atlantic Alliance and negotiations over EC entry, this six-year period also saw a number of key developments which helped shape Spain's international profile. Formal entry into NATO in May 1982 was deeply unpopular, and the PSOE's promise to hold a referendum on the issue helped it secure a crushing victory in the general elections just six months later. However, Felipe González soon discovered that the issue of NATO membership was inextricably linked to Spain's application to join the EC. *Realpolitik* dictated that joining the EC was effectively conditional upon remaining in the Atlantic Alliance. On 1 January 1986, Spain became a member of the EC; just over two months later, on 15 March, the NATO issue was resolved with a referendum vote in favour of continued membership.

Between March 1986 and December 1988, the PSOE government sought to formalise Spain's international relations. This third period in the post-Franco reorientation of foreign affairs established the country's defence commitments. The Nuclear Non-Proliferation Treaty was signed on 5 November 1987, and a year later, on 14 November 1988, Spain became an 'active observer' in the Western European Union (WEU).[2] The following month, two important issues were resolved: a new Defence Co-operation Agreement with the USA was signed in Madrid on 1 December, finally bringing to an end the subordinate relationship first established in 1953; on the same day, NATO's Committee on Defence Plans approved the general outlines of Spain's military contribution to the Atlantic Alliance (Marquina, 1994: 377–80). With these agreements, the reformulation of Spain's foreign and defence policy was effectively concluded.

Ironically, just as Spain was bringing to an end its own international transition, the world saw a remarkable change in the political constants which had marked the international order since the Second World War. The collapse of communism and the end of the Cold War posed major challenges for Spain just as they did for all western nations. Thus, the final period in Spain's international reorientation has been marked by the need to confront and respond to these challenges. The most significant periods of tension have surrounded the Gulf War in early 1991 and the crisis unleashed by the civil war in the former Yugoslavia. In both cases, Spain has sought to fulfil its international obligations as established through membership of the United Nations, NATO and the WEU, in spite of considerable misgivings amongst a population unused to Spanish involvement in overseas adventures.

NATO and Europe: Interlinked Imperatives

The two central points of reference for Spanish foreign policy after the the death of Franco were the EC and NATO. The prospect of EC membership unified Spain's political class, offering the promise of integration with the most advanced European nations. The issue of NATO, on the other hand, was deeply divisive; whilst the UCD had early signalled its desire for Spanish entry, the PSOE remained resolutely opposed. A dual consensus thus emerged: Spain's intention to join the Community would be unanimously supported, but no changes in defence policy would be sought. Instead, bilateral agreements with the USA would remain in force and the question of NATO membership would not be raised (Alonso Zaldívar and Castells, 1992: 196–7). In practice, it became impossible to separate the issues of EC entry and NATO membership, at least in the medium term. Once the dual consensus had been shattered by precipitate moves to join NATO in 1981–2, negotiations over EC entry could not be fully disentangled from the NATO issue.

Spain and NATO Membership

From NATO's point of view, Spain was of considerable strategic significance during the Cold War era. Indeed, regardless of the calibre of the Spanish armed forces at the time, NATO chiefs had every reason to be delighted that Spain joined the Atlantic Alliance in 1982 and immensely relieved that it chose to remain a member following the referendum of March 1986. Possession of the Canary Islands in the Atlantic, Ceuta and Melilla on the Moroccan coast, and the Balearic Islands in the Mediterranean, gives Spain control over a maritime axis of primordial importance (Uxó Palasí, 1986: 47–63). In addition, the long quadrilateral coastline of the Iberian peninsula affords excellent access for more wide-ranging naval deployments. Moreover, as would be demonstrated during the Gulf War, the Spanish landmass offers first-class facilities for air force action and interception (Preston and Smyth, 1984: 15). As a western military attaché told *Le Monde* (12 March 1986) at the time of the NATO referendum, 'If Spain is of interest to her allies, it is with regard to her geography rather than her army.'

Nevertheless, it has also been argued that Spain's real importance to NATO – like that of NATO to Spain – was not so much strategic as political (Herrero de Miñón, 1985; Treverton, 1981: 32, 1986: 35). From the Spanish point of view, political considerations lay at the very heart of the relationship with NATO. They were a powerful motive force behind the urgency of application for membership in 1981. Following the notorious attempted coup led by Lieutenant-Colonel Antonio Tejero Molina in February of that year (see Chapter 3), it was believed that Spanish incorporation into the Atlantic Alliance could play a vital role in establishing a greater respect for democracy within an army renowned for its propensity to interfere in domestic politics. Leopoldo Calvo Sotelo, whose investiture as prime minister following the resignation of Suárez in January 1981 had been interrupted by the so-called *Tejerazo*, promised in his inauguration speech to accelerate moves towards NATO membership. On 20 August, the Cabinet agreed to request authorisation from the *Cortes* to sign the North Atlantic Treaty; debate took place during October, and by 26 November approval had been granted by both parliamentary chambers. Spain formally became a member of NATO on 30 May 1982 (Marquina, 1986: 899–942).

The decision to join NATO was highly unpopular. Opinion polls in late 1981 showed 44 per cent of the population opposed to membership, with just 14 per cent in favour. Indeed, the extent to which Calvo Sotelo had misjudged popular hostility to membership of the Atlantic Alliance contributed to the UCD's decimation in the elections of October 1982. It has been estimated that the promise of a referendum on NATO membership was worth over a million votes to the Socialists (Gillespie, 1989: 417–18).

Opposition to NATO membership existed for a number of reasons. First, the Atlantic Alliance was seen as inextricably linked to the USA, which stood condemned for the support it had offered Franco and for its interventionist approach to Latin America. In May 1975, when it was clear that Franco could not survive much longer, President Gerald Ford undertook an official two-day visit to Madrid, thereby appearing to back the regime even if he spent more time with Prince Juan Carlos than with the dictator (Preston, 1993: 774). Further damage was caused by US secretary of state Alexander Haig's description of the *Tejerazo* as 'an internal matter'.[3] As Felipe González remarked in a speech at the Woodrow Wilson Center in 1986, given past experience, no democratic Spaniard assumes support from the Western democracies for a non-authoritarian Spain. For Spaniards, defence of the West was not synonymous with the defence of democratic values (Maxwell, 1991: 39–40).

Second, and probably more important, there was never any clear perception in Spain of a Soviet threat against which an Alliance would be necessary. Moreover, Franco had used the spurious notion of a communist menace as a legitimising rationale for his suppression of the Second Republic and the maintenance of his dictatorship (Preston, 1993: 149–50 and *passim.*; Southworth, 1986). Opponents of NATO therefore saw in the PSOE the greatest possibility of ensuring Spain's withdrawal. In turn, the PSOE – which had called at its XXVII Congress in 1976 for 'active neutrality' and the removal from Spanish soil of US bases – was in a strong position to capitalise on public misgivings over NATO membership (Santesmases, 1984: 59–67).

The PSOE contested the 1982 election on a manifesto which pledged to freeze NATO integration pending a referendum on the issue, using the slogan '*OTAN, de entrada, no*'.[4] However, the Socialist leadership soon changed tack after its overwhelming election victory. Indeed, the party executive – or Felipe González, at least – seemed to move in the opposite direction to its followers. The promised referendum was consistently put off and, to the consternation of many of its supporters, the government mounted a sustained propaganda campaign in favour of NATO. The campaign reached fever pitch in the final days leading up to the referendum, which was held on 12 March 1986 – the last available date according to the rules on electoral consultations. At no point in the campaign did the government defend its pro-NATO position in terms of defence and security policy; instead, emphasis was placed on the potential political and economic costs if Spain were to say no to NATO.

The referendum question asked if voters supported Spain's continued membership subject to three provisos: participation in the Atlantic Alliance would not involve entry into the integrated military structure; no nuclear weapons would be installed or based on Spanish territory; US military presence in Spain would be steadily reduced (see Exhibit 12.1). Contrary to widespread expectations, the government's efforts were rewarded as it secured a majority vote in favour of continued participation in NATO, although the abstention rate was 40 per cent. Of those who did vote, 52.5 per cent were in favour, 39.8 per cent against, and the remaining 7.7 per cent cast either blank or void votes (Arenal, 1991: 58).

The government's dramatic turnaround on NATO demonstrated the imperious force of pragmatism over idealism. It was argued that membership of NATO did not necessarily increase the threat to Spain

---

EXHIBIT 12.1

**The NATO referendum in Spain, 12 March 1986:
the question and conditionality clauses**

The Government considers it in the national interest that Spain remain in the Atlantic Alliance and resolves that membership should be established on the following terms:

1   The participation of Spain in the Atlantic Alliance will not include its incorporation into the integrated military structure.
2   The prohibition of the installation, storing or introduction of nuclear arms on Spanish territory will be continued.
3   The progressive reduction of the military presence in Spain of the United States of America will proceed.

'Do you consider it advisable for Spain to remain in the Atlantic Alliance according to the terms set forth by the Government of the nation?'

Source: Revista de Estudios Internacionales, 7(1)(January–March 1986), quoted in Rodríguez (1988: 71).

since it was inconceivable that the country could avoid being dragged into any East–West conflict that might arise (Serra, 1985: 63; Blay Biosca, 1985: 1,399). At the same time, the costs of withdrawal from NATO could be high. The USA would be highly unlikely to enter into serious negotiations over military bases should Spain withdraw from NATO. Moreover, once out of NATO, Spain would not be able to count on support in the event of any Moroccan attack on Ceuta or Melilla, which were not covered by the US–Spanish defence agreement. Whilst membership of NATO was no guarantee of protection either, the memory of the 'Green March' on the Spanish Sahara in October 1975 was still fresh in the mind (Villar, 1982). In relation to Gibraltar, it was clear that a negotiated solution to the problem of sovereignty would be virtually impossible should Spain withdraw from the Atlantic Alliance.

Probably more important than these territorial and strategic considerations, however, were economic issues. Indeed, the economic situation of Spain acted as a crucial determinant of foreign and defence policy (Viñas, 1984: 22–4). Incorporation into NATO came to assume a central role in the Socialist government's aim of industrial *reconversión*, or restructuring, towards high technology output. PSOE leaders stressed the industrial and economic benefits to be derived from NATO membership as a key part of their campaign to influence public opinion in the referendum (González, 1986: 27; Sánchez-Gijón, 1986: 15). The military implications of NATO membership were subordinated to domestic political considerations, reflecting in part the very low perception of any immediate threat to Spain.

Defence related production was pinpointed as an area which required urgent modernisation and which could serve to boost what have been termed by some analysts as 'industrialising industries' (Sen, 1984; Smith, 1983) – that is, the group of industries, mostly of strategic significance for the production of military goods, which can serve as the basis ultimately for self-sustaining industrialisation. With the added benefit of breaking Spanish dependence since the early 1950s on the USA for arms procurement, which had a disastrous impact on the indigenous armaments industry, Spain's policy-makers sought extensive involvement in European co-production agreements. Thus, the PSOE government committed itself to the European Fighter Aircraft (EFA) project along with Britain, Italy and Germany, a co-production agreement with France and Germany for the Roland missile system, as well as further projects with France,

Italy and Greece for the development of a naval anti-aircraft missile, an electronic jamming system and a nuclear powered submarine. By 1989, Spanish companies were involved in 24 international defence programmes, representing an investment between 1982 and 1993 of Pta208.5 bn.

The PSOE government's enthusiasm for defence cooperation agreements was also related to its desire to demonstrate its European commitment as well as to secure membership of the WEU. It is therefore deeply ironic that after years of sustained effort, Spain finally achieved a key position within the existing Euorpean order only to see that order almost immediately begin to disintegrate. The end of the Cold War following the collapse of communism generated strong pressures for defence expenditure to be reduced. It became increasingly difficult for the government to persuade public opinion of the virtues of high-level defence expenditure, and after several years of increases in expenditure on arms procurement, sharp cuts in defence spending – the first in a series – were announced in the 1991 state budget. Furthermore, the government withdrew in the early 1990s from several European co-production agreements, including plans to build a new frigate, and backed moves to scale down the EFA project.

Spain's role within NATO in the post-Cold War world will obviously be conditioned by the organisation's own uncertain future. Prior to the collapse of communism, however, the Spanish government had outlined its envisaged model of participation within the Atlantic Alliance. Amidst accusations in the *Cortes* that it was contravening the terms of the referendum, the government set out a series of proposals which were accepted only with hesitation at NATO headquarters in December 1988 (Marquina, 1986: 49–50; 380ff., 1994: 375–8). These proposals included Spain's involvement in all NATO bodies (except the integrated military structure), the adoption of a defence planning procedure similar to that of other allied countries, the participation of Spanish forces in exercises only if they were of strategic interest to Spain, and no involvement in missions under NATO integrated commands without prior co-ordination with Spanish military authorities. In spite of NATO reservations, agreement was finally reached over six missions: to prevent occupation of Spanish territory; naval and air operations in the eastern Atlantic; control of the Strait of Gibraltar and its access routes; naval and air operations in the western Mediterranean; control of Spanish air space and air defence; use of Spanish territory for transit, support and rearguard logistics. Spain's contribution to NATO's military budget was subsequently set at 3.5 per cent of the total (Marquina, 1994: 378).

Spain and the European Community

Long before the PSOE assumed power in 1982, membership of the European Community (EC) was seen as being of fundamental importance to hopes of economic modernisation. Spain's first formal application for membership of what was then the EEC had been made in February 1962, although the dictatorial nature of the Franco regime precluded any chance of success. Nevertheless, Manuel Fraga, minister for information and tourism, stressed that joining Europe was an ineluctable imperative: 'Each step towards European integration is an obligatory step that escapes our volition' (Fraga, 1964: 27). Significantly, Fraga's remarks were made in the journal *NATO's Fifteen Nations*,[5] thereby emphasising perceived interconnections between Europe and the Atlantic Alliance. Twenty years later, ironic echoes of Fraga's stance could be detected in the debate on NATO membership, during which Felipe González argued that if the EC was a system worth belonging to, it was also a system worth defending (Yáñez Barnuevo and Viñas, 1992: 99–100).

There was virtual unanimity amongst political leaders that membership of the EC would represent 'Spain's return to where it belongs historically, culturally and geographically: the West European world' (Serra, 1985: 61). However, negotiations over the terms of entry following Spain's second official application in 1977 were protracted and difficult, this time as a result of economic rather than political issues. Indeed, negotiations did not even begin until December 1978, and soon became entangled with internal EC wrangles over the Common Agricultual Policy (CAP), the size of the Community budget and British demands for a rebate (Alonso, 1985; Armero, 1989: 162–9). Given Spain's own domestic political crises as the UCD government began to break up, little progress was made until the PSOE's assumption of power at the end of 1982. The new Socialist government made entry to the EC the centrepiece of its foreign policy and gave a new impetus to the negotiations.

González made deliberate play of the seeming anomaly that Spain should be accepted by NATO despite the views of a majority of Spanish citizens, whilst EC membership – which had enormous popular support – was proving highly problematic. NATO and EC membership came to be seen as indivisible, and fears of a Spanish withdrawal from the Atlantic Alliance helped unblock talks on European entry. A Spanish diplomatic offensive paid dividends in June 1983 when, under the (West) German presidency, the EC's budget expansion was made conditional upon agreement on Spain and Portugal's entry to the Community (Yáñez-Barnuevo and Viñas, 1992: 92–6). However, negotiations over the details of such entry were marked by tough bargaining which were hardly generous to Iberian interests (Preston and Smyth, 1984: 66–80; Alcaide, 1985; González Campos *et al.*, 1986). Spain was committed to opening its markets to EC competitors and bringing down external tariffs on industrial goods from third countries to the Community average within a period of seven years. In return, it would take ten years for the most competitive sectors of Spanish agricultural output – fresh fruit, vegetables and olive oil – to be phased into the CAP. In addition, Spanish citizens were unable to take advantage of Community rights on the free movement of labour between member states for seven years (Harrison, 1993: 28).

Ultimately, though, reservations over the precise terms of membership were subordinated to the desire to see Spain finally take its rightful place in Europe. The Accession Treaty was signed in Madrid on 12 March 1985, and Spain – together with Portugal – formally became a member of the EC on 1 January 1986. Entry coincided with the Single European Act (SEA), which was signed the following month and came into force on 1 July 1987. The main objective of the SEA was the establishment of a single internal market by 1 January 1993 as a precursor to closer political and economic union. Spain thus joined the EC at one of the most significant moments in the Community's development and was able to derive considerable economic advantage from the economic restructuring required to meet the demands of the SEA (see Chapter 10).

Since entering the Community, Spain has become one of the most committed proponents of European integration and has been a strong supporter of political as well as economic and monetary union (EMU). In January 1989, Spain assumed the EC Presidency for six months, culminating in the Madrid summit at which member states agreed that Phase One of EMU would begin on 1 July 1990. The experience of managing and co-ordinating EC members and institutions not only represented Spain's 'coming of age' within Europe, but also provided vital exposure to the delicate art of diplomatic manoeuvring within the Community (Grugel, 1991;

Alonso Zaldívar and Castells, 1992: 208). In subsequent summits –
notably the Edinburgh meeting in December 1992 – prime minister
González demonstrated forceful negotiating skills in defence of
Spanish demands. These centred on the issue of economic and social
cohesion within the Community, to be supported through a policy of
transfers to less developed regions as well as other measures to
promote growth in the Europe's poorest states (Spain, Portugal,
Greece and Ireland) (Yáñez-Barnuevo and Viñas, 1992: 111–12).

The Socialist government's desire to demonstrate its commitment
to the ideal of European union was reflected in its readiness to
propose initiatives on a variety of fronts. For instance, Felipe
González was a strong proponent of the idea of 'European
citizenship', seen as a third pillar of European union alongside
EMU and a common foreign and security policy. His notion entailed
the creation of 'Eurocitizens', permitted to live, vote and perhaps
even do military service in whichever of the member states they
choose. Carlos Solchaga, minister of the economy from 1985 to 1993,
brokered a fragile compromise in 1990 over the vexed issue of the
European currency unit (ecu) by proposing that 'hard ecus' –
intended to form the basis of a single currency by the end of the
century – should start to be issued during Phase Two of EMU.
Although the debate over the single currency and the hard ecu
continued to rage, EC heads of state accepted Solchaga's suggestion
that Phase Two be postponed by a year until 1 January 1994. Spain
also proposed the establishment of a fixed location for a permanent
secretariat of the Trevi group to serve as a co-ordination mechanism
between European police forces.

Spain and the Wider World

Membership of the EC meant that European priorities have had to
be assimilated in Spain: for instance, Israel was recognised and
diplomatic relations established on 17 January 1986 (Arenal, 1991:
62). In November 1993, an official visit by King Juan Carlos and the
signing of six bilateral co-operation accords set Spanish relations with
Israel on a similar footing to those maintained with European states[6]
(*El País internacional*, 15 November 1993). Equally, for the first time in
its modern history Spain has been able to exert an influence on
European foreign policy orientations, particularly in regard to the
Mediterranean and Latin America.

Political stability in the Mediterranean is a central concern to Spain, which has sought to promote the development of a coherent European policy towards the whole region. Spanish initiatives have been organised around the triple axis of commercial concessions, formal financial protocols, and the stimulation of economic and industrial co-operation (Yáñez-Barnuevo and Viñas, 1992: 114). In response to developing tension in the late 1980s and early 1990s between countries on the Mediterranean's northern and southern rims – mainly as a result of the issue of immigration into Europe via the EC's so-called southern 'soft belly' – the Spanish government sought to establish a permanent agency on security and co-operation in the Mediterranean. The idea, born of a fear that rapid population growth and shrinking economic resources in North Africa could bring the northern and southern shores of the Mediterranean into conflict, formed a central theme of the Conference on Security and Co-operation in Europe (CSCE), held in Palma de Mallorca in 1990. The Conference also expressed particular concern over threats to the ecological security of the Mediterranean region.

For decades, the Mediterranean Sea has been suffering serious damage through the dumping of toxic urban and industrial waste, the over-exploitation of fishing resources, the extinction of certain species, heavy civil and military shipping, environmentally destructive industry and agriculture, and the impact of tourism. Increasingly, Mediterranean regions have been affected by deforestation, overcultivation of farming lands, salinisation and erosion. According to a report by the United Nations Environment Programme (UNEA-MAP) on rising sea levels due to global warming, the alluvial and coastal plains of nearly all the countries in the area, inhabited by nearly 40 per cent of the population, face severe problems through the loss of cultivable land. The Palma de Mallorca meeting of the CSCE identified economic co-operation as central to the protection of the Mediterranean and underlined the need to accelerate social and economic development in the region (Heywood, 1991: 37–8).

In regard to Latin America, Spain has sought to use its historic ties to establish a unique and mutually beneficial link with the EU. Spain has not only attempted to act as an honest broker in defence of Latin American interests, but has also used its influence in the region to bolster its own importance within the Community (Arenal 1994: 286–97). One area in which Spain unsurprisingly took a lead was in promoting democracy and human rights in both Central and South America. The success of its own transition to democracy was thought to invest such efforts with added authority. Spanish policy towards Central America stood in sharp contrast to the attitude adopted by the US government under Ronald Reagan, which saw the 1980s crisis in terms of Soviet-backed incursion via the Sandinistas and supported the Contra rebels as well as providing military aid to 'reliable' regimes. The Spanish government located the roots of Central American political struggles in the gross economic and social injustices which characterised the region (Morán, 1985: 78–84; Piñol, 1988: 5–40). It therefore followed a three-pronged policy of supporting regional peace initiatives (for instance, through the 1983 declaration of support for the Contadora Group and the subsequent Esquipulas initiative), seeking EC political and economic support for them, and opposing military intervention.

Acute differences over Central American policy contributed to tensions between Spain and the USA during the 1980s (Wiarda, 1986). These were eased, however, after elections called by the Sandinista government in Nicaragua resulted in victory for the US-backed candidate (even though, ironically, the USA had expressed no confidence in the democratic process). Moreover, the end of the Cold War led to a change in the international climate, paving the way for efforts at national reconciliation. Spain was at the forefront of negotiating peace settlements in Nicaragua, Honduras and El Salvador: Spanish generals headed ONUCA, the UN Observation Group sent to Nicaragua in 1989 with responsibility for demobilising the Contras, and ONUSAL, the UN peace-keeping force established at the start of 1992 in El Salvador. Spain also gave advice on the reduction and restructuring of armed forces in the region (Arenal 1994: 290–1).

Spain's relations with South America have centred on support for processes of democratisation, promoting awareness amongst its European partners of the scale of debt within the region, and strengthening cultural bonds in the Hispanic world (Alonso Zaldívar and Castells, 1992: 219–25). European aid to South America was almost doubled for the 1991–5 period via the European Development Fund (EDF) and through bilateral cooperation agreements with Argentina, Brazil and the Andean Pact countries (Bolivia, Colombia, Ecuador, Peru, Venezuela) (EUROSTAT, 1992: 244–5). During the late 1980s and early 1990s Spain negotiated flexible debt servicing arrangements with several South American states and also established a series of financial cooperation agreements which sought to foster investment and growth (see Exhibit 12.2). The most important of

EXHIBIT 12.2

Major economic and financial agreements with Latin America, 1988–91

Country	Year	Length	Type of agreement	Main objectives
Argentina	1988	1989–94	General Treaty of Co-operation and Friendship	Promotion of development Promotion of association between firms Scientific, technical and cultural co-operation
Ecuador	1989	–	Global programme of commercial and financial co-operation	Fund development projects Subsidies of Spanish goods and services Debt reduction
Mexico	1990	1990–4	General Treaty of Co-operation and Friendship	Support for development of production and service industries Joint investment projects Scientific, technical and cultural co-operation
Venezuela	1990	1990–4	General Treaty of Co-operation and Friendship	Support for development of production and services industries Scientific, technical and cultural co-operation
Chile	1990	1990–4	General Treaty of Co-operation and Friendship	Support for development of production and service industries Joint investment projects Scientific, technical and cultural co-operation
Bolivia	1990	1990–1	Global Co-operation programme	Funding for development projects Subsidies for Spanish goods and services Promotion of investment
Brazil	1991	1991–5	Memorandum of Bases for Future General Treaty	Scientific and technical co-operation

Source: adapted from Alonso Zaldívar and Castells (1992: 226).

these were with Argentina and Mexico, with whom five year Treaties of Friendship and Cooperation were signed in 1988 and 1990 respectively.

To mark the 500th anniversary of Columbus' 1492 voyage to the Americas, the Fondo Quinto Centenario was established as a channel for bilateral agreements worth $675 mn. In addition, Spain was a leading sponsor of the first summit meeting of heads of state and government from twenty-one Spanish- and Portuguese-speaking nations, held in Guadalajara (Mexico) in July 1991. The resulting Guadalajara Declaration formally inaugurated the Ibero–American Conference, which was to be continued by annual summits aimed at fomenting close relations of friendship and cooperation among participating countries (Arenal, 1992a, 1992b). Spain hosted the 1992 Ibero–American Conference in Madrid, during which the government pledged support for economic restructuring and reform processes underway in South America, as well as trade liberalisation.[7]

Spain's policy towards Latin America has not met with universal approval: during 1992, plans to use celebrations of Columbus's expedition as the basis of a so-called *reencuentro* (literally 're-encounter') met with vociferous hostility from those who saw in them the taint of imperialist condescension. In reality, although Spain has made much play of its role within an emergent Ibero–American community, ever-closer integration into Europe means that Latin America will necessarily come to assume a more peripheral focus – especially after Mexico joined the North American Free Trade Association (NAFTA) in 1993, the establishment of a free-trade agreement (MERCOSUR) between Brazil, Argentina, Paraguay and Uruguay, and plans to carry out similar moves between Chile, Venezuela and Colombia.

Perhaps the most obvious example of how Spain's international concerns have been gradually reoriented towards a more explicitly European focus involves the case of Cuba. In general, Socialist administrations since 1982 have sought to maintain relations based on friendship and co-operation, clearly differentiated from US foreign policy concerns. Tension with the North American administration was particularly evident in November 1986, when Felipe González went on an official visit to Cuba, and in 1992 after the USA attempted to apply laws outside its territorial borders by passing the Cuban Democracy Act (Maxwell and Spiegel, 1994: 83–4). Yet, Spain's own relations with Cuba have been far from smooth: diplomatic co-operation was suspended in 1990 following the so-called 'crisis of the embassies' when Cuban security forces fired on refugees hiding in the Spanish embassy, and in early 1992 the sentencing to death of various Cubans accused of subversion (and the actual execution of one of them) provoked strong diplomatic protests from Spain (Arenal, 1994: 291–2).

Following the establishment of democracy throughout most of Latin America and the former communist bloc, Spain has consistently sought to persuade Cuba that it should stop resisting the democratic current. Various attempts in the early 1990s to set up joint initiatives to promote moves towards democracy in Cuba (for instance, with the Mexican and Venezuelan governments) met with staunch resistance from Fidel Castro's administration. However, in September 1994 the Cuban regime finally agreed to meet three anti-Castro opposition leaders in Madrid, thereby initiating hopes that a negotiated transition to democracy might prove possible (*El País*, 8, 9 September 1994). Although Spain has sought to maintain relations with Cuba on a positive footing, it has refused to provide the financial support which Castro desperately needs following the collapse of the Soviet Union. Ultimately, Spain's international outlook will be conditioned more by its European vocation than by its Hispanic bonds.

Defining an International Security Role

Spain's integration into the EC and the Atlantic Alliance affected not just its diplomatic outlook, but also its defence policy orientation. Until the election of the PSOE government, defence policy had been conducted in a piecemeal fashion, unguided by any overall strategic vision or purpose. The first systematic attempt to outline a coherent set of policy guidelines came in *Una política de paz y seguridad para España*, a PSOE pamphlet published in December 1985 which sought to build upon the outline established in Felipe González's 'decalogue' of the previous year (Exhibit 12.3). The pamphlet underlined Spain's commitment to the defence of western values and its key role in the construction of European security (PSOE, 1985). However, in contrast to the prevailing western outlook which viewed all security issues through the prism of East–West tensions, Spanish concerns centred primarily on North Africa and the Middle East.

The terms of the 1986 referendum on NATO required Spain to reformulate the basis of its relationship with the United States

---

EXHIBIT 12.3

Felipe González's 'Decalogue' on Spain's peace and security role, presented to the Congress of Deputies, 23 October 1984

1　Continued Spanish membership of NATO
2　Non-incorporation into NATO's military structure
3　A change in the bilateral relations with the United States of America towards a gradual reduction in the presence of American forces and installations on Spanish soil
4　The non-nuclearisation of Spain
5　Possible signing of the treaty of nuclear non-proliferation
6　The desirability of joining the Western European Union as the only European organisation with defence capabilities
7　Moves towards a definitive resolution of the Gibraltar issue
8　The strengthening of Spain's role within the European Disarmament Conference and application for membership of the Disarmament Committee of the United Nations
9　The continued development of a network of bilateral agreements on defence co-operation with other west European nations
10　Dialogue between political forces to achieve agreement on a joint strategic plan.

Source: PSOE, *Una política de paz y seguridad* (Madrid, 1985)

(Yáñez-Barnuevo and Viñas, 1992: 115–19). On 1 December 1988 a new eight-year bilateral agreement with the USA was signed in Madrid, built for the first time around the principle of equal partnership rather than Spanish subordination. Its essential components included not just a reduction in the US military presence in Spain – achieved through the removal of the USAF Wing 401 from Torrejón – but also the establishment of a defence accord similar to those which existed between the USA and several of Spain's European partners. In spite of US displeasure over withdrawal from the Torrejón base, the 1988 agreement opened a new and more harmonious phase in relations between Spain and the USA. However, sharp dissension continued to break out on occasion, for instance over the US invasion of Panama in 1989, which Felipe González condemned in the Congress of Deputies (Arenal, 1994: 291).[8] Only with the collapse of communism and the end of the Cold War did a sense of common purpose over defence issues begin to emerge, although neither Spain nor the USA often sees the other as being at the forefront of its international concerns.

Prior to the end of the Cold War, NATO tended to devote most attention to the Central European Front (Aguirre, 1989: 123–68). In contrast, Spain has historically been particularly sensitive to tensions in the Mediterranean region. Frontier disputes, processes of national consolidation, and ideological and religious differences in both North Africa and the Middle East have often been the source of Spanish anxieties, whilst the presence of British-controlled Gibraltar has brought an extra factor of tension to the region. A number of constant factors in the North African environment affect Spanish security interests. For instance, the two Spanish enclaves, Ceuta and Melilla, are seen as vulnerable to a process of 'Morocconisation', whereby they could become Moroccan *de facto* by means of what has been called the March of the Tortoise – the gradual but inevitable outnumbering of Spaniards in the enclaves by local-born inhabitants. Further tensions derived from disputes over territorial waters, exploited to good effect by Morocco in 1983, and the impact on the Maghreb countries of Spain's membership of the EU (Sahagún, 1994: 247–58).

The Mediterranean is a highly militarised geographical area. The presence of nuclear, conventional and chemical weapons, an active arms trade, and the fact that the eastern Mediterreanean is seen as linking the West and the Middle East, have all contributed to the region's instability. In the aftermath of the collapse of communism, Spanish policy-makers identified the CSCE, rather than NATO, as the most appropriate forum for debating security in Europe and the Mediterranean. Since the end of the Cold War, security can no longer be defined only in terms of military balance (CIP, 1990). Instead, it now encompasses such issues as environmental protection, balanced demographic growth, and respect for human rights and national sovereignty.[9] The CSCE was seen as being in a position to promote a new security system based neither on nuclear deterrence, nor on mutual mistrust. In particular, it was hoped that the proposed agency on security and co-operation in the Mediterranean could address the question of arms control and conflict in the Middle East and act as a forum for the exchange of information on military manoeuvres and other defence issues. In the event, Spanish proposals were overtaken by the Gulf crisis and the subsequent political uncertainty it generated.

Nevertheless, Spain was proposed as the most appropriate location for the Middle East Peace Conference of October 1991, which was jointly sponsored by the USA and USSR and which set Israel and the

Palestine Liberation Organisation on the road to their historic mutual recognition. The successful staging of the peace conference – which involved a massive and complex security operation – enhanced Spain's international stature, particularly in the USA. Equally, within the EC it served to bolster Spain's growing credibility on defence and security issues.

One issue which remains deeply contentious in Spain is British sovereignty over Gibraltar. In spite of diplomatic progress since the death of Franco – joint declarations by the Spanish and British governments in Lisbon (10 April 1980) and Brussels (27 November 1984) represented major steps forward – a final solution to the dispute has remained elusive. Whilst the real importance of Gibraltar to the Spaniards remains largely symbolic, UK control of the Rock has become increasingly anomalous since Spain became a full member of NATO and the EU. Felipe González highlighted the issue at the Paris summit of the CSCE in November 1990 and planned to discuss it further with the UK premier, Margaret Thatcher, during an official state visit to the UK later that month. However, the latter's unexpected resignation led to the visit being cancelled. González instead expressed his concerns in a series of interviews with foreign correspondents, in which he accused the UK government of not adhering to the terms of the 1713 Treaty of Utrecht, and complained that the Gibraltarians had refused to implement the Anglo–Spanish agreement on joint use of Gibraltar's airport, signed in 1987. The Spanish leader argued that the UK could hardly claim sovereignty if it allowed the Gibraltarians to halt initiatives undertaken by the national government, which appeared to have no means of enforcing its decisions.

The re-emergence of the Gibraltar issue in the early 1990s was partly motivated by economic considerations, in particular disquiet over smuggling as well as the growing tendency for Spaniards to register companies in Gibraltar and thereby avoid Spanish sales tax. In March 1993, the British foreign minister, Douglas Hurd, proposed Spanish participation in the elaboration of a new constitution for Gibraltar, but would not be drawn on whether Spain would be allowed an administrative role in the colony's future. Ultimately, a solution to the problem will probably involve a return to Spanish sovereignty, perhaps involving some lease-back arrangement. However, a change in sovereignty will remain unlikely so long as Spain retains control of Ceuta and Melilla, its two north African enclaves, and while the Gibraltarians themselves remain intensely opposed to integration into Spain. Indeed, Gibraltar's first minister, Joe Bossano, sees independence as his ultimate aim, even though such an option is expressly ruled out by the Treaty of Utrecht.

Spain in the New World Order

By 1989, Spain had established the basic elements of its foreign and defence policy: membership of the EC had been achieved and a model developed for participation in NATO, the armed forces had been modernised, diplomatic relations had evolved on a coherent basis, and the country had become fully integrated into the international community. However, no sooner had these develop-ments taken place than the constants of the post-1945 world order were turned upside down by the collapse of communism and the end of the Cold War. With the dismantling of the Berlin Wall in 1990, Europe was faced with not only with new opportunities, but also with new challenges. For the first time in its modern history, Spain was able to participate in and help shape Europe's responses to these opportunities and challenges.

The first real test of Spain's new international perspective came with the Iraqi invasion of Kuwait in August 1990. The US-led response to the Gulf crisis called for collective solidarity between members of the United Nations, particularly those in the Atlantic Alliance and related bodies, such as the West European Union (WEU). Although Spain supported a diplomatic solution to the crisis, it offered positive (albeit unenthusiastic) support to the build-up of the West's military presence in the Gulf prior to the 15 January 1991 deadline for Iraq to withdraw.

The Spanish government adopted a triple strategy (Alonso Zaldívar and Castells, 1992: 202–4). First, in line with a decision adopted at a WEU ministerial meeting on 21 August 1990, a small-scale military contribution was made: three warships – a frigate and two corvettes – were sent to the Gulf. During the course of the war, these ships carried out some 3,000 control missions. Second, logistical support was offered to various countries, notably the USA, but also France, the UK, and Turkey. Of particular importance was the use of Spanish air bases: 35 per cent of the total US air deployment operated via Spain, including over 300 missions by B-52 bombers flying out of Morón de la Frontera. In addition, over 230 US ships were received at Spanish ports. For obvious security reasons, details of such support were kept secret. Third, the Spanish government insisted that its forces in the Gulf would not enter direct combat, and also that it would not send ground troops.

The government was obliged to walk a tightrope during the Gulf crisis (Abu-Warda, 1994: 312–5). Public opinion was divided over the causes of the conflict, but broadly opposed to direct Spanish involvement: massive anti-war demonstrations were a regular occurrence in early 1991. The revelation by journalists in late February that B-52s were setting off from Morón sharply increased domestic tension. On the international front, the government anxiously engaged in a damage limitation exercise. Keen to maintain good relations with the Maghreb countries and to leave open the possibility of acting in the role of post-war conciliator, Spain launched a swift diplomatic offensive: the foreign minister, Francisco Fernández Ordóñez, announced visits to Algeria, Mauritania and Morocco. In fact, the Spanish government found itself caught in a near impossible position between trying to appease domestic opinion, maintain good relations with the Arab world, and demonstrate its credentials as a committed member of the Atlantic Alliance. The end of the war, which helped relieve the domestic pressure and allowed Spain to build upon its vision of a permanent Mediterranean security agency, arrived not a moment too soon.

If Iraq's ejection from Kuwait hardly resolved tension in the Middle East, it did highlight the centrality of the United Nations (UN) in the post-Cold War era. Spain has sought to play an active role in the UN – as expressed in addresses to the General Assembly by King Juan Carlos in 1986 and 1991 and by Felipe González in 1985 (Yáñez-Barnuevo and Viñas, 1992: 126) – and in October 1992 was elected a non-permanent member of the UN Security Council.[10] The vote reflected not just Spain's growing international influence, but also recognition of its efforts to work for international peace. Since 1988 Spanish troops have been heavily involved in UN peace-keeping operations, most notably in Central America, but also in Namibia (as part as the Transition Assistance Group) and Angola (overseeing the redeployment and later withdrawal of Cuban troops).

Spain also took an active part in UN missions in the war-torn former Yugoslavia, sending 750 troops in October 1992 to join the 'blue helmet' forces and announcing that it would offer haven to 2,500 refugees. However, Spain resisted NATO pressure in May 1993 to send an entire brigade – up to 5,000 men – to Bosnia in preparation for possible armed intervention by UN forces. Shortly afterwards a Spanish soldier was killed while engaged on a humanitarian mission in Mostar, the first of ten Spanish serviceman to die in the former Yugoslavia between May and October 1993. In September 1993, Spain reached agreement with the UN secretary-general, Boutros Boutros-Ghali, to establish by 1997 a rapid intervention force (*Fuerza de Acción Rápida*) permanently ready to be despatched at the UN's behest to flashpoints around the world.

Within Europe, Spain aims to play a prominent role in the elaboration of a Common Foreign and Security Policy (CFSP), one of the decision-making pillars of the EU which came into being on 1 November 1993 following ratification of the Maastricht Treaty. The CFSP is seen as the precursor of an eventual common defence policy, to which Spain is deeply committed. Spain also plans to contribute to the so-called 'Eurocorps', inaugurated in November 1993 by France, Germany and Belgium and initially consisting of 50,000 troops. The Eurocorps will become the armed wing of the WEU, and play a key role in the eventual integration of European defence policy. At the first Council of Europe summit, held in Vienna in October 1993, Felipe González told a press conference that he was strongly opposed to the rapid extension of NATO to encompass Hungary, Slovakia, the Czech Republic and Poland. The Spanish premier has been a supporter of developing a powerful European defence axis around the WEU, which could eventually replace many NATO functions.

The EU came into being in the midst of major threats to peace and security: civil war in Bosnia, political uncertainty in Russia, and the emergence of nationalist and extreme right-wing movements across Europe were all overlain by a prolonged economic crisis characterised by alarmingly high levels of unemployment. The challenges facing the EU in the final decade of the twentieth century are profound; the manner in which they are confronted will have a far-reaching impact on all its members as they become ever more closely integrated. Spain will contribute in significant measure to the elaboration of a co-ordinated European response. Indeed, for the first time in its modern history, Spain is in a position to play a geo-political role commensurate with its size and geographical position.

Notes

Introduction: Analysing Spanish Politics

1. Gómez Yañez (1989: 807–55) provides a comprehensive bibliography of works on the Spanish transition published up to 1988. For more recent references, see Cotarelo (1992) and Redder San Román (1994).
2. For an insightful comparative analysis of lessons to be drawn from the Spanish transition, see Casanova (1994). On the importance of the emergence of a functioning civil society for the successful establishment of democracy, see Pérez-Díaz (1993).
3. There exists a very wide literature on the 1978 Constitution which is wholly legal in character, concerned primarily with textual exegesis. Other works are aimed at a wider audience, but remain focused on constitutional interpretation. For instance, Editorial Tacos (Madrid) publishes a collection entitled '*Teams Clive de la Constitución española*' (Key themes of the Spanish Constitution). Under the general editorship of Pedro de Vega, the collection consisted of forty-six titles by 1993.

1 Reconciling State and Nation: The Politics of Regional Diversity

1. The First Republic lasted from February 1873 to December 1874 before giving way to the Restoration Monarchy which dominated Spanish politics until the Second Republic (1931–6), which was in turn overthrown by General Francisco Franco during the Spanish Civil War (1936–9). The standard history remains Carr (1982).
2. Linz (1985) has argued that primordial identities (associated with such things as language, culture, distinctive religion or kinship) on their own are insufficient as the basis of nationalist political action. Much more important is territoriality, although primordial elements are instrumental in the creation of the 'invented traditions' characteristic of many nationalist movement.
3. Carlism, officially born in 1833, became an extreme right-wing political movement and still has a vestigial existence. It took its name from followers of the pretender, don Carlos, and won support from northern, conservative, deeply Catholic rural and small-town populations.
4. In February 1994 the Supreme Court decided to seek clarification from the Constitutional Tribunal on the constitutionality of the *Generalitat* promoting the use of Catalan. Behind the decision lay a concern that Spaniards in Catalonia should have the right, but not the obligation, to learn Catalan. The Constitutional Tribunal's found in favour of the *Generalitat*.

5. Arana himself only learned *Euskera* in adulthood.

6. Apparently, blood groups B and AB are proportionately even rarer amongst Basques than amongst their fellow west Europeans. See Collins (1986: 4–5), who dismisses all such claims as being neither scientific nor objective.

7. *Euskadiko Ezquerra* was absorbed by the Basque Socialist Party (PSOE-PSE) at its congress in Bilbao (27 March 1993).

8. To put Galician literary production in a wider perspective, just 0.6 per cent of all books published in Spain between 1970 and 1985 were in *Galego* (Villares, 1989: 512). In Catalonia, by contrast, the 791 titles published in the vernacular in 1976 represented 3 per cent of all books published in Spain; by 1987 there were 4,145 titles – roughly 10 per cent of total Spanish production.

9. The former were initially represented in small and ineffectual organisations such as the *Associación Regionalista Gallega* (1891) and the *Liga Gallega* (1897). However, *Solidaridad Gallega*, founded in 1907, was of rather more political significance, grouping together liberals, federalists and even Carlists in opposition to the corruption of the Restoration system. The *Irmandades de Fala*, which called for the economic 'redemption' of the Galician nation and for the defence of its language, enjoyed a brief existence before a scission at their IV assembly in 1992 led to the creation of the overtly nationalist group, *Irmandade Nazonalista Galega*.

10. Franco was himself from Galicia, born in El Ferrol in 1892. According to Preston (1993: xix), '[h]e was abundantly imbued with the inscrutable pragmatism or *retranca* of the *gallego* peasant.'

11. The EGPGC surfaced in 1987 and claimed responsibility for a number of bomb attacks throughout Galicia and the killing of a civil guard in 1989. These proved to be isolated incidents, and little has been heard of the organisation in the 1990s.

12. The first approach is best represented by Clark (1984 and 1990) and Jáuregui (1985), the second by Zulaika (1988) and Conversi (1992), and the third by Zirakzadeh (1991).

13. The pro-Algerian film *La battaglia di Algeri* (Battle of Algiers) by the Italian director Gillo Pontecorvo achieved a cult status amongst exiled and underground Basque radicals. Pontecorvo's 1979 film *Operación Ogro*, on the assassination by ETA of Franco's prime minister, Admiral Luis Carrero Blanco, received a much cooler reception. By this stage, Pontecorvo had rejected armed struggle in response to the escalating violence and disorder in Italy.

14. Paper given by José María Montero Zabala at St Antony's College, Oxford (10 May 1986). Montero was expelled from *Herri Batasuna* in June 1992 after he published an article arguing that real independence for the Basque Country could be achieved within Spain's existing constitutional arrangements.

15. Birthplace of Castilian, which developed between the ninth and eleventh century as a romance language derived from Latin, this immense region is modern Spain's true heartland, home of historic heroes real and imagined – El Cid, Don Juan, and, of course, Queen Isabel I, whose union with Fernando of Aragón created the basis of present-day Spain.

2   The 1978 Constitutional Settlement

1. The Italian monarchy was rejected by 54.2 per cent to 45.8 per cent in a referendum on 2 June 1946, in spite of King Victor Emanuel III's last ditch attempt at survival by abdicating in favour of his son, Umberto. In Greece, just 31 per cent voted in December 1974 for the restoration of King Constantine II, who had been deposed the previous year by George Papadopoulos. In both cases, the monarchies were rejected because of associations with dictatorial regimes.
2. The precise reasons for this act of political hara-kiri remain a mystery: in Spain, as opposed to Portugal or Greece, there was no 'liberation by *golpe*' or 'exogenous factor' such as defeat in war, leading to regime breakdown. For a thought-provoking analysis of this issue, see Casanova (1983: 929–73). See also Juliá (1988a: 25–40).
3. The *ponencia* was comprised of 3 UCD members (José Pedro Pérez Llorca, Gabriel Cisneros and Miguel Herrero de Miñón), 1 PSOE (Gregorio Peces-Barba), 1 AP (Manuel Fraga Iribarne), 1 PCE-PSUC (Jordi Solé-Tura), 1 CiU/Basque-Catalan Minority (Miquel Roca i Junyent). See Peces-Barba (1988), Solé-Tura (1978), Herrero de Miñón (1988: 65–75).
4. The Constitutional Committee of the Congress had 36 members (17 UCD, 13 PSOE, 2 PCE, 2 AP, 1 'Catalan Minority', 1 PNV); that of the Senate had 25 (12 UCD, 5 PSOE, 2 *'Entesa dels catalans'*, 2 'progressive group', 2 independents, 1 Basque, 1 'mixed group'). The joint committee had 11 members (7 deputies – 3 UCD, 1 PSOE, 1 PCE, 1 'Catalan Minority' and the President of the Congress – and 4 senators – 2 UCD, 2 PSOE). See Aparicio (1988: 361–3).
5. Herrero de Miñón (1988: 73) reveals that the model for drawing a distinction between guiding principles and fundamental rights was the 1948 Constitution of Burma.

3   The Institutional Legacy of Francoism

1. Other *'poderes fácticos'* in contemporary Spain, such as the banks, the bureaucracy, employers' and labour organisations, and political parties are considered in later chapters.
2. The executive agreements on defence – including twenty-two secret clauses signed between 1954 and 1960 though not made public until 1981 – authorised the USA to maintain and utilise military installations *without reference to the Spanish government* and implicated Spain in their policy of containment towards the Soviet Union. It would be difficult to exaggerate the significance of the 1953 agreements in provoking the anti-Americanism which still exists amongst many who fought in the anti-Franco democratic opposition. See Viñas (1981).
3. In 1968, Admiral Luis Carrero Blanco – Franco's right-hand man who was to fall victim to ETA in December 1973 – had warned, 'Let no one

entertain the slightest hope of changing the institutional system in any way, because the Spanish people would never tolerate it – and firm behind them stand the Armed Forces'. Quoted in Piris (1989: 6).

4. That the coup attempt should have taken place at all was in no small measure due to the repeated failure of the UCD government to act firmly against previous essays in *golpismo*. In particular, *Operación Galaxia* in 1978 – conceived by Tejero and Captain Ricardo Saenz de Ynestrillas and in some ways a dry run of 23–F – and a plot in January 1980 involving the senior army general, Luis Torres Rojas, had gone effectively unpunished.

5. In spite of the nine-month provision and the option of doing social work rather than military service, the number of young Spaniards prepared to run the risk of criminal proceedings for refusing to be conscripted reached a record level of some 5,000 in 1994 (The *Guardian*, 27 September 1994).

6. The Socialist administration was subsequently embarrassed when the first civilian head of the Civil Guard, Luis Roldán, escaped into self-imposed exile following his arrest in April 1994 on charges of defrauding the public treasury, embezzlement of public funds and perverting the course of justice.

7. The extensive effort at improving the security forces' image even included the introduction during 1990 of new uniforms for the Civil Guard which dispensed with their notorious tricorns.

8. In the 1980s, the numbers of Spaniards leaving the Church were greatest in precisely those northern provinces that had historically been most Catholic.

9. Such an interpretation should be balanced by the observation that the Church was specifically opposed to active involvement in the creation of a Christian Democratic party, in part through fear of provoking memories of the conflicts which had prefigured the Civil War. This stance was confirmed in the 1986 document published by Spanish bishops, *Los católicos en la vida pública*, which rejected the creation of a confessional party. The Church had neither the resources, nor any compelling reason, to sponsor such a party (Pérez-Díaz, 1993: 170).

10. Suggestions that a libel law be established were opposed by Francisco Tomás y Valiente, president of the Constitutional Tribunal, who called instead for journalists to exercise self-restraint and not step beyond the bounds of acceptable behaviour. See *ABC* (24 November 1989).

11. In an article published in Columbia University's *Gannet Center Journal* in October 1991, John C. Merrill, professor of journalism at Louisiana University, ranked *El País* as one of the twenty best newspapers in the world.

4 Central Government: Monarchy, Core Executive and Parliament

1. The King has been known occasionally to drop in at the popular Café de Oriente, situated opposite his Madrid residence, the Zarzuela Palace.

During his annual holidays in Mallorca, he is renowned for moving freely amongst other holiday-makers. While such activities hardly bring him into contact with a wide cross-section of Spanish society, they are indicative of a style which has endeared Juan Carlos to the public.

2. Members of the *Cortes* are almost certainly rather less interested in the marriage intentions of the heir to the throne than are the so-called *revistas de corazón* (glossy society magazines), which have made the Spanish royal household a focal point of sometimes far-fetched gossip and rumour. In fact, like his father, Felipe, *Príncipe de Asturias* – formally invested as heir apparent on his eighteenth birthday (30 January 1986) – has won considerable affection amongst Spanish citizens and, since coming of age, has played an increasingly prominent diplomatic role.

3. Amongst the more well-known examples of non-elected figures being appointed to Cabinet office was that of the intellectual and former Communist, Jorge Semprún, who headed the Ministry of Culture between 1985 and 1991. His successor, Jordi Solé-Tura was also a former Communist who had never joined the Socialist Party.

4. The specific functions of the President's Office and the structure of the presidency were outlined in *Real Decreto* 2213/1976 (16 September), amplified by *Real Decreto* 1692/1977 (11 January); *Real Decreto* 2761/1977 (28 October), *Real Decreto* 2158/1978 (1 September), and *Real Decreto-Ley* 22/1982 (7 December), in which Article 3.1 established the President's Office as 'an organ of political and technical assistance to the President and Vice-President of the Government', with specific duties laid down by *Real Decreto* 3773/1982 (22 December). See Bar Cendón (1983: 202–7). The precise structure of the president's support network was then codified in the Law on Central State Administration of 16 August 1983. In July 1986, the PSOE government scrapped the Ministry of the Presidency, whose powers conflicted in some respects with those of the vice-president, and replaced it with the less powerful office of Minister of Relations with the Cortes and Secretary of the Government. Other powers, including the influential Presidency of the Commission of Under-Secretaries, were transferred to the vice-president. See Baena del Alcázar (1988: 221–4).

5. In September 1994, in an attempt to shore up the government's damaged credibility following a number of corruption scandals, González agreed to appear weekly in the *Cortes* to answer questions, although he reserved the right to set the general conditions under which they could be asked (*El País internacional*, 12 September 1994).

6. The parallel exists in a double sense: first, those who coined the term '*Felipismo*' claimed that the PSOE government's economic policies had more in common with neo-liberal monetarism than with socialism (see chapter 10); second, like 'Thatcherism', the term has no analytical value, being instead a reductionist and wholly descriptive cliché. See Heywood (1992).

7. The Basque PNV had initially boycotted the Senate debate, but on the final day gave its support to the establishment of the *ponencia*. The PNV's own proposal that 47 specific central state powers be transferred to the Basque Country was rejected.

5 The Judiciary and the 'State of Law'

1. Such an omission is all the more noteworthy given the centrality in Spain of legal interpretations of the 1978 Constitution as a prism through which to analyse politics.

2. In the Burgos trials, staged by a military court, several of the accused – defended by Gregorio Peces-Barba – exposed the torture tactics used by the Franco authorities (De Blaye, 1976: 281–323).

3. As noted in chapter 4, there is no clear separation of powers in Spain between executive and legislature, neither of which is explicitly referred to in the 1978 Constitution; in contrast, the judiciary is specifically mentioned under Title VI (*'Del poder judicial'*).

4. The decision to have an even number of members has been criticised on the grounds that it would make it difficult to resolve any case of deadlock (Lucas Murillo de la Cueva, 1983: 211–2).

5. Writing in 1993, the former president of the Constitutional Tribunal, Francisco Tomás y Valiente, denied the existence of any overt political pressure, although he did reveal that on one occasion the president of an Autonomous Community had sought to persuade him of the logic of his position prior to an important judgement. On another occasion a minister had telephoned him to accuse the Tribunal – after it had reached a particular judgement – of undermining the government (Tomás y Valiente, 1993: 133).

6. Subsequently, the Organic Law on the Judiciary (*Ley Orgánica del Poder Judicial*) of 1 July 1985 introduced significant changes to the Supreme Court's organisational structure. Instead of three separate chambers (*salas*) devoted to administrative issues, a single body was established – divided into seven sections – in order to facilitate the efficient processing of cases. This left the Court with five chambers, dealing respectively with civil, penal, administrative, social and military matters.

7. A maverick self-publicist, Hormaechea had sprung to national attention in November 1990 when he had sounded off to journalists in a bar against leading figures in the *Partido Popular*, the party upon whose support he had relied since 1987 to function as president. His intemperate and, at times obscene, language obliged the PP to break all links and Hormaechea was defeated in a vote of no-confidence. However, he created his own party (*Unión para el Progreso de Cantabria*) and won the regional elections of 1991, since when he had been under investigation for corruption (Martín de Pozuelo *et al.*, 1994: 149–56).

8. The three main professional associations are the *Asociación de Jueces para la Democracia* (AJD), seen as progressive, the more conservative *Asociación Profesional de la Magistratura* (APM), and the moderate *Asociación Francisco de Vitoria*, concerned mainly with technical issues.

9. The matter was referred to the Constitutional Tribunal by the *Grupo Parlamentario Popular*, the main opposition party. The Constitutional Tribunal issed its findings in judgements 45/86 (17 April) and 108/86 (29 July). The Socialist government had sought to justify the change on the grounds that it would counter the innate conservatism of the judiciary.

10. Although the 1988 Law on Demarcation and Building provided for an increase of 57 per cent between 1989 and 1992 in expenditure on the administration of justice, the majority of this sum went towards salary costs. This reflected a rapid growth in the number of judges and magistrates, which had reached 3,224 by 1992 compared to 1,917 a decade earlier. Half of them were under the age of fifty, 28 per cent were women, and just 10 per cent came from families with a professional background in law. Concern has been expressed that many of the new judges were insufficiently experienced, leading to an overall decline in standards in a period when judicial issues had anyway become more complex as a result of the European legislation (Torres, 1993: 29–30).

11. The *Ley Corcuera* allowed for the police under certain circumstances to enter houses without a warrant, as well as to demand identification from any member of the public.

12. One leading judge later remarked, '*No es un cachondeo. Es un desastre.*' (It's not a joke. It's a disaster) (*El Tiempo*, 10 July 1989).

13. The scam, unearthed by an official investigation under the auspices of the High Court judge, Marino Barbero, bore a striking similarity to the 1988 Marseilles 'Urba case', which revealed that the French Socialist Party had for years operated a bogus research office as a front for demanding commissions in return for favours (Mény, 1992). The discovery of Urba's Spanish equivalent was triggered by the revelations of a disgruntled former employee of one of the companies involved, *Time Export*, although the investigation centred on another company, *Filesa*, which gave its name to the entire scandal.

14. For example, the German multinational, Siemens, which won the contract to build the high-speed rail link between Madrid and Sevilla, handed over large sums for 'technical and commercial advice' to firms run by former PSOE officials (*El País internacional*, 1 February 1993). In another scandal relating to the high-speed rail link, the health minister, Julián García Valverde, resigned in 1991 after it was revealed that while he had been in charge of the state railway, *Renfe*, speculators had been tipped off about land due for compulsory purchase (Martín de Pozuelo *et al.*, 1994: 141–7).

6   The Public Sector: Reform and Renewal

1. Public sector employees in the Autonomous Communities (the vast majority of them functionaries) rose from 44,475 in 1982 to 607 309 in 1993 (*La Vanguardia*, 16 August 1993).

2. The PSOE government did, however, announce plans to waive a moratorium on the deregulation of basic telephony until 2003, which had been negotiated jointly with the EU's other 'poor members', Portugal, Greece and Ireland (Chislett, 1994: 26).

7   The Autonomous Committees

1. The central government was particularly concerned at the escalating level of the budget deficit, given that under the terms of the Maastricht

Treaty one of the convergence criteria for entering the first phase of economic and monetary union was that general government deficit should be no more than 3 per cent of GDP. By 1992, Spain's deficit had reached 4.4 per cent of GDP and was increasing rapidly, forcing the central government to hammer out an agreement with the regions and local authorities to reduce their deficit to 0.25 per cent of GDP by 1996 (Chislett, 1994: 39–43)

2. The new system came into effect in 1994, although initially three regions – Aragón, Madrid and the Balearic Islands – were excluded on account of not having completed the full transfer of powers from the central state (*El País internacional*, 11 October 1993).

3. According to government figures, in October 1992 there were 8,085 municipalities, broken down as follows:

Size		% of total
Small (population of under 5 000)	6,972	86.23
Medium (5 001–20 000)	827	10.23
Medium/large (20 001–50 000)	176	2.18
Large (50 001–100 000)	55	0.68
Very large (over 100 000)	55	0.68

See *El País internacional*, 11 January 1993

4. Plans to reform the Senate and give it a genuine role as an assembly for regional interests were announced in September 1994 (see chapter 4).

8 The Electoral and Party Systems

1. Garzón. who had been chosen for his high public profile when investigating political corruption in the early 1990s, subsequently resigned in May 1994 in protest at what he claimed was the government's refusal properly to confront the corruption issue (*El País internacional*, 2, 9 May 1994). When Deputies resign, they are replaced by the next person on the party list for the electoral district in question.

2. The scale of corruption in Italy, which began to be revealed in early 1992, prompted massive attention in Spain as elsewhere in Europe. Inevitably, investigations of corruption cases in Spain prompted comparisons – albeit, largely spurious ones – with the Italian example.

3. As a further example, the devastating defeat suffered by the UCD in the October 1981 regional elections in Galicia, one of its strongholds, followed by an even more humiliating rejection in the Andalucían elections of May 1982, hastened the party's spectacular downfall.

4. Percentage figures refer to the five elections between 1977 and 1989.

5. In June 1994, the PSOE owed Pta 11.7 bn., the PP Pta 5.9 bn, the PNV Pta 2.8 bn, and IU Pta 1.5 bn. Between 1977 and 1994, Spanish parties had received a total of Pta 83.3 bn in state subsidies (with 74 per cent of that sum going to the PSOE and PP), with a further Pta 28.2 bn in electoral expenses (with 67 per cent going to the PSOE and PP). See *El País internacional* (9 January 1995).

6. Further corruption scandals in the early 1990s involved nationalist parties in both Catalonia and the Basque Country, where allegations were made of extortion and collusion with gambling interests (Martín de Pozuelo *et al.*, 1994: 107–17, 173–84).

9   Political Parties: Devalued Defenders of Democracy

1. 82 different parties throughout Spain received votes at the 1993 general elections. See *Anuario El País 1994*: 79. This compares with 61 parties in 1989 and 50 in 1986.
2. As early as 1974, Alfonso Guerra had set up the Instituto de Técnicos Electorales (ITE) to study electoral strategies; the ITE laid the basis for the efficiency and professionalism which would subsequently mark the PSOE's election campaigns. Guerra was acutely aware that electoral success would open the way to rewarding loyal party members.
3. The PSOE's 1993 election victory was widely seen as a personal triumph for González, who called the election early and took charge of the campaign after the party's internal divisions threatened to get out of hand. Although victory further boosted González's own stature, it also intensified the confrontation with the *'guerristas'*. Solchaga's nomination was ultimately backed by 87 to 66 PSOE deputies. However, in May 1994 Solchaga resigned his post and seat, following the imprisonment of the former governor of the Bank of Spain on corruption charges.
4. Perhaps the most striking example was the mismatch between the social-democratic rhetoric of the PSOE and its actions in power (Heywood, 1993: 167–85). It is also arguable that the opposition *Partido Popular*'s claims in the early 1990s to be a centrist christian democratic party were belied by a close study of its detailed policy proposals at the 1993 general elections.

10   Economic Modernisation

1. *Rumasa*, the massive business empire built up by José María Ruiz-Mateos, was expropriated in February 1983 on account of financial irregularities, but most of it was soon re-privatised.
2. Various employment promotion programmes established annually after 1984 saw a marked increase in the number of *temporary* and *part-time* contracts. By 1989, over a quarter of the total number of employees had temporary contracts, and over half the new jobs offered were done so under some form of employment promotion programme (OECD, 1991: 17).
3. The revisions to the plans implicitly acknowledged that the Maastricht terms would themselves have to be revised (see *El País internacional*, 18 and 25 July 1994).

11   The Policy Process

1. The 'power-dependence' framework analyses policy-making in terms of a trade-off between objectives and resources, in which it is recognised

that resources are not only scarce but also unevenly distributed. Amongst competing actors, there is usually a dominant coalition, which enjoys a marked advantage over the regulation of processes of exchange through manipulation of the 'rules of the game'. Strategies range from the 'policy community', in which close interdependence exists between administrators and interest groups in a given sector, through 'issue networks', characterised by exchange relationships, to 'pressure groups', which are usually concerned with single issues and often relatively short-lived. See Furlong (1994: 18–23).

2. Whilst the Franco regime did not develop a comprehensive welfare state, the provision of public services during the 1960s and 1970s in the fields of medicine, education and so forth greatly increased the already very extensive role of the state. The complexities of the transition to democracy gave an added impetus to the role of the state and thus intensified the public sector deficit difficulties which resulted in what 'state overload' theorists identified as a contradiction between 'accumulation' and 'legitimation' functions of the capitalist state.

3. Redondo had been a prime mover behind González's assumption of the PSOE leadership in the early 1970s, when he passed up the opportunity to take on the role himself. His disillusionment with González after the Socialists won office in 1982 was reflected in ever more bitter attacks on the party leader, whom he accused of betraying his true supporters.

4. In particular, Boyer's high-society marriage to Isabel Preysler, socialite stalwart of the gossip columns and former wife of Julio Iglesias, was subjected to extraordinary attention during the late 1980s, when '*los beautiful*' were never far from the headlines.

5. Guerra had a troubled relationship with both Boyer and Solchaga. Whereas in 1985 he was able successfully to resist Boyer being given the rank of vice-president (equivalent to his own), which has been seen as a key factor behind the economy minister's departure from government, he was unable to engineer the removal of Solchaga, who received increasingly explicit support from Felipe González between 1985 and 1993.

6. Although declining union membership was a feature of many industrialised countries during the 1980s, by the end of the decade Spanish figures were far lower than those in (West) Germany (34 per cent), Italy (40 per cent), Britain (41 per cent), Belgium (59 per cent), Denmark (73 per cent) and Sweden (85 per cent). Only in France and the USA were overall rates of union affiliation similar to those in Spain (Visser, 1991: 221; Pérez-Díaz, 1993: 268).

7. Ferrer, a Catalan, shared with the Basque leader of the UGT, Redondo, a commitment to working towards national agreements rather than promoting specific regional demands, an important factor in the development of political cohesion given the historic dominance of Catalonia and the Basque Country in terms of industrial and commercial development.

8. In late 1990 a survey of attitudes amongst young people between the ages of 16 and 22, carried out for the political weekly *Cambio 16*, revealed that in reply to the question of which person they would most like to be,

42 per cent chose Mario Conde. Having assumed the presidency of Banesto in 1987, Conde in many ways embodied the self-confident 'get-rich-quick' culture which swept Spain in the late 1980s, his photograph featuring more often in glossy gossip magazines than in the financial press.

9. The merger operation collapsed as a result of the marital infidelity of Alberto Cortina – known as one of 'los Albertos' along with his cousin, Alberto Alcocer – who owned a 12 per cent stake in Banco Central through the investment company, Cartera Central, headed by Boyer (who had left the Banco Exterior de España to take up the post). 'Los Albertos' were married respectively to the Koplowitz sisters, Alicia and Esther, who had provided the capital with which Cartera Central had been created. Alicia Koplowitz exacted revenge by undermining the merger deal, which finally collapsed when the KIO (Kuwaiti Investment Office) withdrew its stake from Cartera Central.

10. The terms of the purchase, in which Santander beat rival bids from BBV and Argentaria, required that Banesto must operate as a separate institution until at least 1998.

12 Spain as an International Power

1. Suárez was accused of adopting '*tercermundismo*' in an attempt to assume a 'new' role in the international system and to capitalise on prestige in Latin America (Rodríguez, 1988: 61).

2. The Western European Union (WEU) was established in 1954 following the collapse of the European Defence Community. Spanish membership was finally ratified by the *Cortes* in March 1990, but only after severe criticism by the WEU Assembly of Spain's 'ambiguous' position in respect of European defence commitments (Marquina, 1994: 379–80). In 1993 the WEU comprised nine members (Belgium, Germany, France, Italy, Luxembourg, the Netherlands, Portugal, Spain and the UK).

3. President Ronald Reagan later compounded matters on the eve of a visit to Madrid in 1985, when he remarked of the Abraham Lincoln Brigade which fought in defence of the Second Republic against Franco, 'I would say that the individuals that went over there were, in the opinion of most Americans, fighting on the wrong side' (quoted in Maxwell, 1991: 39).

4. The slogan had a deliberate double meaning, which hinged on the two words '*de entrada*': 'NATO, [on the question of] entry, no' or 'NATO, to begin with [i.e., initially], no'.

5. In a special issue devoted to Spain which explicitly called for its inclusion in NATO. The issue was translated and published in Spain as *La España que no pertenece a la OTAN* (Madrid: Ediciones del Servicio Informativo Español, 1964).

6. Israel wanted the visit to take place in 1992, but the Spanish authorities decided to avoid coinciding with the 500th anniversary of the expulsion of the Jews from Spain.

7. The third summit took place in Salvador (Brazil), on 15–16 July 1993, and centred on the theme of development, with special emphasis on social development and programmes of multilateral cooperation. The fourth, held in Cartagena de Indias (Colombia), on 14–15 June 1994, focused primarily on Cuba, as well as economic integration in Latin America.

8. At the General Assembly of the United Nations on 29 December 1989, Spain – in contrast to all other EC states – supported a resolution presented by Cuba and Nicaragua which condemned the US invasion. The resolution was approved with 75 votes in favour, 20 against and 39 abstentions; the only other European states to support it were Sweden, Austria and Finland.

9. The signing in January 1989 by the 35 countries of the CSCE of an agreement on security, human rights, economic, scientific, technical and ecological questions was seen as a clear example of how East–West confrontation could be replaced by conciliation.

10. The UN Security Council has five permanent members (the USA, Russia, China, France and the UK) and ten non-permanent elected members which serve for a period of two years. Spain's membership of the Council commenced on 1 January 1993.

Bibliography

Abel, Christopher and Torrents, Nissa (eds) (1984) *Spain. Conditional Democracy* (London: Croom Helm).

Abu-Warda, Najib (1994) 'Las transformaciones del mundo árabe y sus consecuencias en las relaciones hispano-magrebíes', in Calduch Cervera (ed.).

Aguila Tejerina, Rafael del (1983) 'Los partidos políticos y su lugar en el sistema político español', *Revista de Derecho Político* 17.

Aguila, R. and Montoro, R. (1984) *El discurso político de la transición española* (Madrid: CIS).

Aguilar, Miguel Angel (1981) 'Los oficiales que vienen', *El País* (17 July).

Aguirre, Mariano (1989) 'Looking Southwards', in Dan Smith (ed.), *European Security in the 1990s* (London: Pluto Press, in association with the Transnational Institute).

Alario, Juan (1991) 'Le secteur électrique espagnol: les défis des années 1990', *Cahiers EIB* 17.

Albaladejo Campoy, Miguel (1980) 'Pasado, presente y futuro de la función pública española. Una propuesta de reforma', *Cuadernos Económicos de ICE* 13.

Alcaide, Luis (1985) 'Algunas reflexiones sobre la negociación entre España y la CEE', *Revista de Información Comercial Española* 620 (April).

Alda Fernández, Mercedes and López Nieto, Lourdes (1993) 'El parlamento español: 1977–1993: una revisión de su papel en la transición y en la consolidación', *Revista de Estudios Políticos* 81.

Aldecoa Luzarraga, Francisco (1994) 'La transición y la redefinición de la política exterior española', in Calduch Cervera (ed.).

Allard, Gayle and Bolorinos, José (1992) *Spain to 2000. A Question of Convergence* (London: Economist Intelligence Unit).

Almarcha Barbado, Amparo (ed.) (1993) *Spain and EC Membership Evaluated* (London: Pinter Publishers).

Alonso Olea, Manuel *et al.* (1992) *España y la unión europea. Las consecuencias del Tratado de Maastricht* (Barcelona: Círculo de Lectores/Plaza y Janés).

Alonso Teixidor, L. F. and Hebbert, M. (1982) 'Regional Planning in Spain and the Transition to Democracy', in R. Hudson and J. R. Lewis (eds), *Regional Planning in Europe* (London: Pion Ltd).

Alonso Zaldívar, Carlos and Castells, Manuel (1992) *Spain Beyond Myths* (Madrid: Alianza Editorial).

Alonso, Antonio (1985) *España en el Mercado Común: del acuerdo del 70 a la Comunidad de Doce* (Madrid: Espasa Calpe).

Alvarez Alvarez, Julián (1984) *Burocracia y poder político en el régimen franquista* (Madrid: Instituto Nacional de Administración Pública).

Alvarez Conde, Enrique (1990) *El régimen político español*, 4th edn (Madrid: Tecnos).

Alvira Martín, Francisco and García López, José (1988) 'Los españoles y las Autonomías', *Papeles de Economía Española* 35.

Alzaga, Oscar *et al.* (1990) *Diez años de Constitución* (Zaragoza: Iber-Caja).

Amnesty International (1985) *Spain. The Question of Torture* (London: Amnesty International).

Amodia, José (1977) *Franco's Political Legacy* (London: Allen Lane Penguin).

Amodia, José (1983) 'Union of the Democratic Centre', in Bell (ed.).

Amodia, José (1990) 'Taxonomía e inestabilidad del sistema de partidos en España', *ACIS* 3(1).

Amodia, José (1993) 'Requiem for the Spanish Communist Party', in David S. Bell (ed.), *Western European Communists and the Collapse of Communism* (Oxford: Berg).

Andrés Ibáñez, Perfecto and Pérez Mariño, Ventura (1991) 'La justicia: entre Constitución y crisis', in Vidal-Beneyto (ed.) (1991a).

Aparicio, Miguel A. (1988) *Introducción al sistema político y constitucional español*, 3rd edn (Barcelona: Ariel).

Aragón, Manuel (1980) 'La monarquía parlamentaria', in A. Predieri and E. García de Entierra (eds), *La Constitución española de 1978* (Madrid: Civitas)

Aragón, Manuel (1989) *Constitución y democracia* (Madrid: Tecnos).

Aranzadi, Claudio (1989) 'La política de desinversiones en el INI', *Papeles de Economía Española* 38.

Areilza, José María (1977) *Diario de un ministro de la monarquía* (Barcelona: Planeta).

Areilza, José María (1983) *Cuadernos de la transición* (Barcelona: Planeta).

Arenal, Celestino del (1991) 'Democracia y política exterior: el largo camino hacia el cambio', in Vidal-Beneyto (ed.) (1991a).

Arenal, Celestino del (1992a) 'Las Cumbres Iberoamericanas y la Comunidad Iberoamericana de Naciones', *Tiempo de Paz* 24–25.

Arenal, Celestino del (1992b) 'La Comunidad Iberoamericana de Naciones: entre la utopía y la realidad', *Revista de Occidente* 131.

Arenal, Celestino del (1994) 'La política exterior española en Iberoamérica (1982–1992)', in Calduch Cervera (ed.).

Armero, José Mario (1978) *La política exterior de Franco* (Barcelona: Planeta).

Armero , José Mario (1989) *Política exterior de España en la democracia* (Madrid: Espasa Calpe).

Attard, Emilio (1982) *La Constitución por dentro* (Barcelona: Argos Vergara).

Aumente, José (1985) 'Apuntes para una teoría del felipismo', *El País* (7 September).

Baena del Alcázar, Mariano and Pizarro, Narciso (1982) 'The Structure of the Spanish Power Elite, 1939–1975', *EUI Working Papers* 55.

Baena del Alcázar, Mariano (1988) *Curso de ciencia de la administración* (Madrid: Tecnos).

Balfour, Sebastian (1989) *Dictatorship, Workers, and the City* (Oxford: Clarendon Press).

Bañón Martínez, Rafael (1988) 'The Spanish Armed Forces During the Period of Political Transition, 1975–1985', in Rafael Bañón Martínez and Thomas M. Barker (eds), *Armed Forces and Society in Spain Past and Present* (Boulder: Columbia University Press).

Bar Cendón, Antonio (1982) 'El sistema de partidos en España', *Sistema* 47.

Bar Cendón, Antonio (1983) *El presidente del gobierno en España: encuadre constitucional y práctica política* (Madrid: Editorial Cívitas).

Bar Cendón, Antonio (1984) 'The Emerging Spanish Party System: Is There a Model?', *West European Politics* 7.

Bar Cendón, Antonio (1985) '¿Normalidad o excepcionalidad?: para una tipología del sistema de partidos español, 1977–1982', *Sistema* 65.

Barciela, Fernando (1981) *La otra historia del PSOE* (Madrid: Emiliano Escolar).

Bardavío, Joaquín (1980) *Sábado santo rojo* (Madrid: Ediciones Uve).

Barnes, Samuel, McDonough, Peter, and López Pintor, Antonio (1986) 'Volatile Parties and Stable Voters in Spain', *Government and Opposition* 21(1).

Bell, David S. (ed.) (1983) *Democratic Politics in Spain* (London: Frances Pinter).

Beltrán Villalva, Miguel (1990) 'La administración pública y los funcionarios', in Giner (ed.).

Ben-Ami, Shlomo (1983) *Fascism From Above. The Dictatorship of Primo de Rivera in Spain 1923–1930* (Oxford: Clarendon Press).

Bennett, R. J. (1987) 'Tax assignment in multilevel systems of government: a political-economic approach and the case of Spain' *Environment and Planning C: Government and Policy* 5.

Bermeo, Nancy (1987) 'Redemocratization and Transition Elections: A Comparison of Spain and Portugal', *Comparative Politics* 19.

Beyme, Klaus von (ed.) (1988) *Right-wing extremism in Western Europe* (London: Frank Cass).

Blanco Valdés, Roberto L. (1990) *Los partidos políticos* (Madrid: Tecnos).

Blas Guerrero, Andrés de (1992) 'El sistema español de partidos', in Guerra and Tezanos (eds).

Blas Guerrero, Andrés de (ed.) (1983) *Introducción al sistema político español* (Barcelona: Teide).

Blay Biosca, Vicente (1985) 'Defending the Strait of Gibraltar', *International Defence Review* 9.

Bonime-Blanc, Andrea (1987) *Spain's Transition to Democracy* (Boulder, Colorado: Westview).

Borja de Riquer, Jordi (1989) 'Cataluña', in Fusi (ed.).

Botella, Joan (1988) 'Spanish Communism in Crisis. The Communist Party of Spain', in Michael Waller and Meindert Fennema (eds), *Communist Parties in Western Europe. Decline or Adaptation?* (Oxford: Blackwell).

Botella, Joan (1989) 'The Spanish "new" Regions: Territorial and Political Pluralism', *International Political Science Review* 10.

Brassloff, Audrey (1989) 'Spain: the state of the autonomies', in Murray Forsyth (ed.), *Federalism and Nationalism* (Leicester: Leicester University Press).

Brenan, Gerald (1963) *The Literature of the Spanish People* (Harmondsworth: Peregrine).

Britton, Andrew and Mayes, David (1992) *Achieving Monetary Union in Europe* (London: Sage/Association for the Monetary Union of Europe).

Bull, Martin and Heywood, Paul (eds) (1994) *West European Communist Parties After the Revolutions of 1989* (London: Macmillan).

Busquets, Julio (1984) *El militar de carrera en España* (Barcelona: Editorial Ariel).

Cacho, Jesús (1988) *Asalto al poder. La revolución de Mario Conde* (Madrid: Temas de Hoy).

Cacho, Jesús (1989) *Duelo de titanes. Asalto al poder II* (Madrid: Temas de Hoy).

Cacho, Jesús (1994) *M.C. Un intruso en el laberinto de los elegidos* (Madrid: Temas de Hoy).

Caciagli, Mario (1984) 'Spain: parties and the party system in the transition', in Pridham (ed.).

Caciagli, Mario (1986) *Elecciones y partidos en la transición española* (Madrid: CIS).

Caciagli, Mario (1989) 'La parábola de la Unión de Centro Democrático', in Tezanos, Cotarelo and Blas (eds).

Calduch Cervera, Rafael (ed.) (1994) *La política exterior española en el siglo XX* (Madrid: Ediciones Ciencias Sociales).

Callahan, William J. (1990) 'Catholicism', in Kern (ed.).

Camiller, Patrick (1986) 'Spanish Socialism in the Atlantic Order', *New Left Review* 156.

Camiller, Patrick (1994) 'Spain: The Survival of Socialism?', in Perry Anderson and Patrick Camiller (eds), *Mapping the West European Left* (London: Verso).

Capo Giol, J. (1981) 'Estrategias para un sistema de partidos', *Revista de Estudios Políticos* 23.

Capo Giol, J., García Cotarelo, R., López Garrido, D. and Subirats, J. (1990) 'By consociationalism to a majoritarian parliamentary system: the rise and decline of the Spanish Cortes', in Liebert and Cotta (eds).

Carcassonne, Guy *et al.* (1979) *L'espagne démocratique* (POUVOIRS (Revue Française d'Études Constitutionnelles et Politiques) 8; Paris: Presses Universitaires de France).

Cardona, Gabriel (1990) *El problema militar en España* (Madrid: Biblioteca Historia 16).

Carr, Raymond (1982) *Spain 1808–1975* 2nd edn (Oxford: Clarendon Press).

Carr, Raymond (1986) *The Civil War in Spain* (London: Weidenfeld & Nicolson).

Carr, Raymond and Fusi, Juan Pablo (1981) *Spain. Dictatorship to Democracy*, 2nd edn (London: George Allen & Unwin).

Casanova, José (1983) 'Modernization and Democratization. Reflections on Spain's Transition to Democracy', *Social Research* 50(4).

Casanova, José (1994) 'Las enseñanzas de la transición democrática en España', in Redero San Román (ed.).

Castellano, Pablo (1992) 'El parlamento y el gobierno', in Tusell and Sinova (eds).

Castells Oliveres, A. (1987) 'Financing regional government in Spain: main trends and a comparative perspective', *Environment and Planning C: Government and Policy* 5.

Castells, Luis (1989) 'País Vasco', in Fusi (ed.).

Cavero, José (1990) *Poderes fácticos en la democracia* (Madrid: Espasa Calpe).

Cavero, José (1991) *El PSOE contra la prensa* (Madrid: Temas de Hoy).

Cebrián, Juan Luis (1989) *The Press and Main Street* (Ann Arbor: University of Michigan Press).

CES (1994) *España 1993. Economía, trabajo y sociedad* (Madrid: Consejo Económico y Social).

Chislett, William (1994) *Spain: at a turning point* (Madrid: Banco Central Hispano).

CIP (1990) 'Tendiendo puentes. La CSCE y una ecoseguridad integral en el Mediterráneo', *Informes* (Madrid: Servicio Informativo del Centro de Investigación para la Paz).

CIS (1985) *Encuesta sobre las condiciones de vida de los españoles in 1985* (Madrid: CIS).

Clark, Robert P. (1979) *The Basques: The Franco Years and Beyond* (Reno, Nevada: University of Nevada Press).

Clark, Robert P. (1984) *The Basque Insurgents. ETA 1952–1980* (Madison: University of Wisconsin Press).

Clark, Robert P. (1987) 'The Question of Regional Autonomy in Spain's Democratic Transition', in Clark and Haltzel (eds).

Clark , Robert P. (1990a) 'Basques', in Kern (ed.).

Clark, Robert P. (1990b) *Negotiating with ETA. Obstacles to Peace in the Basque Country, 1975–1988* (Reno, Nevada: Nevada University Press).

Clark, Robert P. and Haltzel, Michael H. (eds) (1987) *Spain in the 1980s* (Cambridge, Mass.: Ballinger).

Claudín, Fernando (1980) *¿Crisis de los partidos políticos?* (Madrid: Dédalo).

Claudín, Fernando (1983) *Santiago Carrillo. Crónica de un secretario general* (Barcelona: Planeta).

Colino Cámara, César, Delgado Sotillas, Irene, and López Nieto, Lourdes (1994) 'Political studies in Spain', *European Journal of Political Research* 25.

Collins, Roger (1986) *The Basques* (Oxford: Basil Blackwell).

Colomé, Gabriel (1992) 'The «Partit dels Socialistes de Catalunya»', in José María Maravall *et al.*, *Socialist Parties in Europe* (Barcelona: ICPS).

Colomé, Gabriel and López Nieto, Lourdes (1989) 'Leadership Selection in PSOE and AP', *Working Papers* 06/89 (Barcelona: Institut de Ciències Politiques i Socials).

Company, Enric and Arroyo, Francesc (1989) *Historia del socialismo español (1977–1988). La salida del túnel* (Barcelona: Conjunta Editorial).

Conversi, Daniele (1990) 'Language or race?: the choice of core values in the development of Catalan and Basque nationalism', *Ethnic and Racial Studies* 13(1).

Conversi, Daniele (1992) 'How Culture Can Influence Political Choices: Language Maintenance and its Implications for the Catalan and Basque National Movements', *History of European Ideas*.

Conversi, Daniele (1993) 'Domino Effect or Internal Developments? The Influences of International Events and Political Ideologies on Catalan and Basque Nationalism', *West European Politics* 16(3).

Cotarelo, Ramón (1983) 'Los partidos políticos', in Blas Guerrero (ed.).

Cotarelo, Ramón (1985) *Los partidos políticos* (Madrid: Editorial Sistema).

Cotarelo, Ramón (1989) 'El sistema de partidos', in Tezanos, Cotarelo and Blas (eds).

Cotarelo, Ramón (1991) 'La jefatura del estado', in Vidal-Beneyto (ed.) (1991a).

Cotarelo, Ramón (1992) 'Los partidos políticos', in Cotarelo (ed.).

Cotarelo, Ramón (ed.) (1992) *Transición política y consolidación democrática. España (1975–1986)* (Madrid: Centro de Investigaciones Sociológicas).

Cotarelo, Ramón and Bobillo, Francisco J. (1991) 'El sistema de partidos', in Vidal-Beneyto (1991a).

Cotarelo, Ramón and López Nieto, Lourdes (1988) 'Spanish Conservatism, 1976–1987', in Beyme (ed.).

Cristóbal, Ramiro (1989) 'Las técnicas de Alfonso Guerra para manipular la televisión', *Cambio 16* 933 (16 October).

Cuenca Toribio, José M. (1994) 'La transición española, modelo universal', *Nueva Revista de Política, Cultura y Arte* 37 (December).

De Blaye, Edouard (1976) *Franco and the Politics of Spain* (Harmondsworth: Penguin).

De la Cuadra, Bonifacio (1991) 'Poder judicial nuevo, problemas viejos', *Anuario El País 1991* (Madrid: Ediciones El País).

De la Cuadra, Bonifacio (1993) 'La política asedia los tribunales', *Anuario El País 1993* (Madrid: Ediciones El País).

De la Dehesa, Guillermo (1990) '¿Cómo será la economía española en 1999?', in Antonio Alférez (ed.), *España 1999* (Madrid: Temas de Hoy).

De la Dehesa, Guillermo (1993) 'Political and Economic Reform in Contemporary Spain', paper presented at the conference on 'The Political Economy of Policy Reform', Institute of International Economics, Washington DC (14–16 January).

De Riquer Permanyer, Borja (1989) 'Cataluña', in Fusi (ed.).

De Vega García, Pedro (1985) *La reforma constitucional* (Madrid: Tecnos).

Delibes, Miguel (1979) *Castilla, lo castellano y los castellanos* (Barcelona: Planeta).

Di Palma, Giuseppe (1990) *To Craft Democracies* (Berkeley, Cal.: University of California Press).

Díaz López, César (1985) 'Centre-Periphery Structures in Spain: From Historical Conflict to Territorial-Consociational Accommodation?', in Yves Mény and Vincent Wright (eds), *Centre-Periphery Relations in Western Europe* (London: George Allen & Unwin).

Díaz, Elías (1963) 'Teoría general del estado de derecho', *Revista de Estudios Políticos* 131.

Díaz, Elías (1979) *Estado de derecho y sociedad democrática*, 7th edn (Madrid: Ediciones Cuadernos para el Diálogo).

Díaz, Elías (1982) *Socialismo en España: el partido y el estado* (Madrid: Mezquita).

Díaz, Elías (1987) *La transición a la democracia* (Madrid: Eudema).

Donaghy, Peter J. and Newton, Michael T. (1987) *Spain. A Guide to Political and Economic Institutions* (Cambridge: Cambridge University Press).

Douglass, William A. and Zulaika, Joseba (1990) 'On the Interpretation of Terrorist Violence: ETA and the Basque Political Process', *Comparative Studies in Society and History* 32.

Duverger, Maurice (1957) *Political Parties: Their Organisation and Activity in the Modern State* (London: Methuen).

Economist, The (1992) 'After the Fiesta: A Survey of Spain' (25 April).

Eguiagaray Ucelay, Juan Manuel (1992) 'El Estado Autonómico', in Guerra and Tezanos (eds).

Elliott, Larry (1992) 'Why Maastricht should be anathema to the Labour Party's philosophy', *The Guardian* (17 August).

Ellwood, Sheelagh M. (1992) 'The Extreme Right in Post-Francoist Spain', *Parliamentary Affairs* 45(3).

Escudero, Manuel (1984) 'El Estado de las Autonomías', *Leviatán* 18.

Espadas Burgos, Manuel (1988) *Franquismo y política exterior* (Madrid: Ediciones RIALP).

Esteban, Jorge de (1992) *El estado de la Constitución (Diez años de gobierno del PSOE)* (Madrid: Libertarias/Prodhufi).

Esteban, Jorge de and López Guerra, Luis (1982) *Los partidos políticos en la España actual* (Barcelona: Planeta/Instituto de Estudios Económicos).

Esteban, Jorge de *et al.* (1977) *El proceso electoral* (Barcelona: Labor).

European Commission DG XVI (1992) 'Spanish Regions: Evidence that Regional Policy Really Exists', *Regional* (Special Issue) (July).

EUROSTAT (1992) *Europe in Figures*, 3rd edn (Luxembourg: Office for Official Publications of the European Communities).

Fernández Rodríguez, Z. (1989) 'El alcance del proceso privatizador en España', *Papeles de Economía Española* 38.

Fernández, Carlos (1982) *Los militares en la transición política* (Barcelona: Argos-Vergara).

Fishman, Robert M. (1990) *Working-Class Organization and the Return to Democracy in Spain* (Ithaca: Cornell University Press).

Ford, Richard (1974) *Las cosas de España* (Madrid: Caro Raggio).

Foweraker, Joe (1989) *Making Democracy in Spain* (Cambridge: Cambridge University Press).

Fraga Iribarne, Manuel (1964) 'Spain and the mission of Europe', *NATO's Fifteen Nations* 9(2).

Fraga Iribarne, Manuel (1983) *La leal oposición* (Barcelona: Planeta).

Fraga Iribarne, Manuel (1992) 'Galicia in the Context of the European Regions', *El Comercio Hispano Británico* (April).

Fuentes Quintana, Enrique (1991) 'Economía y economistas españoles', *Revista de Economía*.

Fundación Friedrich Ebert (1983) *Elecciones generales 1982* (Madrid: EDIS).

Furlong, Paul (1994) *Modern Italy. Representation and Reform* (London: Routledge).

Fusi, Juan Pablo (1984) *El País Vasco* (Madrid: Editorial Alianza).

Fusi, Juan Pablo (1989) 'La organización territorial del estado', in Fusi (ed.).

Fusi, Juan Pablo (ed.) (1989) *España. Autonomías* (Madrid: Espasa Calpe).

Gallagher, Tom and Williams, Allan (eds) (1989) *Southern European Socialism. Parties, elections and the challenge of government* (Manchester: Manchester University Press).

Galy, Michel, Pastor, Gonzalo and Pujol, Thierry (1993) *Spain: Converging with the European Community* (Washington DC: International Monetary Fund).

García Canales, Mariano (1991) *La Monarquía Parlamentaria Española* (Madrid: Tecnos).

García de Enterría, Eduardo (1981) 'La posición jurídica del Tribunal Constitucional en el sistema español: posibilidades y perspectivas', *Revista española de Derecho constitucional* 1.

García Delgado, José Luis (1990) 'Claves de unos años decisivos', in García Delgado (ed.).

García Delgado, José Luis (ed.) (1990) *Economía española de la transición y la democracia (1973–1986)* (Madrid: CIS).

Garzón, Baltasar (1994) 'Prólogo', in Martín de Pozuelo *et al.*

Gellner, Ernest and Waterbury, John (eds) (1975) *Patrons and Clients* (London: Duckworth).

Gibbons, John (1990) 'Political Change in Galicia in the Regional Elections of December 1989', *ACIS* 3(2).

Gillespie, Richard (1989) *The Spanish Socialist Party. A History of Factionalism* (Oxford: Clarendon Press).

Gillespie, Richard (1990a) 'Regime consolidation in Spain: party, state, and society', in Pridham (ed.).

Gillespie, Richard (1990b) 'The Break-Up of the Socialist Family: Party-Union Relations in Spain, 1982–1989', *West European Politics* 13(1).

Gilmour, David (1985) *The Transformation of Spain* (London: Quartet).

Giménez y Martínez de Carvajal, José (1984) 'El Concordato español de 1953', in Joaquín Ruíz Giménez (ed.), *Iglesia, estado y sociedad en España. 1930–1982* (Barcelona: Argos Vergara).

Giner, Salvador (1984) 'Ethnic nationalism, centre and periphery in Spain', in Abel and Torrents (eds).

Giner, Salvador (ed.) (1990) *España. Sociedad y política* (Madrid: Espasa Calpe).

Giner, Salvador and Moreno, Luis (1990) 'Centro y periferia: la dimensión étnica de la sociedad española', in Giner (ed.).

Giner, Salvador and Sevilla, Eduardo (1984) 'Spain: from corporatism to corporatism', in A. Williams (ed.), *Southern Europe Transformed* (London: George Allen & Unwin).

Gómez Reino, Manuel, Francisco Orizo, Andrés and Vila Carro, Dario (1976) 'Sociología política', in Fundación FOESSA, *Estudios sociológicos sobre la situación social de España, 1975* (Madrid: Editorial Euroamérica).

Gómez Yáñez, José A. (1989) 'Bibliografía sobre la transición a la democracia en España', in Tezanos, Cotarelo and Blas (eds).

González Campos, Julio *et al.* (1986) 'El ingreso de España en las Comunidades Europeas y los efectos del Acta de Adhesión', in Eduardo García de Enterría, Julio D. González Campos and Santiago Muñoz Machado (eds), *Tratado de derecho comunitario europeo. Estudios sistemáticos desde el derecho español*, 3 vols (Madrid: Editorial Civitas).

González Encinar, José Juan (1983) 'La organización territorial del Estado', in Blas Guerrero (ed.).

González Fernández, Sara (1993a) 'Monetary policy', in Almarcha Barbado (ed.).

González Fernández, Sara (1993b) 'Telecommunications and transport policy', in Almarcha Barbado (ed.).

González, Felipe (1986) 'Ten points for NATO', *ENDpapers* 12.

González, Miguel (1990) 'La reforma de la carrera militar solivianto el ánimo de los cuarteles', *Anuario El País 1990* (Madrid: Ediciones El País).

Graham, Helen (1991) *Socialism and War. The Spanish Socialist Party in power and crisis, 1936–39* (Cambridge: Cambridge University Press).

Graham, Robert (1984) *Spain. Change of a Nation* (London: Michael Joseph).

Greenwood, Davydd J. (1977) 'Continuity in change: Spanish Basque ethnicity as a historical process', in Milton J. Esman (ed.), *Ethnic Conflict in the Western World* (Ithaca: Cornell University Press).

Grugel, Jean (1991) 'The Spanish Presidency of the European Community: The External Dimension', *CMS-Occasional Paper No.2* (Bristol: Centre for Mediterranean Studies).

Guerra, Alfonso and Tezanos, José Félix (eds) (1992) *La década del cambio. Diez años de gobierno socialista, 1982–1992* (Madrid: Editorial Sistema).

Gunther, Richard (1985) 'Constitutional Change in Contemporary Spain', in Keith Banting and Richard Simeon (eds), *The Politics of Constitutional Change in Industrial Nations: Redesigning the State* (London: Macmillan).

Gunther, Richard (1987) 'Democratization and Party Building: The Role of Party Elites in the Spanish Transition', in Clark and Haltzel (eds).

Gunther, Richard (1992) 'Política y cultura en España', *Cuadernos y Debates* 36 (Madrid: Centro de Estudios Constitucionales).

Gunther, Richard, Giacomo Sani and Goldie Shabad (1986) *Spain After Franco. The Making of a Competitive Party System* (Berkeley, Cal.: University of California Press).

Harrison, Joseph (1993) *The Spanish Economy. From the Civil War to the European Community* (London: Macmillan).

Hebbert, Michael (1987) 'Regionalism: a reform concept and its application to Spain', *Environment and Planning C: Government and Policy* 5.

Hebbert, Michael (1989) 'Spain – A Centre-Periphery Transformation', in Jens Christian Hansen and Michael Hebbert (eds), *Unfamiliar Territory* (Aldershot: Avebury).

Heiberg, Marianne (1989) *The Making of the Basque Nation* (Cambridge: Cambridge University Press).

Heidenheimer, A. J., Heclo, H. and Adams, C. T. (1983) *Comparative Public Policy – the politics of social choice in Europe and America*, 2nd edn (London: Macmillan).

Hennessy, C. A. M. (1962) *The Federal Republic in Spain* (Oxford: Oxford University Press).

Hennessy, C. A. M. (1989) 'The renaissance of federal ideas in contemporary Spain', in Murray Forsyth (ed.), *Federalism and Nationalism* (Leicester: Leicester University Press).

Heras, Raúl (1994) *La guerra de las rosas* (Madrid: Temas de Hoy).

Hermet, Guy (1985) *Los católicos en la España franquista*, 2 vols (Madrid: CIS).

Hermet, Guy (1988) 'Emerging from Dictatorship. The Role of the Constitution in Spain (1978) and Portugal (1976)', in Vernon Bogdanor (ed.), *Constitutions in Democratic Politics* (Aldershot: Gower).

Herrero de Miñón, Miguel (1979) 'Les sources étrangères de la Constitution', in Carcassonne *et al.*

Herrero de Miñón, Miguel (1985) 'NATO as a Weapon in Domestic Politics' in Shub and Carr (eds).

Herrero de Miñón, Miguel (1988) 'La elaboración de la Constitución', *Cuenta y Razón* 41.

Heywood, Paul (1989) 'Spain', *Electoral Studies* 8(3).

Heywood, Paul (1990) *Marxism and the Failure of Organised Socialism in Spain, 1879–1936* (Cambridge: Cambridge University Press).

Heywood, Paul (1991) *Spain's Next Five Years: A Political Risk Analysis* (London: Economist Intelligence Unit).

Heywood, Paul (1992) 'The Socialist Party in Power, 1982–1992: the Price of Progress', *ACIS* 5(2).

Heywood, Paul (1993a) 'Spain and the European Dimension: The Integrated Market, Convergence and Beyond' (Glasgow: *Strathclyde Papers on Government and Politics* No.94).

Heywood, Paul (1993b) 'Rethinking socialism in Spain: *Programa 2000* and the social state', *Coexistence* 30(3).

Heywood, Paul (1994a) 'The Spanish Left: Towards a Common Home?', in Bull and Heywood (eds).

Heywood, Paul (1994b) 'Political Corruption in Modern Spain', in Paul Heywood (ed.), *Distorting Democracy: Political Corruption in Spain, Italy and Malta* (CMS *Occasional Paper*, No. 10; University of Bristol: Centre for Mediterranean Studies).

Heywood, Paul (1995) 'The Emergence of New Party Systems and Transitions to Democracy. Spain in Comparative Perspective', in Geoffrey Pridham and Paul Lewis (eds), *Rooting Fragile Democracies: Comparing New Party Systems in Southern and Eastern Europe* (London: Routledge) – forthcoming.

Hollyman, John (1974) 'The press and censorship in Franco's Spain', *Iberian Studies* III(2).

Holman, Otto (1989) '*Felipismo* or the Failure of Neo-Liberalism in Spain', paper presented to Political Studies Association Annual Conference, University of Warwick.

Hooper, John (1986) *The Spaniards* (Harmondsworth: Penguin).

Hooper, John (1995) *The New Spaniards* (Harmondsworth: Penguin).

Hopkin, Jonathan (1993) 'La desintegración de la Unión de Centro Democrático: una interpretación organizativa', *Revista de Estudios Políticos* 81.

Hughes, Robert (1992) *Barcelona* (London: Harvill).

Huneeus, Carlos (1985) *La Unión de Centro Democrático y la transición a la democracia en España* (Madrid: CIS).

Huntington, Samuel P. (1991/92) 'How Countries Democratise', *Political Science Quarterly* 106(4).

Jáuregui Bereciartu, Gurutz (1985) *Ideología y estrategia política de ETA. Análisis de su evolución entre 1959 y 1968*, 2nd edn (Madrid: Siglo XXI).

Juliá, Santos (1988a) *La desavenencia* (Madrid: Aguilar/El País).

Juliá, Santos (1988b) 'Transiciones a la democracia en la España del siglo XX', *Sistema* 84.

Juliá, Santos (1990a) 'The Ideological Conversion of the Leaders of the PSOE, 1976–1979', in Frances Lannon and Paul Preston (eds), *Elites and Power in Twentieth Century Spain. Essays in Honour of Sir Raymond Carr* (Oxford: Clarendon Press).

Juliá, Santos (1990b) 'Sindicatos y poder político en España', *Sistema* 97.

Junta Electoral Central (1994) *Ley orgánica del régimen electoral general* (Madrid: Publicaciones de la Cortes Generales).

Keating, Michael (1993) *The Politics of Modern Europe* (London: Edward Elgar).

Kellas, James G. (1991) 'European Integration and the Regions', *Parliamentary Affairs* 44(2).

Kellner, Peter and Crowther-Hunt, Norman (1980) *The Civil Servants: an Inquiry into Britain's Ruling Class* (London: Macdonald).

Kern, Robert W. (ed.) (1990) *Historical Dictionary of Modern Spain, 1700–1988* (Westport, Conn.: Greenwood Press).

Krutwig, Federico (1963) *Vasconia* (Buenos Aires: Erbait).

La Souchère, Elena de (1964) *An Explanation of Spain* (New York: Vintage Books).

Lancaster, Thomas (1989) *Policy Stability and Democratic Change. Energy in Spain's Transition* (Pennsylvania: Pennsylvania State University Press).

Lancaster, Thomas and Prevost, Gary (eds) (1985) *Politics and Change in Spain* (New York: Praeger).

Lannon, Frances (1987) *Privilege, Persecution and Prophecy. The Catholic Church in Spain, 1875–1975* (Oxford: Clarendon Press).

Lasuén Sancho, J. R. (1987) 'The Autonomous Communities: politics and economics', *Environment and Planning C: Government and Policy* 5.

Lawson, Kay and Merkl, Peter H. (eds) (1988) *When Parties Fail* (Princeton: Princeton University Press).

Letamendía Belzunce, Francisco ('Ortzi') (1994) *Historia del nacionalismo vasco y de E.T.A.*, 3 vols (San Sebastián: R&B Ediciones).

Liebert, Ulrike (1990) 'Parliament as a central site in democratic consolidation: a preliminary exploration', in Liebert and Cotta (eds).

Liebert, Ulrike and Cotta, Maurizio (eds) (1990) *Parliament and Democratic Consolidation in Southern Europe* (London: Frances Pinter).

Linz, Juan (1973) 'Early State-Building and Late Peripheral Nationalisms Against the State: the Case of Spain', in S. N. Eisenstadt and Stein Rokkan (eds), *Building States and Nations* (London: Sage).

Linz, Juan (1980a) 'The new Spanish party system', in Richard Rose (ed.), *Electoral Participation: A Comparative Analysis* (London: Sage).

Linz, Juan (1980b) 'Religion and Politics in Spain: From Conflict to Consensus above Cleavage', *Social Compass* 27.

Linz, Juan (1985) 'From Primordialism to Nationalism', in Edward A. Tiryakian (ed.), *New Nationalisms of the Developed West* (London: George Allen & Unwin).

Linz, Juan (1990) 'Transitions to Democracy', *The Washington Quarterly* (Summer).

Linz, Juan and Montero, José Ramón (eds) (1986) *Crisis y cambio: electores y partidos en la España de los años ochenta* (Madrid: Centro de Estudios Constitucionales).

López Aranguren, Eduardo and García Ferrando, Manuel (1991) 'Nacionalismo y regionalismo en la España de las Autonomías', in Vidal-Beneyto (ed.) (1991b).

López Garrido, Diego (1987) *El aparato policial en España* (Barcelona: Ariel).

López Guerra, Luis (1980) 'Sobre la personalidad jurídica del Estado', *Revista del Departamento de Derecho Político* (Madrid: UNED).

López Nieto, Lourdes (1988) *Alianza Popular: Estructura y evolución electoral de un partido conservador (1976–1982)* (Madrid: Siglo XXI/CIS).

López Pina, Antonio (ed.) (1987) *División de poderes e interpretación* (Madrid: Tecnos).

Lucas Murillo de la Cueva, Pablo (1983) 'Los órganos constitucionales', in Blas Guerrero (ed.).

Lyrintzis, Christos (1984) 'Political Parties in Post-Junta Greece: A Case of 'Bureaucratic Clientelism'?', in Pridham (ed.).

Ma Valles, Josep and Cuchillo Foix, Montserrat (1988) 'Decentralisation in Spain: a review', *European Journal of Political Research* 16.

Machin, Howard and Wright, Vincent (eds) (1985) *Economic Policy and Policy-Making under the Mitterrand Presidency, 1981–1984* (London: Frances Pinter).

Mainwaring, Scott, O'Donnell, Guillermo, and Valenzuela, J. Samuel (eds) (1992) *Issues in Democratic Consolidation* (Helen Kellogg Institute for International Studies, Notre Dame: University of Notre Dame Press).

Mair, Peter (1990) *Understanding Party System Change in Western Europe* (London: Frank Cass).

Máiz, Ramón (1986) 'El nacionalismo gallego: apuntes para la historia de una hegemonía imposible', in F. Mercadé Hernández (ed.), *Estructuras sociales y cuestión nacional en España* (Barcelona: Editorial Ariel).

Máiz, Ramón and Portero, Xose A. (1988) *As institucións politicas no Estatuto de Autonomía* (Santiago: Parlamento de Galicia).

MAP (1990) *Reflexiones para la modernización de la administración del estado* (Madrid: Ministerio para las Administraciones Públicas).

MAP (1992) *Plan de modernización de la administración del estado* (Madrid: Ministerio para las Administraciones Públicas).

Maravall, José María (1979) 'Political cleavages in Spain and the 1979 general election', *Government and Opposition* XIV.

Maravall, José María (1984) *La política de la transición*, 2nd edn (Madrid: Taurus).

Maravall, José María (1992) 'From opposition to government: the politics and policies of the PSOE', in José María Maravall *et al.*, *Socialist Parties in Europe* (Barcelona: ICPS).

Maravall, José María and Santamaría, Julián (1989) 'Transición política y consolidación de la democracia en España', in Tezanos, Cotarelo and Blas (eds).

Marcus, Jonathan (1983) 'The Triumph of Spanish Socialism', *West European Politics* 6(3).

Marquina, Antonio (1986) *España en la política de seguridad occidental, 1939–1986* (Madrid: Ediciones del Ejército).

Marquina, Antonio (1994) 'La evolución de la política de seguridad española (1982–1992)', in Calduch Cervera (ed.).

Martín de Pozuelo, Eduardo, Bordas, Jordi and Tarín, Santiago (1994) *Guía de la corrupción* (Barcelona: Plaza & Janés).

Martín Villa, Rodolfo (1984) *Al servicio del Estado* (Barcelona: Planeta).

Martínez Cuadrado, Miguel (1980) *El sistema político español y el comportamiento electoral regional en el sur de Europa* (Madrid: Instituto de Cooperación Intercontinental).

Martínez Inglés, Amadeo (1989) 'El Ejército español no sirve para nada', *Cambio 16* 930 (25 September).

Martínez-Alier, Juan and Roca, Jordi (1985) 'Viejas ideologías y nuevas realidades corporativistas', *Revista Española de Investigaciones Sociológicas* 31.

Martínez-Alier, Juan and Roca, Jordi (1988) 'Spain after Franco: from corporatist ideology to corporatist reality', in Andrew Cox and Noel O'Sullivan (eds), *The Corporate State* (Aldershot: Edward Elgar).

Mateos, Abdón (1993) *El PSOE contra Franco* (Madrid: Editorial Pablo Iglesias).

Maxwell, Kenneth (1991) 'Spain's Transition to Democracy: A Model for Eastern Europe?', in Nils H. Wessell (ed.), *The New Europe: Revolution in East-West Relations* (New York: *Proceedings of The Academy of Political Science* 38).

Maxwell, Kenneth and Spiegel, Steven (1994) *The New Spain. From Isolation to Influence* (New York: Council on Foreign Relations).

Meaker, Gerald H. (1974) *The Revolutionary Left in Spain 1914–1923* (Stanford, Cal.: Stanford University Press).

Medhurst, Kenneth (1973) *Government in Spain* (Oxford: Pergamon Press).

Medhurst, Kenneth (1977) *The Basques and the Catalans* (London: Minority Rights Group).

Mella Márquez, Manuel (1992) 'Los grupos de interés en la consolidación democrática', in Cotarelo (ed.).

Mendoza, Cristina and Mendoza, Eduardo (1989) *Barcelona modernista* (Barcelona: Planeta).

Mény, Yves (1992) *La corruption de la République* (Paris: Fayard).

Merkel, Wolfgang (1992) 'After the golden age: is social democracy doomed to decline?', in José María Maravall *et al.*, *Socialist Parties in Europe* (Barcelona: ICPS).

Michels, Roberto (1958) *Political Parties. A sociological study of the oligarchical tendencies of modern democracy* (Chicago, Illinois: Free Press).

Ministerio de Defensa (1986) *Memoria de la legislatura 1982–86* (Madrid: Ministerio de Defensa).

Ministerio de Economía y Hacienda (1989) *Desarrollo del proceso autonómico en el periodo 1986–1989* (Madrid: Dirección General de Coordinación con las Haciendas Territoriales).

Molas, Isidre and Pitarch, Ismael E. (1987) *Las Cortes Generales en el sistema parlamentario de gobierno* (Madrid: Tecnos).

Monreal, Antoni (1986) 'The New Spanish State Structure', in Michael Burgess (ed.), *Federalism and Federation in Western Europe* (London: Croom Helm).

Montero, José (1988) 'More than Conservative, less than Neoconservative: Alianza Popular in Spain', in Brian Girvin (ed.), *The Transformation of Contemporary Conservatism* (London: Sage).

Montero, José Ramón (1989) 'Los fracasos políticos y electorales de la derecha española: Alianza Popular, 1976–1987', in Tezanos, Cotarelo and Blas (eds).

Montero, José Ramón (1992) 'Las elecciones legislativas', in Cotarelo (ed.).

Montero, José Ramón and Gunther, Richard (1994) 'Sistemas 'cerrados' y listas 'abiertas': sobre algunas propuestas de reforma del sistema electoral en España', *Cuadernos y Debates* 49 (Madrid: Centro de Estudios Constitucionales).

Moore, Barrington (1967) *Social Origins of Dictatorship and Democracy* (London: Allen Lane The Penguin Press).

Morán, Fernando (1985) 'El papel de Europa en Centroamérica', *Tiempo de Paz* 7.

Morán, Fernando (1990) *España en su sitio* (Madrid: Plaza y Janés/Cambio 16).

Morán, Gregorio (1985) *Miseria y grandeza del Partido Comunista de España, 1939–1985* (Barcelona: Planeta).

Morán, Gregorio (1991) *El precio de la transición* (Barcelona: Planeta).

Moreno, Luis (1990) 'Las fuerzas políticas españolas', in Giner (ed.).

Morodo, Raúl (1984) *La transición política* (Madrid: Editorial Tecnos).

Mujal-León, Eusebio (1983) *Communism and Political Change in Spain* (Bloomington).

Muñoz Alonso, Alejandro (1984) *Las elecciones del cambio* (Barcelona: Argos-Vergara).

Muñoz Alonso, Alejandro (1988) 'Las instituciones democráticas, 10 años después', *Cuenta y Razón* 41 .

Naylon, John (1981) 'Iberia', in H. D. Clout (ed.), *Regional Development in Western Europe* 2nd edn (London: John Wiley).

Nieto García, Alejandro and Gutiérrez Reñón, Alberto (1991) 'La administración pública', in Vidal-Beneyto (ed.) (1991a).

Nieto, Alejandro (1984) *La organización del desgobierno* (Barcelona: Editorial Ariel).

Niskanen, W. (1973) *Bureaucracy and Representative Government* (Chicago: Aldine Atherton).

OECD (1991) *Spain* (Paris: OECD Economic Surveys).

Oporto del Olmo, Antonio (1992) *Emigración y ahorro en España 1959–1986* (Madrid: Ministerio de Trabajo y Seguridad Social).

Orizo, Andrés Francisco (1983) *España, entre la apatía y el cambio social* (Madrid: MAPFRE).

Ortega y Gasset, José (1931) *La redención de las provincias y la decencia nacional* (Madrid).

Paramio, Ludolfo (1990) 'Los sindicatos y el sistema político en la España democrática: de la clandestinidad a la huelga general', *Sistema* 94–95.

Paricio, Jesús M. (1983) *Para conocer a nuestros militares* (Madrid: Tecnos).

Payne, Stanley G. (1987) *The Franco Regime, 1936–1975* (Madison: University of Wisconsin Press).

Payne, Stanley G. (1990) 'Army', in Kern (ed.).

Payne, Stanley G. (ed.) (1986) *The Politics of Democratic Spain* (Chicago: Chicago Council of Foreign Relations).

Peces-Barba, Gregorio (1981) *La Constitución española de 1978: un estudio de derecho y político* (Valencia: Fernando Torres).

Peces-Barba, Gregorio (1988) *La elaboración de la Constitución de 1978* (Madrid: Centro de Estudios Constitucionales).

Penniman, H. R. and Mujal-León, E. M. (1985) *Spain at the Polls. A Study of the National Elections of 1977, 1979 and 1982* (Durham, Mass.: Duke University Press).

Pérez Francesch, Juan Luis (1993) *El gobierno* (Madrid: Tecnos).

Pérez Henares, Antonio, Malo de Molina, Carlos and Curiel, Enrique (1989) *Luces y sombras del poder militar en España* (Madrid: Ediciones Temas de Hoy).

Pérez Royo, Javier (1994) *Curso de derecho constitucional* (Madrid: Marcial Pons).

Pérez-Díaz, Víctor (1987) 'Neo-corporatist experiments in a new and precariously stable state', in Ilja Scholten (ed.), *Political Stability and Neo-Corporatism* (London: Sage).

Pérez-Díaz, Víctor (1987) *El retorno de la sociedad civil* (Madrid: Instituto de Estudios Económicos).

Pérez-Díaz, Víctor (1993) *The Return of Civil Society* (Cambridge, Mass.: Harvard University Press).

Petras, James (1990) *El socialismo español, camino de Marbella* (Madrid: Editorial Revolución).

Petras, James (1993) 'Spanish Socialism: the Politics of Neoliberalism', in James Kurth and James Petras (eds), *Mediterranean Paradoxes* (Oxford: Berg Publishers).

Pierson, Christopher (1992) 'Democracy, Markets and Capital: Are there Necessary Economic Limits to Democracy?', in David Held (ed.) *Prospects for Democracy* (special issue of *Political Studies*, Oxford: Blackwell).

Piñol, Joan (1988) 'Las relaciones españolas con Centroamérica: el período de los gobiernos socialistas (1982–1988)', *Afers Internacionals* 14–15.

Piris, Alberto (1989) 'El ejército español durante la guerra fría' (unpublished manuscript).

Pollack, Benny (1987) *The Paradox of Spanish Foreign Policy* (London: Pinter).

Powell, Charles T. (1991) *El piloto del cambio* (Barcelona: Planeta).

Preston, Paul (1984) 'The agrarian war in the south', in Paul Preston (ed.), *Revolution and War in Spain, 1931–1939* (London: Methuen).

Preston, Paul (1986) *The Triumph of Democracy in Spain* (London: Methuen).

Preston, Paul (1988) 'The Decline and Resurgence of the Spanish Socialist Party During the Franco Regime', *European History Quarterly* 18.

Preston, Paul (1990) *The Politics of Revenge* (London: Unwin Hyman).

Preston, Paul (1991) 'El discreto encanto del general Franco', *ACIS* 4(1).

Preston, Paul (1993) *Franco. A Biography* (London: HarperCollins).

Preston, Paul (1994) *The Coming of the Spanish Civil War*, 2nd edn (London: Routledge).

Preston, Paul and Smyth, Denis (1984) *Spain, the EEC and NATO* (London: Royal Institute of International Affairs).

Pridham, Geoffrey (ed.) (1984) *The New Mediterranean Democracies* (London: Frank Cass).

Pridham, Geoffrey (ed.) (1990) *Securing Democracy: Political Parties and Democratic Consolidation in Southern Europe* (London: Routledge).

Przeworski, Adam and Sprague, John (1986) *Paper Stones. A History of Electoral Socialism* (Chicago: University of Chicago Press).

PSOE (1985) *Una política de paz y seguridad para España* (Madrid).

PSOE (1991) *Manifiesto del Programa 2000* (with Introduction and Conclusion by Willy Brandt, Felipe González, and Alfonso Guerra) (Madrid: Editorial Sistema).

Puigjaner, Josep-María (1989) *Catalonia. A millenial country* (Barcelona: Generalitat de Catalunya).

Ramírez, Manuel (1982) 'El sistema de partidos en España tras las elecciones de 1982', *Revista de Estudios Políticos* 30.

Ramírez, Manuel (1988) 'El sistema de partidos en España, 1977–1987', *Revista de Estudios Políticos* 59.

Ramírez, Manuel (1989) *Partidos políticos y Constitución* (Madrid: Centro de Estudios Constitucionales).

Ramírez, Manuel (1990) 'El sistema de partidos en España tras las elecciones in 1989', *Revista de Estudios Políticos* 67.

Ramírez, Manuel (1991) *Sistema de partidos en España (1931–1990)* (Madrid: Centro de Estudios Constitucionales).

Redero San Román, Manuel (ed.) (1994) *La transición a la democracia en España* (issue 15 of the journal *Ayer*; Madrid: Marcial Pons/Asociación de Historia Contemporánea).

Redondo, Nicolás (1992) 'La llegada del neoliberalismo', *Tiempo*, 10th anniversary edition (24 February).

Reig Tapia, Alberto and Merino Marchán, Emilio (1994) 'El sistema político español', in Manuel Pastor (ed.), *Fundamentos de ciencia política* (Madrid: McGraw-Hill).

Rivases, J. (1988) *Los banqueros del PSOE* (Barcelona: Ediciones B).

Robinson, Robert (1989) 'Coalitions and Political Parties in Sub-National Government: The Case of Spain', in Colin Mellors and Bert Pijnenburg (eds), *Political Parties and Coalitions in European Local Government* (London: Routledge).

Roca i Junyent, Miquel (1988) 'The Reception of the Constitution in Parliament and the Country', in María Antonia Turner and Alejandro N. Nayfeld, *The 1978 Spanish Constitution* (Columbia University: report on a symposium held at the Spanish Institute, New York, 7 June 1988).

Rodríguez Aramberri, Julio (1980) 'Origen y evolución del sistema de partidos en la España democrática: un ensayo de interpretación', in Claudín (ed.).

Rodríguez Lara, Emilio (1993) 'Media policy', in Almarcha Barbado (ed.).

Rodríguez, Emilio A. (1988) 'Atlanticism and Europeanism: NATO and Trends in Spanish Foreign Policy', in Federico G. Gil and Joseph S. Tulchin (eds), *Spain's Entry into NATO* (Boulder and London: Lynne Reiner).

Rose, Richard (1981) *Do Parties Make a Difference?* (London: Macmillan).

Rose, Richard (1991) 'Prime Ministers in Parliamentary Democracies', in G. W. Jones (ed.), *West European Prime Ministers* (London: Frank Cass).

Rovira y Virgili, Antoni (1916) *El nacionalismo catalán* (Barcelona).

Rubio Llorente, F. and Aragón Reyes, M. (1979) 'Enunciados aparentemente vacíos en la regulación constitucional del control de constitucionalidad', *Revista de Estudios Políticos* 7.

Ruedo Ibérico (1972) *Horizonte español 1972*, 3 vols (Paris: Ruedo Ibérico).

Ruiz, David (ed.) (1993) *Historia de Comisiones Obreras (1958–1988)* (Madrid: Siglo XXI).

Sahagún, Felipe (1994) 'España frente al sur', in Calduch Cervera (ed.).

Salmon, Keith G. (1991) *The Modern Spanish Economy* (London: Pinter).

Salmon, Keith G. (1992) 'The modern Spanish economy – integration into the European Community and the world economy', *ACIS* 5(1).

Sánchez Agesta, Luis (1980) *El sistema político de la Constitución española de 1978* (Madrid: Ed. Nacional).

Sánchez Asiaín, José Angel (1992) 'El sistema financiero español ante la unión económica europea', in Alonso Olea *et al.*

Sánchez, José Antonio and Santos, Roberto (1990) *La conjura del zar* (Madrid: Ediciones Temas de Hoy).

Sánchez-Gijón, Antonio (1986) 'The Spanish Navy after the Referendum', *Naval Forces*.

Santesmases, Antonio (1984) 'PSOE y OTAN', *Leviatán* (II^a época) 17.

Santillán, Sergio (1993) 'Industrial relations and trade unions', in Almarcha Barbado (ed.).

Sarasqueta, Antxon (1991) *La agonía del duque. El enigma de Adolfo Suárez* (Madrid: Temas de Hoy).

Sartori, Giovanni (1976) *Parties and Party Systems* (Cambridge: Cambridge University Press).

Schneider, P., Schneider, J. and Hansen, E. (1972) 'Modernization and Development: the Role of Regional Elites and Noncorporate Groups in the European Mediterranean', *Comparative Studies in Society and History* XIV.

Seara Vázquez, Modesto (1980) *El socialismo en España* (Mexico: ENEP-ACATLAN).

Seco Serrano, Carlos (1984) *Militarismo y civilismo en la España contemporánea* (Madrid: Instituto de Estudios Económicos).

Segura, Julio (1990) 'Del primer gobierno socialista a la integración en la CEE: 1983–1985', in García Delgado (ed.).

Sen, Gautam (1984) *The Military Origins of Industrialisation and International Trade Rivalry* (London: Pinter).

Serra, Narcís (1985) 'Spanish Security Policy: the Plan and the Process', in Shub and Carr (eds).

Sevilla Segura, J. V. (1987) 'Financial aspects of political decentralization in Spain' *Environment and Planning C: Government and Policy* 5.

Share, Donald (1988) 'Spain: Socialists as Neoliberals', *Socialist Review* 1.

Share, Donald (1989) *Dilemmas of Social Democracy* (Westport, Conn.: Greenwood).

Shub, Joyce Lasky and Carr, Raymond (eds) (1985) *Spain. Studies in Political Security* (Washington, DC: Washington Papers).

Shubert, Adrian (1990) *A Social History of Modern Spain* (London: Unwin Hyman).

Sinova, Justino and Tusell, Javier (1990) *El secuestro de la democracia* (Barcelona: Plaza y Janés).

Smith, Merrit Roe (ed.) (1985) *Military Enterprise and Technological Change* (Cambridge, Mass.: MIT Press).

Solé-Tura, Jordi (1978) *Los comunistas y la Constitución* (Madrid: Forma).

Solé-Tura, Jordi (1988) 'The Significance of Consensus', in María Antonia Turner and Alejandro N. Nayfeld, *The 1978 Spanish Constitution* (Columbia University: report on a symposium held at the Spanish Institute, New York, 7 June 1988).

Solé-Vilanova, Joaquim (1989) 'Spain: developments in regional and local government', in Robert J. Bennett (ed.), *Territory and Administration in Europe* (London: Pinter).

Solé-Vilanova, Joaquim (1990) 'Regional and Local Finance in Spain: Is Fiscal Responsibility the Missing Element?', in Robert J. Bennett (ed.), *Decentralization, Local Governments, and Markets* (Oxford: Clarendon Press).

Soto Carmona, Alvaro (1993) 'Comisiones Obreras en la transición y consolidación democrática. De la asamblea de Barcelona a la huelga general del 14-D (1976–1988)', in Ruiz (ed.).

Southworth, Herbert J. (1986) *El mito de la cruzada de Franco* (Barcelona: Plaza y Janés).

Spourdalakis, Michalis (1985/86) 'The Greek Experience', *Socialist Register*.

Stoetzel, Jean (1982) *¿Qué pensamos los europeos?* (Madrid: MAPFRE).

Story, Jonathan (1991) 'Spanish External Policies: Towards the EC Presidency', *CMS-Occasional Paper*, No. 2 (Bristol: Centre for Mediterranean Studies).

Subirats, Joan (1990) 'Modernizing the Spanish Public Administration or Reform in Disguise' (Barcelona: Institut de Ciències Politiques i Socials, *Working Papers* 20).

Subra de Bieusses, Pierre (1983) 'Constitutional Norms and Central Administration: Reflections on Some of the Articles of the 29 December 1978 Constitution', in Bell (ed.).

Sullivan, John (1988) *ETA and Basque Nationalism* (London: Routledge).

Tamames, Ramón (1989) 'Los planes de desarrollo (1964–1975)', *Información Comercial Española* 676–7, Vol.1.

Temprano, Emilio (1988) *La selva de los tópicos* (Madrid: Mondadori).

Terrón Montero, Javier (1981) *La prensa de España durante el régimen de Franco* (Madrid: Centro de Investigaciones Sociológicas).

Tezanos, José Félix (1989a) 'Continuidad y cambio en el socialismo español: El PSOE durante la transición democrática', in Tezanos, Cotarelo and Blas (eds).

Tezanos, José Félix (1989b) 'Modernización y cambio social en España', in Tezanos, Cotarelo and Blas (eds).

Tezanos, José Félix (1992) 'El papel social y político del PSOE en la España de los años ochenta. Una década de progreso y democracia', in Guerra and Tezanos (eds).

Tezanos, José Félix, Cotarelo, Ramón and Blas, Andrés de (eds) (1989) *La transición democrática española* (Madrid: Editorial Sistema).

Times Mirror Center for the People and the Press (1991) *The Pulse of Europe: A survey of political and social values and attitudes* (Los Angeles: Times Mirror Center).

Toharia, José Juan (1989) *Cambios recientes en la sociedad española* (Madrid: Instituto de Estudios Económicos).

Tomás y Valiente, Francisco (1993) 'El Tribunal Constitucional', *Anuario El País 1993* (Madrid: Ediciones El País).

Torres Boursault, Leopoldo (1993) 'La división de poderes en la España de hoy', *Sistema* 117.

Treverton, Gregory F. (1981) 'The Strategic Significance of the Iberian Peninsula', *NATO's Fifteen Nations* (June-July).

Treverton, Gregory F. (1986) *Spain: Domestic Politics and Security Policy* (Letchworth: International Institute for Strategic Studies).

Tsoukalis, Loukas (1991) *The New European Economy. The Politics and Economics of Integration* (Oxford: Oxford University Press).

Tuñón de Lara, Manuel (1985) *Tres claves de la Segunda República* (Madrid: Alianza Editorial).

Tusell, Javier and Sinova, Justino (eds) (1992) *La década socialista* (Madrid: Espasa Calpe).

Uxó Palasí, General José (1986) 'El eje Baleares-Estrecho-Canarias como principal lineamiento de la defensa española', in Fredo Dannenbring *et al.*, *España dentro de la Alianza Atlántica* (Madrid: Instituto de Cuestiones Internacionales).

Varela, Manuel (1989) 'El Plan de Estabilización como yo lo recuerdo', *Información Comercial Española* 676–7, Vol. 1.

Vázquez Montalbán, Manuel (1984) *La penetración americana en España* (Madrid: EDICUSA).

Velarde, J., García Delgado, J. L. and Pedreño, A. (1991) *Apertura e internacionalización de la economía española* (Madrid: Colegio de Economistas).

Vera Fernández, Rafael (1989) '¿Pocos o demasiados policías?', *Anuario El País 1989* (Madrid: El País).

Vidal Prado, Carlos and Iglesia Chamarro, Asunción de la (1994) *Guía electoral* (Pamplona: Ediciones Universidad de Navarra).

Vidal-Beneyto, José (ed.) (1991a) *España a debate. I. La política* (Madrid: Tecnos).

Vidal-Beneyto, José (ed.) (1991b) *España a debate. II. La sociedad* (Madrid: Tecnos).

Vilar, Sergio (1987) *La década sorprendente, 1976–1986* (Barcelona: Planeta).

Villalaín Benito, José Luis *et al.* (1992) *La sociedad española de los 90 y sus nuevos valores* (Madrid: Fundación Santa María).

Villar, F. (1982) *El proceso de autodeterminación del Sáhara* (Valencia: Fernando Torres).

Villares, Ramón (1989) 'Galicia', in Fusi (ed.).

Viñas, Angel (1981) *Los pactos secretos de Franco con Estados Unidos* (Barcelona: Grijalbo).

Viñas, Angel (1984) 'Coordenadas de la política de seguridad española', *Leviatán* (II^a época) 17.

Viñas, Angel (1984) 'Spain, the United States and NATO', in Abel and Torrents (eds).

Vincent, Mary (1995) 'Spain', in Martin Conway and Tom Buchanan (eds), *Political Catholicism in Europe, 1918–1965* (Oxford: Oxford University Press) – forthcoming.

Visser, Jelle (1991) 'Tendencias de la afiliación sindical', in Informe de la OCDE, *Perspectivas del empleo* (Madrid: Ministerio de Trabajo y Seguridad Social).

Walker, David (1991) 'Convergència Democràtica de Catalunya: Its Successes and Its Problems', *Regional Politics & Policy* 1(3).

Walsh, Michael (1989) *The Secret World of Opus Dei* (London: Grafton).

Wiarda, Howard J. (ed.) (1986) *The Iberian-Latin American Connection. Implications for US Foreign Policy* (Boulder, Col. and Washington, DC: Westview Press/American Enterprise Institute).

Yáñez-Barnuevo, Juan Antonio and Viñas, Angel (1992) 'Diez años de política exterior del gobierno socialista (1982–1992)', in Guerra and Tezanos (eds).

Zirakzadeh, Cyrus Ernesto (1989) 'Economic Changes and Surges in Micro-Nationalist Voting in Scotland and the Basque Region of Spain', *Comparative Studies in Society and History* 31.

Zirakzadeh, Cyrus Ernesto (1991) *A Rebellious People. Basques, Protests and Politics* (Reno, Nevada: Nevada University Press).

Zulaika, Joseba (1988) *Basque Violence: Metaphor and Sacrament* (Reno, Nevada: Nevada University Press).

Index